Further Pi

"This haunting autobiography is a major contribution to the newly growing body of Holocaust-survivor-children's memoirs. Its two-part title says much: *Piecing Scattered Souls* highlights the care in the centripetal organization of the three-generation narrative dealing with the author's survivor parents, his own generation of Holocaust-survivor children and their wives, and the next generation of his four children. The tome's subtitle, *Maine, Germany, Mexico, China, and Beyond*, highlights the macrocosmic venue in which the events unfold. David O. Solmitz's evocation of his professor-father, Walter Solmitz, a survivor of the post-Crystal-Night weeks-long incarceration in Germany's first concentration camp, Dachau, is comprehensive: In his analytical portrayal, Solmitz is sensitive to the all-pervasive survivor guilt that led to his father's suicide in his fifties. Employing Helen Epstein's path-breaking work, the author convincingly shows how that survivor guilt was projected onto Walter's only child—leading to David's lifelong activities as community organizer, teacher, and peace activist. The rich collection of firsthand documentary material throughout the memoir makes the narrative real and believable. Particularly compelling is the detailed, comprehensive report by Walter Solmitz that serves as the volume's first appendix: a rare account of the Jewish prisoners' daily lives in Dachau at the end of 1938. The words I would use to characterize this unique volume are: 'honest,' 'engaging,' 'self-probing,' and 'thoughtful.' Not only was Walter Solmitz a philosopher in the best sense of the word, his son, David, is one as well."

—Steven Cerf

George Lincoln Skolfield, Jr., Professor of German and Holocaust Studies, Bowdoin College, Maine

"Guided by the twin shibboleths of his father—a philosopher, holocaust survivor, suicide—Socrates' 'Know thyself' and Pindar's 'Become who you are,' David Solmitz takes us on a searing pilgrimage of pain, healing, and redemption. Shuttling between past and present, across five generations, three continents, he weaves, like Wordsworth's poet, a rich tapestry of 'relationship and love.' An unforgettable memoir."

—L. S. Asekoff

Poet and Professor of English
Brooklyn College, New York City

"Even as he survived the Holocaust, and despite a tragically foreshortened life, Walter Solmitz never ceased in his intellectual pursuit of truth as a teacher, scholar, and believer in democracy. In this riveting account of his parents' escape from the horrors of war in Europe and their courageous attempts to make a meaningful life in a new country and culture, their son, David, has given us a moving family history and a record of his own intellectual and spiritual growth, accompanied by a profound meditation on the state of our lives today. As I read this beautiful book, I couldn't help thinking how proud his father would be of his son, who embodies his ideals in his own teaching, writing, and citizenship—ideals we need to hold to if we are to survive as a self-aware people in a free society."

—Peter Anastas

Former student of Walter Solmitz
Author of *No Fortunes* and *Decline of Fishes*

Piecing Scattered Souls

Piecing Scattered Souls

Maine, Germany, Mexico, China and Beyond

David O. Solmitz

Polar Bear & Company
Solon Center for Research and Publishing
Solon, Maine

One or more names in the text have been changed for anonymity.

First edition 2011
15 14 13 12 11   2 3 4 5 6 7 8

Polar Bear & Company™
PO Box 311, Solon, Maine 04979 U.S.A.
207.643.2795, www.polarbearandco.org

Library of Congress Control Number: 2011925686
ISBN 978-1-882190-04-1

Cover art & design, Ramona du Houx
All photos courtesy of author.

Manufactured in the U.S.A. by Thomson-Shore, Inc., an employee-owned company—certified by the Forest Stewardship Council and a member of the Green Press Initiative—using soy ink and acid-free, recycled paper of archival quality, at paper permanence specifications defined by ANSI.NISO standard Z39.48-992: "The ability of paper to last several hundred years without significant deterioration under normal use and storage conditions in libraries and archives."

In fond memory of my parents, Elly Reis Solmitz and Walter Moritz Solmitz, and to my wife Jing Ye, who encouraged and supported me to write this book, and to my children, Oliver, Justin, Sonnet, and May.

Contents

All the world's a stage,
All the men and women merely players;
They have their exits and their entrances;
And one man in his time plays many parts,
His acts being seven ages. At first the infant,
Mewling and puking in the nurse's arms;
And then the whining school-boy, with his satchel
And shining morning face, creeping like a snail
Unwillingly to school. And then the lover,
Sighing like furnace, with a woeful ballad
Made to his mistress' eyebrow. Then a soldier,
Full of strange oaths, and bearded like the pard,
Jealous in honor, sudden and quick in quarrel,
Seeking the bubble reputation
Even in the cannon's mouth. And then the justice,
In fair round belly with good capon lined,
With eyes severe and beard of formal cut,
Full of wise saws and modern instances;
And so he plays his part. The sixth age shifts
Into the lean and slippered pantaloon,
With spectacles on nose and pouch on side;
His youthful hose, well saved, a world too wide
For his shrunk shank; and his big manly voice,
Turning again toward childish treble, pipes
And whistles in his sound. Last scene of all,
That ends this strange eventful history,
In second childishness and mere oblivion;
Sans teeth, sans eyes, sans taste, sans everything.

—Jaques' monologue
William Shakespeare's comedy
As You Like It

Foreword

Walter Solmitz was my teacher in the Introduction to Philosophy course that he held in the fall of 1961 and the spring of 1962, and David was my classmate in the Goethe course that Frtiz Koelln held in the fall of 1962 and the spring of 1963: the academic years at Bowdoin College, my junior year and senior year, which were separated by the summer in which Walter Solmitz died.

Walter Solmitz's death is the beginning of David's story, and he brings it to an end with the death of his mother, Elly Reis Solmitz, forty-two years later. He voyages backwards from his father's death into their past and present as a family, or as several families—his father's, his mother's, and his own—and then finally directs a tentative gaze, beyond his mother's death, in an epilogue, toward a future which he hopes to be able to shape into something worthy of that past: into something not capable of redeeming it, but of putting it, nonetheless, to the most human possible use.

David revisits horrors of which his father's death was a not-so-distant echo. But he also examines the involuted cultural, spiritual and psychological equilibriums, which, in his own particular family, those horrors and the immediate history from which they descended could only throw desperately awry; and in doing so he addresses states of mind and modes of thought of which the strengths and weaknesses are fatally intertwined, and even at times indistinguishable from one another. David takes on the task of coming to nourishing terms with all the forces, ancestral or not, which come into play within his life, and whether they are positive or negative from any other point of view than his own is finally immaterial. The motto that controls his narrative—from Pindar, from his father, from his father's teacher Paulus Geheeb—is "Become who you are," and values, in that light, are positive or negative only insofar as they promote or hinder the pursuit of such a goal. The fortitude which allowed his mother to rescue his father from Dachau plays out somewhat differently in her relationship with her son, just as the gift of all-overwhelming compassion that preserved his father's humanity in the face of unspeakable trials was likewise a force, no matter how moving and eminently attractive, that David would have to learn somewhat differently to modulate.

David has undertaken this voyage primarily for his own benefit. And in doing so, he offers an example. There are pains he refuses to avoid or dampen, embarrassments from which he refuses to hide, recollections he refuses to suppress. There are also joys and satisfactions that he is careful to acknowledge and revere. Gratitude is one of the emotions he seems most ready to express. But there are also numerous ways in which his voyage is more than personal. Self-liberation—becoming who and what one is—is no end in itself. The liberated individual is a person who is able more fruitfully to engage with other human beings, which in David's case is a question not only of intimate or personal relationships, but also of his chosen work as a courageous and unconventional educator. That is the kind of liberation that David has chosen to seek.

David, too, has performed a special service for those of us who knew his father, and who were very much affected by him. One knew him with great intensity, but one did not know him well. He was more like a moral force than a true and proper individual. That had something to do with what he may have seen as a necessary distance between teacher and student, but there were other, more intimate distances as well. David, now, has enabled us to know him somewhat better, and that's something for which I personally am very grateful.

Henry Martin
Author, art critic, translator
Fié allo Sciliar, Italy

Introduction

THERE ARE NOT LESS THAN 36 TZADDIKIM—RIGHTEOUS PERSONS IN THE WORLD WHO RECEIVE THE SHEKHINAH—THE DIVINE PRESENCE.

—B. T. SANHEDRIN 97B, SUKKOT 45B

The Thirty-Six Unknown

The notion of the thirty-six righteous ones appears in the Talmud, the oral tradition of Judaism, as a teaching of one of the Babylonian rabbis, Abbaye. In Abbaye's teaching, the world required a minimum of thirty-six righteous individuals in order to exist. There follows an argument about what happens if there are not thirty-six in the world. How will the world be redeemed? The idea may have been suggested by the famous story in the Bible of Sodom, in which Abraham argued with God to save the wicked city (Genesis, chapter 18). God agreed, if ten righteous individuals could be found there. Abraham won the argument but lost the fight; Sodom was destroyed, seemingly because the minimum, ten righteous individuals, could not be found. That's the shadow side of the story of the thirty-six: it's a minimum, and sometimes the world may not contain thirty-six righteous individuals.*

In later Kabbalistic (Kabbalah) folklore, the thirty-six hidden ones have the potential to save the world, they appear when they are needed, and one of them might be the Messiah. They come at times of great peril, called out of their anonymity and humility by the necessity to save the world. Because they can, and because we need them. We Jews began to get familiar with them, referring to them in Yiddish as the *lamed vov-niks* (*lamed vov* is Hebrew for thirty-six), and seeing them everywhere in the anonymous acts of good people who rise to great acts in difficult circumstances. And because one of the lamed vov-niks, one of the

*From the Web site of Todd Weinstein, a photographer in New York City, www.lichtensteiger.de/todd.html.

anonymous thirty-six might be the Messiah, we tended to treat strangers with kindness and the possibility that he or she could be the one. It could be the person we least suspect, because the thirty-six, like all the sustaining notions of the world in the Kabbalah, are hidden. They may appear, they may not appear. If they do appear, they may be known, they may be unknown. In each generation, we look for them everywhere.

The first time I met David Solmitz and his parents, David must have been about five—possibly six—years old, because he was born in 1943, two years before my own first child. My husband, Bill, had begun his short teaching career at Bowdoin College in 1946, teaching philosophy and psychology, commuting from my family's retirement farm on Prince's Point, where we had been caretaking during World War II, waiting for my parents to return—about seven miles from the Bowdoin campus. Bill, who was legally blind, could not drive, so made the commute, either driving in with our neighbor, who taught in the mathematics department, or cycling in and back on his Raleigh bicycle. In the evening, I would drive in and pick him up for the trip home, unless he was cycling.

But in September 1946 we decided to move into town, and were lucky enough to be offered a year's rental by the head of the German department, Fritz Koelln, who, along with his family, was to be in Germany for a year's Sabbatical leave.

I expect it might have been at a party put on by Ann, the wife of the head of the philosophy department, Newton Stallknecht, that we first met Elly and Walter, David's parents. Walter was teaching in the German department, but also taught an occasional class in philosophy—and clearly would have loved to be in the department full-time.

I liked them both very much, and admired Walter, although his natural courtliness and reserved manner made it a bit difficult to feel completely at ease with him for a natural "leveler" like me. However, as I came to know him better over time, I became very fond of him, and realized more and more clearly that his reserve was a necessary cloak for a great deal of intense feeling—a man of profound beliefs and a kind and caring nature, yet also a deeply troubled person. He smiled but seldom, but when he did, it was turning on a brilliant light.

I too had a lot to hold back—although not on the same grounds as Walter's nor to the degree of urgency. Even so, its existence must have created a kind of unspoken inner bond for me. I learned from Bill that Walter had actually been in a concentration camp but had been rescued by Elly's persistent efforts—which made me admire them both even more.

Elly herself was a very calm, thoughtful person, also sensible and deeply caring—and David was an oddball kind of little kid—but then, so was my Billy. David was probably preoccupied with his little cars, lying on the floor and supplying the background motor noises needed to bring them to life, while Elly and I chatted about this and that.

It was only many years later, after Bill's thesis had been written and accepted, and he had taken a job teaching in Texas, and then, after nine years, another one at the State University of New York at Albany, that we heard—perhaps from Ed Pols at Bowdoin—that Walter was suffering badly. I became deeply troubled at this news, and even telephoned him to ask if I could come to Brunswick for a short visit and talk with him. There was something about the dynamic I was sensing in the situation that connected with what I was undergoing myself—although I could not have specified what that was. Of course, he thanked me very politely but said no, not just now—or something equally gentle but firm. The next news we heard was that he had taken his life.

It couldn't have been a lot later than my call. In my own hour of profound unmet need I had attempted to reach out to him on a very deep level, soul to soul, as it were—from the "place" where we are all one, perhaps. Of course it was not possible as a potentially successful strategy to prevent suicide—but that was not the level at which I was operating. His refusal to engage with me on the level of action in a real world was predictable and rational, and served to jolt me back to a better sense of my own reality. But for him that outer reality had ceased to function as an adequate anchor against the chaos and despair within.

Does this story mean that we are, after all, alone in our separate worlds, unable to reach out to one another in the hour of need? Is the myth of the lamed vov-niks which I quote above merely a wishful fantasy created by a people who had been living for centuries without hope of kindness and acceptance by their fellow men? If so, then, the question must go beyond to the further one: Is the whole concept of God's profound sense of justice and kindness in the face of mass human indifference, self-centeredness, and evil also a self-serving myth? And what happens if you concur, and decide just to live as part of a world that believes this to be true? Some modern-day churches seem to operate as though it were both possible and realistic to do so, while still clinging to the old shibboleths of their faiths. Newton Stallknecht once quoted to us his father's term for them as "mouth Christians."

Perhaps it is possible to find a humanistic solution to the age-old religious issue of "faith and works"—but I'm not sure. What I do believe is that we human beings are destined to live our lives in the light of our earliest experiences and, most crucially, the influence of our parents and siblings—whether "for" or "against"—or, if we are lucky, or work hard at it, in an Hegelian synthesis of the two! In this manner, the culture we derive from our forebears, for good or evil, is perpetuated in our offspring, and continuity is thereby assured for the survival of that culture, with both its faults and its virtues.

I remember reading somewhere that if indeed God is a human invention, then He is one we need to make, if we are to learn to live according to the best that is in us, not the worst! And we need also to give profound respect to those who live in the world as though the myth is real, and God in fact does demand of us that we live a life of justice and mercy, of righteousness—the life of tzaddikim, holy ones—to the best of our ability to become them! In that sense, it makes a great deal of difference what kind of God we are giving our allegiance to—whether our God is one who has been reified by some religious group or is inherent in the outlook on life being embodied in our parents. It is in this sense, I believe, that both Walter and Elly Solmitz, and their son David no less, could be said to be Jewish despite a lack of formal connections with any institutional group—and how it happened that Elly saw herself as Jewish enough at the end of her life to ask for a visit from a rabbi. Such identification comes from within, and does not depend on external connections.

These, then, are the kinds of underlying themes that I experience David Solmitz as exploring in his faithful rendering of all these lives in their historical settings. It is a worthy inquiry indeed—especially in the context of the profound changes we seem to be undergoing in modern society. It sometimes seems to me that Nietzsche's "transvaluation of values" is taking place under our very noses, fulfilling the chillingly prophetic poem of William Butler Yeats, *The Second Coming*, which ends:

The darkness drops again; but now I know
That twenty centuries of stony sleep
Were vexed to nightmare by a rocking cradle,
And what rough beast, its hour come round at last,
Slouches towards Bethlehem to be born?

With all of these profound changes taking place in human society, I wonder whether or not one can adopt a way of life based on a belief one may doubt is actually true, in the literal sense of truth, and yet be necessary for the perpetuation of life on earth—and thus, in a sense be taken as true on the profoundest level of truth. Can we invent a God who functions as the source of goodness, truth and humanity, without being verifiable as actually existent under the rubrics of either science or nature?

This is one of the questions I have elicited from David's detailed and very moving accounts of the lives of his parents and of himself. He provides us with many innate questions—and, by the strength of his love and devotion, with his personal answers. His faithfulness to the lives of his parents, and, by his own words and deeds, to both the love they gave him and the teachings they instilled into him from birth onward, gives us all the answers he needs.

David has arrived at these truths as a result of a great deal of living—of soul searching—of trial and error. Like his father, David has striven to live his life according to the teachings of the Greek lyric poet Pindar, which became the motto of the Odenwaldschule which his father attended in his youth—*Werde der du bist*—"Become who you are." And, I would add, also those of the Oracle of Apollo at Delphi as echoed by Socrates—*gnothi seauton*—"Know thyself!" Also like his father, David sometimes worries about his own ability to live up to those ideals and still be faithful to the harder truths about himself—but unlike Walter, David received the blessing that Walter was not fortunate enough to have been given, of a childhood filled with love and joy, of acceptance and support. Not an ideal childhood, I'm sure, but what childhood is?

Walter and he were both fortunate enough to have married faithful, intelligent, well-balanced women (although for David that came only after many years of pain)—but for Walter the childhood of family comfort and status he was born into was not enough to balance out the dark forces that continued to work within him throughout his lifetime. Some of them were no doubt inherent in the many historical forces operating in the lives of most Jewish families—but in his case, there was also a direct heritage of conflict and dysfunctionality within the family severe enough to create mental illness in his sister and the suicidal deaths of both his grandfather and his father. This dysfunctionality was also embedded in non-Jewish German culture of the times. David writes of his father's childhood:

> He grew up in a Prussian-like, rigid Germany, while the German empire seemed to be at its prime. Born in 1905, his childhood seemed pitifully formal and lonely. I see pictures of little

> Walter dressed in a wide-collared sailor shirt, tucked neatly into smoothly pressed shorts, beneath which he wore dark tights. Narrow, ankle-high, multi-laced shoes add to the stiffness of his appearance. The large stone house in which he was growing up in Braunschweig reflects the stuffy living conditions of an extended family of well-to-do Jewish business people.

Walter's early life reminds me of that of Ludwig Wittgenstein, who grew up in a very rich, successful Jewish family in Vienna—and whose inner life was always suffused with profound depression and self-doubt. The ending of his life reminds me of that of the Italian chemist Primo Levi, whose book *Survival in Auschwitz* details the horrifying conditions under which he and the other inmates were forced to survive—and who finally also took his own life after having endured both the camp and the equally appalling circumstances of his long trip back into the postwar world—and who seemed to have finally taken it back up again, apparently a happy, successful businessman and writer, only to succumb to the dark inner forces that still lived within him.

I do not claim to understand completely everything that haunted Walter Solmitz throughout his lifetime, which contaminated his post-Holocaust life throughout the outwardly—or potentially—happy years of his professorship at Bowdoin College, and which ultimately took his life.

My concern is to accept the terms of all of those lives with which David presents his readers so vividly, and to try to learn from them something more about the meaning—the enigma—of life, and how we are to live it! It seems to me that there is a great deal to be internalized and learned from within the compass of these deeply felt, expressively shaped histories, reminiscences and musings that David Solmitz has offered to us, his readers, in *Piecing Scattered Souls*.

My friend Rabbi Zalman Schachter-Shalomi says, "We are all *Meschiach* (the Messiah) now"—that we need to learn to live our lives as though God had sent us to "save the world"—or, I might say, as though we might be, unknownst to ourselves as well as to others, one of the hidden lamed vov-niks whom God has decreed are necessary to save the world.

Mary Leue
Educator
Ashfield, MA

Preface

Many Americans who attempt to trace their families a few generations back end up feeling lost. More than likely these ancestors came from near and far, from beyond the borders of the United States, from Mexico and Latin America, England, Ireland, and the European continent, Russia, the Middle East, Asia, and the African continent. Furthermore, many Americans today spend their lives moving between divorced parents and different partners as well as between jobs. How can one not feel uprooted and disconnected?

Therefore, this book is a story about journeys, connections, and healing. It is a family chronicle discovering surprising links from around the world that form a matrix of stories. These reach from Dessau, Germany, to Monterey, Mexico, to Roma, Texas, to Braunschweig (Brunswick), Germany, and from there to Brunswick, Maine. From Brunswick, Maine, the links continue to Zurich, Switzerland, to Shantou and Shanghai, China, and back to Maine. This narrative, like so many stories of families, is borderless as regards race, ethnicity, cultural backgrounds, and creed. It becomes a journey to different places both figuratively and literally. It fosters the realization that we are one people huddled together on our small, fragile planet Earth.

This particular saga is seen through the eyes of the only child of Nazi Holocaust survivors. By writing in the third person, I find I become less of a narcissist, feel a little more humble, and am better able to see myself more clearly. By reflecting on the place of David, the son, in these stories, they become a healing process by allowing me to break through prejudice and misconceptions, resulting in new and lasting friendships. In visiting my parents' hometowns of Braunschweig and Hamburg, Laim, a suburb of Munich where they lived following their marriage, and the Nazi concentration camps, especially at Dachau and Theresienstadt, I felt directly akin to them. Guided by the wisdom of those who came before, the bonds they made, and the understandings they fostered, I intimately offer my insight of a continually evolving community through life, death, and rebirth.

Waterville, Maine
June 2010

DOS

Acknowledgments

This book was made possible thanks to the encouragement and support of my wife Jing Ye. Her suggestion to seek and develop connections as opposed to an autobiographical text made the process of discovery exciting, uplifting, and balanced. Jing came up with the title for the book. My mother, to whom I became close again during her last years of life, shared stories from her childhood, her youth, her life in Germany and America that touched me deeply. Her recollections demonstrated the humble yet tenacious person she was. I am grateful to my father's colleague, Professor Edward Pols, at Bowdoin College for his courageous affirmation of my father during his years at Bowdoin. Although I knew he had brought my father into the philosophy department, only when talking with him did I realize the difficulty he, as a Catholic, had in the mid 1950s to bring a Jew into the department. I am grateful to several of my father's students who shared their stories of my father and their appreciation for him. These include among others Louis Aeskov, Henry Martin, Frank Scmit, and Kent Spriggs. I am particularly grateful to Mary Leue, who wrote the moving foreword to this book.

After nearly sixty years, on reading in several educational journals about Mary Leue and the nationally recognized alternative school, the Albany Free School, that she founded and directed for many years, I wrote to her. I wondered whether she was the same Mary Leue I fondly remembered as a small child. Her husband, Bill, a philosopher, was a colleague of my father's at Bowdoin College. As a result we reconnected, forming a beautiful friendship for which I am deeply appreciative. Mary has seen how as an educator I have followed my father's example and become a progressive teacher in my own right.

I am thankful to Roger Phelps, who has offered encouraging feedback throughout my process of writing. As the book nears completion, I am indebted to my Academic Dean, Thomas Edwards of Thomas College, Waterville, Maine, who directed me to a friend of his in the U.S. Consulate. This gentleman put me in touch with the Regional Archives in Munich and the Archives at the concentration camp at Dachau.

I am thankful to Dieter and Liliana Goldstein de Kühne of the Jewish Community in Braunschweig, who provided a fascinating tour of the temple—its current state and history—as well as the City of Braunschweig, and who introduced me to Reinhard Bein. Mr. Bein showed me the actual graves of my grandfather, great- and great-great-grandfathers, as well as giving me his recent book on the cemeteries of Braunschweig, *Ewiges Haus, Jüdische Friedhöfe in Stadt und Land Braunschweig.* With unrelenting zeal, he continued to help me search further about my family in Braunschweig. He spent many, many hours in Braunschweig's archives searching for further information on the Solmitz family and transcribed the old handwritten script into legible typewritten form for me. We have become fond friends. His partner, Regina Blume, translated gravestones of my family from German into English, for which I am deeply grateful.

I am very grateful for the significant information that Dr. Werner Gorssert and Dr. Bernd Ulbrich of the Jewish community in Dessau, Germany, provided me. They were able to discover information about my grandmother's family, the Sanderses of Dessau, on my father's side, who were from that town near Berlin. Together with Werner Grossert and Reinhard Bein, we were able to discover the gravestone of Alexander Wolf Sanders, my great-great-grandfather on the Sanders side of the family. I am obliged to Terry Sanders, grandson of my grandmother's brother, Maurice, who gave me a copy of the Sanders family tree. Hollis Pruitt, whose wife Sandra is a Sanders of Little Rock, has furnished me relevant information on—and old photos of—the Sanders family.

I am also indebted to Professor Joist Grolle of Hamburg, who has written a book about my father, answered numerous questions about him, and given me a tour of the university at which Walter studied, the Warburg Library where he worked, and the Jewish quarter where my mother grew up. His knowledge of Hamburg is invaluable to my understanding of both my father and mother.

I am most grateful to Kari Hopperstead for hours of patience and outstanding work in editing the book. I am indebted to Paul Cornell du Houx, editor of Polar Bear & Company, who enthusiastically accepted this book with much interest, appreciation, and dedication. My deep appreciation and gratitude to Ramona du Houx for her moving artistic interpretation for the book's cover. Last but not least, I am indebted to my daughter, May Ye, who was always ready to rescue me with computer expertise.

THE DUAL AND RECIPROCAL FUNCTION OF HISTORY IS TO PROMOTE OUR UNDERSTANDING OF THE PAST IN THE LIGHT OF THE PRESENT AND OF THE PRESENT IN THE LIGHT OF THE PAST.

—EDWARD HALLETT CARR, *WHAT IS HISTORY*

Piecing Scattered Souls

1

Quiet Thunder in August

THURSDAY, JUNE 9, 1963

David writes in his journal:

> The last time I saw you, Daddy, Mummy was taking me to Harvard Summer School in Cambridge. You encouraged me to make up the biology course I failed at the University of Maine. Although you seemed your usual self as you stood on the porch, cigarette in hand, to wave us good-bye, you were more relaxed. After all, the semester had ended for you, and you had turned

in your final grades just the day before. I remember the moment clearly. It was a cool morning in late June, and you were wearing that loose, light, purplish-gray zipper jacket, zipped part way up over the worn yellowed dress shirt and dark-gray slacks with an elastic waistband, and those funny brown cloth shoes with beige rubber soles you really liked. Standing by the steps, you gently waved good-bye as we headed off, I at the driver's seat and Mummy next to me. My last sight of you was through the rearview mirror of our battleship-gray 1959 Rambler American: you had turned around and were already opening the screen door to enter the house.

Weeks later, on the morning of August 23, Mummy came to pick me up from Harvard Summer School. She had spent a few days with friends from Germany in Belmont, minutes away from Cambridge. Never in my wildest dreams could I have imagined when Mummy and I arrived home, we'd find a note on the banister, so different from those I was used to, which usually said: "Munky, wake me up at 3:00 p.m."

THURSDAY, AUGUST 16, 1962

His wife and son having left just hours ago, Walter feels he finally has the window of opportunity to end his despair. Sitting at his desk in his small, dark, smoke-filled study, he writes the following note to his son, whom he lovingly calls Munk.

Dear Munk,

Mummy left a few hours ago, and I feel like sending you a greeting. I cannot write any more—
except
giving you my love.
Daddy
Walter

David has little interest in attending college. He needs to escape from his home environment and his fear of being unable to live up to his father's expectations—or at least those he imagines. At age 19, he doesn't fully understand his father. He doesn't have much compassion for the accumulation of horrific experiences and events that has caused his father much suffering, severe anxiety, and depression. He doesn't really appreciate the wisdom and insight into the human condition that his father, a brilliant classical philosopher and scholar, has developed. Nor is he aware that his father feels guilty for his inability to face demons from his past and shameful that his wife has been working as a secretary to help pay for his frequent hospitalization and medical expenses.

Walter is anguished that his son chose to attend the University of Maine that mandated Reserve Officers Training Corps participation, rather than attend Bowdoin, where he is teaching. Graduating from a prestigious college may offer David more and better career opportunities. And how could David deal with ROTC when he has strong reservations against the military? Walter, whose own conviction as a pacifist grew out of his experiences during the Holocaust, fears sending his son off to war. The war in Vietnam is in its beginning stages, and tensions between the United States and the Soviet Union over the construction of the Berlin Wall could escalate into war.

Friday, August 17, 1962

Elly, his wife, telephones, just to stay in touch. Walter feels relieved. Accepting her suggestion, he enjoys a good goulash meal and heads out for a walk, stopping on the way to mail Elly a brief note.

David with his parents, 1960

WALTER HIKING IN BAVARIA, CIRCA 1936

Although seeking solace and inspiration in the beauty of nature, he is despondent, anguished, and even desperate that he might not have the ability to teach his upcoming courses.

Leaving the house on the last side street off Brunswick's Maine Street, he walks slowly but deliberately, taking in the smells of sweet fern and freshly cut late-season hay and the melodious chirping of birds. He heads towards a scenic outcrop above Dionne's farm. Standing at a small, abandoned rock quarry filled with water, he looks over the mowed fields below, the neat white farm and tall silo of Granite Hill Dairy in the distance, and forests of mixed hardwoods and conifers. As he notices the early signs of fall—orange and red on maple trees—he thinks lovingly of his wife. In Maine the first signs of fall always occur around her August 10th birthday.

The worried face of his professor in Hamburg, the philosopher Ernst Cassirer, appears in his mind. "Walter," Cassirer speaks softly, "you are a brilliant man. I am impressed by your work. However, you take on so many questions that you seem unable to pursue one to completion."

That was thirty years ago. He flinches, looks onto the granite outcrop on which he is standing, thinking that he still cannot pursue his work to completion—he cannot even complete his course preparation for the coming fall term. He looks down at the still, dark water of the little quarry pond, thinking of Ed, his department head and close friend, and of his family, "I can't meet Ed's expectations. I can't burden Elly and David. I can't continue…"

He calls to mind the image of the kindly director of the Warburg Library for the Science of Art, Fritz Saxl, for whom he worked as a research assistant in Hamburg back in the early thirties. Having noticed that Walter was finding it difficult to balance his dissertation and research project, Saxl sat down with him over coffee. "Why not take a break from our work together, so that you can focus on your thesis? I encourage you to spend time in the countryside. There, in the nature you so much love, you will surely be able to work uninterrupted without the headaches and challenges of your research work with us."

He recalls the time he spent nearly thirty years ago living for several months with a kind family at their Bavarian farm. From his small, gabled room, he used to look out over the barnyard in which ducks, geese, and chickens freely roamed. He could hear the farmer's pigs grunting and growling in their pen. Two workhorses often stood silently by the gangplank to a wooden frame barn. Looking beyond the farmyard, he used to relish the rolling meadows bordered by dark fir forests.

He walks alone on gravel lanes and paths across meadows and through woods, obsessing over his inability to work effectively on his doctoral dissertation. Always new thoughts arise, preventing him from completing earlier concepts. Now unable to break from this pattern, he feels more alone, frustrated and even at times hopeless without Elly by his side to encourage and support him.

Saturday, August 18, 1962

He is disappointed that no letter from Elly appears in the mailbox. That afternoon, in his usual manner of jotting down notes, he writes to Elly in their native German. After his lengthy hospitalization during the previous winter's recurring mental breakdown, he now dwells in constant fear that he may not be able to continue teaching, and that he will become a burden to his wife and son. He tries to disguise his anxiety a little, but he cannot help expressing his dependence on her.

> No letter from you, also none to answer since you telephoned. It serves me right to experience what it is like when I don't receive a letter from you. It serves me right when I find that it is not there.
>
> Yesterday afternoon I went for a long walk above Dionne's farm—to bed at 10,
>
> up at 5.
>
> — constantly smoking too much
> — in the office put together books for my courses
> — began the reading list and additional schoolwork
> — also preparing in case I won't be able to return
> — Ed informed me that he wants to see my list by the end of the week.

Humid day, but cool at home and at the office—so beautiful and green here.

Undisciplined—home at 4 for dinner. Have already eaten pea soup. Writing this while potatoes cook—so that I can put this in the mailbox before 5.

Can you give yourself a little pleasure? Would like that. And buy a dress? (that would please me)

And now to the mailbox—and then to the potatoes!

Love,

Elly,
Your,
Walter.

SUNDAY, AUGUST 19, 1962

He reflects on Nietzsche, as he often quoted to his son whenever he felt discouraged, "What does not destroy you, makes you stronger." *I am at the end*, he thinks, *for it appears to me now that I cannot deal with having more trouble and worry than joy. Therefore, it seems that the time has come to disappear, even if it it's difficult.*

By this time, especially as the day of Elly's and David's return is drawing closer, he has to make a final decision. No longer can he waver back and forth.

MONDAY, AUGUST 20, 1962

He writes his final letter to his son.

What I may do seems necessary although it is deeply wrong—towards myself, towards you, towards Mummy.

(One part of it was the smoking).

Teaching philosophy was perhaps a little too much for me. You may do simpler things, and you will do them decently. You know, you are a good boy. In spite of what I have done, you will have and give joy.

Having written this, he feels some relief. His spirits seem a little lighter. Although wavering, he remains serious about carrying out his plan.

Tuesday, August 22, 1962

In his usual logical manner, he draws up a list.

Contra	Pro
Possibly not succeeding	Smoking
Elly, David	In case of mental disability
Betrayal to the good	Giving up this year will be hell for Elly and me
Hard to do	This year, can I face it? Will I make it? Exams

Major meetings. (regular meetings with students)
Majoring in philosophy
Breaking out of crisis again.

Before going to bed, he writes a short note to Elly.

Dearest,

Writing is a little difficult for me, but to tell you what I know, that I love you, is not hard for me to say. At least I want to send you a greeting before the post office closes.

Love,

Your,
Walter

Wednesday, August 22, 1962

As the morning dawns, he writes a note that he never mails, probably to Elly.

I have probably put it off—first because of exams [he was thinking of David's exams at summer school], then not sure whether I would succeed. I had wanted that everything would be in order before you arrived. Now it has become very late. Keep well!

Greeting also to friends. You know of whom I always think.

Later that morning, he drafts a letter to his closest friend, Professor Fritz C. A. Koelln. Fritz and Walter had met in the mid 1920s as philosophy students at the University of Hamburg and had remained steadfast friends ever since. Fritz, who was not Jewish, emigrated together with his wife and eldest daughter to the United States. In 1929 he became a professor of German at Bowdoin College, to which he brought Walter as an instructor in German.

The humidity from Monday has dissipated. The weather is once again clear, warm and dry. Midafternoon, he picks up the letter addressed to Fritz. Holding it, he hesitates, then sets it down again on his desk. Grabbing his ballpoint pen, he adds on the envelope: "Do not open until Friday." He descends the stairs from his smoke-filled study. As he opens the front door of the house, a cool sea breeze greets him. Lovingly, he inhales a deep breath of fresh air. He heads towards Fritz's house, about three-fourths of a mile down Maine Street. Across from the college, he turns onto Page Street. Hesitating a moment at 7 Page Street, he hears Fritz, a portly, cheerful gentleman with a crop of white hair. He is playing the piano inside. He musters his courage, ascends the front steps, rings the doorbell. Fritz opens the door, happy to see his friend. "Come in!" he beckons.

Walter in his office, Bowdoin college, 1957

"Just for a moment. I have a letter here for you that I ask you to open only on Friday," Walter says. He enters the house and follows Fritz to the first room on the left, his study.

"Sit down," Fritz says, "I've just been playing Beethoven sonatas." Seating himself at the old upright, he turns to Sonata, Op. 10, No.3, begins to play the lively *presto* first movement. Walter relaxes on the little German love seat. Enjoyment of music bonds the two men. Following the Sonata:

"Such beautiful music

brings me peace. However, I must go now. I still have much work to do for my courses," Walter says.

"Oh, Walter," Fritz replies, "stay a little longer. It's so good of you to stop by. Let's just enjoy a little more music."

"I must go."

"And how are Elly and David?"

"David wrote me such a nice letter the other day. He is determined to return to the University of Maine. Finally, I've come around to accept his decision. After all, when I am not well, it is hard on both Elly and David."

"But, Walter, you are in fine shape, better than I have seen you for some time," Fritz replies.

"Ah, yes, but I really must go. Greet Bine [Fritz's wife] for me."

Looking back at Fritz, who remains standing at the door, Walter descends quickly for the walk home. On the one hand, he feels reassured. On the other, he is wavering. *Fritz is such a dear friend,* he thinks, *he'll miss me.*

He is also becoming more anxious. *Will I be able to do it? Will I succeed?*

Thursday, August 23, 1962

Upon his waking, the early morning sun radiates through his window and birds are signing cheerfully. He rises, lights a cigarette, sits at his desk to draft his last letter to Elly.

> Thursday
> Dear Elly,
>
> I don't believe that I will ever be well again. Therefore, I don't believe I can withstand the temptation of taking the sleeping pills. You can tell the police that they should come to check. It is terrible that I am doing this just before David's exam, but the opportunity is right here now. Do not forget that you have done more than everything you can for me and that I know how much you have suffered on account of me. You feel it better, feel it deeply and remain silent. Don't forget the joy and that you are dearly loved more than you can ever imagine. And also the boy very much in another way.
>
> Your,
> Walter

He then takes the note written to David on Monday but not yet mailed and adds:

> Thursday
> Your letter almost (and for a while) almost kept me from doing it.

Before the clock strikes 6:30 a.m., he places a note on the capital of the banister leading upstairs, laying a stone on top of it. He places the letters to Elly and David on the green bureau that sits above the stairs by the bathroom door. He places a second note to Fritz by the banister downstairs. He goes to the bathroom, takes a bottle of sleeping pills from the white medicine cabinet above the sink. With water, he swallows all.

About an hour later, he is mortified to wake up. In his despair, he quickly scribbles a message to the bottom of his letter to Elly.

> The sleeping pills haven't worked. Shall I try something else? I cannot think of you when I do this.

By 9:00 a.m. Thursday morning, Elly arrives at Perkins Hall, a Harvard University dormitory, to pick David up from summer school. The botany exam is over. He has learned that he passed by the skin of his teeth. *Oh well*, he thinks, *it's over with.*

He is, however, sad to leave behind Betty, a kindergarten teacher from upstate New York. From the moment he met her at the summer school's cafeteria, he had been enamored of her, a small, slender woman in her mid twenties with blue eyes and sandy-colored hair. Not only is her hair short like his mother's, but also her interests and values are similar to those instilled in him by his parents. They had enjoyed going to Boston's Museum of Fine Arts and attending lectures and concerts together. They attended a lecture by the aging socialist, Norman Thomas, whose humanity and activism impressed them. On Hiroshima Day, they had listened to a young peace activist, Brad Lyttle, both feeling that his radical approach to peace was frightening. Betty had remarked, "How insane to grasp hold and climb on the propeller of a submarine."

"Yes," David had replied, "doing things in the extreme usually have a bad ending."

As mother and son drive out of the city on this warm summer day, he thinks lovingly of Betty. Just a few days ago, after the Pete Seeger concert, David had written in his journal:

> Betty is so sweet. She is lively and at the same time such a gentle and warm person. She is delicate, which brings out her charm, her sweetness, her pure pleasantness. She is so sincere and so kind and lovable. Imagine, being brought up in an orphanage and now teaching sub-primary! . . . We talked about Emerson and Thoreau. She said that he and Thoreau saw what life really is and tried to understand it. They saw a purpose to life and knew what it is.

He now looks forward to a short stay at home before returning to the University of Maine. He anticipates that during these last days of summer Daddy and he can hike in the Camden hills.

Reaching the Kennebunk rest area off of the Maine Turnpike, they stop for lunch at the Howard Johnson's. Following their usual meal of meatloaf, green peas, and instant mashed potatoes, they finish with a traditional strawberry sundae.

The closer they come to Brunswick, the more excited the son becomes. He is eager to see the petunias that he had planted on new traffic islands in the middle of Maine Street. As he would be away for the summer, he had asked the fire department to water them. They did. They even purchased a special nozzle for a hose for their No. 1 tank truck.

At one in the afternoon, the weather couldn't be more beautiful. Puffy clouds in a clear blue sky and a strong breeze cause the summer temperature to feel just right. The son parks the car in front of Day's Newsstand. He jumps out, crosses the street to admire the petunias. Wow! Beautiful! Bushes of well-watered and nourished deep-red flowers have grown so large that they hang over the island's curb. Crossing the street back to the car, he joins his mother chatting with Fritz, who has just come out of the store, the day's *New York Times* in hand. Elly offers to drive Fritz home, a proposal he accepts. After dropping him off, mother and son head home three-fourths of a mile up Maine Street.

On entering the front door, they catch sight of folded pieces of paper held down by a stone on the capital of the banister. Father often left messages there, be they "Wake me up at 3:00 p.m.," or "Gone for a walk." This note, however, orders: "Do NOT go upstairs." David's heart sinks into his stomach. In spite of his mother's firm mandate that he not follow her up the stairs, he pursues with a heavy heart and an agonizing feeling of anxiety.

Although sleeping pills and the son's blood-stained knife both failed, he has successfully slit his wrists with a razor blade under water in the bath tub, where they find him now. In shock, the son dashes downstairs and reads the note written to Fritz the previous day.

> Elly and David can be expected to be here around or after 1 o'clock Thursday. I had hoped to arrange things so that they would know before leaving Boston. But I could not decide fast enough. Then I must ask you to see to it that they'll know before entering the house—and the body be removed and everything cleaned up before they'll come. Would you wait here for them to tell them before their entering the house?
>
> (My mother is buried on the "Hand in Hand" cemetery in Boston. People here may get in touch with Solomon Funeral Home in Boston. Everything as simple as possible.)

The mother immediately telephones Fritz and Ed, Walter's department chair, from the upstairs phone. Too shocked to cry, the son then notifies the police department from the downstairs phone. Chief LaBelle arrives promptly, but Ed arrives first, speechless and frightfully pale. After the police chief leaves, Ed immediately takes charge by asking Elly for a pail and Comet bleach detergent.

A short while later Fritz arrives out of breath, having walked from home as fast as he could. "Elly, if only I had opened Walter's letter. I honored his request as a friend. I never imagined—" Tears burst forth; he sobs uncontrollably.

Within minutes, a black hearse from Brackett's funeral home pulls up behind the black-and-white police car. Two dignified men in dark gray pinstriped suits alight from the long, black Cadillac with drawn black curtains on its rear side windows. They walk stern faced to the back of the vehicle, pull out a stretcher, and proceed quickly up the front steps. The son opens the door. Without uttering a word to each other or to the son, they head upstairs.

Neighbors have been gathering on their front lawns wondering what is going on at the Solmitzes'. As the son comes out of the house, their next-door neighbor, Jean Walker, comes over crying. From across the street, Mario and Theresa Tonon, approach. Mario, a former student of Walter's on the GI plan, now the stern principal of the son's high school, doesn't mince words: "You'll be going to Bowdoin in the fall. Your mom, needs you at home. I'll contact Bill Shaw, director of admissions."

Theresa, his bride whom he rescued while serving in Poland during

World War II, returns to their house. A few minutes later, she brings David a plate with a fried egg and piece of bread.

The son is standing by the front steps, when the door opens. The two undertakers bear a stretcher with his father covered in a white sheet. They wheel the stretcher toward the back of the hearse, open the rear door, and slide his father in. A moment later, the Cadillac pulls away from the house.

The son strolls toward the house of the other neighbors, the Russells, solid Maine stock from Presque Isle and Orr's Island. Mrs. Russell, a sixth-grade school teacher, stands alone in her driveway.

"He took his own life," the son explains.

"I'm so sorry," she quietly says.

The son senses her thoughts have turned to her older son, who drowned several years earlier. She returns slowly to her house.

As Ed and Fritz are cleaning up the bathroom, Elly is telephoning her husband's nephew, Fred, a lawyer who lives in Wellesley, Massachusetts. Walter had requested to be buried next to his mother just outside of Boston in Jamaica Plains. Fred's wife urges mother and son to drive down immediately to stay with her and her family. "Fred will help you make the necessary arrangements for the funeral and burial. We will host a gathering for your friends and Walter's colleagues who will be coming from Brunswick to attend the service."

Elly packs a small suitcase with a suit in which the son's father will be buried. When mother and son leave a little while later, the wind has died down. The pink, puffy clouds have disappeared, leaving the sky a cobalt blue. During the entire trip to Wellesley, they remain silent. As he drives, occasionally he glances toward her. She sits straight in her seat next to his in the Rambler. She looks out at the scenery, the woods and fields she so much loves. Black-eyed Susans are now dotting the fields together with delicate Queen Anne's lace and the season's first goldenrod.

In his journal the following day, the son writes:

> Saturday, August 25, 1962
>
> Daddy wouldn't like this [paying $650 for a coffin], nor do I. It would be so wonderful if he could be just gently laid in a simple wooden plank coffin and go back to the simple earth from which we all originated. He was a humble man, and never wanted lushness or luxury. The country was home to him. It was peace. The birds sang sweetly in the trees. It is quiet in the country. Here Daddy could think, away from the intensity of people and city

> noise. I am convinced that it was in the country where Daddy accomplished his best thoughts . . . It was the quietness and serenity of the country, which gave him hope, because it was here where he always was at his peak, most calm and most wonderful.

Walter's colleagues from Bowdoin attend his funeral in Brookline. They are present when he is laid to rest next to his mother at the Hand in Hand cemetery in Jamaica Plains. A small, simple, flat stone plaque rests embedded in the grass.

The eulogy Ed Pols delivers at the October 8, 1962, meeting of the Bowdoin faculty reflects the truth of Walter's life.

> For him philosophy was a way of life. The great maxim of Socrates has been invoked so often through the centuries that one hears it now perhaps a little inattentively. Walter Solmitz never heard it so, and he never said it glibly: "The unexamined life is not worth living." If he ultimately despaired of life, it was never because he thought that the philosophic and examined life was not worth living. It was a despair rather at the persistent return of an old and only half-intentioned unhappiness, at the persistent effect of an old and only half-understood weakness—a fear, if you will, that he might not be able to live life in accordance with that high ideal. Those who were closest to him in his last hard year saw the courage with which he tried to overcome his own inner troubles; they saw too the tenacity with which he fought to carry out his duties in the face of what became as time went on a complete physical exhaustion; they know that his despair left life—life qualified by that high ideal—in a sense untouched. It was part of the bitterness of his end that he always felt that the examined life *was* worth living. His students and friends will always remember that.

Professor Fritz Koelln, who made it possible for Walter to join the faculty of Bowdoin in 1946 as instructor in the German department, speaks at the memorial service on 3 October, 1962, for his friend and colleague. He, too, reflects that Walter's compassion fed his despair.

> There was a quality in him which showed itself at the end of his life sometimes to an unbearable degree: he felt the suffering of other people as his own suffering. When he had to disapprove of

a student he felt the sting of this disapproval often stronger than the one against whom it was directed. The general exhaustion with which he had to struggle during the times of his ill health had a great deal to do with this unusual degree of self identification with anyone whom Walter Solmitz saw suffer. If this contributed greatly to his final total exhaustion, we must also remember that it was also the root of the great effect his deep personal concerns had on so many lives of his students and his friends.

Within two weeks of his father's death, David learns of the suicide of one of his father's students who had graduated that June. In his suicide note the student, Timothy, had written that he could no longer live without the support of his mentor Professor Solmitz. David had met Timothy on a sunny, warm day that spring, when he had accompanied Walter for lunch at their home. Unlike other Bowdoin students whom David had met over the years, Timothy didn't talk with him. He appeared shy and withdrawn. David wondered why he had painted a few blobs of white on his nose. The meal was silent. Timothy and the father talked briefly in the living room before he left.

David calls the dean of the college to ask whether he may accompany him and several faculty to Timothy's funeral in the small central Maine mill town of Jay. The kindly dean asks whether the son is sure he wants to come along. It would be a long service—a Catholic Mass in Latin. Without hesitation, the son says yes. They drive along the Androscoggin River amidst farmed fields, mixed soft- and hardwood forests, and rolling hills. The dean drives the college's big Checker car. The other passengers besides the dean and David include Walter's colleague Ed and their friend from the English department, Roy Greason. There is silence—no conversation—on the three-hour round trip. Yet David is glad to be attending the funeral, both out of respect for his own father and for Timothy. Maybe he identifies with the loneliness that each felt in their lives.

One further death occurs next autumn, fifteen months to the day after his father's passing. On returning home from classes on a typically cold and gray November day, the son turns on his tiny, turquoise portable radio. It had recently been sent to him as a present from his father's close friend, the Gestalt psychiatrist, Kurt Goldstein. Instead of hearing the folk music to which he had been looking forward—Joan Baez; Pete Seeger; Peter, Paul and Mary—he learns that President John F. Kennedy has been shot. He goes downstairs to turn on the family's little black-

and-white television. Yes, according to the report by NBC News anchors Chet Huntley and David Brinkley, President Kennedy has been shot by Lee Harvey Oswald. Oswald, they say, was a U.S. Marine who had defected to the Soviet Union and later returned to the United States with his Russian wife, Marina. *An evil Communist*, the son sarcastically thinks as images flash through his mind: his father's grim face bemoaning the fact that Alger Hiss was one of the victims in the late 1940s and early 1950s of a national witch hunt of alleged Communists. Two days later Oswald is shot by a Dallas nightclub owner, Jack Ruby.

That evening as he sits at his father's desk, where he has studied ever since his father's death, he drafts a condolence letter to Oswald's wife. He feels compassion for this Russian immigrant who must be suffering greatly from the national outrage and from the often vitriolic news coverage of her husband's alleged crime. The son recalls that just three months before, neighbors had gathered around his house on the arrival of a police car and then a hearse. He recalls feeling awkward and anxious. He remembers the relief he experienced when his high-school principal expressed understanding for his father's actions, the comfort he felt when others showed compassion for his mother and himself. He wants Marina Oswald to know that there are some Americans who feel her pain and who are standing by her during these trying times.

Over the years, reflecting on his father's troubled life leads David to learn more about him and his family. As he explores the past that is his father's, he learns, too, of his mother's heritage. Slowly, in time, he will come to see and appreciate the multitude of international connections, not coincidences, that arose to create the diverse cultural world that he, their Maine-raised and Maine-rooted son, inhabits.

2

Oma, Roma, and the Mexican Connection

Cambridge, Massachusetts, September 1956

A white nightie covers her frail body. Her head is propped on white pillows, so she can look out of the bay window of her room. At 91, Sophie, Oma (German for grandmother), is the last boarder at Mary Menton's boarding house. This rapidly dilapidating house at the corner of Trowbridge and Broadway was, without a doubt, a beautiful home in its heyday. Fifty-five years later, her grandson David recalls for instance the small black-and-white tiles of the bathroom floor and lower walls, the marble threshold, the large white porcelain sink standing freely on its ribbed porcelain column. Now water constantly drips from the ornate, brass faucets, causing a brown rust stain in the bowl. The large bathtub rests on four feet that look

Sophie Solmitz holding her grandson, David, 1943

like bear claws. It, too, has genuine brass fixtures. The toilet fascinates her grandson, as he has to pull a chain from a tank above the commode. A chandelier heavily coated with dust hangs from the bathroom ceiling.

In contrast to the dark, damp bathroom, the dingy hallway, the greasy treads of what once was red floral carpeting on the stairway, and the smell of cat urine and feces that permeates the rest of the house, Oma's room is bright and clean. The furnishings are sparse: a dresser, a night table by her brown tubular metal-framed bed, and a couple of chairs. The wooden floor is covered with a sheet of well-worn floral patterned linoleum that is brittle, cracked, and in places completely torn. She used to sit in the cushioned armchair by the window, enjoying her view onto the little park at the end of which was Cambridge's brownstone public library. Before she became completely bedridden, watching kids play ball there and seeing the traffic go by brought Oma a little pleasure in her otherwise lonely existence.

Besides keeping the room clean and well-aired, Mrs. Menton, a bubbly, gray-haired woman in her mid fifties, cares for Oma with genuine warmth. She makes sure she is kept clean, well fed, and comfortable. Oma, according to David's parents, never reciprocates Mrs. Menton's kindness. She looks down at her as a lower-class servant.

A very few times during the year, when David and his parents come to Cambridge, he visits Oma. Without fail, she welcomes him saying, "My, how you have grown." She then asks him to hand her the big, black leather handbag resting on the nightstand. With shaking hands, finding her little change purse, she opens it, takes out a nickel. Closing the purse and putting it back into the bag, she tells David to return the bag back to its place. Then she hands him the nickel. "Go to the market across Trowbridge Street to buy yourself an ice-cream sandwich." He has no choice in the matter: it has to be an ice-cream sandwich. She makes him show it to her on his return.

Following the ice cream that he eats in her presence, he goes downstairs to visit with Mrs. Menton. For him it is boring to sit around while his parents try to chat with his Oma. Mrs. Menton welcomes him into the living room, a large darkened room to the right of the house's entrance. Heavy, dusty and smoke-filled drapes completely cover the room's large windows. Thick dust coats every piece of furniture, the lamps, and the knickknacks sitting on the built-in shelves. The stuffing peeks out a stained and dirty brown from the arm rests of the once maroon-colored sofa on which he sits. Mrs. Menton's husband sits passively in an equally shabby armchair in a particularly dark corner of the room. There, between sips of rum from a glass he occasionally fills from the bottle resting next to his chair, he chain smokes cigarettes. He has lost his job as a skilled salesman at a men's clothing store, taking measurements for the tailor-made suits or for alterations on store-bought suits. Whether he had been fired because of his alcoholism or whether men with his skills were no longer needed, David doesn't know. Mrs. Menton, who has no children of her own, enjoys David's company. She asks him about his pet beagle, his school, his garden. Never having been in Maine, she is curious to know about the rural state.

Following Oma's 1957 death, on a visit to Cambridge in 1959—when he has his driver's license—David visits Mrs. Menton. He invites her to go to an Alec Guinness movie with him and have a snack at Brigham's restaurant. He is not surprised to find that Mrs. Menton's house has fallen apart even further. Several front steps are completely rotten in places. Balusters in the porch railing are falling out, and columns supporting the porch show signs of severe rot. He learns that her husband has died, that she lives all alone in the big house. Although she obviously enjoys being together with him again, she no longer asks him about his activities or his parents. Much of their time is spent in silence. When he drops her off, he watches her slowly ascend the dilapidated steps to her home, sensing that this will be the last time he ever sees Mrs. Menton, that an era has passed. Driving back to Maine, he thinks about his Oma.

He recalls visiting her at Mrs. Menton's when he was a young child. His father helped her cautiously down the greasy carpeted stairs, and they crossed Broadway to stroll in the park in front of the library. There she walked with a cane. David wonders why, when his father brought her one summer to a "rest home" in Topsham, across the bridge from Brunswick, she never visited at their home. Were there tensions between her and his father? David remembers his father once telling him that Sophie had little patience for her ethereal son. As he was growing up, she resented his scholarly interests and desires. He seemed too much like his father, a man of no professional ambition whose interests were primarily literary and who differed from his own brothers—one a lawyer, the other a banker, both holding professions worthy of Jewish men.

David still sees his father sitting at the foot of his mother's bed during family visits to Cambridge, while he stands by his father. David's mother stands in the background, then sits in Oma's chair by the window. Why does Oma ignore her? David eventually realizes that she resents Elly, just as she resented her own husband, Otto. Although Elly is Jewish, she is not only from a lower-class family, she is an artist. Therefore, Oma believes, instead of persuading Walter to take on a more respectable profession, Elly continues to support his intellectual pursuits.

Where did Oma's social pretension come from? After all, she was born in 1866 in Roma, Texas, a tiny town on the Rio Grande, directly across from Mexico. Even today the town is still small with a population of under nine thousand, ninety-eight percent Spanish speaking. Her grandfather, Alexander Wolf Sanders, was originally from Dessau, Germany, while his wife, Henriette, was from Braunschweig.

Born February 6, 1837, Fred was one of their eight children. Alexander was a scribe at the Synagogue in Dessau, where he also taught children calligraphy. He earned 142 *Taler* a year, on which a family of ten could not survive. In desperation, he sent a letter to the Duke and Duchess of Anhalt-Dessau in 1840 and two in 1845, less than a year before his death, on September 18, 1846.

In pleading for help to "The Most Illustrious Duchess Friederike von Anhalt-Dessau" he addressed her "as your royal highness, love-filled mother to all those who are hard pressed and in need of your help." He wrote that he found himself in such need that only the charitable help of her excellence could save him and his family. He explained how he had to give every bit of his meager wages to his creditors and didn't have enough money to sustain his family of children. He was unable to pay the rent and must vacate his apartment in the coming weeks. Even by selling or pawning his beds, he would be unable to satisfy his landlord. The duchess sent him a small amount of money, but it did not make any significant difference to his dire situation.

Following Alexander's death in 1846, the family was left completely destitute. They were at the mercy of charity from the Jewish community and from whatever other sources they could ask for help.

According to Fred's obituary, he emigrated in 1854 from Dessau to Monterrey, Mexico, where he had relatives. It is possible that he actually settled in Roma, Texas, where his older brother had established a business. However his wife Fannie, to save embarrassment to the family, may have given this information to the Little Rock, Arkansas, newspaper. After all, had he left the United States during the American Civil War, he might have been thought of as betraying his new homeland.

More than likely these relatives, like so many others, had left the economic turmoil of 19th-century Germany after being lured by letters, books, and newspaper articles describing the untapped potential of Texas. These described the beautiful landscape, the availability of large plots of fertile land, and the abundance of wild game to hunt.

Fred's relatives were probably drawn to settlements created by the Adelsverein, an organization that was formed in 1842 by a group of twenty-one German nobles to provide economic relief for the German working class. By creating new settlements in Texas, they hoped to produce large amounts of natural resources from the land, such as cotton, set up new trade markets to supply markets for German industry, and promote German maritime commerce. They promised settlers comfortable and spacious ships, reasonable travel charges, and free transportation to their settlements, but the Adelsverein organizers were idealistic, totally unprepared for the conditions awaiting the settlers. When the first immigrants arrived in Texas in December 1844, they found themselves stranded, often without adequate shelter.

Between October 1845 and April 1846, a total of 5,257 emigrants arrived in Texas. By the end of 1847, the Adelsverein was facing bankruptcy. According to the *Handbook of Texas Online:* "The chief causes of its failure were not greed or the mean-spirited parsimony of its members, however, but their lack of business sense, the intrigues of land speculators and some members of the society, the naïveté of the nobles involved, and a lack of trust even in their own officers in Texas."

When Fred's relatives discovered that the information they had gathered in Germany turned out to be false, that the hardships they encountered were unbearable, they headed for Monterrey, Mexico. With the American victory that ended the war with Mexico in 1848, Fred's relatives surely heard that better opportunities existed for them there.

Exactly what Fred's relatives did for work in Monterrey is not known. However, it is likely that the husband began as a "Jewish peddler." He might have even set up a stall at a Monterrey market and eventually started his own business. Fred was a very bright boy, both interested and gifted in languages. Besides his native German, he studied Hebrew and quickly became fluent in French and English. He was already filled with the spirit of adventure, and the idea of exploring a new life in America free of the burdens at home appealed greatly to him. His older brother, Moritz, probably came first, established a business in Roma, Texas, and then brought Fred and their younger brother Alexander Jr.

As Roma was located on the Mexican border, Moritz could easily trade with Mexican towns. He hired his brother Fred, who had picked up Spanish easily, to manage the business relationship with Mexico. Also, being located on the Mexican border, the brothers, who opposed slavery, could easily escape to Mexico to avoid being drafted into the Confederate Army during the American Civil War that began in 1861. The brothers developed friends in Mier, directly across the border from Roma, and had business relations in Mier, Los Aldamas, and Monterrey.

Through his business contact, Fred met his future wife Fannie, a Jewish girl from an Oberdorf in Germany (there are numerous Oberdorfs), who was living with her brothers in Monterrey.

Years later Fred wrote a letter to his younger brother Alexander containing the following story. As Fred's story goes:

> I had become angry with my brother Moritz for treating me as a stranger as opposed to a brother, yet demanding that I accomplish more than I had. As I had expected patience and understanding from my brother, I didn't feel badly to take off. Having a tendency for adventure, I befriended Don Francisco Naranjo.* He was a lieutenant in the Mexican state of Nuevo León, having been sent to Tamaulipas by President Juárez, president of the Mexican republic, in order to suppress the constantly reoccurring revolutions of small farmers against the wealthy, conservative landholders. Juárez was ruling Mexico from Veracruz. Although he had won the election in 1859 he had to flee the city because of an uprising led by conservative generals. I was sympathetic to the rebellious Rojos since the brothers of my girlfriend, Fannie, were members of this political party. The party represented the illegally suppressed majority.
>
> In Mier, directly across the Rio Grande from Roma, I was sitting on this occasion at lunchtime in the hotel. Across from me sat Mr. Naranjo. A friendly yet testy conversation evolved. It didn't take much logic on my part to prove that the president was wrong to suppress the rebellion of the majority by supporting the small and financially weak party. Suddenly, Naranjo pulled me aside, "You should advocate for your point of view by taking up arms and fighting in the field. I'd like to talk about this with you." How could I trust him? Trying to control my emotions, I made a fist in my trousers' pocket. If I had contradicted him, I would have lost. After all, I was among a group of officers who belonged to the same army as Naranjo. As I would have been laughed at, I left without comment. Several days after this incident, Moritz sent me to nearby Los Aldamas for business. I was careful to take my be-

*Francisco Naranjo later became Mexico's minister of war and head of the Mexican Railway Administration. He was two years younger than Fred.

longings—my dishes and weapon—with me. Los Aldamas was still under the control of the province of Nuevo [León]. I punctually took care of my tasks. Instead of returning humbly to Moritz in Roma, I decided to go to a section of Las Aldamas, a place I knew well, to join the rebels—the Rojos. Soon there would be an encounter at Mier. Our goal was to free the region from the control of Nuevo León. We therefore, sought an advantageous position to resist our rival. With pounding heart I awaited the first sign of an attack. On March 8th the Nuevo Leóners appeared. An officer bearing a white flag for peace soon appeared and quickly departed. The leaders of both parties held a conference that circumvented the battle. We received the order to return home. But I? I no longer had a home! To return to Moritz and beg to be taken back? No way! I went to acquaintances on the coast to reflect as to what I should do. I then returned to Roma and got a light job: collecting debts, smuggling, etc., providing me enough money to stay afloat.

In May, my acquaintance, John Vale, arranged for me to go to Monclova, a city in the Mexican district of Coahuila, north of Monterrey. On my trip there, I went through Mier. There my friends advised me to get a military transit pass. As the territory was being thoroughly patrolled, such authorization would be helpful should I encounter difficulties. Seeing the value of this advice, I went to the commander to obtain the permit. Barely had my request been granted, Naranjo entered. For a moment he stopped short. Then as he stepped toward me yelling, "Señor general, a spy!" and drew out his sword. "Surrender!" With a few words he explained to the general that I am not Mexican and that I am armed, intending to resist those in charge. Therefore, within a few moments I was disarmed, seized and brought to the lockup. Now I was captured. As a spy, there is no doubt in the world, I would be shot dead. Yet, I do not believe that I was fully aware of my predicament, for as I pricked up my ears I detected conversation among soldiers.

Two officers were playing chess. I watched their game and became engrossed in it. As Naranjo entered, the game stopped. They spoke of the country's political devastation. In the south the Republicans were fighting against Maximilian.* In the north they

*That Fred mentions Maximilian I, emperor of Mexico from 1864 to 1867, suggests a little confusion about the time frame of his narrative. Fred must have

fought side by side. "Yes," I said, " if only the Mexicans could unite. If only they could put their private quarrels aside. But that they won't do." It's as if I had stepped on Naranjo's painful toe. He glared at me. "You are a bastard, an outrageous liar, a . . . a . . ." He wanted to pierce me with drawn blade. His comrades stepped in and sat me on a bench."

"You are a coward," I yelled at Naranjo. "You can do that to a defenseless prisoner. I would like to see what kind of a grimace you'd make if we were standing on equal footing." Then I stretched out on the bench using my hands as a pillow and looked up at the ceiling. Naranjo's comrades shoved him out the door.

At noon I was given a good meal, "Therefore, the last supper," I thought to myself, unable to touch it. I lay down on the bench again and watched the flies on the ceiling. Soon I fell asleep.

The entrance of armed men woke me, "You must come with us," the sergeant said.

"To campo santo [the cemetery]?" I asked.

No answer. I smiled rather bitterly to myself. A long strap was fastened to my right leg. A soldier wound the loose end around his fist. Then they took me between them.

My letter continues. Dear brother,* allow me to give you an inkling about my thoughts. In the streets of a city where I have been

---

written this account at the earliest in the late 1860s when he was already living in Texas. As Austrian Archduke, Maximilian was denied a share in the imperial government by his reactionary older brother, Emperor Francis Joseph. Since Napoleon III wanted to extend the French empire, he promised the idealistic Maximilian military support if he agreed to become emperor of Mexico. On June 10, 1864 Maximilian and his wife Carlota were crowned in the cathedral of Mexico City. To the dismay of the wealthy, conservative landowners, Maximilian upheld former president Benito Juárez's land reforms, and educated the Indians and the poor. Fred and Fannie's two brothers also backed the reforms of Juárez. When in 1866 Napoleon ordered French troops to withdraw from Mexico, Maximilian remained. A short while later he and his small army surrendered at Querétaro. Maximilian and his two leading generals were condemned to death and promptly shot.

*Probably referring to his younger brother Alexander. Literally translated would be "dear child."

greatly respected, I am surrounded by a band of armed warriors, soldiers wearing shirts and sandals, as opposed to uniforms. I am twenty-two years old and with a head full of highfalutin plans.

I thought of our poor mother, of your and my brother Moritz, who lives only nine miles from here. In any case he knows my predicament. I also thought of my girlfriend, my flame. Like every sailor as he plunged from the mast into the sea cried out: "I am dying for my fatherland." However, that I should not yet have been shot, about that I thought the least. I was imprisoned in the courtyard of the city office complex. It was surrounded by an eight foot high wall. I was confined to a cell with a heavy iron door. There I sat on the bare floor. The door being a very strong iron gate, allowed me complete view of the empty courtyard. Guards were stationed at the gateway. They often checked on me here. Abandoned, imprisoned, condemned to death! My wonderful youthful life, my hopes, my castles in the air. Everything, everything thrown away! I did not cry, dear brother. I passed the time in the damp cell. It felt like an eternity until the guard would be relieved. At that time, a man came by with my blanket and pushed it through the gate. Another shoved my supper the same way through the gate. I was hungry and ate, though only a little. I then took the blanket to prepare a comfortable seat. A scrap of paper fell out. I first observed it as I lay on the blanket. Then I noticed that something was written on it: "doce de la noche." I read it. I took it in my hands. "No soy cobarde. Esté V. alerta a las doce de la noche para que salgue de aquí. Lo más se verá. (I am not a coward. Remain awake around midnight so that you can get away from here. More will turn up.)"

What does that mean for me? I thought Naranjo was a coward. Does he want to let me free? Perhaps! Perhaps to appease me! Be calm and pay attention. Hour upon hour passed. I lay on my blanket and pretended to sleep. The guard often came to check on me. Finally, finally! At midnight the guard was released from his shift. Someone came to the gate. It was Naranjo himself.

"Señor Sanders!"

"Don Pancho!"

"I am not a coward. You must get out of here."

I stood up. Immediately the door opened. "Here is your weapon. Your horse is already saddled by the back wall. Don't forget your blanket. So now climb onto my shoulders. You must go, quickly and silently." In a few moments I was free and on the back of my magnificent horse. With a strident gallop we rushed to the Rio Grande and by daybreak crossed the river to the American side. Freedom, freedom, freedom! With this kind of freedom, I felt giddy with joy accompanied a bitter taste. I sometimes wondered how I would feel if I should return to Mexico.

"What would have been my purpose?" Nonsense, Fred. Life is for the living. Shortly after daybreak I arrived in Roma. I went to my friend Don Pedro Torres. I quickly told him my story, some of which he already knew. "What should I do now, Don Pedro?" A war council of friends was called together. The council agreed that a duel would effectively settle our differences. Don Máximo Mancillas would bring word of the duel with pistol in hand to Don Pancho Naranjo at eight the following morning on the island of Sabinitos. Further agreement could be reached with the combatants at the battlefield.

The answer: "Accepted with great pleasure, Naranjo."

Shortly after seven I arrived at the designated battlefield. The time approached eight o'clock on my watch. There was no sign of Naranjo. Nine o'clock? What does that mean? We had expected the best. Mancillas went to Mier; I waited for him here. He returned at noon: "The troops left early this morning at six. Naranjo with them." This adventure that took place in the spring of 1860 has come to an end.

18 September 1863 in Monterrey, Nuevo León

My wedding should take place on the 22nd. I just have come from the jeweler from whom I bought a ring. Troops from Puebla are marching past. Don Pancho Naranjo is riding at the head of a regiment. I recognize him in spite of his colonel's uniform.

About two in the afternoon I leave my bride to go to my hotel for my siesta. From the distance I see Naranjo, who doesn't recognize me at the moment.

With intent to meet him, I said: "Don Pancho Naranjo?"

"'With whom do I have the honor?'

"Sanders, Frederico Sanders, as you like. We have a bone to pick."

"Your hand, Don Federico, I am willing to forgive you. I am no longer a coward and perhaps in your eyes no longer belonging to that sort of people who stay at home and squabble, giving the enemy of the republic a free hand. I have been in Puebla, and you know it. Now, I only have to say to you: We pulled out of Mier without warning at six that early morning. I couldn't even write you a few lines. Now, after three years, I have come home. I have been awarded numerous honors. I am now going to my parents in Lampsos. Still you should not be satisfied with the offer for an appropriate apology. Anyway, we could meet tomorrow afternoon, someplace you would like. Please decide."

"I, Don Pancho, will be married in four days."

"Well, well, getting married! I congratulate you! And the duel?"

"I am ready to recognize your merit. You want to make up. That is all that I am able to ask for and request under the present circumstances."

"Well, then we'll meet this evening at Vidal's wine bar. Bring your friends along. Also, I will bring witnesses.

The evening at Vidal's. Naranjo is there with a variety of officers. I am there with my future brother-in-law and several friends. Mutual introductions.

Naranjo: "Gentlemen. About three years ago I abused this man as a prisoner condemned to death. Herewith I retract the terrible words I said in the heat of the moment and present Mr. Sanders to you as my best friend. Toast him my gentlemen!"

I: "My opinion of Colonel Naranjo's behavior at the time was justified. Still Don Pancho did the unbelievable: he saved my life and gave me freedom. By speaking out, I punished Don Pancho because of his lies about his wartime deeds. I'm glad that I am able to consider this gentleman my friend. There is no better patriot and cavalier in Mexico. Three cheers to him!"

Fred and Fannie's first child, Louis, was born in 1864 in Monterrey. Eager to return to the United States at the end of the American Civil War, Fred brought his family back to Roma in 1865. Fred's two brothers settled in Mexico. Alexander is said to have later emigrated to Peru following the murder of his brother Moritz in Monterrey.

Fred worked for another merchant in Roma. It is possible that he

*The Sanders had relatives in Holland. In 1838, Solomon Pareira, a clothing merchant, together with his wife left Holland for the United States. They settled in Providence, Rhode Island, where in 1847 he became the first president of the Jewish community there.

FANNIE SANDERS

worked with Issac Pareira who was born in 1840 in Holland.* In 1857, at the age of eight, Issac's younger brother immigrated to Roma. It is likely that with the declaration of the American Civil War, Issac and his brother also left for Mexico. Following the Civil War, like Fred, Solomon returned to Roma where he may have worked for the same merchant as Fred. He left Roma in 1857.

On occasion, Fred was employed in nearby Rio Grande City, the seat of Starr County, as a court interpreter. On November 9, 1866, his second child, Sophie, who would become David's Oma, was born in Roma. Shortly after the birth of Fred and Fannie's third child, Henry, the family moved to Memphis to be closer to Fannie's sister and brother Wilhelm. Apparently not content with his life there and eager to try his hand at farming, Fred then moved his family to Richwoods, Stone County, Arkansas, in the Ozark Mountains, where according to his son Henry he failed miserably at farming.

Fred's son Henry, who died in 1956, left behind *Henry Sanders: An Autobiography of Amusing and Entertaining Anecdotes from 1868 to 1912.**

In the book, Henry described his childhood:

*Henry's nephew Arthur recalled his unexpected death. "One evening he walked the half block from Aunt Flora's house to catch the bus to return to his hotel [in Little Rock]. He mounted the two or three steps of the bus and was reaching in his pocket for the fare when the bus driver started the bus without closing the doors. Uncle Henry was jerked backwards, hit his head on the curb, cracked his skull and ended up unconscious in the gutter. A television cameraman happened to be on the spot and that night on the news we saw Uncle Henry, immaculately dressed—as always—lying in the gutter. He was taken to the hospital, but did not make it through the night (Sanders 2000, 5).

Fred Sanders

Why my father selected such a poor, God-forsaken country has always been a puzzle to me. We were forty miles from the railroad, the Ozark Mountains; poor, rocky land. My father erected a log house, and tried to farm, something he had never had any experience in—and to add to his miseries, his health gave way and had it not been for the goodness of an uncle, Ben Rieser,* who traveled from Memphis by boat, train and horseback from Mississippi, we all would have starved. My uncle brought us some food and some money to buy the necessities of life. (Sanders 2000, 7)

After a few days, their uncle took Henry and Sophie back to Memphis to live with an aunt there. Sophie was eight at the time, Henry six. Louis, the oldest son, was responsible for keeping the farm going during their father's illness. Henry wrote, "Memphis was a revelation to my sister and me, as we had no recollection of ever being on a railroad train before" (Sanders 2000, 8).

The day following their arrival, the two children were sent to school. They remained in Memphis for four unhappy years. Henry wrote, "The least said about these four years the better, as I do not wish to revive an unpleasant recollection or write evil of an aunt that passed on several years ago" (Sanders 2000, 9).

In the meantime three more children were born to Fred and Fannie. By the time Henry and Sophie, who was now twelve years old, returned to Arkansas, the family had moved to Little Rock. Henry described their arrival.

*Who had a plantation in Mississippi.

> My father met me with a spring wagon which he used to peddle vegetables. We were living at Eleventh and Rock Streets, where my mother took care of a small grocery store and a big family. The store and living rooms were all in the one-story frame building, which was owned by an old blacksmith bachelor, living next door. We had a big back yard with fruit trees and a stable for the horse and a shed for the cow. Little Rock was not much more than a country town then—when many families kept their own cows and a horse or two. (Sanders 2000, 9)

After selling vegetables from his wagon for several years at a market on the corner of Fifth and Main Streets, Fred finally found a position as a bookkeeper in a seed and feed business, while his wife continued to manage the grocery store.

Henry noted:

> My father was one of the best educated men that I ever met. He was really a walking encyclopedia, but a poor business man. He started out with a "magic lantern"* and lecturing tour, covering many southern states and Mexico where he was stranded. My mother had to eke out sufficient income from the little grocery store to bring him back home. He drifted into the tintype and photo business. (Sanders 2000, 12)

As Fred and Fannie continued to produce children, they barely could feed their large family. Therefore, in 1880, when Sophie was fourteen, Fred sent her to Braunschweig, Germany, to be raised by his sister Bertha, eight years older than him. Sophie was not happy suddenly to be told by her father that she would be leaving her brothers and sisters to be raised by an unknown relative in a foreign land. Though Sophie had no choice in the matter, at least she could fantasize that by being raised in a wealthy family, she could become a famous dancer and actress. Bertha's husband had died in January 1879, and Bertha, wealthy and childless, had paid for Sophie's voyage.

Sophie's father brought her the forty miles to the nearest railroad station. From there she had to travel alone. On occasion she had to change

*The Magic Lantern, developed in the 1840s, was the forerunner of the modern slide projector. Originally used primarily for entertainment, it projected images from glass plates.

SOPHIE AND HENRY SANDERS, BROTHER AND SISTER

trains until she reached Galveston, Texas. There she boarded a steamship for Hamburg. As the story goes, the ship travelled via Argentina, where it picked up, among a host of passengers and goods, a middle-aged man. He, who had been collecting butterflies, became enamored of the fourteen-year-old Sophie. On disembarking in Hamburg, he gave her a flat, wooden box of butterfly pupae. When she arrived at her aunt's home in Braunschweig, she set the box atop a wardrobe. Several weeks later as the metamorphosis became complete, beautifully colored butterflies fluttered throughout the large, stone house.

Sophie Sanders as a young woman in Braunschweig, Germany

Bertha's husband, Marcus Aronheim, had been the chief partner of Aronheim and Company, a textile wholesale firm. He had married Bertha when he was 42 and she 18. Businessmen in Germany at the time would sometimes marry later in life if they felt they needed first to acquire a fortune, but that was not necessary for Marcus. His parents had provided well for him, and when his mother died in April 1847, she left him considerable assets. Within six months of his mother's death, Marcus married Bertha, and it is probable that his delay in marrying had been imposed on him by his mother, who either didn't want her son to marry at all, or forbade him to marry Bertha, a woman of a lower social class.

Then how did Marcus meet Bertha in the first place? Her grandfather,

Otto as a young man in Braunschweig, Germany

Michael David Engel, came from Poland to Braunschweig in 1795. He became the proprietor of a cotton mill that was located by the old Jewish Synagogue. He also was the synagogue's clerk, choir leader, and eventually its cantor. His wife, Friederike, must have joined him later, as their daughter, Henriette, was born in Poland in 1796. In 1824, Henriette married Alexander Wolf Sanders of Dessau. She likely met him while he was visiting his brother Samuel Wolf Sanders, also, from Dessau.

Samuel Wolf had become a business assistant to Abraham Samson in Braunschweig. It turns out that both Samuel and later Moritz Solmitz, David's great grandfather, were apprentices to Mr. Samson. In fact, they both lived at 775 Breitan Strasse, the home of Abraham Samson. Bertha, who was born in 1829, may have visited her uncle Samuel and her grandfather, who was well into his second marriage. As the Samsons, Aronheims, and Solmitzes were not only acquainted through their business in Braunschweig's textile industry, but also as members of the same Jewish congregation, Bertha could have easily met Marcus Aronheim. Who knows, she may even have been employed by him and his mother as a maid in their home.

The change from inexorable poverty in a developing city in the wilds of Arkansas to living in a stone mansion in an old German burg couldn't have been easy for Sophie. Although she was not fluent in German when she arrived in Braunschweig, she at least was familiar with the language, as both her parents communicated primarily in German. Nor was she used to the formality of her aunt's fashionable, well-to-do household. She ate her meals separately from her adults, yet had to learn her place in the social hierarchy as an upper-class youth with servants to command. When attending services at the synagogue, she, like all the other women, sat in the balcony separate from the men. Although she found the lifestyle stifling, she enjoyed taking dancing lessons and accompanying Bertha to the opera and the theater. Sophie dreamed of becoming a professional actress or dancer, but she was forbidden by her adopted family. Such a life, according to her aunt, was for less-sophisticated, lower-class people.

Sophie remained in close contact with her family in America. In 1888, after she had been in Braunschweig for eight years, Bertha arranged for her to visit her family in Little Rock. During Sophie's tenure with her aunt, Bertha remained close with her husband's former partner, Moritz Solmitz, and his wife Therese. Moritz, who had apprenticed for Abraham Samson at the same time as Samuel Sanders, had become the director of Aronheim and Co. by 1848 and continued to run the textile business as sole proprietor after the departure of both Marcus Aronheim and Joseph Loeb, the other original partner. His success and wealth are evidenced by the recording of his name in 1866 on a list of the most heavily taxed property holders and businessmen in the Duchy of Braunschweig. He was, therefore, eligible to vote in the provincial parliament.

Moritz and his wife had three children, Selmar, Otto, and Ernst. Selmar became an investment banker in Berlin and served on Berlin's city council. Selmar preferred to study history, law, and modern languages; however, his father insisted that he become a merchant to take over the family business. Ernst became a banker in Hamburg, while Otto, the middle son, remained in Braunschweig, living off the inheritance of his father. He traveled to London, where he became fluent in English and developed a passion for Shakespeare. On a childhood visit to his grandmother in Braunschweig, Selmar's son, Werner, observed that Otto liked to gather the family in their sitting room to read to them from Shakespeare, Goethe, and other classic authors. Noticing that Otto's mother, Therese, dozed off while he was reading, Werner realized that she had become quite bored with her son's intellectual pursuits and ethereal lifestyle.

3

Two Brunswicks

SOPHIE IS STILL UNMARRIED AT AGE TWENTY-SEVEN. She is a lovely, slender, blue-eyed woman with long, wavy, sand-colored hair. Bertha wants to be sure that Sophie marries into a well-to-do family, so that she will be able to lead a comfortable and secure life. After all, throughout her childhood and youth, Bertha suffered extreme poverty. Since Otto is still living with his mother Theresa, she helps to arrange Sophie's September 1893 marriage to him. She also hopes Otto will make enough money that Sophie can support her unpredictable father, her mother and younger siblings in Arkansas. Following their marriage, Sophie and Otto honeymoon in Luzern, Switzerland, where they stay at the Frankfurter Court Hotel.

Their marriage turns out to be unhappy. He continues to Dundee, London, and cities on the continent. From there he writes short letters to Sophie and his two daughters in metered verse. While at home, he prefers to lock himself in his study to pursue scholarly interests. On occasion he takes the streetcar for about ten minutes on the Wolfenbüttelerstrasse to the family garden, located on about 433 acres of land that his father had purchased as an investment. He has no interest in business, nor for the society life that Sophie is eager to lead. As a result, he experiences increasing bouts of depression. Finally, in 1907, two years after his son Walter is born, Otto takes his own life.

With her husband's death, Sophie's dreams of becoming an actress, a star on stage, are wiped out. She worries how she will hold onto her social status as a member of one of Braunschweig's elite families and survive financially. On top of these fears, she now has to raise her three children as a single mother. In reality, the task of raising two-year-old Walter falls to his sister, Edith, who is eleven years his senior. Edith is stubborn and domineering, yet extraordinarily beautiful. Like the evil stepmother who felt threatened by Snow White's beauty, proud Sophie becomes envious of Edith's glamorous appearance. The middle child, Annaliese, less physically attractive than her sister, is emotionally unstable and possibly schizophrenic.

For Walter the home atmosphere feels stifling. He is caught between two resentful, competing, and overbearing women, as well as a mentally ill sibling. Luckily, throughout his entire childhood, he has one friend: Wolfgang Ölicher. Walter, a loner, later tells his son that his happiest times were when he was able to escape the house and take the tram to the

Sophie and Otto Solmitz

family garden, where he enjoyed the calmness of being alone, weeding, planting, and picking vegetables.

In May of 2005, on his journey to learn about his parents and their families, David visits his father's home town of Braunschweig. As the train pulls into the station at 11:08 a.m., precisely on schedule, he sees the official blue sign with white lettering that says BRAUNSCHWEIG: BRUNSWICK, YOUR HOME TOWN.

Coming out of the postwar station together with a couple from the Jewish community who met him there, he feels a little disappointed to see that the station is a large, plain, concrete structure, lying on the outskirts of town. He had imagined the terminal as a huge covered hall from which all trains had to back out in order to continue their journey. During his father's childhood that had been the case, but now trains either whiz through the station at a high speed, or stop at a designated platform for a moment before continuing on their way to the next destination.

David sees a grassy expanse in front of the station through which run streetcar tracks. He is a little surprised that the grass hasn't yet been mowed. Grass is also growing between the tracks: quite un-German in comparison to the meticulous neatness in Hamburg. To the right of the station is a well-preserved steam locomotive: black with bright red wheels, a monument to the days of steam that came to an end only in the late 1950s. At least this locomotive is well preserved in comparison to engine #470 that pulled Maine's last passenger train in 1954; 470 is now rusting away, robbed of all its brass instruments, on its pedestal in Waterville. David feels a little better knowing that the Braunschweig community does seem to take pride in its Old Glory.

Around the grassy square are concrete and stucco buildings, all postwar. David isn't surprised, as he had been told that Braunschweig was badly bombed during World War II, that it is now a modern city of concrete, steel, and glass.

A couple from Braunschweig's Jewish community meet David at the station. On the way to his hotel, they have to take a roundabout way to avoid a large demonstration going on in the center of the town. His escorts explain that during the darkness of a recent night, workers had entered the park in which the palace of Braunschweig's duke had been located, and cut down the ancient trees to make way for a modern shopping center. Even though the palace had been badly bombed during the war, and the deteriorating ruins had been hauled away during the 1960s, the park with its beautiful trees had remained a treasure for the citizens of Braunschweig. The demonstrating protesters not only were outraged by the secretive felling of trees, but also vehemently opposed a shopping mall of chain stores in the middle of their beloved park.

David calls to mind an early March evening years ago when he joined his parents at Brunswick's annual town meeting. He was a teenager, maybe fifteen. He was eager to attend the meeting even though he had to sit in the balcony and was still too young to vote. He wanted to witness the discussion and vote for or against the destruction of the old town hall, the icon of Maine Street, to make way for a new J. J. Newbury chain store. He had no sentimental feelings for the high-ceilinged and spacious brick building with its tall clock tower. Sure, as a child he had enjoyed going to the marionette show there, but later, as a fifteen-year-old, he could care less for puppets. By ripping down the old and replacing it with the new, progress would be made. As part of the project, a new, small and efficient town office building would be constructed on Federal Street next to the town's recreation center. Sitting in the balcony, David listened to the arguments for and against, feeling ever stronger that the yeah votes, those for progress, should win. When the moderator finally called for a vote, he watched with bated breath as the hands rose. "The yeahs have it," Bowdoin professor of oratory, Herbert Ross Brown, announced with clarity and dignity. David felt relieved and elated. His father and mother voted to preserve the old town hall. They felt that the great heart of the town was being threatened; in the old town hall the community gathered to practice democracy in its most basic form as well as to participate in a variety of social and cultural functions. As David reflects on his lack of wisdom in favoring corporate modernization over preservation of the past, he can only hope that were he a teenager in Braunschweig, he would be part of that demonstration.*

David's hotel, Hotel Frühling (Spring), is a renovated, original façade in the old city, directly across from the synagogue. He imagines meeting

*When David returns to Braunschweig in April 2008, he sees the new shopping mall. It has been built out of stone, using remains of original columns from the old palace, with a facade made to look like the original building. Entering through the main portal, the interior appears like a renovated palace from antiquity. This portion houses a gallery, as well as the regional archives. The entrance to the mall is toward the far side of the palace. It consists of a modern green glass addition to the building creating a uniquely harmonious and tasteful contrast between the restored façade and the new mall. It is a far cry from David's imagination of a façade—the fake wooden fronts of Wild West towns seen in old Gene Autry cowboy-and-Indian movies.

an aging rabbi clad in black with a black yarmulke atop his long gray hair. Spectacled eyes peer from his face encompassed by a neat, bushy gray beard. Walking tall and straight, he would represent the modern-day rabbi. But David does not see the rabbi, who serves several small communities. This Sabbath he is conducting services elsewhere.

David's mind drifts sentimentally back to Richmond, Maine, on the Kennebec River. During the 1950s his father had liked to take him to Richmond. Although his father spoke no Russian, he seemed to feel comfortable in this little community with its two quarreling Russian Orthodox churches—one whose parishioners were of Ukrainian ancestry and the other whose descendants were from Byelorussia.* The priests were always dressed in black, wearing black hats that appeared to David's eyes like soft, round cans. Walter enjoyed taking his wife and son to a little restaurant to have borscht and Russian goulash. He met with the director of a church choir who was the grandnephew of Leo Tolstoy. Walter showed David the home in which a cousin of the former czar lived. He pointed out the raised vegetable beds tended by women dressed in their traditional, long, dark dresses, their heads covered with a kerchief. The beds were like those Walter had had in the family garden in Braunschweig. He brought David to the shoemaker, who reminded Walter of the cobblers back home in Germany. This elderly man made tall, black leather boots lined with sheep's wool in his tiny Main Street storefront. David felt he was in the old world from which his father had emigrated, eventually landing in Brunswick, Maine. Was this in a way a little like growing up in Brunswick, Germany?

In the early spring of 1970, David brought a group of sophomore high-school students from a small mill town in which he was teaching, to experience the Easter celebration at the one remaining Russian Orthodox Church in Richmond, the Ukrainian Alexander Nevsky Church. While preparing for this trip, David learned that the Russian Orthodox community in Richmond, like the Jewish community in Braunschweig, no longer had a permanent priest. Performing the service was a young monk from the Orthodox monastery in upstate New York. Twenty-five years later, the little church still remains. Its congregation is small, consisting of second- and third-generation Russian immigrants who are still living in the area. The large Victorian house that had been the residence of the priest has long since been sold. Notices on the

*A Russian baron had bought land cheaply here in order to set up a community of refugees from the 1917 revolution.

Braunschweig Synagogue before it was destroyed by the Nazis.

bulletin board in front of the church are no longer in Russian but in English.

As David reflects on the two communities, the Russian in Maine, and the Jewish in Braunschweig, he feels some affinity with the Jewish community in Braunschweig. The large, old community had been annihilated by the Nazis. Only now signs of a revival are beginning to appear. Yet many of the younger generation show little interest in the faith. For instance, the family who met him at the train station has two children. The older boy has gone to Israel, wanting to experience Judaism more fully, while the younger daughter refuses to set foot in a synagogue.

The secretary of the synagogue, like most of the new parishioners, is a Russian Jew. She left her homeland for Germany together with her family eleven years ago to escape deteriorating economic conditions. Her mother had been killed in a pogrom in 1942. Her father, who at seventeen enlisted in the Russian army and fought on the front lines, survived. He remains in Russia. "Isn't religious freedom for Jews now common in Russia today?" David asks her. "Yes, but the quality of life there is terrible. We had to get out."

Braunschweig's synagogue is a huge concrete bunker that the Nazis built following their Crystal Night (November 9, 1938) burning of the original synagogue. Because the synagogue was attached to neighboring buildings, the Nazis ordered the fire department to burn only the inside of the temple. Then a crane was used to tear down the ornate façade. The corner building adjoining the synagogue, the home of the rabbi and cantor, was not destroyed. The Nazis used this as headquarters for the local police. Following the war, the building was returned to the Jewish community. In one small room is the temple. There is an office for the rabbi and his secretary, a small kitchen, and conference room. Upstairs rooms are rented to students. This summer a small, new temple will be built extending from the present structure into a courtyard adjoining the Nazi bunker. Although the current Jewish community has grown to 180 members, the number is a far cry from the nearly 2000 prewar participants.

David asks himself whether he fits in this Jewish community. No, he doesn't. But why? He has come to Braunschweig to find some of his roots that happen to be within Jewish ethnicity. Neither his parents nor grandparents were practicing Jews. Yet, like his father, he feels affinity for the ethnic group. He recalls how proud his father was that the Jews were among the first to believe in a universal supreme being, a belief he felt could help bring about a more peaceful world. He has also come to Germany to visit the places at which his family suffered, and to see the Jewish cemeteries in which his ancestors are buried.

THE NAZI BUNKER THAT REPLACED THE SYNAGOGUE.

David is surprised to find these graves, as he had been told by relatives in the United States that they no longer existed. However, he is most fortunate to get in touch with a *Gymnasium* teacher of German and political science, who has researched the cemeteries of Braunschweig. They agree to meet at 10:00 a.m. in front of the Frühling Hotel. A gray-haired, balding, blue-eyed man wearing dark-blue slacks and a red, finely striped, open-collared polo shirt strolls up the sidewalk. *Can't be Jewish*, David thinks to himself, but he has such a kind and warm expression David immediately recognizes him as Herr Bein. They shake hands firmly, chat briefly before getting into Herr Bein's car to begin their visit to the Jewish burial grounds.

Alongside a wide road consisting solely of postwar buildings, they park by an iron gate. As they get out of the car, Herr Bein, carrying a large book, asks whether David has brought a hat with him. He's forgotten. He'd already been reminded in Hamburg of the need to cover the head entering Jewish cemeteries. Herr Bein puts on his cap, but, well, unless David places a paper hankie on his head that will undoubtedly fly away, he has no head covering. As Herr Bein unlocks the gate, David follows bare-headed into the small, old burial ground.

Rows of simple markers, the oldest in the form of the two tablets containing the Ten Commandments Moses received from God, rest among ancient trees, grass, and ivy-covered paths. Once inside the gate, Herr Bein opens his book *Ewiges Haus: Jüdische Friedhöfe in Stadt und Land Braunschweig* (Eternal House: Jewish Cemeteries in the City and State of Brunswick). He takes a computer printout from the book that he hands to David. It is a complete printout of David's family tree in Braunschweig. He then pulls from his pocket a sheet that shows where every individual's grave site in the cemetery lies.

As they walk to the back of the cemetery, David feels he is being guided back into the past. In the shade of a large tree stands the grave of Jehuda Levi Solmitz. David envisions him, a tall, balding, stern-faced man, wearing a suit. In his front vest pocket is a gold watch attached to a gold chain. He was born in 1788 and died on the 19th of February, 1853. The front of the old gravestones are inscribed in German, while the back sides are in Hebrew; according to the Jewish calendar his death date on the gravestone is 11 Adar 5613. Levi grew up in nearby Peine, a very small town where he started a horse-trading business. Eager to expand his business with a move to the larger city, he petitioned Braunschweig in 1832 but was refused by the city council. Unwilling to give up, he contacted an influential person in the state of Lower Saxony, to which Braunschweig belonged. This official made it possible for him and his wife, Minka, to move to Braunschweig. Besides horse trading, his business grew to include all the necessities for horses, including saddles and harnesses, as well as carriages and wagons. David is amused to think that Levi started what today would be a car dealership. He recalls his father's Bowdoin College student from Lewiston, Sheppard Lee, son of immigrants from Russia, who started a car dealership that is now a statewide franchise, of which Sheppard became president. If Levi had lived in modern America, he would undoubtedly be president and CEO of a chain of car dealerships.

David at first believes that Levi was his great-great-grandfather. However, that turns out not to be the case. His great-great-grandfather Salome (Salomon) died in Peine. Salome had been married twice. After his first wife died when he was 53, he then married her younger sister, who was 28 at the time. The only child of this second marriage was Moritz, David's great-grandfather.

Moritz's son, Selmar, in his unpublished memoir, told about his grandfather Salome. "He was a reputable, good-natured man, who worked as a merchant barely able to earn enough to sustain his large family. The situation severely worsened following a fire about 1820 that nearly destroyed their home. His wife is said to have saved only their large tin coffeepot that she convulsively held onto until the fire was extinguished."

When Moritz was twelve, his parents sent him to Braunschweig for a better education, as well as for economic reasons. There he lived with his uncle Blumenhoff, a jovial horse dealer. At the age of fourteen, Moritz began an apprenticeship in Braunschweig in Samson's English-German wholesale business of manufactured goods. He eventually became a textile merchant. Moritz served as a city councilor for Braunschweig. He was head of the Jewish community from 1853 to his death in April 1879. While he was treasurer of the synagogue, he invested 50,000 Reichsmarks from an Italian banker, Nathalieon. Within ten years the money doubled in value. With those monies, the sale of the old synagogue, along with a donation from the city of Braunschweig, a new, elegant temple was built in 1874. One year before he died, he established the Moritz Solmitz Foundation for "simple individuals of good character."

Herr Bein tells David, "I have found nothing in the archives about your grandfather in relation to his line of work. Did he take over his father's wholesale textile firm? More than likely he did not. He seems to have lived off the inheritance of his father and pursued his intellectual interests."

Wondering how the family name Solmitz came about, David asks Herr Bein. "Jews, prior to the Napoleonic occupation of Westphalia and Niedersachsen in which Braunschweig lay, used their given names. During his rule, Jerome, the French appointed king of Westphalia, insisted that Jews had to give themselves a surname. Salome came up with the name Solmitz by combining Itzig and Salomon. Many Jews simply chose the name of their profession like Goldschmidt (Goldsmith). After Napoleon's defeat, the Jews maintained this tradition."

Having seen the graves of Levi and Moritz, Herr Bein says: "Now you want to see the grave of your grandfather, Zadek Otto, don't you?"

"Why, of course," David replies with anticipation.

"Well, he was buried here," continues Herr Being, "but his body was exhumed, and now he lies in a cemetery started in the early 1930s. This is because the city decided to widen the street. As a result they had to take land and graves from the cemetery."

"The Nazis allowed his remains to be transferred?" David asks, surprised.

"Yes, it is surprising that the Nazis didn't simply destroy the graves. This is, however, most unusual," Herr Bein concluded.

As they leave the burial ground, Herr Bein hands David his book *Ewiges Haus*. With a smile he says: "This is for you. I am so glad you are interested in your heritage. I always welcome you back to Braunschweig." In the book he has inscribed: "In memory of your days in Braunschweig, Reinhard Bein." David is touched; he feels bonded to Herr Bein as if they have known each other for years.

They drive to a huge cemetery that is divided into various sections. The majority belong to the Protestant (Evangelical) Church. There is also a section for those who gave up their membership in the Church, signing an official document at city hall so they no longer have to pay a church tax. The extraordinary number of graves of Braunschweig residents who died during the bombing raids and hometown soldiers killed during the war are memorialized by small, flat, stone markers. Jews have their own burial ground here, a neatly, well-maintained grassy area shaded by large trees. A new section was recently created for the many Turkish Muslims who continue to immigrate to Germany.

A few steps into the Jewish section, at the corner of a passage between graves, stands an obelisk, the monument of David's grandfather, Zadek Otto Solmitz, who died at age 55 when his son Walter was but two years old.

You must have inherited your grandfather's interest in learning and his sensitivity as a human being. How sad that you really didn't get to know him. I lost you when I was nineteen. How I wish you were still alive today—or at least for many more

David at his grandfather's grave in Braunschweig, 2005

years after your premature death. I feel that we would have had a lot to share from our mutual distaste for war and belief in pacifism. You would have supported my position as conscientious objector to the Vietnam War. You would have had many ideas as to how to make my ideals as a democratically oriented teacher become successful.

Beneath the obelisk but above the base is a rectangular block with the inscription for Annaliese (Anna Elisabeth), Walter's sister who died at age 38. As she died in Freiburg/Breisgau, Herr Bein believes that her ashes were brought here to be buried together with her father's remains.

Having seen the graves of his forefathers, David is eager to find the ornate house in which his great-grandparents lived. He remembers a picture of Walter hanging in his mother's Cambridge Massachusetts apartment. At age seven, he is seated on a stone post in the ornate portico to his grandfather Moritz's and grandmother Therese's home at Gördelingerstrasse 43. As Herr Bein takes him there, he tells David that the house was badly bombed, yet the ornamental entrance remains preserved. David is awed at the magnificence that this house once was.

Herr Bein also shows David houses in which his grandmother, Walter, and his sisters had lived. One of these was Allenstrasse No. 3, a four-story building consisting of several apartments. As this house was close to Wolfenüttlerstrasse, Herr Bein and David drove along this wide street to the outskirts of Braunschweig, where the family had a large garden. This was located on 400-plus acres that Walter's grandfather,

Walter circa 1910 at the entrance to Moritz Solmitz's home in Braunschweig that was bombed during WWII.

Moritz, had purchased as an investment. Walter would often take the streetcar there. Recently the land has been developed into attractively laid out town housing with plenty of trees and space for small gardens.

Later, Reinhard shows David a different part of the city where families have established little communities in which they own small plots of land. Here they have set up little cottages. Some members use their entire plot for a vegetable garden. Others have a few fruit trees and lawn. When David and Reinhard stop at one "garden community,"

The same entryway as it stands today (2010).

several members—both men and women—are using wheelbarrows to carry gravel to improve the walkways. Not the same as in his father's time, David thinks.

In the vicinity of these little gardens, his father used to hike near artificial ponds built by monks in the 16th century, are restored thatched-roof farmhouses and barns made into fashionable homes, as well as several new houses that attempt to imitate the old style. This was the setting in which a Braunschweiger helped his Austrian-born friend, Adolf

Walter and sisters Edith (left) and Annaliese

Hitler, become a citizen of Germany. Although Braunschweig still shows the scars of Hitler's devastation, remains of the old city have been preserved and restored. David can imagine the beautiful and powerful walled, medieval city in which his father grew up.

He finds himself unexpectedly comfortable and welcome, not only in Braunschweig but also in Germany as a whole. The country appears orderly, neat, and clean, the atmosphere civilized. Adjoining nearly every city sidewalk are bicycle paths on which people of all ages pedal. Experimental hydrogen-powered buses can be found on city streets. People are polite, if not especially friendly, and helpful. David does not encounter the cultural deterioration of youth violence, coarse sex, homelessness, drug-related crimes, and a high murder rate that he encounters in America.

As Herr Bein and David chat, David learns that he is a high-school teacher of history and social studies. He easily pictures Herr Bein in the classroom, his eyes shining with excitement for the subject he is teaching. Always attentive to his students, his enthusiasm is contagious. When he tells David he will retire within a few years to devote more time to his genealogical studies, enjoy the outdoors and travel, David doesn't imagine that he, too, will retire from teaching a few years later to pursue his interests in writing and painting. Soon after returning home to Maine, David receives a warm letter from Herr Bein in which he has enclosed glossy photos he took of different homes in which David's father had grown up.

WALTER ON HIS HOLLANDER, CIRCA 1911

As a child David was not oblivious to his parents' suffering, even though he was unaware of the facts. Although neither of his parents shared their experiences with their young son, when he was about fourteen his father took him to see a documentary on Nazi Germany and the death camps. He witnessed his father's acute pain as he sat very tense with slumped shoulders glaring at the movie screen. David realized his father must have experienced the horrors they were watching. He understood why his mother only as an elderly woman returned to Germany, and only then to visit a friend from her youth. Gertrude, a Christian, had risked her life to look after Elly's parents before they were sent to Theresienstadt (concentration camp). On meeting Germans who appeared "typically" German, David always cringed. Yet, as a result of David's friendship with Reinhard, the spiral of hate that David experienced has been rapidly dissipating.

A few months after David's visit, Reinhard sends David drawings of his parents' passport photos, taken December 27, 1938. David left these photos with Reinhard during his visit to Braunschweig, and Reinhard commissioned the artist who illustrated his book *Ewiges Haus* to create these drawings.

As David continues his research into his family's origins, Reinhard spends hours in archives seeking information that he shares with David

WALTER ABOUT AGE 12

in great detail in his letters. In one he writes to David: "It seems we truly have similar biographies. We are somewhat similar as we both were teachers and worked for 39 years in the same profession. It also appears that in many ways we are quite similar . . ." He signed "your friend Reinhard."

As David reads this, a sensation of warmth fills his entire being. He is incredibly grateful. Reinhard is a genuine friend. Not only do they have experiences and interests in common, the friendship became even deeper when he informally signed "your friend." This may be common in America; however, David grew up believing that Germans are always rigid and formal.

As the letters continue to come, David is surprised to learn that in 1982 Reinhard had developed a friendship with his own dear family friend, Nellie Friedrichs. Reinhard met Nellie when he brought his 12th-year students to the opening of an exhibit on Braunschweig, focusing on the Nazi period. Nellie's mother, Ella, who often visited David and his family in Brunswick had been an intimate friend of Sophie and Otto in Braunschweig. Nellie often returned to Braunschweig to visit with classmates and childhood friends she had made there from 1912 to 1937. Following Nellie's death in the late 1990s, a street in Braunschweig was named after her. It was Nellie whom David telephoned in the early 1980s when tensions between his mother and him intensified. Beloved by both David and Elly, she helped to mediate the discord between the two.

When Reinhard sends David a description from Nellie's memoir, David can easily picture the formality of this family of Braunschweig socialites. For New Year's Eve 1925, Mr. and Mrs. Fred Sanders, Jr. from Los Angeles (one of Sophie's brothers who eventually opened a china shop in Little Rock), who spent several months in Braunschweig, invited Ella's mother, Ella, and her daughter Nellie, together with Sophie and her son Walter, to Café Lüeck in the Park Hotel. Nellie wrote,

> I had never experienced such high society. Following a fantastic festive meal there were all sorts of different performances. They were particularly appealing as we were familiar with the performers. There were singers and actors from the county theater. The master of ceremonies was the Santa Claus from our childhood, Hermann Mesmer. All of this was followed by music and dancing. Suddenly Walter Solmitz [age 20 at home for the holidays from his studies] discovered a former classmate from the *Odenwaldschule* [the progressive boarding school near Frankfurt to which Walter was sent at age thirteen]. He was the young painter, Ulfert Wilke. Wilke shared with us that he had just returned from Paris.

As David reads this, he pictures the contrast between his grandmother and father. She relished Braunschweig's high society, while he preferred the solitude of his study. Walter undoubtedly felt uncomfortable in this milieu, though he appreciated Ella, an independent woman and lover of classical music, especially Chopin and Liszt.

During the 1917–1918 school year, while attending the *Gymnasium*, the German college preparatory high school, David's father develops severe headaches that force him to miss much of his schooling. As the First World War is raging, the already unbearable family tensions at home are worsening due to the country's deepening economic crisis and the family's deteriorating financial situation. Walter is already developing a passionate antipathy for the arrogance that leads a country to war and conquest.

On his thirteenth birthday, January 19, 1918, Walter's mother accompanies him to Braunschweig's train station. Together, with a

*Max's son, Kurt, marries Selmar's daughter, Eva. Kurt becomes an art historian. Eva, who is a close friend of Edith Geheeb, teaches at the Odenwaldschule. Eva develops a close friendship with Rainer Maria Rilke. In 2009 their correspondence is published in Germany, edited with comments by Sigrid Bauschinger.

certificate from a psychiatrist confirming his severe headaches, they board the train for Frankfurt, from which they then walk to Badhombach. There he begins a six-year stay at the Odenwaldschule. The school in the Oden Forest is not only an educationally progressive boarding school, but Germany's first-ever coeducational school. It is the continental equivalent of A. S. Neil's Summerhill School in England.

Walter's sister Edith has made the necessary arrangements for her brother to attend this school—as their family has a long-standing connection with the Cassirer family. Max Cassirer provides his daughter Edith Cassirer Geheeb and her husband Paulus Geheeb with the funds with which to purchase property and start in 1910 their progressive school, the Odenwaldschule. Edith's and Walter's uncle Selmar is a close friend of Max Cassirer, who owned a cellulose factory in Silesia and a lumber business in Berlin.*

Although Walter is considerably relieved to leave home tensions behind, he undoubtedly experiences anxiety as well. Upon his arrival, he is welcomed by Edith Geheeb. Edith, who is thirty-three, nearly twenty years younger than his own mother, becomes a loving second mother to him, just as Paulus has stepped into the role left by the father he barely knew. Looking up to this tall man with long dark hair, a beard reaching down to his chest, wearing knickerbockers and sandals when not completely barefoot, Walter admires his idealism. Growing up in a war-fearing nation, he values Paulus's romanticism, his knowledge and love of philosophy, and his courage to establish an international, coeducational school, the purpose of which is to foster humanity.

Thanks to Paulus, Walter is introduced to old and new philosophers and poets: Pindar and Plato, Herder and Goethe, and a contemporary friend of Paulus, Christoph Schrempf. Before the noontime meal, Paulus reads from classical and contemporary authors whose ideas reflect his own hope regarding the betterment of humankind. He often quotes Pindar whose dictum, "Werde der du bist [become who you are]" is the maxim for his school.

On Christmas Eve of 1961, Walter gives David a small, blank notebook entitled *Quotations*, in which he hopes his son will write words of people he admires. Walter introduces his concept by writing a few of his favorite quotations, the first being Pindar's aphorism. He also quotes Schiller, one of Paulus' favorites:

> Von der Menschheit—du kannst von ihr nie gross genug denken;
> Wie du im Busen sie trägst, prägst du in Taten sie aus.

(You can never think too highly of humanity,
As you feel compassion in your heart, you practice it in deeds.)

Walter and Paulus often take walks together through the woods and feed wild deer; Edith also accompanies him on long hikes. Just as he enjoys working in his parents' garden in Braunschweig, Walter faithfully tends the school's garden. During his years at the school, Walter develops friendships with both boys and girls. One lad in particular, Raymond Klibansky, becomes Walter's close lifelong friend. Born in 1905 in Paris, he is the same age as Walter. Both have similar academic and humanitarian interests. He tells *Le Devoir* in 1992, "My ambition was to understand what it is to be human. And to do so required starting at the beginning, with Greek thought and Greek language—of the philosophers, but also of the poets, not to mention visual expression of spirit that can be found in art (*McGill Reporter* 1992)."

As Klibansky teaches at Oxford University's Oriel College and McGill University in Montreal, he on occasion visits Walter and his family in Brunswick. David remembers driving with his father in the evening the 40 minutes to Yarmouth Junction. There they meet the Grand Trunk steam-powered train from Montreal on its last stop before ending its journey in Portland. Raymond, with long, wavy black hair and deep-set dark brown eyes always greets David warmly. Although engrossed in long philosophical discussions with Walter, he always finds time to chat with David during his visits and inquires about him in letters to his parents. Whenever Raymond visits, Elly feeds the family at the dining-room table. Such a feat she accomplishes only on the rarest of occasions; in this case, she wants to show her respect and fondness for Wal-

Walter at the Odenwaldschule, Ober-Hambach, Heppenheim, Germany

Paulus and David at the Ecole d'Humanité in Goldern, Berner Oberland, Switzerland

ter's devoted friend. He continues to correspond with her until shortly before he dies in Montreal at age 99.

Having successfully completed preparation for the tough German university entrance exam—*die Abitur*—it's time for Walter to leave the school he so much enjoys. Without a doubt, these years were some of the happiest times of his life. In a letter to Walter's mother, Paulus writes that Walter's health has significantly improved. The year he completes his studies at the Odenwaldschule, 1923, is a year of tremendous inflation. As a result, the remainder of his mother's assets vanishes.

What could Walter do? Encouraged by Paulus to study philosophy, Walter becomes engrossed in his study of philosophy and classical philology. Apparently with some success, both Edith and Paulus try to persuade Sophie to seek help from her relatives to support her son's academic future.

As Edith's cousin Ernst Cassirer is a recognized philosopher at the University in Hamburg, she arranges for Walter to meet with him. Even during their short encounter, Cassirer is impressed. Walter initially joins his close lifelong friend from the Odenwaldschule.

Raymond Klibansky is teaching at the University of Heidelberg. However, after the first semester, he transfers to Hamburg to study un-

Paulus and Edith Geheeb circa 1915, founders and directors of the Odenwaldschule

der Cassirer. There he becomes friends with a fellow student, Fritz Carl Augustus Koelln. Fritz leaves for America in the early 1920s together with his wife. On coming to America in 1940, Walter is soon accepted at Harvard Graduate School to complete his doctorate and is employed as a teaching fellow in German. When he begins looking for a permanent teaching position, he seeks employment through a refugee contact organization. There he discovers his old friend, Fritz Koelln, chairman of the German Department at Bowdoin College. Delighted to hear from Walter, Fritz is able to arrange for him to become an instructor in German at Bowdoin. Walter leaves alone in early August 1946 to meet with Fritz and his colleagues at Bowdoin, and to find an apartment for his family. On a rainy day in late August, Elly and their three-year-old son take a local train to Boston's North Station. From there they board a train that will stop in Brunswick on its way north to Bangor, Maine. David vividly remembers his father standing under a black umbrella on the platform in Brunswick and grabbing his son as he tries to climb down the steep steps of the coach. A connection from Braunschweig (Brunswick), Germany, to Brunswick, Maine, has become a reality.

4

Bonded in Hamburg

THE YEAR IS 1914. DAVID'S MOTHER, ELLY, is a cheerful little girl of four, growing up in Hamburg, Germany. There is excitement in the air—the virulent patriotism of Germans supporting their Kaiser Wilhelm as he leads them off to war. Having seen the Kaiser in a parade, she rushes home. Thrilled, she tells her mother: "I saw the Kaiser. He was standing in an open car. He wore a full uniform with a big spiked helmet."

Elly's mother cannot participate in her daughter's enthusiasm. With sadness, she replies: "He is leading our country to war." The little girl does not understand.

A few days after seeing the Kaiser, Elly brings the daily mail to her father. He has been in bed for days with a severe case of bronchitis. He immediately grabs a letter from the imperial government addressed to him. As he opens it, his wife and daughter stand by his side. His face turns gray, his body tightens, his head droops: "I have been drafted into the Kaiser's army. On Monday, I have to report for duty," he says solemnly. As he is too ill on Monday to report for duty, an army doctor comes to the apartment. At the time they already have an *Einquartierung*, a soldier billeted in their apartment. To Elly he is a shy, dull man who keeps to his room and prefers eating with the maid in the kitchen.

When Elly's father finally has to leave, her mother explains gently, "Daddy has to go away, maybe for a very long time. Therefore, we will have to board the train for Lübeck—only about an hour's trip—to stay with your relatives."

The little girl is overcome by fear. Something awful is going on—does it have to do with the Kaiser, she wonders? Why must her father be sent away? What are the big parades about, the uniformed soldiers marching goose-step to martial bands? Those marches are so different from the folk songs and classical melodies that her mother, Stephanie, plays on the piano.

While in Lübeck, Elly becomes somewhat aware of the war. She watches a train with wounded soldiers slowly pulling into the station while she and her mother are walking above across a bridge. Elly experiences anti-Semitism for the first time while living in Lübeck. Kids call her names, ridiculing her for being Jewish.

Elly and her mother stay with her uncle Ignatz and his wife Else in Lübeck. He is a medical doctor who has developed a muscular disease. He and his wife soon move to Berlin to seek medical help. After Else and Ignatz leave for Berlin, Elly and her mother move into a furnished apartment for the spring and summer of 1917 in Bad Schwartau, just outside Lübeck. There she spends some of the most pleasant times of her childhood, playing with neighbor children and with her cousin Vinzent, who sometimes comes to visit with his mother.

In the fall, Elly and her mother move back to Lübeck, where they live with her grandfather, a very stern gentleman, a successful grain merchant. In typical German fashion, he commands the household. His wife, Elly's grandmother, lives submissively in his shadow, but is close to her daughter and granddaughter. This kindly lady tells Elly stories, takes her for walks, and sticks up for her to the other adults.

During her years in Lübeck, Elly makes friends with other children. Her closest is Adelheid, a non-Jewish girl. On occasion, during their summer vacation, their mothers take their daughters on an inexpensive train to the beach at Travemünde; sometimes Adelheid's mother alone takes them to the ocean. There they enjoy the sandy beach and the ice cream they purchase from special carts on the curbside. Travemünde is a real *Badeort*, a fancy resort with elegant hotels and restaurants.

When her father comes home on leave from the war, he never describes the horrors he experienced fighting in the trenches, where he became deathly ill with typhoid. Already an introvert, he withdraws into a deeper silence and melancholy. Elly has always seen her father Herman as an unhappy man, who represses his feelings by rarely speaking. As a boy, he yearned to become a professional pianist, but his parents forbade him to take piano lessons. "Little boys do not take piano lessons," they sternly insisted. Since his arranged marriage to her mother, Stephanie, he has worked selling buttons to agents for a raincoat factory—a job he hates. He is often humiliated because of his poor salesmanship, and fails to earn enough money to support the family. Herman had been promised his father-in-law's grain business, but it is given to his unreliable brother,

Elly's parents, Herman and Stephanie Reis, under the Nazis, 1940

Hubert, upon his return from the United States with his young American wife.

Naturally fond of her father, Elly enjoys picking blueberries with him in the Sachenswald forest. Yet they rarely talk, even when they take walks together. Unable to communicate with her father, Elly feels he doesn't understand her. One time on leave from the army, he buys her a pair of elegant boots that she refuses to wear; they aren't the simple style she enjoys, in contrast to the elaborate dress found at the fancy hotels at Travemünde.

Fear of lack of acceptance in the broader community haunts Elly throughout her childhood. From the time she begins kindergarten in Lübeck, she is scared. Even in kindergarten, the curriculum is rigid. Teachers are strict and impersonal. Although many of the children at her schools, both in Lübeck and Hamburg, are Jewish, she doesn't find it easy to associate with them. Many come from affluent families. As she grows older, she lacks confidence and tends to withdraw. She particularly dislikes math. She dares not ask her teachers for help. Not only are they impatient, they ridicule their students. When her father tries to teach her, he impatiently remarks, "It's so simple, you just do this, this, and this, and you have the answer." Still she doesn't get it.

The war is not yet over when, on April 15, 1918, Elly's brother Hans is born. As an eight-year-old, she is delighted to have a little brother to look after, to hold and rock. Living in poverty with barely enough to eat, she becomes very protective of her little brother. Even if she doesn't have enough to eat herself, she gives him some of her morsels. And they have fun together. One day she takes the toddler Hans with her to buy a loaf of bread at the bakery. She stuffs the many bills of inflated money in their little red wagon and has her brother sit on top so the money won't blow away. He giggles happily as she pulls the wagon along the cobblestone streets. Elly particularly enjoys playing art teacher, creating fanciful designs and encouraging Hans to draw the cars and trucks that were beginning to replace horse-drawn wagons.

In spite of her enjoyment of her little brother, Elly often feels anxious as severe economic depression overtakes Germany, and the hardships of poverty mingle with the solemn, angry, and vengeful mood stemming from Germany's defeat in the Great War. How will their family survive? Will she ever be able to fulfill her dream of going to art school?

She feels heavy hearted on a daily basis when her father comes home from work. His face is drained of color, his shoulders bent, and his clothing rumpled. Another day of selling buttons; another day that is less than successful. Sullen, rarely speaking a word, he slinks into the bedroom.

Her husband's despair affects Elly's mother. She is no longer the

Elly and her brother Hans (John) with their parents, March 1922

spirited and cheerful woman Elly knew just a few years before. Elly wishes her father were supportive of her mother's talent for singing and her love of opera and the theater. If only he were not so tightly bound by the tradition of the man as breadwinner, Elly mutters to herself, her mother would work for the opera and the family would be happier. Elly is convinced that if her father could get a job at a fashionable restaurant playing the piano while her mother Stephanie sings, they'd be happy, even if they'd bring home less money.

Finally, the night before Stephanie is to begin work as a secretary for the director of the Hamburg Opera, a job to which she is tremendously looking forward, she hears a thump in the kitchen. She goes to see what has happened. Herman has fallen from a chair in front of the gas oven. He had opened the door in order to inhale the poisonous fumes. Stephanie calls the doctor, who is able to revive him. As a result of his suicide attempt, she has to give up the position at the Opera to take care of her husband.

Several years later, Herman jumps into the Elbe River near Blankenese, by Hamburg. A well-to-do man rescues him and brings him home. If her parents' misfortunes were not enough, the return of Stephanie's oldest sister to Hamburg only increases tensions. Greta, a sickly woman who has never married, moves in with them at their Grindelhof apartment in Hamburg's Jewish quarter. Elly has to share her bedroom with this cranky person. Greta is often developing bronchitis and suffering from asthma attacks. She coughs throughout the night. Eventually, annoyed and frustrated, Elly puts a nightstand between the two beds so that Greta can spit out her phlegm into a bowl rather than get up at night, causing even more disturbance. A few years later Greta will die of pneumonia.

Elly's fondness for art leads to her determination to become a commercial artist. In this profession she could support herself and also help out her family, and, she figures, she might be able to draw and paint on the side, maybe even exhibit and sell her paintings at a small gallery. At the age of seventeen, she goes to the *Realschule,* a vocational school, of Dr. Löwneberg in Hamburg.

In 1928, she is delighted to be accepted as an apprentice to the commercial graphic artist Karl Schreiber. She enjoys lettering and hand delivering his posters; however, she quickly develops a strong dislike for this short, balding man, with dark eyes and beautifully sculpted hands. Originally from Czechoslovakia and father of two small children, he is purely interested in making money. He is a shrewd businessman who knows how to get plenty of customers by charging them high prices.

Elly's poster from 1931

At least, according to government regulations, he pays her the standard wage for her three years of apprenticeship. The only other employee in the office is Walter Wendt, a good-looking, tall young man with longish, brown hair brushed neatly behind his ears. Although Elly and he share a common interest in art and hiking, she refuses his passionate advances, because she feels she is too young.

At the completion of her apprenticeship, Elly is able to claim unemployment and therefore attend art school at the *Landeskunstschule* (the state art school) at Lerchenfeld free of charge. Although she particularly likes life-drawing classes with a modern artist named Willy Tietzi, she continues her training as commercial artist.

Elly is elated to be studying at the *Kunstgewerbeschule* (an applied art school). Within her first year at the school, she wins first place in a citywide poster competition. Her poster *Schutz, Licht und Luft dem Kinde* (Protection, Light and Air for the Child) is distributed throughout the city for Floral Days, the 5th and 6th of September, 1931, as part of a charity project to collect money for poor children in Hamburg.

Also, during her first two years at the school, she develops close friendships with two other art students, Loni and Gertrude, neither of whom are Jewish. Elly particularly appreciates Loni's artistic ability and enjoys her vibrant energy, her good nature and sassy personality. Elly meets Gertrude at a state business school where commercial-art students attend lessons once a week in the business aspects of commercial art, learning stenography and typing. Gertrude actually studies at another of Hamburg's art institutes, concentrating on lithography. The young women share similar interests in art and music. Both are enthusiasts of Bauhaus architecture and enjoy the innovative forms and creativity of contemporary art. Together they go to museums and take afternoon walks along the Elbe River or in city parks in Hamburg. On weekends, they enjoy hiking in the countryside.*

Elly's friends are liberal thinkers, idealists, communists and socialists. Elly and her friends dress unconventionally in shorts; she and her female friends bob their hair. On weekends the young men and women hike, sing, flirt, and dance their way through the *Lüneburger Heide* (Lüneburg heath) and the Harz mountains. They pass their nights in farmers' hay barns, climbing a ladder into the hayloft, the ideal place to experiment with sexual play. Together with these lively friends, Elly develops a taste for freedom and rebellion from the otherwise stern and rigid demeanor

*As Gertrude is not Jewish, she remains in Hamburg during the Second World War. At that time, she risks her life by visiting Elly's parents, bringing them food and other necessities of life, and keeping Elly informed of their perilous situation. When Elly and her family visit Hamburg in 1997, she tries to telephone Gertrude. The man who answers the phone informs her that Gertrude passed away the year before. Elly is shocked and hurt; she never recovers from the blow. She feels guilty, as during the last years their friendship had become strained and their contacts less frequent. Gertrude, who never married, became increasingly bitter with her life. Following the recent death of their lively, life-loving, bubbly friend Loni, Gertrude became more sullen and isolated. Loni, who had been married to a successful Esso executive in Hamburg, had throughout her life looked after Gertrude.

of German society. After all, it's not unusual for artists to be free-thinkers, nor for youth to be steeped in their parents' unspoken political leanings. Elly relates to her Uncle Ignatz and his wife as active socialists in conservative Hamburg, who continue their political activities in Berlin.

However, the idealism and hope prevalent during the Weimar years (Germany's democratic republic from 1919 to 1933) become tainted by fear. Although initially she and her friends talk about politics, they soon abandon such chatter for fear of arrest. They quickly realize that there always are untrustworthy people amongst them, such as spies planted by the police or by a *Sondergruppe*—a "special organization" with Nazi ties.

In 1932, at the end of her second year at the Kunstgewerbeschule, she is informed that, as a Jew, she can no longer attend the art school. Disappointed and frustrated at being forced to terminate her education, she begins looking for a job to support herself and her parents, with whom she still lives. The ugly head of Nazism is sprouting everywhere. The streets are filled with Nazi soldiers, troops formally goose-stepping in their brown uniforms. Nazi sympathizers are spreading the word of hatred toward the Jews.

When Elly is about 19, she goes to a Jewish hospital in Hamburg, suffering from a kidney problem. She is given water injections and told to drink lots of tea and water. She finds herself attracted to the young, well-dressed, well-mannered doctor who treats her, Hans Loeb. Shortly thereafter, she meets him by chance at the annual *Künstlerfest* artists' festival. A friendship evolves. She is enamored of his finely-sculpted face; with this tall, athletic man with dark-brown eyes and dark hair, so unlike her other friends, she experiences her first true love.

Hans comes from a very *Spiesser* (bourgeois) family, but Elly introduces him to more liberal ways of thinking, as well as to the beauty of nature. They go for long hikes in the countryside, during which they talk and share intimate feelings. They often take walks through the heath, Elly wearing a beige skirt and Hans in a beautifully tailored suit. He delights in Elly's liveliness and her appreciation of nature. To be away from the stress at his job in the hospital and together with an attractive and easygoing young woman is a happy contrast to his stifled childhood and youth within the conceited and rigid confines of his bourgeois family. Their friendship peters out when his job in Hamburg ends, and he moves to Cologne, where he continues to practice medicine.

By early 1934, Elly has a job working mornings as a secretary for a Jewish banker, Hermann Reichenbach, a friend of her mother's friend, Frau Danziger. He is cultivated but not distinguished, a kindly gentleman in his fifties. Elly appreciates the plays that he writes, as well as his friendly demeanor. Afternoons she does secretarial work for the firm of N. J. Kallmes and Alfred Levy, real estate brokers. Here she meets and befriends H. A. Rey, who will later become famous in the United States for his *Curious George* books. Rey is a friend of Alfred Levy, working for the firm on an informal basis.

During this time, Elly decides to take an introductory course in philosophy that meets once a week at *Volkshochschule* (people's high school), a school organized by the Jewish community for adults who want to further their education as well. It is located at the Jewish Community Center. There, before the first class, she spots a tall man pacing back and forth in front of the building, smoking a cigarette. She asks this handsome, black-haired, brown-eyed man whether he knows the room in which Herr Solmitz will be teaching a philosophy course.

He responds, "That is I." Together they enter the building and head directly to the classroom. Sitting near the front of the room, Walter takes out notes from his briefcase. When he stands up to begin his lecture, Elly can't keep her eyes off him, this *gebildeter Mann* (educated, cultivated man). As the weeks pass, she comes to admire him more and more. As

Jewish synagogue and Community Center where Elly and Walter met, Bauhaus design by Walter Gropius.

she prepares to leave class on the evening following their fourth session, Professor Solmitz asks her to have a cup of coffee with him. She gladly accepts.

Together they go to a little café a few blocks from the community center. Sitting at one of the four little, round tables, Elly orders coffee with cream and a little sugar, while Walter orders his usual black—pure black. They quickly realize that they have interests in common: art, art history, music, and the love of the outdoors. Elly is mesmerized by Walter's sad eyes, his gentle smile, deep voice, and delicate, soulful smile. He is attracted to her youthful vigor, her excitement about art, her practical and positive outlook on life.

From that point on, they meet frequently after class at the little café. As they sip their coffee, he with a burning cigarette between his fingers, Elly notices that occasionally his eyes appear glazed. He doesn't seem to be present. When she breaks such silences, his shoulders jump slightly.

On some evenings they explore his lectures further. The course is on Plato, and Elly's interest is piqued by Socrates' remarks on the immortality of the soul in his dialogue *Phaedo*. Socrates said, "Only in death is it possible for the soul to actually gain true knowledge." In spite of all that they have in common, Elly finds she is too practical to fully deal with this concept that suggests the possibility of a next life.

"How can that be?" queries Elly.

"The point, my dear, is that the soul exists before the body takes shape; the soul becomes the body's master. Therefore, our actions will have consequences in the next life."

"Now really," Elly winces, replying with a tinge of stubbornness.

Walter calmly assures, "This ancient Greek concept referred to in *Phaedo* is similar to the Buddhist and Hindu recognition of Karma." Walter continues his explanation by referring to his teacher, Aby Warburg, who has explored cultural history through iconology, leading him to discover patterns in early Renaissance paintings.

On weekends Elly and Walter go for hikes in the countryside, finding peace and solitude in the gentleness of nature. Elly brings her Leica to photograph the heath she loves, as well as the old architecture she admires in such little towns as Lüneburg. In the city, she photographs the modern, functional Bauhaus style, so different from the heavy, robust Prussian architecture with which she had grown up.

She also carries with her a little sketchbook. To her surprise, on one of their early walks along a path through a lush meadow, Walter stops by a sprawling tree and pulls a little pad from his jacket pocket to quickly sketch this tree. In his sketch, the tree is like a generous, protective umbrella in the vast meadow, with the forest and the distant hills outlined in the background. From then on, they occasionally do quick drawings together, although Walter denies any artistic ability—as he will continue to do throughout his life, in spite of the beautiful sketches he will make from time to time on family vacations by the sea or in the mountains.

At first Elly and Walter meet in front of the original building of Hamburg University, built in 1911. Later, he picks her up at her home in the Jewish quarter, just minutes away on foot. Before he could pick her up at her family's apartment, she has to introduce her lover to her parents. Her mother expresses delight. "I am so happy for you." Yet she fears how the two will survive, as their desired careers in commercial art and academia are being gradually eliminated by the Nazis. Still she tries to reassure herself and them. "You are such a happy and gifted couple. You will make it through the hard times we are facing. Elly has secretarial skills that will help you both, I'm sure."

Her father is amenable to their relationship but is too depressed to express any feelings on the matter.

As their relationship evolves, Elly and Walter commiserate over their shared fate of being forbidden by the Nazis to continue to their studies—Elly at the Kunstgewerbeschule in Hamburg, and Walter at the University in Hamburg.

WALTER, 1936

Walter feels betrayed and abandoned, not only by the loss of his place at the University. His professors have left Germany. His closest friend from their days together at the Odenwaldschule, Raymond Klibansky, is already established at Oxford. His mother and other relatives disapprove of his academic lifestyle. His sister Annaliese is institutionalized with tuberculosis and schizophrenia. His mother, with whom he has little contact, will probably be returning to America.

He explains to Elly that all of

Elly, 1936

these circumstances cause him to feel depressed and distraught, unable to generate the motivation necessary to pursue his doctoral thesis. Yet Elly gives him encouragement. She emboldens him to go to Munich to start work again on his thesis, reassuring him that she will always stand by him. However, depression strikes a severe blow when he learns in November 1935 that his sister, Annaliese, has taken her own life at the sanatorium in which she was a patient. Hearing of this, Elly, still living in Hamburg, wishes more than anything to be lovingly by his side.

For Christmas of 1935, Walter invites Elly to visit him in Munich. As the train pulls into Munich's central station, she spots Walter pacing the platform. He is delighted to see her again, as is she to see him. However, his face has become gray; bags hang heavily beneath his beautiful, dark brown eyes. As they hug on the platform, she assures her Walter that he will recover from his sister's death, complete his thesis, and become a great professor.

Since Elly has to return to her job in Hamburg, the visit is much shorter than either would like. On the way to the station to drop Elly off for her return to Hamburg, Walter suggests they stop for coffee. As they are unusually early (Walter has a lifelong habit of being late), Elly agrees. Realizing his depression and inability to work on his thesis as promised, he tries to look her in the eye as he hesitatingly and gently ushers in the topic foremost on his mind. "Elly, I ah, well, I ah . . ."

"Yes?"

"You know how difficult it is for me to make decisions."

"I do."

"I have made a decision. I, ah, I want to ask you for, I mean, to ask you to marry me."

Without hesitation, Elly responds with a firm "yes."

Walter feels as if a heavy burden has been lifted from his shoulders. Elly really appreciates him; yes, she loves him. He has found a companion who can help stabilize his life. They agree to marry the following summer in Munich.

Marriage of Elly and Walter in Munich together with Lotte Pariser, July 1st, 1936

As Elly boards the train, taking a window seat facing the platform and opening the glass so she can watch her beloved as the train departs, she notices that Walter looks happier and more relaxed compared to the day she arrived. As the train slowly chugs out of the station, Walter walks aside the coach, trying to keep pace. He smiles and waves his white handkerchief and even whistles a Bach minuet as Elly gazes out the train window with longing eyes, waving.

Elly quits her job with Herr Simonis just prior to the firm's dismantling and joins Walter in Munich. Shortly after she leaves, the Nazis close all Jewish businesses throughout Germany. She and Walter see anti-Semitic slogans everywhere, written on once-thriving Jewish shops, now permanently closed.

With some apprehension but also with happiness, Walter travels with Elly to his home town of Braunschweig to introduce his fiancée to his family.

His mother, Sophie, and older sister, Edith, are cold to Elly. Desirous of Walter marrying into a well-to-do, professional, and highly cultured Jewish family, they reject Elly, who comes from a poor family and is not, in their words, *gebildet.*

Elly likewise develops a strong dislike for Walter's family. She views Sophie as a stupid woman with a narrow outlook upon life: rich people should only associate with other rich people. Elly feels insecure around Edith, whom she considers more beautiful than herself. She had also met Annaliese before her premature death and perceived her to be a lonely and peculiar person, who was exceedingly strict with herself and with others.

During the early months of Elly's stay in Munich, Walter suffers severe depression. She arranges for him to recuperate for several weeks at the clinic of Dr. Laudenheimer, a psychiatrist Walter had befriended when he was a student. Dr. Laudenheimer helps Walter reorganize his thesis, this time dealing with themes related to Goethe. He encourages Walter to follow through on one topic at a time, while Elly types Walter's scholarly work.

Walter's anxiety and depression frighten Elly, but she never discusses her concerns with Dr. Laudenheimer. Uncertain how to deal with Walter's fears, his mood swings, and his bouts of depression, she knows only that she loves him dearly, and so she must stay with him. Elly and Walter are married on the 1st of July, 1936, in Munich.

The only witness to their marriage before a justice of the peace is their friend Lotte Pariser. Walter became acquainted with her when he was a student at the Odenwaldschule, at which she spent much time.

Lotte is deeply involved in intellectual circles, through which she befriended Rainer Maria Rilke and the Austrian artist Gustav Klimt. Lotte, who will remain in Munich during the war, is arrested by the Nazis during the summer of 1942. She is sent to Theresienstadt and from there on October 26, 1944, to Auschwitz, where she perishes.

Many years later, Elly's and Walter's son meets and befriends a fellow progressive educator, Emanuel Pariser. He lives just three blocks from the son's home in Waterville, Maine. Lotte, the son learns, was Emanuel's great-aunt.

5

From Hamburg to Terezin

On his trip to Germany in the spring of 2005, David's first stop is Hamburg. Within the hour of his arrival, he waits for his host, Herr Grolle, in front of Hotel Wagner. David feels tense and ill at ease as he spots Herr Grolle, an older gentleman, short in stature, wearing a beige trench coat and tweed cap, and bearing a briefcase under his arm.

When David was preparing his trip to Germany, he had corresponded with Herr Grolle, who had written a biography of his father, *Account of a Difficult Life: Walter Solmitz, 1905 to 1962, Pupil of Aby Warburg and Ernst Cassirer.* He arranged the hotel at which David would stay, a short walk equidistant between the University and the Jewish quarter.

When they actually meet, David feels as if he were a child, lacking any sense of authority, feeling intellectually inadequate before this man. Even though this person wrote kindly about his father, David feels an entrenched prejudice toward Germans coursing through his veins. For David, Herr Grolle represents the stereotype of a German: rigid, as in Prussian military style. As David becomes acquainted with Herr Grolle over the next few days, he observes the older man's reluctance to understand the worldview of younger generations. Herr Grolle represents a way of thinking and being that is very different from David's father's intellectual and rational approach.

For instance, Herr Grolle speaks with pride of one son who is an international journalist for a prominent, national magazine in Germany. Yet he implies that his other son, Daniel, a Tai Chi instructor and author of a thick book, *Understanding Tai Chi: A Playful Way to the Source of Natural Freedom*, does not reflect the status of his other son. David tells Herr and Frau Grolle about his Chinese wife, an instructor of Tai Chi. The following evening when he has supper at this gentleman's home, Frau Grolle presents him with a copy of their son's book. In the introduction to the book, Daniel shares his passion for cultures vastly different from his own that offer ways to advance harmonious presence. "Since kindergarten I have greatly admired my great-aunt, Christel Proksch, her husband and their family. A family filled with stories and adventures. Finally when Christel under dramatic circumstances disappeared to Asia and reappeared just as dramatically, she visited us and brought the magic of Tai Chi into our home. When she began a Tai Chi class in Hamburg, I joined in."

As David tries to come to terms with his negative feelings, he recalls his mother had also visited Herr Grolle in Hamburg. Since she felt ill at ease with him, it is understandable that she may have negatively influenced David. At least subconsciously, he will not betray her. Even though she remained in close contact with her art school friends Gertrude and Loni until their deaths in the 1990s, she maintained throughout her life a bitter taste for Germans in general. David wonders what role Herr Grolle may have taken as a young man during the War. Did he write this book to ease a guilty conscience? Did he want to tell about the sad circumstances and fate of students like Walter who had studied under Hamburg's famous scholars, Warburg and Cassirer? David is deeply grateful to Herr Grolle for showing him around Hamburg, yet, he can't overcome his aversion to Herr Grolle's intimidating character.

On arriving in Hamburg, David has easily found the little Hotel Wagner, occupying the first floor of the former Dammtor-Palais. The cozy, meticulously neat and clean single room, with a huge window, feather bed, and modern bathroom, suits him perfectly. The surprise that makes this hotel even more special is yet to come.

Standing on the small, tree-lined street beneath billowing white-and-pink clouds in a clear blue sky, Herr Grolle gestures to a little shaded park across the street from the hotel. "It is a memorial to Hamburg Jews, including your mother's parents. They were brought here to be transported to Theresienstadt. From there many were sent to other concentration camps."

As Herr Grolle and David cross over to the park, they stand in silence. David imagines seeing a large crowd of people, his grandmother and grandfather among them. Herman is carrying a small, battered suitcase. Both look worried and tired. However, Stephanie's eyes are bright, her gait firm. Herman, on the other hand, moves slowly, as if all energy has been sucked from him.

Through the trees across the main thoroughfare, David sees a sleek, red train glide by. It was on these tracks that his mother's parents were shipped in cattle cars through Poland to Terezin, in what is now the Czech Republic. Suddenly, he envisions the rumbling of a freight train, hears the puffing of the steam engine. He sees its gray smoke filling the air, his mother's parents squeezed with others into a cattle car, one of many such wagons on the train. At this moment, David resolves to see Theresienstadt during this trip—to see where his grandparents perished.

Leaving the little park, Herr Grolle and David walk along the wide, tree-lined avenue, the railroad tracks on their right. Within moments they reach the original domed building of Hamburg University, constructed in 1911. This modest edifice reflects the grace of many buildings he sees in Hamburg, so unlike the heavy, massive edifices he has seen on earlier trips in Germany. A long semicircular, columned portico adorns the façade atop of which more columns are separated by large, arched windows surrounding the dome. Under the dome is the spacious lecture hall in which David's father attended lectures by Ernst Cassirer and Aby Warburg. David imagines him listening intently, taking notes, jotting down questions, always with a burning cigarette between his fingers.

Retracing their steps toward the little park, Herr Grolle and David pass a tall, concrete office building. Herr Grolle proudly notes that the philosophy department occupies several floors here. "We'll come back, but let us continue to Grindelhof, where your mother grew up. It is very near."

They head down a narrower street with red-brick buildings. Stepping onto a stone-paved square inscribed with a pattern of black stripes, Herr Grolle explains, "This was the Jewish synagogue, the largest in northern Germany. It was set on fire by the Nazis on Crystal Night."*

David pictures his mother as a young girl often passing this synagogue, sometimes together with her little brother, John.

Herr Grolle continues, "Realizing that Nazi takeover was imminent, Rabbi Carlebach sent his wife and seven children to England. He remained here only to be arrested and sent to a concentration camp, at which he was killed.

*Crystal Night (*Kristallnacht*)—night of broken glass—November 9–10, 1938, was an anti-Jewish pogrom, supposedly sparked by the assassination of a German diplomat, Ernst vom Rath, by a German-born Polish Jew. From small towns to large cities throughout Germany, Jewish store windows were smashed, Jewish homes destroyed, and synagogues demolished; 25,000 to 30,000 Jewish men were arrested and sent to concentration camps. Others were beaten, and some were killed.

"Look at this building." Herr Grolle points to a plain, five-story structure with large rectangular windows, sitting at the edge of the square. It reminds David of a Holiday Inn. "This was built as a Nazi bunker shortly after the burning of the synagogue. Now it has other uses."

David wonders, *How could this have been a bunker?* He expects a bunker to be a large windowless concrete fortress.

Within moments they reach Grindelhof, a street lined with prewar homes. David's heart sinks as he realizes he does not know the building number at which his mother and her family lived. He imagines this to have been a quiet, peaceful neighborhood, as so much of Hamburg is.

Beckoning in the direction of the university, Herr Grolle says, "Now that we have seen where your mother grew up, let us return to the Moorweide and Dammtor, as these are sites I would like you to see."

Upon reaching Moorweide, a park close by the heavy traffic of a thoroughfare, Herr Grolle points to a large, round, red-brick, windowless structure with a cone-shaped roof that is somewhat hidden by sprawling trees. When he explains this was built as a Nazi bunker, David is again surprised at the unique architecture. This one blends rather well into the surroundings.

In a nearby open space to its left is the Henry Moore sculpture which Herr Grolle was responsible for securing for Hamburg. Having this graceful modern sculpture so close to the Nazi bunker seems incongruous.

Leaving the park, Herr Grolle and David cross the broad avenue, walk through the Dammtor station lined with fast-food stands serving sandwiches and pastries, a fresh juice stall, and, alas, a McDonalds.

A bright, airy, comfortable hall in which to purchase train tickets stands beside this gallery. As they come out the other side, they climb a series of steps onto a wide path passing two monuments. The first is a heavy, rectangular, concrete block surrounded by bas-relief profiles of marching soldiers. This monument was built in the mid 1930s by the Nazis. A few yards further is a postwar sculpture graphically representing the firestorm that destroyed much of Hamburg following Allied bombings of the city. Burnt faces and bodies are symbolized in this iron-and-stone memorial.

Continuing on the wide walkway, they come to the entrance to a botanical garden on their right. Directly beyond, an arched, steel bridge traverses a deep gully with a view onto a pond surrounded by woods. Herr Grolle tells David that it is a mere half-hour walk to Lake Alster and the city center, causing him to appreciate the proximity of his hotel even more.

The two return through Grindelhof to make their way to Herr Grolle's home, no more than a half-hour walk, for supper. He lives on Isetrasse, a quiet, wide, tree-lined street with the *U-Bahn*, the elevated city train, rolling on an iron grid high above the street's center.

In Boston, Chicago, and New York, where David has seen elevated trains, they are very noisy rumbling across dirty and rusting iron trusses. Yet in Hamburg he is amazed at the delicate, painted gray wrought ironwork of the U-Bahn, and at how quiet the trains are. From Herr Grolle's spacious third-floor apartment, one can hardly hear them passing.

Herr Grolle's home is located in a row of elegant prewar apartments. High ceilings, huge windows, and a balcony add to the spaciousness of the home. A wax plant surrounds the floor-to-ceiling window of the living room. The walls and bookshelves are painted white. Oriental carpets bedeck the hardwood floors. Paintings and drawings decorate the walls. Largely modern furniture, some of which reflects the Bauhaus style, embodies the sophisticated taste of the home. Frau Grolle serves a delicious meal with white asparagus and, for dessert, strawberries.

The following morning Herr Grolle takes David to the synagogue and Jewish Community Center where his parents met. It is no longer a synagogue but a music hall, yet David is impressed by the grace of this simple, concrete structure.

Leaving here, professor Grolle brings David to the Aby Warburg library. A picture of his father hangs prominently in a little office to the right of the entrance. The library has been completely restored to its original appearance. On this visit David learns that Aby, the oldest son of a wealthy family, gave his birthright to his brother Max, so he could devote his life to studying art history. Therefore, in order to build his library, he needed his brother's permission to take money from the family account. They reluctantly agreed. David wonders whether Walter ever took Elly here to show her where he studied and introduce her to the scholars for whom he worked.

With Herr Grolle's help, David finds in the library's archives a letter from Edith Geheeb, wife of Paulus Geheeb, director of the Odenwaldschule, to Kurt Goldstein, the psychiatrist and family friend, written following his father's death, confirming the suicide of both Walter and his sister Annaliese.

Following their visit to the Library, Herr Grolle takes David to an enormous park—a cemetery. Save seeing gravestones scattered throughout, one would never recognize this as anything other than a beautiful park with a pond, huge trees, little woods, and grassy fields and lawns. Herr Grolle shows David the ancient Jewish graveyard: stones in the shape of the Ten Commandments engraved in Hebrew with dates according to the Jewish calendar. This burial ground is hidden in a forest among old trees and rhododendron. From there they drive to another

Warburg Library, Hamburg

part of the cemetery to see a separate burial ground for Jewish soldiers who died fighting for Germany during both World Wars. Of course, there are hundreds if not thousands of stone markers of residents of Hamburg who died during the Second World War.

Herr Grolle and David conclude their day's tour at the Landeskunstschule Lerchenfeld where Elly studied art. Herr Grolle tells David that the school was designed by a famous architect, Fritz Schumacher, and built in 1911.

David is amazed at the country atmosphere, the lake and park surrounding the school. He envisions Elly as young woman with short hair carrying her portfolio through the huge, high-ceilinged lobby, up the stairs to her studio or classroom. There, enthusiastic and happy, she meets her friends Gertrude and Loni. During lunch they go to the park, sit near the water's edge to chat and eat.

On David's third day in Hamburg, he takes the route around the city suggested by Herr Grolle. Following a pleasant day downtown, he leaves the chaos of the city center and, within minutes, finds himself entering a forested park. Walking down a steep hill, crossing a waterfall, and following a path along the pond, then walking up another hill, he is amidst red, orange, purple, and white rhododendron. He realizes this is the park Herr Grolle and he viewed from Dammtor. In the quiet and solitude of nature, unable to see any buildings, David finds it hard to believe that this haven is located in the heart of the city. Several people sit on benches set alongside gravel paths amidst plants, shrubs, and a little stream. Further up are glass greenhouses. This park must have been here when Elly was a child, but David can't imagine why she never mentioned it to him.

During his last night in Hamburg, David suddenly awakens. He is scared. Does he hear bombs exploding, or are these fireworks? Can't be fireworks; there's been no holiday. Did he dream? He gets up, pulls the curtain aside a little to peek out. All is silent except for an occasional quiet hum of a passing car. He feels comforted by a slight warm breeze coming through the open window. David is at peace, being reminded how lucky he is to be here at a time so different and pleasant than when Elly was growing up.

The next morning David leaves Hotel Wagner. He experiences an emotional farewell to Hamburg as he walks along the gravel path that intercepts the tree-shaded park from which his grandparents were transported to their death.

On his way to Theresienstadt in the Czech Republic, David spends a couple of nights in Krakow to visit the death camps of Auschwitz-Birkenau. Because these have been preserved as a museum, David feels the atmosphere has sanitized—almost to the point of sterility—the unspeakable horrors that took place there.

For example, the lawns are mown; the buildings are spotlessly clean. Items such as piles of human hair to be made into Nazi uniforms, lampshades made of human flesh, are neatly displayed behind glass. Yet tourists coming here as couples or in groups ooh and ah at the atrocities committed here. Under these circumstances, is it even possible to fathom the degree of torture and suffering that occurred there?

He takes a bumbling local train from Krakow to Katowice, whence he'll take the intercity train to Prague. The little train passes through lush, green, rolling countryside, fields and meadows bordered by small forests and little compact villages with tiled roofs. It stops at every station—some of which appear to be merely a platform amongst trees and fields. As the train pulls into a larger town, David spots a convoy of carcasses: old, rusting steam locomotives. Some are small, regional engines with attached coal tenders, while others are larger steam locomotives with separate tenders that pull long-distance trains.

As much of the country, locomotives have changed. Did the locomotive engineers of the big steam engines, the drivers of the switching locomotives, or the workers who coupled the wagons and engines together know that they were hauling thousands upon thousands of people to their death? Did they ever wonder why cattle cars were overflowing with terrified people?

David is afraid to think what he might have done had he been a railroad worker at the time. Would he have been frightened at the pathetic sight of these trains filled with scared people of all ages including children? Would he have cared? Would he have resisted doing his job? Maybe not, knowing that the Nazis had occupied his country. Had he a wife and child, had he resisted, not only would he have lost his job and possibly be part of the next trainload of "undesirables," his wife and child would undoubtedly have been punished as well.

On the intercity train from Katowice to Prague, David's spirits rise. It is a warm spring Friday afternoon as he looks out the window of the train and spots two women who have laid their bicycles by the side of a path. They are sitting relaxed in a field, chatting.

On a little road with woods on one side and a large field on the other, a family has parked their red car. They have set a blanket in the field on which the three of them are enjoying a picnic. Later, David spots a group of five young men and women picnicking in a field adjacent to a small pond, their bikes, also, resting by a pathway. He thinks of the happy, youthful excursions his mother told him of, and pictures her among these people.

From Prague David takes a regional bus the next morning to Terezin, an hour's trip mostly along the expressway flanked by rolling hills, broad fields, and scattered patches of woods. The bus passes a large burial ground with a huge iron Star of David. It travels past the fortress that was used as the concentration camp, crosses a bridge over a river, next to which is a disused, ancient, many-arched bridge, and comes to a stop at a large tree-lined square in the quiet, small town of Terezin. Along with the other passengers, David gets off to begin the two-kilometer walk back to the fortress.

At 10:00 in the morning, there are few tourists here. David walks slowly alone through the courtyards of the old barracks built in the late 1700s near the junction of the Elbe and Ohre rivers. *Gosh, isn't this similar to old Fort Popham*, he thinks, reminded of the old fort at the mouth of the Kennebec River in Maine, built for the War of 1812, that he and his father used to explore when he was a child. Father and son had been struck how cold and dismal the fort was, how terrible it must have been for prisoners of war to be held there.

Coming to the burial ground, he walks past each grave row by row, looking for a marker with the names of Herman and Stephanie Reis. Some have no markers. Some are missing portions of names. As he reaches the end of the last row by the fortress wall, he feels sad and defeated. Maybe they were not buried here, he thinks. Possibly they were dumped into a mass grave somewhere else. They may have died just before or right after liberation by the Russians.

Unable to find a marker with the names of his grandparents, David enters the fortress by crossing a wide bridge over the now-grassy moat, and passing through a large, arched gateway. The thick wall, like the rest of the fortifications, is covered with grass. Inside the wall is an office, where David pays to enter the memorial. He inquires whether he can go to the archives to find out about his grandparents.

"I'm sorry," the lady informs him in broken English. "The archives are closed today."

His heart sinks. *Why didn't I have the common sense to realize that, of course, on Saturday the archivists do not work*, he ponders. The lady gives him a form to complete, assuring him that the archivist will send him an e-mail with the information he desires. David will complete and mail the form, upon

Entrance to the fort that became the concentration camp at Terezin.

his return home to Maine. However, he never receives a response. He will send several more e-mails, but to no avail.

Now at Theresienstadt, David passes through barracks once heated by little coal stoves lined with typical wooden bunks. He feels sad and alone. For the first time he experiences the sensation that he is together with his mother's parents whom he never got to know. They are elderly, frightfully thin and frail. Their sunken eyes look downwards. Stephanie's long gray hair, that used to be tied neatly behind her head, now is dragging in strands beside her ears. Though they are together, they are silent.

David walks through a 500-meter tunnel. At points along the tunnel walls are openings, little portholes for guns. At the end of this underground passage is the place where prisoners were executed. As he comes out, instead of the usual gravelly ground, David enters upon a grassy area. He climbs up a steep grassy slope onto the top of the fortress wall. Here, amidst some low bushes, he sits in the warm sun relishing a gentle breeze wisping through tall grass as he overlooks the town of Terezin. In the background he sees the silhouettes of high blue hills. Tears come to his eyes as he senses the strong presence of his grandparents. He thinks of his mother, trying desperately with the help of her close friend from art school, Gertrude, and the American Red

A Theresienstadt office and the sign: Work Makes You Free.

Cross to find her parents, to secure their liberty, and to bring them to America.

He thinks of his parents as they were in 1940, experiencing a relatively happy new beginning in America, yet with the war still raging in Europe. Elly agonizes about her parents. Are they still in Hamburg? Are they surviving the war? Or, like so many Jews, have they been arrested and sent to their death in the camps? At such thoughts she shudders and is overcome by a cold sweat. She makes it her goal to locate them and bring them to America. She learns from a cousin in Sweden that she has sent them food packages. The cousin gets the signed receipts back, but Elly's parents never receive the parcels. With the help of the Red Cross and the Jewish World Federation, Elly learns that they have been deported to the concentration camp at Theresienstadt.

On April 3, 1944, Elly writes to the National Refugee Service, Inc. in New York City.

Dear Sir:

I understand that you have some information about Jewish people from Germany who have been deported to Theresienstadt. May I ask you to let me know whether my parents are to be found on your list?

The names of my parents are:

Herman Reis, who was born January 26, 1879, in Lübeckk, and Stephanie Schlomer Reis

Their last address was Hamburg, Frickestrassse 24. They have been deported from Hamburg in the beginning of the month of June 1942.

Showers at the concentration camp at Terezin

> In fall 1942 some relatives of mine in Sweden found out that at that time my parents were in Theresienstadt and that my mother's number was: L425. Some time later on, however, communications from Sweden were returned with the remark: "unknown."
>
> We have not been able to establish any contact with them since, and would be very grateful indeed for any news you can give us or any suggestions how to contact them.
>
> Very truly yours,
> Elly Solmitz

On June 28, 1945, she receives a notice from the National Refugee Service that states:

> According to information received recently, a list of internees in Theresienstadt contained the name of Mr. Herman REISS, aged 72, previous address, Hamburg. Judging by this date, this might be your father.
>
> We are aware of the fact that things have changed in the Theresienstadt situation in the last few months and our information may not be up-to-date any more. In case we receive any more news, we shall notify you immediately.

A year later, she learns that her parents died of starvation at Theresienstadt. Her words of their death still haunt her son: "At least they were both spared to die in the gas ovens, what kind of things one had to be grateful for!"

David gets up slowly, walks down the slope and back through the fortress. Before leaving, he passes through the museum, hoping to find pictures of his grandparents. However, as he does not recognize them and names of those shown are not those for whom he is looking, he solemnly departs through the thick entrance wall, crosses the moat, and turns left to walk among the graves again, wanting to believe that his grandparents are lying here peacefully.

He returns to the quiet little town of Terezin, walking across the old arched bridge and through a courtyard surrounded by large antiquated buildings that were once used to house Jewish prisoners. These were part of the Jewish ghetto—an attempt on the part of the Nazis to present a false image to the world that they were creating an ideal community for the Jews.

David continues to walk along the neat side streets lined with rows of simple, two-story stone houses. Some are graced with handsomely carved wooden doors. He finally sits on a bench in the shade of a tree-lined path that circles the town square. On this Saturday afternoon it is very quiet, except for the happy songs of many chirping birds. A few people, young and old, sit contentedly on park benches. As the bus for Prague pulls up to the stop, he boards. Still sad, yet grateful to have had this opportunity to experience Theresienstadt, he watches through the window as the bus passes the heavy walls of the camp, the iron Star of David, and into the lush countryside of small farms, fields, and little forests.

He returns to his room on the third floor of an old building near the center of Prague, just one stop from the famous art museum. Following a day in Prague, he leaves by train for Munich early on Monday.

6

Bitter and Sweet

In the days following their marriage, Elly and Walter leave the city for a cottage at a lake near Munich with a view of the distant mountains. Hills and woods are in back of the house. Here in the peace of the countryside, away from the growing political unrest, they hope to stay some time. This setting seems ideal for Walter to work on his thesis, and it is an easy commute to the university in Munich. After a few relaxing days of hiking, swimming, candlelight meals at the cottage, their landlord tells them that the people in the village are inquiring as to whether Elly and Walter are Jews.

Feeling under pressure, guilty, and not wanting to hurt the newlyweds, he awkwardly says, "If you want to stay here longer into the fall, no one can harm either you or me, because I am joining the Party."

Disappointed, uncomfortable, and even fearful to stay, they decide to move back to Munich. In the suburb of Nymphenburg, they rent two furnished rooms in the house of a Jewish widower.

David's mother often wonders how she and Walter will endure this period. They are surrounded by Nazis—in the streets and in the shops—always clad in their brown uniforms. They goosestep for hours through the city. Even when the newlyweds are hiking in the countryside, they see and hear Nazis partaking in military exercises.

Yet Walter seem oblivious to the gradual heightening of Nazi terror. Why hasn't he thought of leaving Germany, especially as he witnesses the flight of his closest friend, Raymond Klibansky; his professor, Ernst Cassirer; and the entire Warburg Library and its staff? After all, since his mother's family is American, he could emigrate to the United States more easily than if his entire family were German. He spends hours writing down reasons, pro and con: *if* this happens, *then* that will happen. Of course, he never comes to a conclusion. Like Paulus from the Odenwaldschule, Walter is idealistic. He tries hard to believe in the goodness of humankind, refusing to acknowledge the impact Nazism is having on the Jews.

Fearing the worst, unwilling to rely on her husband's optimism, and aware of his pattern of procrastination, Elly telephones Walter's close friends at the Warburg Institute in London, Fritz Saxl and Gertrude Bing, to seek their help in getting visas as trans-migrants. Such status would allow them to stay in England until their American quota number is reached. She also contacts Walter's close friend, Raymond Klibansky, who is already teaching at Oriel College in Oxford, and Theo Sanders, Walter's mother's brother, an architect in Little Rock, Arkansas, who offers to sponsor by affidavit their flight to America.

When David's parents arrive home from the city on the afternoon of November 9, 1938, they enter the house as usual, intending to head upstairs to their little apartment. Their landlord's maid approaches them with great excitement and deadly fear in her eyes.

"Nazis were here just two hours ago. They arrested our landlord, and said they would be back to arrest Herr Solmitz." At that time, they had no idea that this was the onset of Crystal Night. Nor did they know that Walter was just one of many Jewish men to be arrested that evening.

Elly and Walter's 2nd floor apartment at the time of his arrest, Nov 10, 1938

In shock and dismay, they thank the maid, rush upstairs to their apartment. Walter, tense and anxious, immediately lights a cigarette. Elly fills the kettle with water, lights the gas stove to prepare some tea. What could they do? Under Elly's directive, Walter calls Dr. Laudenheimer to tell him of their predicament, but neither he nor any of their other friends take the risk of hiding them.

They continue to talk in the privacy of their little flat. "There is no place that we can hide. We can't flee. We really have no other choice than to turn ourselves in to the Gestapo at the Wittelsbacher Palace (their headquarters in Munich)," Elly explains pragmatically and calmly.

In his typical style of reasoning, for and against, Walter asks, "But is this the only alternative we have? We have to be reasonable, Elly. We must be sure our decision is the best decision. Let us figure out, carefully, the pros and cons of this matter."

"Walter, this is no longer the time to figure out such things. I know this is the most reasonable thing to do," she replies. "There simply is no prospect for escape. All railroad stations and roads are controlled. Furthermore, we can't stay with our non-Jewish friends, as we are placing them in danger. You know, Walter, I will never, ever let you down. You know as well as I do of brutal arrests that have already taken place. It is far better that we turn ourselves in. I will do everything in my power to help you and us, so that we can leave this country," she says lovingly.

In the late afternoon, Elly and Walter sadly leave their apartment. They walk slowly the ten-minute walk to the Laim station to board a local train to Munich's main railroad terminal. From there they take two different streetcars to reach the Gestapo headquarters. With adrenaline rushing to her head, Elly, holding her husband's arm, walks past the SS guards and numerous other soldiers. The corridor is full of empty beer bottles. In the office at which they report are ghastly looking SS men. When she asks whether she may accompany her husband, an officer bluntly informs her with a curt no. Elly, however, does spot one official who seems to have some humanlike features. Courageously she approaches him, asks him his name and whether she may come back to inquire about Walter. Not only does he tell her his name, Peter Schmidt, but also that she may return to check on her husband's status.

By the time Elly leaves the Gestapo headquarters, darkness has befallen the city. As she waits for the streetcars on her return to the railroad station, she sees stones flying onto—and fires raging fire in—Jewish shops, homes, and synagogues. She feels sick at heart as she witnesses young boys, soldiers, grown men, and old-timers with happy smiles and intense aggression as they release their rage at every conceivable symbol of Jewish life and culture. With adrenaline still surging in her veins, she walks briskly to the streetcar stop. She cringes as she hears glass breaking and the crackling of fires. Catching the local train, she takes the first available seat. As the train creeps through the suburbs via Nymphenburg, the night sky lights up from the multitude of fires. During the short walk home from the Laim station, along a broad, quiet road, she passes soldiers, skirts stones thrown by young hoodlums, and spots damaged storefronts.

The house at 59 Wotanstrasse in which she and Walter live is dark. She unlocks the door, climbs the narrow staircase to their two rooms. As she is getting ready for bed, she occasionally hears people outside screaming. Lying alone, she feels despair, yet she is determined to do whatever she can to save her Walter. On the following morning, she telephones Bing and Saxl in London and Raymond at Oxford to inform them of Walter's arrest and to urge them for help. Raymond immediately predates a letter before Crystal Night inviting Walter to his college.

The next day David's mother returns to the Gestapo headquarters. As she walks up the long approach to the Wittelsbach palace, two SS men stand guard at the entrance. When she gets there they cross their guns. She does not hesitate to tell them that she wants to see Officer Schmidt. They issue her a number, so that she can get out again. From that day on, she goes regularly to ask Herr Schmidt about Walter's whereabouts—always without success. After a couple of weeks, she receives a censored postcard from Walter from Dachau, the concentration camp just outside Munich, to which Walter was trucked, then nothing.*

In his *Report on Dachau* (see full report in Appendix A), Walter accepts his arrest and incarceration philosophically. He observes that to be arrested en masse is much more tolerable than being arrested all by himself. As the arrests on Crystal Night are a collective action throughout Germany, there is some public awareness; Walter realizes and is thankful that the SS have been ordered to restrain their actions towards the prisoners.

However, having no idea as to how long he and the others who have

*Dachau was the first Nazi concentration camp. It was located in an abandoned munitions factory about ten miles northwest of Munich. Construction began in 1933 and was completed in mid August of 1938. It was built largely by political prisoners, many of whom were Communists, who opposed the Nazi regime. They continued to remain as prisoners following the camp's completion. As a result of Crystal Night, on November 9 to 10, 10,000 Jewish men were arrested and sent to Dachau. Many from this group were released a few weeks to a few months after proving they had arrangements to emigrate from Germany.

Dachau concentration camp, photo taken at the museum in 2009

been arrested will be in captivity, overnight or forever, is troubling. To receive a letter from his wife about three weeks after his arrival at the concentration camp brings him some relief. Yet, all letters, which are limited to a maximum of ten lines, are, of course, censored. Ultimately, Walter is in Dachau for six weeks. During that time the weather is relatively good, so he remains healthy; snow arrives the day after his release. Had he been sick while at the camp, he would not have been freed. Of the 200 in his portion of the camp, he knows of six who died during his term at Dachau.

As a philosopher, Walter has empathy for his captors. He understands that people who are unfulfilled in their lives or unhappy in their personal relationships and their economic situation tend to take their anger and frustration out on those they perceive as different from and who are weaker than they are. As the collective attitude of the government and the society grows to sanction violence toward the disenfranchised groups, the crimes become less secretive, more overt, and more horrific. Drawing upon his knowledge of human behavior, Walter later prepares a report commissioned by the British government in 1939.* In the report, he predicts the escalation of Nazi violence toward the Jews and the atrocities that will occur during the war in death camps like Auschwitz and Bergen-Belsen.

> When we were brought by truck to Dachau, the truck ran out of gas. [Dachau is only about twenty minutes from Munich.] The young, smart aleck, SS officer who drove the truck got a can of

*As Walter was among the earliest refugees to arrive in England from the concentration camp, the British government requested that he describe conditions in the camp. With this information the British might be able to assist those incarcerated and help others who were threatened to be sent to the Nazi concentration camps. Walter wrote his report in German.

> gas from a nearby gas station. He poured it into the tank. Next to him stood one of the repulsive men in civilian dress, smoking a cigarette. He was one of those who had been busily occupied with us during the night at the Wittlebacher Palais. The SS officer told the guy smoking a cigarette so that all could hear:
>
> "Stand back with your cigarette or else the whole caboodle will go up in flames. That wouldn't be a shame at all, but I can't take responsibility for it." I asked myself: *Would it really be a pity? Would it really be a shame if this little heap of Jews would no longer exist? No. If that's really the case, maybe it wouldn't be so bad if the SS officer himself were no longer either.* If one begins to think in this way, that is, what would be a shame or what would not, then there is little left that would truly be a shame. The national socialists think that way. In regard to the Jews, it would not be a shame. On the contrary, it would be their good fortune if there weren't any Jews left. They are bad luck! They alone are the blight, the vermin that spoils everything. They must be destroyed, why don't they exterminate us like rats and mice that are wiped out? They could line us Jews up and shoot us. Why don't they do that? Why can't they take the responsibility? Is it the rest of humanity that prevents them from doing it? (Solmitz 1939)

Walter raises other questions: Why are Jews imprisoned when they can just be handed over to the angry SS? Why did vom Rath [the German ambassador to Czechoslovakia] have to be murdered [allegedly by a Jew] before the Jews could be arrested [two days later, on Crystal Night]? These questions lead Walter to a philosophical inquiry about the difference between a *guilty conscience* and a *true conscience.* He writes:

> Embodied in Hitler, one finds the guilty conscience of humanity—at least that of the European capitalistic world. I am referring to the guilty conscience not conscience itself. True conscience recognizing a guilty conscience tries to come to terms with it. The aim is to make the guilty conscience no longer appear burdensome but good. Therefore, the guilty conscience must be made to disappear not by denying, suppressing or combating it, but on the contrary, placing a high value on the evil act by making the act appear as if it were a good deed.
>
> I will try by giving an example to clarify my point. A poor pickpocket steals a wealthy lady's pocket book, which contains

> twenty marks. He is arrested and confronted by the lady. His excuse is that he desperately needs money. If he were to return the money, it really would make no difference to the lady if she had twenty more or less marks. Besides, she belongs to the rich who keep the poor oppressed. To this the lady has no answer. The man is right; he appealed successfully to her guilty conscience. He not only used it, he embodied it. He has become her guilty conscience. To carry this example further, the man having had success with this excuse continues to steal even when stealing is no longer urgent. He always gives the same reason: to help the holy cause of the oppressed classes until in the end he believes his excuse himself. Even after he has become a real criminal, his arguments will be accepted by the rich who have been robbed. Their own social guilty conscience has become no better. The ideologically sanctioned criminal embodies the guilty conscience. He knew instinctively how to touch the sore spot. The guilty conscience allows no peace of mind. It must constantly renew and document its morality by committing new crimes. To carry the example even further, a factually, justifiable, historically necessary movement of the disadvantaged classes steps into action. The movement will serve the ideological criminal and it in turn carries him to new heights. So the politically justified movement becomes an "historic necessity." The argument pertaining to the "historical necessity" and the mission of a just cause hits the guilty social conscience of those who are attacked. In this way, one can understand the insecurity and conflict in judging the ideologically sanctioned criminals by the attacked nations and social classes. (Solmitz 1939)

Walter believes that, had the capitalists introduced social reform, then the conditions of the destitute that brought about the rise of Nazism would not have been possible. He writes in his report:

> The need for power and the hostility of the poor and unemployed was in essence directed against *capitalism,* the *capitalists*, and their money. The need for power and hate among the impoverished was directed by the regime to the Jews. After all, the Jews were typically considered representative of the money hoarders. (Solmitz 1939)

In his report, Walter writes without hatred about the suffering of others at the abusive hands of those who held power in the camps:

> During the marching and especially at roll call the four rooms of the barrack come together. Immediately in front of us stood the smallest men, including the very young to the very old from the neighboring rooms. One of these people from the neighboring section could not go any further on the way to the roll call square. We supported him and massaged him as best we could during roll call. Afterwards, two young men from our group, who always energetically seized the opportunity to help, brought him to the infirmary. He was not admitted and sent back to the barrack. For days he had not been able to eat and the episodes of weakness occurred repeatedly. He was again brought back to the infirmary. Once more, he was kicked out.
>
> The capo, the section leader of my part of the barrack, was a baker from Mainz—a huge, powerful man. He, like all section and room leaders, was a political prisoner. Although he had a sly expression, he had a humorous and an indifferent air, as well as a furiously brutal chin. (He was in the camp because his wife had denounced him.) This capo could be quite pleasant and cheerful. However, this totally inconspicuous little man became the target of his scorn. The third time that he was brought back to the infirmary he was literally kicked out with actual blows and kicks. He was brought back to the barrack from which he was bolted out by the section leader. That evening money was distributed. Therefore, we had to stand in the cold following the evening roll call. We wanted to put this man in the lobby at least until our turn came. This would occur later as his name started with "S." Having noticed that comrades had brought him into the lobby, the section leader kicked him out again. He had to stand with us. He died the following night. In view of cases like these, one can presume that the room leaders were given a quota by their superior officers demanding that a certain number of people die. Although this cannot be confirmed, it is not improbable. (Solmitz 1939)

As Walter's *Report on Dachau* reflects upon his experiences in that concentration camp, it reveals a man who is contributing important intellectual understanding and reasoning for the rise of Nazism and the viciousness that it encompassed. In spite of the brutality he experienced at the hands of the SS, the suffering he underwent and anguish he witnessed others endure, his humanity remained unscathed. Throughout this report, he attempts to offer explanations for why his captors behaved as they did:

> It can be that the SS themselves are taught and drilled in a very brutal, cynical, and chastising manner. In part this might be meant as a Spartan-like toughening process. The outcome of this cynical and unconstrained system, which is perhaps intentional, forces them into degradation in such a way that it progressively and greatly intensifies their need to take revenge for this suffering, disgrace, and pain. This creates a lust for power way beyond natural limits. It creates a person of indiscriminate lust for power for whom everything is all in order to satisfy himself. It is also expressed in the form of conviction to serve a great cause, a totality for which he himself is not responsible. The result is a continuous extortion and far reaching destruction of natural solidarity. (Solmitz 1939)

In his honest and dispassionate evaluation of the conditions at Dachau, Walter even suggests that the *Aryans* who were political prisoners at the camp and who were in charge of the Jewish prisoners encountered worse circumstances than the Jews:

> I could not and cannot resist my impression that in spite of the cruel treatment and intentional degradation, we Jews occupied a "privileged" position. The Jews who were arrested on November 10th were in Dachau for weeks or months. The Aryans were there for years—maybe forever. The Aryans had to work for us: to cook, write, clean and repair the streets, even serve as barbers. The "Browns" had to clean the septic system and transport the foul smelling refuse in open carts. We were spared all of these things. Even the SS seemed worse off than the majority of Jews. In fact, they seem to look toward the Jews with some envy as Jews were able to leave. (Solmitz 1939)

Several days following Walter's arrest, some well-to-do neighbors, whom Elly knows only by sight, come to the house in order to confiscate their silver, camera, and other possessions of value. They rifle through their drawers, read their letters, and place everything they want into the hall. They become very disappointed and angry because they do not find much. While these men are ransacking their little flat, their friend Lotte Pariser telephones. Sensing that something is wrong in the way Elly answers the telephone, she promptly calls the police. Before these men are through, the bell at the outer garden gate rings. The men storm out to see who it is. A single policeman standing by his bicycle outside the gate tells them timidly that the *Aktion* is over and looting is no longer allowed. The neighbors depart, leaving their loot behind. Elly, distressed by this experience, calls the Laudenheimers. Without hesitation, they immediately ask her to move in with them. She gratefully accepts.

During Walter's incarceration at Dachau, Elly is busy collecting papers in order to get passports. She has to show receipts from the gas and electricity companies, and bank accounts, among other paperwork. Since these offices are closed to the public by eleven in the morning, she has to get from one to another by taxi. One taxi driver, realizing her rush to get to different bureaus on time, reassuringly says, "Green light, we'll make it."

At the *Finanzamt* (the tax collecting agency), she encounters a helpful official. After he has given her a statement confirming that she and Walter don't owe any taxes, she asks whether she may get the same statement for Dr. and Mrs. Laudenheimer. The elderly couple, Elly explains, is desperately waiting for this statement in order to get passports to accept his cousin's invitation to England. The official pulls out the Laudenheimers' application, looks at it and says, "It's written in such an awful handwriting, I can't read it." After Elly helps him decipher it, he gives her the necessary statement.

Elly finally is issued the passports at the police headquarters in Munich. When the elderly police officer at the desk hands them to her, he quietly but firmly says, "Now watch out, the Gestapo will ask you to send your husband's passport for him to sign at Dachau. Do not give it to them. You will neither see the passport nor your husband ever again."

Elly is particularly grateful for this man's kindness. After all, he is a full-fledged German police officer. Had his advice been discovered, he would definitely have lost his job and more than likely been sent to Dachau or another concentration camp.

Elly alone has to make all decisions needed to arrange their departure once Walter is released from Dachau. She has to decide what to take along, what to have sent to America, and what to leave behind. This is an unusually difficult task. She, like other Jewish emigrants, is forced to pay a tax to the Nazi regime of 100 percent of the value for everything they want to take along, 200 percent for new things. Since they have been married for only two years, most of their belongings are new. She has to hire an appraiser to assess everything from books to handkerchiefs. In addition to their belongings, they can only take ten marks per person out of Germany. As she deals with the preparations, Ellly keeps reminding herself, *The only thing that matters is to get Walter out of Dachau and then for the two of us to get out of Germany.*

Elly packs her husband's books and working materials as well as some household goods that she puts into storage at the *Freihafen* (free port) in Hamburg.* She pays in advance for the freight so that the boxes can be shipped to the United States when their quota number to the U.S. is reached and they may leave for America.

On June 1, 2005, David anxiously visits the concentration camp at Dachau in which his father was incarcerated sixty-seven years before, during the dark, dismal days of November and December, 1938. On entering the camp, David sees the huge roll call square now, like the rest of the camp, covered neatly with gravel—as if it were a park. Of course, it is no longer a concentration camp; it is a well-maintained memorial. To the right is the museum and administration building, to the left a poplar-lined street with concrete slabs, the only remnants of the barracks that bordered both sides of the street.

On this warm, sunny morning, chills overtake his body. He imagines his father standing there on a cold, damp November morning together with hundreds of other prisoners, as Nazi soldiers and SS officers are yelling humiliations while taking roll call.

David walks quickly across the roll-call square to the archives located at the far end of the museum complex—all part of the original buildings. He rings the bell outside the wooden door, enters a clean, white office complex. The offices are sparsely furnished. This one has two large rectangular tables, a computer, and large gray filing cabinets. Explaining his purpose, he is brought to Dr. Albert Knoll, director of the archives. Having corresponded with him via e-mail from Maine, Dr. Knoll is expecting David's visit. A gentle man in his mid thirties, he tells David to go to the next room to wait for him while he completes his search on Walter. As only a large glass wall separates the two rooms, David heads toward the clear, glass partition. "No, you must go out the door here,

*The fact that the Nazis opened the boxes while they were in storage and stole some of the contents becomes evident when a friend of theirs finds one of Walter's books with his name in it on sale at a bookstore in Hamburg. The friend purchases the book and, after the war, sends it to them in America.

and enter the door over there," Dr. Knoll explains. He sits down at his computer.

While waiting, it is hard for David on this sunny, warm June morning to picture the scene his father encountered 67 years ago. As David looks out the large window from the wooden table at which he is sitting, he sees a large concrete wall, before which is a high, barbed-wire fence. From the other side of the wall come the sounds of the constant flow of automobile traffic. Several minutes later Dr. Knoll returns with a file that he shows David. Walter, he learns, was registered at Dachau on November 11, 1938. His custody number was 2034, and he was identified as a "Jew in Protective Custody."

Dr. Knoll gives David other documents to examine, including an essay by Werner J. Cahnman, who also was arrested on November 9, 1938, and incarcerated in the same barrack section as Walter. Dr. Knoll then presents David with a photocopy of the handwritten registration of Walter's admittance to the camp. "You may keep this copy," he says.

Dr. Knoll also gives David a document regarding the Crystal Night "action" taken against the Jews in Hamburg on November 9 and 10. Of the 10,911 who were brought to Dachau as a result of that event, 10,451 from all over Germany were released from Dachau before August 1939. The number of dead is given at 185.

On departing the office of the archives, David is once again standing on the roll call square. He walks across to view a sample barrack. Only the washroom is exactly as his father describes it in his report. The barrack is bare except for new bunks and seems sterile.

David leaves to walk down the street, on either side of which once were barracks. Only concrete slabs remain. He stops before the former #24 barrack to take a photo of small purple flowers growing beneath the poplar trees before the barrack's cement slab. In the background is a watchtower. He hears birds singing. He thinks of his father, how much he enjoyed listening to birds and how he would have loved to see these little flowers. Knowing this little scene would give his father peace, David continues down the street.

As he comes to the end, he crosses over a large gravel square in which a Mercedes Unimog truck is parked. In the very rear of the truck are several, large blue-and-yellow plastic tanks with sprayers attached, chemicals to kill weeds in the gravel. David passes the vehicle and heads to a large monument between two blackened stone walls into which he must descend. At the bottom is a chimney-like opening. On looking up the chimney, one sees a menorah reaching into the sky. On leaving the monument David sees two middle-aged men in blue work shirts lifting two iron lids by the side of the wall to his left. David hears the two men laughing. Next to them stand two of the plastic canisters with attached sprayers. Overcome by chills, David suddenly imagines that they are the truck driver and his assistant who drove the truck that brought his father to Dachau. As the young man lit a cigarette, the driver said, "Stand back or the whole caboodle will go up in flames." At that moment, David imagines that he is in his father's shoes, that the two workers are Nazi soldiers humiliating him. David pulls his thoughts away from this image. He quickly flees from these two men and from the memorial, heading back to the tree-lined street.

On reaching the street, he takes in deep breaths of air, embraces the warmth of the late spring sun. Strolling along this street, he encounters a group of noisy, flirting and giggling teenagers. Accompanied by their teacher and a guide from the museum, the girls are wearing tight jeans and low-cut tight tops; the boys are clothed in jeans, loose t-shirts and light jackets. Three boys straggling behind are picking up pebbles and throwing them at each other, laughing as they hit one another. An image creeps before David eyes that these youth are being transformed into the Aryan prisoners, section leaders, harassing Jewish inmates. David feels hopeless. These kids just do not understand what has happened here more than fifty years ago. To them that would be ancient history. Do they even know what crimes former members of their families may have committed? Then he thinks of his father. He realizes he is coming here all the way from America well over half a century later to learn about Walter and intentionally try to experience his presence here.

David sits on the edge of one of the barracks feeling the warm sun on his shoulders. Looking up at the hazy blue sky with billowy white-and-pink clouds, he feels very much alone. He wonders, do people *really* comprehend what has happened here? And even if they do, will people ever have the courage to prevent new atrocities from occurring? All he can do now, sitting here, is to take in this experience, breathe in, breathe out, embrace Walter's efforts at consoling others.

Suddenly the sun goes behind a cloud. A cool breeze picks up. David still hears birds chirping cheerfully, yet he remains heavy-hearted as he rises. He walks toward the museum, feeling obligated to at least walk through it. Maybe he will see his father in a photograph there. David passes quickly through the exhibits. Teenagers laugh and giggle while some gasp with horror and sorrow as they look at the displays. The photos are primarily taken at the time of the camp's liberation. Of course Walter is not in them.

With passports in hand, the big question remains how Elly will get her Walter out of Dachau. On the morning of December 23, 1938, delirious with the flu and fever, Elly carefully leaves Walter's passport at home and goes again to see Officer Schmidt. The guards at the Wittelsbach palace uncross their guns allowing Elly to enter. As she walks into his office she surprises herself, saying half-jokingly, "Herr Schmidt, tomorrow is Christmas. Can't my husband come home for Christmas?"

A faint smile comes over the officer's face. Never before has a Jewess spoken to him in this way. Saying nothing, he rises from his desk chair, turns toward the wall to his left. Reaching into a large filing cabinet, he pulls out an endless list of names. Turning back toward Elly with the list in hand, he scans down until he reaches Walter's name. There in the margin next to his name, he makes a little red cross. He places the long list on his desk, takes a few steps toward Elly. As he looks at her with his kind blue eyes, he holds out his hand, "All will be well for you."*

As Mrs. Laudenheimer has had a minor accident, Elly can't stay with them any longer. However, feeling safer and more hopeful and encouraged that Walter is about to come home, she returns to their own two rooms only to find that the radiators have frozen and broken.

Her instinct is correct: she has touched the heart of Herr Schmidt. That evening Walter climbs the stairs to their apartment. As they embrace, Elly notices how thin and pale her husband has become. His shaven head, the work of his captors at Dachau, only adds to the sadness, fatigue, and anxiety in his appearance.

*Herr Schmidt's kindness was not the only factor that contributed to Walter's early release. In May 1938, the Nazis had demanded of Jews that they provide detailed information about all of their property, financial assets, and insurance policies to the taxation authority. Hermann Goering was in charge of a program to calculate the value of Jewish property, which would be used to provide necessary funding for the forthcoming war. However, on Crystal Night, when Jewish businesses and homes were plundered, robbed, and destroyed, the wealth that Goering was planning to confiscate was lost. On November 21, 1938, a new law was passed: *Sühneleistung der Juden* (Jews' atonement tax). Jews now had to pay 20 percent of all of their properties. The rationale that the Nazis gave was that the Jews had to pay for damage created on Crystal Night! When Walter

Because of the frozen pipes, Elly and Walter anxiously seek a hotel in which to stay for a few days. They aren't sure whether any hotel will accept them, as anyone can tell what has happened to Walter. Terribly ill at ease, they find a hotel at which they stay for a few days until they can move in with their friend Lotte Pariser.

With Walter's release, Elly immediately begins to make reservations to fly out of Germany for London. At the same time, Walter comes down with a severe case of tonsillitis. As it is impossible for her to visit her parents in Hamburg before their January 13 departure, Elly can only talk with them over the phone, a sad goodbye, a goodbye forever.

Photo in Walter's German passport issued December 28, 1938.

At the airport Elly's brother John is there to see them off. He, too, has been recently released from Dachau and will soon be on his way to England.* However, at the airport both Elly and Walter become fearful that the plane will take off without them. Each has to undergo thorough personal searches. Finishing with one, they encounter more bureaucracy and additional searches. They have almost lost all hope for escape when the plane's departure is delayed for deicing the wings.

---

was in Dachau, the authorities in Braunschweig knew of the 400-plus acres the Solmitz family owned on the outskirts of the city. Apparently Walter's name was the first on the list of inheritors of that property. Therefore, he was required to pay the *Sühneleistung*.

Robert Solmitz, an attorney in Hamburg, who had been arrested on November 10, and was behind bars for several days, promptly sold the land to Braunschweig on behalf of the heirs for 60,680 Reichsmarks. The city of Braunschweig then paid 15,000 Reichsmarks to the taxation authority in Hamburg. It was there that Robert had signed the sales contract in order "to recompense the obligation of Walter Solmitz and his wife Elly, born Reis, living in Munich 38, Wotanstr. 59." The result was that the tax Walter owed had been paid and another barrier to Walter's release from Dachau had been surmounted (Reinhard Bein research.)

*In England John will work for a few months on a farm. With the outbreak of the war, he joins the British army. Following the war, he permanently settles in England.

Photo in Elly's German passport issued December 28, 1938.

As the plane takes off through the cold, heavy, gray clouds, Elly and Walter are not even able to get a last glimpse of Munich. When the plane lands in Brussels, they take their first breath of freedom. Then off to London.

Arriving at London's airport, each has to be checked by the British Health Authority. Fear creeps through their veins again. Will they be denied access because of Walter's tonsillitis? A doctor examines Walter's throat. "Not too bad," he says. Relieved, they walk through the double doors into freedom, where they meet their friend Gertrude Bing. In the late afternoon light, she drives them through London, a huge and strange city, to Dalgarno Gardens. She drops them off at the community center of this new housing project constructed in slum clearance in North Kensington. Here Miss Rachel Alexander has reserved a flat for refugees. Elly and Walter may stay here until two doctors from Berlin, a brother and sister, arrive to claim the flat.

When the two doctors arrive, Miss Emily Jenkinson, the warden of the community center, who has taken Elly and Walter under her wing, lets them have her former flat in the center. This kindly woman has moved into a neighboring house, since she did not have a minute's peace and quiet while staying in the center: children and adults constantly came knocking at her door with requests.

Elly and Walter are happy at Dalgarno Gardens. Nearby Wormwood Scrubs is a playground with swings and beautiful green lawns for the children of the housing project; however, most of the children prefer to play on the cement-covered streets and courtyards around their dwellings.

When Walter comes home from the Warburg Institute (the former Warburg Library of Hamburg) the day war is declared, young children in this slum clearance call after him, "Mr. Solmitz, we like you!"

They must have heard from their parents, the very poor, that Elly and Walter are refugees. David's parents are especially touched because they, the "refugees," are so much better dressed than the local residents. They could take only ten marks each out of Germany, so they had purchased clothes for the next few years before leaving, as they had no idea where and how we were going to make a living.

When Elly and Walter tell people that they live near Wormwood Scrubs, they are met with laughter, because Wormwood Scrubs is also the name of one of the sternest prisons in London.

Eventually, Miss Jenkinson arranges with Miss Rachel to have Elly and Walter move into a flat in the housing project at a very low rent. By this time Walter has a job at the Warburg Institute, working on *Corpus Platonicum,* a body of work that Walter's friend Raymond Klibansky finished editing several years later.

One afternoon, soon after war has been declared, on returning to their flat, Elly finds a note from the local police in their mailbox. Terrified she reads the letter, "Please report to the police station tomorrow morning or afternoon, whatever suits you better." She reads the note again, shares it with Walter when he returns. They both are touched and relieved by the politeness of the note—a request from a police force, so different from the one they rightfully dreaded in Germany.

Very early the next morning they walk to the police station. A police officer gets up from behind his desk asking politely, "What can I do for you?" They show the officer the note they received. The officer offers them a seat.

"Do not worry," he says. "You see, the Nazis have smuggled in a number of spies with passports marked with a "J" for "Jews," the way they mark all Jewish passports. Because of this, our government has asked that all refugees must register as aliens. This you will be able to do right here and now. Later you will be asked to attend a tribunal to determine whether you may stay in England or be deported to Canada or Australia. I am sure, Mr. and Mrs. Solmitz, that with letters from the director of the community center and from Mr. Solmitz's employer, you will be all set."

Although worried, Elly and Walter appreciate the assuring manner in which the officer has spoken with them. Shortly thereafter, they learn that quite a few Jews have been deported, as the British government has no way of telling who is friend or foe.

A few weeks later, they appear before the tribunal. The judge readily clears Elly and Walter. He permits them to stay in England until their quota number is reached and they have received their visas for the United States.

In the meantime, Walter has notified his uncle in Little Rock, Oma's brother Theo, that he has been released from Dachau and that he and Elly are now in England. Theo writes back most warmly on February 24, 1939:

My dear Walter,

Today we received your interesting letter, which we have eagerly awaited, ever since we heard of your safe arrival in England. Immediately upon receiving your post-card announcing your arrival in London, I wrote to you and enclosed a check for a sum of money which I was sure you and Elly could make use of. I trust you have received this check as it would be most unfortunate if it had been lost in the mail. Your relatives here are also anxious to send you some good, warm clothing and now that I know your address, I will send them word to forward the packages to you. Also we would all like to know if there are any particular articles which you and Elly could use, which we can supply you with.

Your good, loyal wife has earned the respect and admiration of all who know what was accomplished through her courageous efforts and we sincerely hope that the reward will come in many, many years of happiness and peace for both of you.

With kindest greetings and best wishes to both of you, I am

Affectionately,

Uncle Theo

Needless to say, Elly and Walter are grateful to Theo. Yet life in London is not at all easy. After war has been declared, even though the bombing has not yet started, the children are evacuated to the countryside, but shortly thereafter are returned home. As the schools remain closed, the center asks Elly and Walter to help out teaching some classes. They both enjoy working with children, teaching reading, spelling, and drawing. Particularly for Elly, drawing with the children becomes the highlight of her day. Once again, she can release and share her creative energies.

Elly, of course, agonizes about her parents. She and Walter therefore approach Miss Rachel for advice as to how to get her parents out of Germany. They leave with the impression that Miss Rachel is unconcerned, but a week later when Elly and Walter come home in the evening, a note from Miss Rachel is in their mailbox. "Sorry to have missed you," the note reads. "Would you please fill in the enclosed form that I have signed as a guarantor for a visa for your parents. Do you think they would prefer to live in London or in the country?"

Several years later Elly learns that her parents were unable to secure a visa even before the outbreak of the war; with the eruption of the war in 1939, to obtain the needed documents became impossible.

At last, in May 1940, Elly and Walter receive their visas to the United

States. The Cunard Line notifies them that within two weeks a ship will be sailing. An exact date is not given, as shipping is kept secret due to the danger of submarine attacks.

Just before their departure, Dr. Laudenheimer, who also fled to London in 1939, gives them a gift: an original letter by Johann Wolfgang von Goethe, written on April 1, 1815, in Weimar, to his official successor, a certain von Voigt in the Ministry of Mines. In his cover letter of May 30, 1940, Dr. Laudenheimer writes:

> I transfer this valuable letter to our dear young friends Elly and Walter Solmitz.
>
> As today you are forced to leave Europe in flight from Hitler's evil scheme, may this symbol of the good German spirit accompany you to your new American home.

Elly and Walter are notified that their boat is ready to sail the day before it departs. Already packed, they catch a train for Liverpool. There, on May 31, they board the *Antonia.* While some emigrants have to spend a week or more on board ship in Liverpool before departure, the *Antonia* sails the same day they embark. The ship departs in a convoy that includes a heavy cruiser and several smaller ships, as well as planes flying overhead.

As they are sailing out of the harbor, they pass a ship that has been sunk. Only the funnel and masts are still visible. Several hours later the rest of their convoy returns to port, except for one other ship and the heavy cruiser. The planes return to the mainland. The two remaining ships zigzag back and forth all the way to America to protect the *Antonia.*

Every day all passengers and crew take part in safety drills. Passengers are asked to participate in submarine watch, a pointless exercise; by the time a submarine is spotted, their ship would already have been attacked. Elly notes that every whale they see looks like a submarine.

The weather is beautiful, the ocean calm, the trip relatively relaxing. Elly and Walter sleep through the only exciting moments of the trip, when, already on the St. Lawrence River, they encounter an Italian ship. Shots are exchanged, because Italy has declared war on the Allies. However, the incident passes easily as the Italian ship quickly flees.

After thirteen days at sea, Elly and Walter arrive on the morning of June 12, 1940, in Montreal. They find the weather to be quite chilly for mid June. Canadian immigration officials take their traveling documents and put Elly and Walter in a taxi that brings them to the railroad station, where they board a train for New York City. Only after they cross the U.S. border do they get their papers back.

The train often stops at little country towns with white wooden churches. Walter imagines how nice it would be to become a librarian in such a little town. As they look out the windows, they are astonished to see people wearing light summer clothes; they don't realize that the train is air conditioned. When they arrive in New York, they are struck by the heat. Walter's cousins meeting the train easily recognize them by their heavy tweed suits, felt hats, and heavy shoes.

The relatives rent them a room with a bath on the fifteenth floor of the Beekman Tower Hotel for two weeks. To their delight, their room overlooks the East River. Walter begins searching for academic employment, meeting with various people in New York, at Bryn Mawr, Pennsylvania, and finally in Cambridge, Massachusetts.

After spending a few days in a dorm at Harvard Summer School, they stay in the homes of a lawyer, and two professors, who are on vacation. By summer's end the Refugee Committee in Cambridge helps them find a furnished room to rent. Walter, who has received permission to study at Harvard's Weidener Library, does research for an art historian who lives North Carolina.

Elly takes courses in typing and shorthand at a secretarial school in Cambridge. In the fall, Walter receives a fellowship at Harvard to work towards his PhD in philosophy; later he becomes a teaching fellow in the German department. Elly works unhappily as a secretary in the Germanic Museum for a few months until she secures a job she relishes under Professor Harlow Shapley at the Harvard Observatory. There she does lettering on astronomical charts.

Within a few weeks, Elly and Walter find a delightful flat in a pleasant brick apartment building at 13 Ware Street, a lane a few minutes' walk from Harvard Yard. Furnishings for their apartment, including two high-backed oak chairs, a desk chair, silverware, and a bread knife that Elly and Walter later bring with them to Maine, are donated by the three different families in whose homes they spent the summer of 1940. David and his family still use this as their only bread knife.

Sometimes they walk to the nearby Window Shop for lunch. This European bakery, café, and restaurant was created by a group of Cambridge residents to provide a safe harbor for hundreds of German and Austrian refugees who fled from Hitler to America. The continental cuisine brings back fond memories of delicacies Elly and Walter had enjoyed in Germany. Many European intellectuals, who fled to Cambridge, gather at the Window Shop. Here Elly and Walter make lasting friendships.

As the years roll on, the Window Shop is transformed from a bakery of European pastries, café and restaurant into a fine clothing store for women. Until its closing in the mid 1970s, Elly visits the Window Shop whenever she goes to Cambridge from Brunswick, on occasion purchasing a blouse, skirt, or dress. Her friend Mary Mohrer, a refugee from Austria who also lived at 13 Ware Street, runs this tasteful shop.

Within two years of settling in Cambridge, Walter's mother, Sophie, moves into a rooming house two streets down from their apartment on Ware Street. Elly and Walter are forever grateful to have escaped Germany, to be welcomed and supported by Walter's American family, and to have encountered the kindness of many people who made their new beginning in the United States one of hope and happiness.

7

Warrior for Peace

DURING THE EARLY AUTUMN OF 1942, DAVID'S father walks between rows of maples along the gently flowing Charles River in Cambridge. He stops, spotting a leaf gliding like a feather on the river. Suddenly he is taken aback as he sees the reflections of trees and buildings in the placid water, and amidst the buildings and trees, he recognizes many faces. They are sad, bewildered, torn with pain, beseeching him: "Tell our families that we are still here in Dachau. We love them. Tell them they are not safe; leave Germany as quickly as they can. Even if we are never released from here, we want to know they are safe."

Walter recalls an elderly Jewish judge during morning roll call. He is being commanded by the SS to step out in front of the crowd. He is ordered to hop like a frog. Stumbling, falling, he is brought back to his feet, forced to repeat his ordeal before being sent back into line, exhausted and relieved. The officer again demands that he face the detainees to repeat his routine. Within moments he collapses on the ground, unable to get up.

Seeing in the river reflections of trucks passing, to Walter's mind's eye they become army vehicles overfilled with the families he was never able to reach upon his release from the camp. Distraught with guilt, David's father also feels enormous gratitude for having been granted refuge in the land of individual and academic freedom. As World War II continues to rage out of control throughout Europe and England, Walter has become obsessed with the notion of world peace. He must do all that he can to bring about worldwide disarmament.

As he returns to his little apartment at 13 Ware Street, Elly greets him warmly. Yet, he seems oblivious to her affection and heads toward his desk. She does not ask what he has been thinking about. She knows better. She hopes he has come up with more thoughts for his thesis.

With pencil in hand, he sits jotting down ideas—thoughts about the propaganda that the Nazis used to win power in Germany and the failure of anti-Nazi propaganda. In order to come up with a realistic plan regarding disarmament, one must fully understand how the Nazis came to power. "There are two kinds of propaganda," he writes. "Negative propaganda—as an instrument promoting war, and positive propaganda—preparing and propagating a peaceful and lawful organization of social and transnational cooperation."

The Nazis came to power, he argues, in part because of "the lack of another positive idea which was stronger than the prevailing idea and which offered a constructive solution to the economic, moral and political crisis, say of 1929." But how can one resist the Nazis? "Create an atmosphere of trust by means of truth (exact information), sincerity, trustworthiness, and reason—all factors that the Nazis do not apply." However, the strength of Nazi propaganda, he realizes, is its emotional appeal, and its tendency "to make people stupid and non-thinking" (Solmitz 1942).

His spirits drop; he lights a cigarette adding more blue haze to the smoke-laden air of their little apartment. He recalls the leaf floating gently down the river. Picking up his pencil again, he writes,

> Anti-Nazi propaganda has to appeal to the individual as a fellow-man. It needs to stress common interest in the "We." Anti-Nazi propaganda cannot appeal to the "real" Nazis—but has to be directed to the indifferent masses, the half-Nazis and to the people who are opposed to Nazism. These people need encouragement and a scope for the future. (Solmitz 1942)

Walter believes international solidarity is necessary to halt Nazi aggression by bonding such socialistic organizations as cooks, barbers, printers, along with scientific, scholarly, and artistic organizations. Hitlerism was not the cause, but only a symptom and expression of an international civil war: economic instability and depression, unemployment and overproduction. Therefore, anti-Nazi propaganda should focus on cooperative economies, as opposed to capitalism that focuses on the individual. To bring about civil peace, international civil propaganda must offer a strategy to achieve this goal with specific plans and spelled-out projects. The anti-Nazi propaganda should be a "simple appeal to the natural honesty of the average German" (Solmitz 1942). Exact information about Germany and occupied countries, including information about concentration camps, deportation of the Jews, and terrorism in occupied countries needs to be presented to prick the Allied and Axis consciousness.

He lays down his pencil, lights another cigarette, and rises from his desk. Elly has already prepared supper, for which he is grateful.

As the war progresses, Pearl Harbor is attacked; Walter becomes more obsessed with finding a peaceful solution. He begins by delineating a list of obstacles to the establishment of a lasting peace. Among these are people who:

- Find the idea of lasting peace ridiculous
- Believe war is good for moral reasons, progress, and efficiency
- Like war for adventure, fun, excitement, uniforms, and fond memories
- Are professionals in the military and those involved in the armament industry
- Have become more prosperous and socially secure as a result of war
- Indulge in brutality, cruelty, and crime
- Are in desperate straits from which violence is the only way out

In typical manner, he concludes his notes with questions: What type of people could be expected to have a strong potential desire for lasting peace? What motives are apt to increase the desire for lasting peace? What kind of motives might transform that desire into action towards peace? What means can be devised to overcome all of these obstacles?

Following the outlining of these difficulties, he derives a declaration of intent for lasting peace. He writes:

> Peace implies the establishment of methods other than physical violence to solve any conflicts arising between individuals, or between groups, or between groups and individuals. (Solmitz 1944)

The first step has to be negotiation. If that step fails, arbitration will come next. Should arbitration fail, a court of law must intervene. Only if the court's warning is followed by the failure of economic sanctions, would the court authorize armed force. This, then would be the only lawful means to use armed force to settle conflicts.

As the war years intensify, Walter becomes increasingly discouraged and dejected. The dropping of the atom bombs on Hiroshima and Nagasaki on August 6 and 9, 1945, sends shock waves throughout his entire being. As horrific as Hitler's atrocities were, he is convinced that United States' action to end the war in this manner is unconscionable.

However, a few days earlier, July 28, when the United States Senate voted to approve the United Nations charter by a vote of 89 to 2, Walter does feel a glimmer of hope. His faith is confirmed when the United Nations officially becomes legitimate on October 25, 1945, following the ratification of its charter by twenty-nine nations.

Even so, the plight of the Jews continues to obsess Walter. In early 1948, he becomes deeply depressed. He fears the worst for the Jewish people if a separate state of Israel is to be established with or without the support of the United Nations. Following a week of recuperation at Brunswick's little hospital, barely two months before May 15, the deadline by which the British are to leave Palestine, he gives a chapel talk at Bowdoin.* In that speech, he accurately predicts the international conflagration regarding Israel that continues today. He offers a viable solution based on the concept of a sanctuary for the outcast who existed in so-called primitive societies and religions. Here the outcast is safe, as he may not be removed by force or violence. He tells his audience:

> What is going to happen in Palestine when the British will have left? The Arabs will attack. The United Nations have recommended a partition of the small country; this recommendation is greatly welcomed by the political Zionists because it fulfills their hope of establishing an independent Jewish state. It is bitterly opposed by the Arabs, who feel that the Jewish state is being built at their expense, and that they are deprived of their political self-determination; even the right of a plebiscite is not given to them. The Arabs will attack in great force. The Jews who, after all their persecutions seemed to have found something like a home, will resist passionately, but in vain. They are in the minority hopelessly. The Jews will be slaughtered, and virtually destroyed *unless* they

*At that time, the college set aside a number of days per semester at which all students were required to attend mid-morning chapel. These talks were given by Bowdoin faculty members and by the college president.

are helped by the United Nations, or by some nation or nations. If they are helped by any nation, a war is most likely to originate which, in all likelihood, will not remain confined to the country of Palestine. And the Jews will be considered as those who formed the cause of this war.

The alternative is either the Jews will be slaughtered, or there will be a war. I happen to favor neither alternative; I have a different view. As long as the war is postponed, there is still a *chance* of its being avoided altogether.

The issue is complicated further by the fact that the case appears to be, or is made to appear, a *test case* of the United Nations. This situation poses a further dilemma.

The United Nations is the only institution we have so far which is supposed to work towards the organization of a normal and peaceful life of the nations. The case of Palestine is the first case in which this organization has arrived at some sort of a decision. This first decision appears to be a test case.

If the United Nations will not stick to their decision, and will back out, just as the League of Nations did in the case of Manchuria and Abyssinia, then the United Nations will be done with—and even this small beginning towards a reasonable organization of civilized life will be gone.

If the United Nations will stick to its own decision, and show that it is strong enough to enforce it, there will be a war. Thus, either the United Nations abandon their decision, and abandon the Jews; and the Jews in Palestine will be slaughtered, and the United Nations will be done with. Or else the United Nations will stick with its decision and fulfill the wishes of the political Zionists, and the paradox will occur that the very organization which is intended to procure peace, will lead the world into war.

Is there any way out?

Theoretically, there exists the possibility of a way out: It is the establishment of a transnational sanctuaries and asylums and prototype of such transnational sanctuaries, as a Zone of Peace, under a Truce of God.

What would this mean? It would mean the establishment of an extra-national territory—at least for a limited period of time—from which nobody could be removed by force, and the peace of which would be guarded not by any one nation, and not by the inhabitants themselves, but by a truly transnational administration, and a truly transnational police force, which would have no reason to interfere as long as the inhabitants get along among one another, and are not disturbed from the outside.

What would this imply and require?

A sanctuary for both the "outcasts" of the group of Western nations and for people of the Eastern nations, might become a meeting point for East and West, so that the land of the Holy Grave would not become the unholy grave of civilization, but the starting point for its resurrection.

The main requirement would be *moral sacrifices* by all parties involved. It would involve sacrifices on the parts of Arabian nationalists, on the part of the Jewish nationalists, and on the part of the United Nations.

The most significant sacrifice would be that of the United Nations. They would have to sacrifice the resolution they have made concerning Palestine, and they would have [to] give up considering it a test case of their strength of character and their physical strength. Stubbornness is often mistaken for strength of character. If they were able to revise their decisions and create for this partial but central question a new form of organization, it would be much more than a test case of their strength in stubbornness; it would prove their wisdom, the possibility of their growth in wisdom—it would be a test of their ability [for] growth and development.

Let me add, in parentheses, that it would require also a sacrifice on the part of those perfectionists who believe that anything towards peace can be achieved only *after* a world government has been established. What would be required here, would be a "world" action, a truly centralized and transnational action [on] a very limited, on a very small scale. To be sure, it would make the inhabitants of such extra-national territory the first actual citizens of the world.

It would require a sacrifice on the part of the Jewish nationalists—a sacrifice that must be very hard indeed on them; and since they *are* nationalists, the sacrifice would hardly be made easier for them by the fact that it is a sacrifice made for the sake of humanity and universal peace. But it might be made easier by the sober realization of the fact that the actual existence of a really independent Jewish state is doomed in any case.

Now, I must add one word here. I personally am not a Zionist.

> I do not think that the establishment of an independent Jewish state and the establishment of an independent military Jewish force is very much in line with those Jewish prophets of the Old Testament who envisaged the promised land as the nucleus of a world in which the swords would be turned into ploughshares.
>
> This is perhaps incidental. And it must be realized that among those Jews who have become Nationalists there are many who have been driven to it because there seems to be no home for them, no refuge, no shelter if not in an independent state. Nobody who has not experienced the kind of unimaginable persecution, complete deprivation of everything, [and] unbelievable cruelty can fully understand the passion of their desire for a home. To the extent to which they will be reassured of their having a home and security, their interest in nationalism must decrease.
>
> The sacrifice of the Arabs and their participation in a transnational project would be very hard indeed. Just having awoken to nationalism, it must naturally be most difficult for them to jump over one stage of development at once. For the sacrifice to be made easier, if the territory for which they would have to give up their claims would not be taken over by any one nation, but would be theirs as much and as little as anybody else's.
>
> Such sacrifices made by the United Nations, by the Jews, and by the Arabs would express and demand that sincerity on which mutual trust alone can rest. Trust implies a minimum of risk at least and always. If this risk were taken, the first small nucleus for the rebuilding of trust in this world would be formed. (Solmitz 1948)

If Walter were still alive in 2006, he would be horrified by the June war that Israel unleashes on Hezbollah. He also would realize that even though Israel had won wars in the past, their loss in this war reflected his foreshadowing of the demise of Israel. After all, he had stated that either the establishment of a Jewish and Palestinian state by the United Nations, or other nations supporting Israel in war against the Palestinians would be catastrophic. Like his father, his son supports a solution to this conflict in a letter he writes May 6, 2006 to his local newspaper, *The Morning Sentinel*, of Waterville, Maine.

> As the son of Jewish immigrants who survived the Nazi Holocaust, I feel proud to live in Waterville. After all, this is a city

> that has among its various communities one Jewish and another Lebanese. However, I am saddened and distressed that Israel is causing untold suffering by relentlessly bombing Lebanon. I am also ashamed that the Bush administration upholds Israel's bombing of Lebanon. Unfortunately, the concept of supporting Israel as an ally in America's "War on Terrorism," fuels hatred that is bringing the entire world into a deadly morass.
>
> A glance at history may help to understand why Israel feels an urgent need to crush Hezbollah. The United Nations following World War II created Israel out of 60 percent of British-occupied Palestine. Although the Jewish settlers comprised only one third of the population, the Arab majority tried immediately to force them out of Israel. Since then Israelis [have] waged several wars against their Arab neighbors during which they gained territory. With intense Arab and Middle Eastern hatred toward Israel, her need to survive is understandable. However, her violent approach is both misguided and a dangerous approach. Dennis Kucinich and twenty-three other Congressmen have drafted a Congressional Resolution I believe can defuse the current crisis. They demand an immediate ceasefire, multiparty—including the U.S.—negotiations with no preconditions, and an international peacekeeping force in southern Lebanon to prevent cross-border skirmishes during multiparty negotiations. Let's encourage the Bush administration to give this approach a try. (Solmitz 2006)

As he writes the letter to the newspaper, David recalls that his father was an admirer of the British statesman and scholar B. H. Liddell Hart, who would have reminded the Bush administration that it was neglecting its role as a world power, as an effective negotiator for peace. In 1943, Liddell Hart had accurately observed in his book, *Why Don't We Learn from History?* "A long historical view not only helps us to keep calm in a 'time of trouble,' but reminds us that there is an end to the longest tunnel. Even if we can see no good hope ahead, an historical interest as to what will happen is a help in carrying on" (Hart 1971, 12).

Two years later, December 27, 2008, Israel launches a war on Gaza with the intent to stop Hamas rocket attacks on southern Israel and arms smuggling into Gaza. The Israeli operation begins with an intense bombing of the Gaza Strip targeting Hamas bases, police training camps, police headquarters and offices. Civilian infrastructure, including mosques, houses, medical facilities, and schools, are also attacked. Israel states that many of them were being used by combatants, and as storage spaces for weapons and rockets.

Hamas intensifies its rocket and mortar attacks against targets in Israel throughout the conflict, hitting previously untargeted cities such as Beersheba and Ashdod.

On January 3, 2009, the Israeli ground invasion begins. By January 18, 2009, when a unilateral ceasefire between Israel and Hamas is announced, over 1,400 Palestinians and 13 Israelis have been killed. Four thousand Palestinian homes have been destroyed, leaving tens of thousands of Palestinians homeless.

David's father again would be devastated. Again the consequences he predicted have come true. However, he would be heartened by an organization called Jewish Voices for Peace, which realizes that Israel's aggressive actions are self-destructive. Not only would he contribute money in support of the organization, he undoubtedly would express his own views. With a growing number of such people, he, like David, couldn't help but feel some hope in the midst of despair because of these courageous activists. The following letter from Jewish Voices for Peace sent to its membership in 2008 reflects both Walter's and David's perspective. The plea is written by a 77-year-old grandmother, who immensely wants her grandchildren and all the children in the area to have a future to look forward to.

> Dear [member],
>
> How will the terrible devastation in Gaza make us safer? Not in USA?
>
> I write to you as a Jewish woman who is both American and Israeli. I have lived in Israel for over 50 years, and I can tell you that I have had enough of wars and insecurity.
>
> America keeps on sending us billions of dollars in weapons every year. And yet, Israel has become the least safe country for Jews to live in (except for war zones such as Afghanistan, where no one is safe).
>
> Nowhere else in the world since WWII have we Jews lived through 12 wars/battles/campaigns—all in less than 61 years.
>
> Nowhere else in the world since WWII have so many Jews been killed in violence—over 23,000 since Israel came into being.
>
> Nowhere else in the world have so many Jews been injured.
>
> And yet, we have no security. Sixty-one years of the use of force have not brought us Israelis one iota of security.

> To make matters worse, those of us who are seeking peace find ourselves harassed by the Israeli police. A number of my colleagues have had their computers confiscated, been called to interrogations, or have been made to sign declarations forbidding them to talk with one another. To add insult to injury, the police actions were carried out on Israel's Memorial Day to send a subtle message to the public that our activism may compromise Israel's security.
>
> Our crime? We dared to ask questions. We dared to ask whether militarism was the only way. We are undeterred. We will continue asking.
>
> It is your time to ask too. If you are an American, please take a moment right now to call on Congress to ask the question: what happened with your US tax dollars in Gaza? If you live in another country, ask yourself whether your government is involved in this trade of weapons and destruction.
>
> Here in Israel, we do not need more US weapons. We need you to help us achieve peace—real peace.
>
> There can be no peace, however, until the Palestinians have justice. The Palestinian catastrophe since 1948 has included expulsion from their homes and lands, and for those who remained in the West Bank and Gaza, extra-judicial executions, land confiscations, no freedom of movement, nor the freedom to build homes and communities, Palestinians live always with the fear of Israeli military incursions. Since September 29, 2000, Israel has killed 6,248 Palestinians. 1,487 of these have been children.
>
> Israel's Memorial Day is the saddest day in the year for me, not only because of those who are already buried, but because of all those who might be killed for generations to come unless you help us achieve a just peace. (Jewish Voices for Peace 2008)

Of course Walter, who dies in 1962, does not live through most of this deepening conflict. However, in the early 1950s, as Senator Joe McCarthy's Red Scare takes over the country, David's father becomes distraught, fearing the demise of America's democracy. He sees parallels to the failure of the Weimar Republic, leading to the rise of Nazism. David recalls his father sitting at the kitchen table saying: *"Verrückt! Das kann nicht sein!"* (Insane! that cannot be!)

"What is the matter?" David asks.

"Ach," he answers, "Alger Hiss has been found guilty of spying for the Russians. *Ich weiss* (I know) he is innocent."

"Who is Alger Hiss?"

"He is a great man. He worked for the Justice Department. Later he coordinated American foreign policy. Then, employed by the Carnegie Endowment for Peace, he advocated for an end to the cold war with the Soviet Union."

"So why is he accused of being a Communist?" David wants to know.

"*Furchtbar* (terrible). You can't understand," Walter solemnly says.

"Why not?"

His father explains, "Fear is taking over our country and destroying our government. Congress is investigating thousands of individuals and many organizations because they think they are subversive."

"What is subversive?" David asks.

"Well, it means that people are accused of wanting to overthrow our country. Really, they are not. All they want is peace."

During the 1952 presidential race of Adlai Stevenson versus General Dwight Eisenhower, David's parents actively work for Adlai Stevenson's campaign. At the end of the summer, Stevenson comes to Maine on a campaign and fundraising trip. A family friend, Peggy Packard, accompanies Elly and Walter to a lobster bake at Pemaquid with Stevenson. Peggy later recalls Stevenson walking out onto the rocks admiring the sunset over the ocean and remarking that this is the most beautiful campaign stop he has experienced.

Unfortunately, the crowd of about 400 is rather small. As people mill about, Peggy notices that a couple who seem to be Walter's and Elly's age are constantly looking at them. Peggy asks Elly whether she knows these people. "No," Elly replies, "but they are survivors of the Nazi concentration camps."

"How do you know?" Peggy asks with curiosity and interest. "Do they have numbers tattooed on their lower arms?"

"No, they don't," Elly answers with sadness. "Survivors of the camps are always able to recognize each other."

In October that year, Walter becomes particularly discouraged and grieved when a columnist whom he admires, Dorothy Thompson, writes a piece for the *Boston Globe,* "A Vote Against Trumanism." Although she writes that all things being equal she would not choose any general for president, yet she believes that a vote for Stevenson is a vote for the status quo.

> For the same organized groups, forces, pressures, influences

> and personalities who have directed American policy, domestic and foreign, to its present condition. These forces have directed us toward unlimited wars; toward a formidable Federal apparatus absorbing more and more of the functions of the whole of society; toward dependency in the place of self-reliance; toward the depreciation of the currency; toward an unlimited and apparently, in their eyes, an illimitable national debt; toward a cynicism regarding integrity, honor and loyalty, producing not one administration scandal, but a whole succession of them. (Thompson 1952)

Wherever Walter is, whatever he is doing, going for a thinking walk, conducting his classes, talking over a cigarette at the dinner table, he obsesses over how he can persuade this liberal thinker to change her position. He acknowledges this to her in a lengthy letter, "Since I have read your article . . . I have had many discussions with you (in my mind)."

After all, Dorothy Thompson is a highly respected columnist; Walter believes her words can help sway the electorate towards Stevenson. In his letter, he argues that Stevenson is much more intellectually independent than Eisenhower. To be tied to Truman is no different from following McCarthy and Nixon. He expresses his belief that Eisenhower was nominated because he had effectively coordinated various and divergent factions as an administrator. His moral decency and modesty as a famous military leader have caused him to be admired and well liked. His popularity, and "the myth that goes with a successful military leader" may secure his election and maybe even bring unity to the nation, yet Walter fears that hero worship, especially of a military commander, results in unquestioned authority. With McCarthy's Red Scare underway, to support Eisenhower for president, Walter feels, will be most dangerous to America's principles of justice.

Ms. Thompson is impressed not only by Walter's thorough and impassioned response to her column but also by his appreciation of and humility towards her. Walter writes:

> I am aware of the fact that in writing to you personally, I am doing something no Emily Post can approve of. A person whom you do not even know personally has probably no business of writing to you in the vein I have followed. Still, as your reader, and perhaps, not only as your reader, I owe you much.
>
> Thus, I don't like to talk about you "behind your back," or

> even to think "behind your back," and I trust that I shall feel more at ease after having made my confession to you yourself. (Solmitz 1952)

In her personal response to Walter, Ms. Thompson says,

> The source of my affliction is my conviction that Western civilization is approaching the end of its tether, for which I see every symptom, including all that accompanied the fall of Rome. Were I a saint or more of a philosopher I should say, "So what?" Each civilization serves its turn, for better or worse, lives its life, passes, and gives way to something else, and when its time comes it must go, etc. etc. My affliction is not to have such detachment. (Thompson 1952)

Years later, as David reads the correspondence between his father and Ms. Thompson, he realizes that direct, well thought-out correspondence, personally typed and signed by the renowned writer, doesn't exist any longer. Today, a letter is answered by a "personalized" form letter with a photocopied signature of the eminent person to whom it was written. Even to receive an e-mail response from such a person, especially one with a lengthy, thoughtful response, is improbable.

Haunted as he is by the McCarthy Red Scare, Walter feels the town meeting remains the foundation of American democracy, and he actively participates in Brunswick's annual democratic event. At the March 3, 1954, meeting, Walter speaks up during a lengthy debate on raising the salaries of public school teachers. David likes to think that it is partly due to his father's persuasive words that the teachers receive a small salary increase to an annual income of $2,700! However, his father becomes quite upset when he reads an account of the meeting in the *Brunswick Record* later that week. At the supper table that evening, he reminds his son and Elly of the dangers of not speaking up. He is concerned that a few lines in the article on the meeting "might possibly be open for misinterpretation" at a time "in which the situation of democracy is somewhat precarious." He decides to address his concern by sending a letter to the paper, written diplomatically and with humility.

> Since these lines seem to be of general interest in that they

may have some bearing on the future of the Town Meeting, I have been wondering whether you would like to have these passages brought to your attention.

He then quotes the lines in print that introduced the article:

> This town meeting turned out to be one of almost record-breaking length as oratory, acrimony, and stupidity continued to prolong the Wednesday evening affair for four and a half hours as voters sweltered in an overly-heated hall and frequently exhibited impatience and boredom.

Rather than attack the author, Walter gently encouraged his readers to reflect upon the dangers implied by the words that appear to encourage the demise of the town meeting:

> These lines are, perhaps, read best simply as a humorous description. Still I have asked myself this question: Suppose I had not been present at the town meeting, how would I feel now? Would I not say to myself: "Oh, now I am certainly glad that I did not go to the town meeting. I certainly saved myself from sweltering, and boredom, and unpleasantness. And certainly I will not attend the next town meeting.
>
> Thus, it seems to me that if these lines are not read with the necessary sense of humor, but are taken seriously, they can easily be read, or misread, so as to discourage readers from ever attending a town meeting again, and thus to impair the significance and effectiveness of the town meeting.
>
> A reader who takes these remarks seriously might ask these questions: Does Mr. Downing [the reporter who wrote the article] wish to slight the town meeting? Does he want to abolish the town meeting? And does he want to do so by influencing people in this indirect manner instead of persuading them in a frank discussion? (Solmitz 1954)

Although Walter describes the meeting as "pretty good, pretty exciting, and useful," he is eager to see continued improvement of the town meeting process. He persists with his serious reflections upon the fragile state of America's democracy.

> I feel that one can hardly be too careful in the use of words, and in making sure that they are understood correctly, e.g. "boredom." A little boredom now and then goes not only with the Brunswick Town Meeting, but goes with any democratic procedure (as it goes with every job well done). The reader with a sense of humor knows that. And he knows that a little boredom now and then is not too high a price to pay for democracy. But the reader without a sense of humor may easily be discouraged from taking further interest in the democratic process if that is made to appear to him as just so much boredom. Indeed it is the fascist mass rallies that are arranged so as to avoid boredom and provide entertainment for the masses. (Solmitz 1954)

The McCarthy era eventually fades, in part due to the courage of people such as Maine's Senator Margaret Chase Smith and CBS News reporter and commentator William R. Murrow. However, America's fear and belligerence toward the Soviet Union continues while the Soviets build the Berlin Wall.

In late August 1961, Walter meets one of his former students, Louis Asekoff, on the steps of Widener Library at Harvard. Walter is agitated, nearly shouting—quite unlike his usual, quiet demeanor. He is particularly distressed by the bellicose spirit of Americans, believing that such an insensitive attitude will surely result in war. He actually sees war approaching and repeats several times, "It's going to happen; it's going to happen."

Louis later recalls, "It seemed that nightmares of his past were coming back to haunt him."

Days later Walter and Elly drive their son the hour and a half to the University of Maine in Orono to begin his freshman year of college. Walter is severely depressed, and David's decision to go to the University of Maine in spite of the Reserve Officers Training Corps (ROTC) requirement torments him all the more. He knows this was a decision that weighs heavily on his son. Within two weeks of their son starting college, Elly brings Walter to a sanatorium, Baldpate, in Georgetown, Massachusetts, for psychiatric treatment.

David has written to the dean of students requesting an exemption from compulsory ROTC service. The dean responds saying that he must take ROTC "without any mental reservations" or withdraw from the university. After much deliberation, David decides that he will face up to ROTC to see whether he can learn to understand the military mind as a means to try even harder to work for peace. He is issued a dark-green, military dress uniform along with black shoes that he is required to polish before each use with a "spit shine." However, when on the first day he is ordered to sign a loyalty oath that would require him to defend his country with arms, his heart drops. He refuses to sign. The captain tells him that if he does not sign, he will be removed from the university. David remains firm.

Several days later David goes to the college infirmary, as he has been experiencing diarrhea. Although he thinks the nurse will just give him some pills, she insists that he sees the doctor. Dr. Graves immediately asks whether anything is troubling him.

"Well," David replies, "I am required to take ROTC, and I am opposed to war."

The doctor looks him straight in the eye. "I understand," he says. "I am opposed to war, too. I served in the Korean War. However, whenever I was required to shoot, I shot my rifle in the air."

David is surprised and touched by his understanding. However, not knowing what to say, he remains silent.

The good doctor then asks, "Would you like me to pursue a medical excuse for you, so that you can be free from ROTC?"

Feeling shy, uncomfortable, and guilty, David replies, "Yes, I appreciate your kindness. Thank you so much."

Besides issuing David a bottle of Lomotil pills, Dr. Graves sets up another appointment to discuss the process David must pursue to get out of ROTC. Upon David's return to the infirmary several days later, Dr. Graves beckons him into his private office. Sitting behind his desk, he looks serious and sad. "We have stirred up a hornet's nest," Dr. Graves explains. "Dean John, Dean of Students, is furious. He said that you agreed to come to the university under the condition that you would take ROTC. However, he won't prevent me from giving you a medical excuse, but you will have to sign the loyalty oath."

What a decision for David to make. Thoughts quickly rush through his mind: *Would I be a coward if I signed the loyalty oath? Would I be giving up all the principles in which I believe and on which I stand firmly? Do I have an obligation to Dr. Graves, who stuck his neck out to help me? What would I gain from remaining in ROTC? I will still be reluctant and antagonistic toward the military, won't I? And this damned diarrhea, will it finally go away if I get out of ROTC?*

He then and there agrees to sign the loyalty oath. Dr. Graves lets out a sigh of relief. Smiling gently he says, "I know, David, this was a terribly hard decision to make for a principled boy. I believe you did the right thing, and that you will continue your struggle for human justice." David, too, feels greatly relieved. That afternoon he brings the medical excuse to the ROTC office and signs the loyalty oath.

In early January, David encounters his former ROTC captain in front of the physics building. The captain kindly asks David how he is doing. He then bends over, takes some snow in his hands saying, "You know war isn't that bad. It's just like throwing a snowball over the physics building hoping that it will kill those on the other side." David feels enormously relieved that he no longer is a part of ROTC.

When he bumps into the captain, David is carrying a self-portrait of Käthe Kollwitz. He had bought this original lithograph at an exhibition at the University's art museum. He believes that his parents will be as moved as he by her drawings of Nazi Holocaust victims. After all, they had introduced him to her work. The Kollwitz self-portrait is to be David's present for his father's birthday on January 19. On bringing the lithograph home and showing it with excitement to his mother, David becomes anxious and disappointed. Elly encourages him not to give it to his father, "You know Daddy is not well. Käthe's sad face will disturb him. It will bring back terrible memories from Germany."

The following fall, after the death of his father in August 1962, David returns home to attend Bowdoin College in Brunswick. The Vietnam War is in its early stages. Gradually, Bowdoin students, together with a professor, a Unitarian-Universalist minister, as well as a local business leader and the editor of the *Brunswick Record*, start the Brunswick chapter of Turn Toward Peace. By 1964, the national organization has already brought together more than thirty national peace, labor, religious, veterans', and public affairs organizations "who seek to build a major public support throughout the country for a disarmed world under law, safe for free societies and democratic values" (Turn Toward Peace 1964).

As part of an antiwar effort by Turn Toward Peace, David circulates throughout the college and town communities a petition that John Cole, the newspaper editor, has written to President Lyndon Johnson opposing the war. Quoting from a policy speech that president Johnson had made at Johns Hopkins University in April 1965, the petition expresses support for "his fine words." It urges the president "in earnest hope that you will try to turn this nation's course from cruelty to compassion, from destruction to healing, from retaliation to negotiation, from war to peace" (Cole 1965).

Together with the Peace Center and Bowdoin's International Club,

David helps to sponsor a lecture by the well-known physicist, Linus Pauling, who received the 1960 Nobel Peace Prize for his persistent struggle to generate public awareness of the genetic dangers of nuclear fallout. As vice-president of Bowdoin's International Club, David also arranges the visit of Arthur Waskow, a Civil Rights and peace activist. Waskow authored *The Worried Man's Guide to World Peace* and *From Race Riot to Sit-in, 1919 and the 1960s.* As he is preparing his introductory remarks for Waskow's talk, David remembers that his father had read to him a poem by the ancient philosopher and mystic, Lao Tzu, a poem that reflected Walter's own beliefs about the ways to achieve peace among nations. David quotes the verses in his introduction, drawing Waskow's appreciation.

> A skillful soldier is not violent;
> An able fighter does not rage;
> A mighty conqueror does not give battle;
> A great commander is a humble man.
>
> You may call this pacific virtue;
> Or say that it is mastery of men;
> Or that it is rising to the measure of God,
> Or to the stature of the ancients.
>
> (Blakney 1955, 121)

Following graduation from Bowdoin in 1965, David, with the help of Maine's Senator Edmund Muskie, receives a waiver from his draft board to teach at the Ecole d'Humanité. (During the war Paulus Geheeb had moved his school, the Odenwaldschule, which David's father had attended, from Germany to Switzerland, where it was known as Ecole d'Humanité.) While there, in early 1966, David applies for the status of conscientious objector to war. He is clearly influenced by the legacy of Paulus Geheeb on his father, and, therefore, on himself. The works of Thoreau, Emerson, Dostoevsky, Gandhi, and later William James, author of *The Will to Believe*, help David realize the need to have faith in searching for the truth in approaching difficult and often unknown ways of life.

Although one of the stipulations for applying for conscientious objector status is belief in a Supreme Being, David reflects on these thinkers. He writes in his application:

God exists often hidden in every living person as the "Inner Light." The Deistic view that god created the world and has left it up to mankind to make of it what he can has been expressed by Thomas Jefferson, third president of the United States. Ralph Waldo Emerson, also, spoke similarly in that each person must rely upon his strengths to stand upright for what the inner voice has bade him to seek: justice, peace, righteousness. "Nothing can bring you peace but the triumph of principles," wrote Emerson in his essay, *Self-Reliance.* Each must rely upon himself to *become* in the words of Pindar, *what he is!* This means that each person must develop his individuality. Each must continuously strive to develop his own abilities (mechanic, teacher, architect, musician, artist, doctor, etc.) to his fullest. Sometimes his artistic talents are herein included. A person must learn to fulfill these strengths as playing a musical instrument, painting, partaking in a non-competitive sport, caring for plants and many others, because he, spiritually inspired, will become a more complete and sensitive individual. Furthermore, by means of these experiences, his ability to love, the highest capability that man has above animals, becomes greater. Love is to help another *become what he is!* As he develops this ability, he will be able to help others in the worst of distress. I further believe that love includes everybody's equal right to live and develop his abilities. Nobody has the right to end by his own hand the life of another. Man will thus become better capable to of performing his duties to God and society.

The rearing of children in the home, and, ideally, at school, a difficult question which is much discussed, shall help to clarify my opposition to the use of force between individual persons on account of personal reasons and prejudices. Professor Rudolf Dreikurs in his book *Children: The Challenge* spoke of democracy not autocracy in the family. The parents, by treating the child with love and rationality, should try to win its cooperation and should allow it to learn from its own experiences. Corporal punishment should under no circumstances be used. This method is not force; it is careful guidance with the foresight on the part of the parents. It is my belief that the child should have the opportunity to discover his own way in life and develop social and human duties, which are to respect the equal rights of each person, the individuality, and above all the Supreme Being, which exists however hidden in every human being. (Solmitz 1966)

The draft board never officially acts on his request for status as conscientious objector. During the two years he teaches at the Ecole d'Humanité, David meets and marries a fellow English teacher, Esther Bircher of Zurich. Upon their return to the United States during the summer of 1967, their first son is born. As the father of a single son and as a public school teacher, David is automatically deferred from the draft.

8

Brilliant Mind, Troubled Soul

During the evening hours of June 1, 1943, Elly announces that her time has come. Walter anxiously calls a taxi to take them to Mt. Auburn Hospital by the Charles River in Cambridge. As fathers are not permitted to participate in the birthing process, Walter returns home to their apartment at 13 Ware Street. He can't sleep that night. Drinking neither warm wine nor hot milk has any effect. Although he is ecstatic about his soon-to-be-born child, he worries whether he will find a teaching job, become an accepted member of the faculty at an American college, and be able to financially support his family.

The following morning when he arrives at the hospital with a bouquet of flowers, he smiles a rare, broad smile seeing Elly holding their son, David. He was born in the early morning hours of June 2. Despite spotting a mouse running across the floor of her hospital room, Elly feels blessed to have borne her child in a land in which both she and Walter feel safe. Now that they have a child to free their minds from the hardships of adjusting to a new country, Elly sees their mission to joyfully and successfully raise their son in their new homeland. Walter, she believes, will complete his doctorate at Harvard and become a prestigious professor like those under whom he has studied in Germany and at Harvard. Although she understands that her husband is preoccupied with his studies and teaching, she feels sad that unlike other graduate students he never finds time to accompany his wife and baby for walks along the Charles River, in the Cambridge Commons, or through Harvard Yard.

As the years pass, David's mother sorrowfully realizes that her husband has never finished his doctoral dissertation. She recalls her disappointment and frustration strolling alone with her son in the baby carriage without his father's company. Memories of Walter's hospitalization in Munich following the death of his sister revive old anxieties.

David with Elly in Harvard Yard
April 1944

Within two years of his appointment as an instructor of German at Bowdoin College, Walter succumbs to a severe bout of depression. The kindly college physician, Dan Hanley, admits him for a week of recuperation in Brunswick's tiny general hospital. Even as a small boy, David knows something is not right with his father. He notices his father becoming tense, irritable, jumping at the slightest noise, and staring vacantly. Always a cigarette is in his hand, while a cup or thermos of black coffee is never far away.

In spite of spells of depression even during his youth, Walter has always been considered highly intelligent and gifted. When he begins his studies in Hamburg during the winter semester of 1925–26, Walter is among only 210 people invited to attend a lecture by his professor Ernst Cassirer, Freedom and the Necessity of Renaissance Philosophy, for the opening ceremony of Professor Aby Warburg's Library for the Scientific Study of Art.

Walter looks up to Cassirer not only as his teacher, but as a father from whom he can seek advice. During this time, Walter falls in love with Ernst Cassirer's daughter, Anna. She, who studies the violin and voice in Berlin, will become a concert pianist. Because Walter is deeply engrossed in his intellectual world and is emotionally unstable, both Anna and her parents develop misgivings as to whether their relationship can last. During the year he spends in Bavaria working on his doctoral thesis, Walter makes three trips to visit her in Hamburg and Berlin, yet he soon learns that she has become engaged to Kurt Appelbaum, a pianist in Berlin. She marries him on February 1, 1933. Walter is crushed. He speaks for three hours with Anna's father and briefly with her mother, to no avail. Her mother, Toni, in a letter to Edith Geheeb dated October 22, 1932, writes, "For the first time in all these years, Walter has reacted like a normal person. That I had an unhappy but not a desperate man with me, was at this moment a great relief to me" (Grolle 1994, 21).

When Walter expresses a desire to write his doctoral thesis on Euripides' philosophic aspects of Greek tragedies, Cassirer feels incompetent in this specific field to be his advisor. After all, he is more interested in 18th-century German philosophers and art history of the Renaissance. Furthermore, he finds Walter's topic to be too broad. Shortly thereafter, Cassirer is offered a position at the University in Frankfurt. If Cassirer is to go there, should Walter follow? Or should he continue his work and foster his developing interest in art history with Warburg at the Warburg Library? At the last moment, Cassirer decides to stay in Hamburg and continue his collaboration with Warburg. What a relief Cassirer's decision must be for Walter. However, less than half a year later, in October 1929, Warburg dies. In spite of the shock, loss, and sadness he experiences, Walter continues his work and studies at the Warburg Library. The new director Fritz Saxl and his partner Gertrude Bing admire, respect, and bond with Walter. Saxl entrusts him, for instance, to put together a scientific work for publication that he and art historian Erwin Panofsky* are writing, *Classical Mythology in Medieval Art.*

Walter becomes deeply interested in Warburg's work exploring the relationship between the pagan cultures from which mythology arose and the impact of mythology on Eastern and Western art throughout the ages. Warburg accepted Freud's interpretation of evolutionism that looks to "primitive" cultures for a common cultural origin. However, he rejected Freud's notion of primitivism as barbarism, transcended by evolution, and looked instead toward C. G. Jung's interpretation. To Jung, evolutionism meant the loss of something precious and authentic. In fact, Jung looked at primeval cultures in developing his ideas on archetype and manifestation.

*Panofsky, like Walter, also came to the United States, in his case to teach at Princeton University. Walter and he not only corresponded with each other, he visited Walter's family in Brunswick. They took him to the small coastal town of Wiscasset on a rainy, summer day. There, David recalls, he rhymed the couplet:

> The trains in Maine drive you insane,
> But in Wiscasset they are an asset.

In September 1896, Warburg went to New York to attend the wedding of his brother Paul. Soon thereafter he left New York, a city that he described as the "practical foundation of this over-richly assorted, largest department store in the world," for Arizona and New Mexico (Steinberg 1995, 59).

Realizing that native cultures worldwide were declining, he extended his American stay for nearly two years to compile an ethnographic study of the Pueblo Indians. In April 1923, back in Germany, he gave a lecture illustrated with his own photographs, "Images from the Region of the Pueblo Indians of North America," at the psychiatric hospital at which he was a patient. He concluded his talk:

> The modern Prometheus and the modern Icarus, Franklin and the Wright brothers, who invented the dirigible airplane, are precisely those ominous destroyers of the sense of distance, who threaten to lead the planet back into chaos.
>
> Telegram and telephone destroy the cosmos. Mythical and symbolic thinking strive to form spiritual bonds between humanity and the surrounding world, shaping distance into the space required for devotion and reflection: the distance undone by the instantaneous electric connection. (Warburg 1923, 54)

As Walter's interest in art history intensifies, he realizes in a letter to Edith Geheeb that, "in philosophy, one becomes ever more isolated in oneself, becomes critical and argumentative toward the world as a whole and unworthy of nature's love. On the other hand, in studying art history, one actively learns from one another. If one wants, in this field, one can lead a lively, rich, intellectual life" (Grolle 1994, 11). Even with this realization, why Walter chooses philosophy, a path that leads him deeper into self-isolation, remains unclear.

Following his father's death, David sorts through his father's desk drawers to determine what should be saved or tossed. At the bottom of a drawer beneath a large stack of manila folders filled with notes, he discovers several astrology magazines. He is shocked that his father would read such common trash.

Recalling this experience many years later, David realizes that Aby Warburg and Walter were only able to understand the mythology of pagan cultures at an intellectual level. They were yet unable to comprehend the wisdom of the ancients, even though Walter studied and appreciated the texts of Buddhism and Lao Tzu. However, he never seems to have been introduced to quantum physics, the branch of science that deals with discrete, indivisible units of energy called quanta, which contain many clues as to the fundamental nature of the universe. Though quantum physics is relatively new science, the concept that all matter is densely packed light, was understood and practiced by the ancient Laika shamans of Peru.

Alberto Villoldo's 2008 book, *The Four Insights: Wisdom, Power, and Grace of the Earthkeepers,* explains how, for millennia, the Laika shamans of Peru knew about the luminous nature of light. They understood that the human body is enveloped by a luminous energy field. "Over millennia, the Laika learned to access the biological blueprint of light and assist Spirit in the unfolding of creation. They also learned how to heal disease and create extraordinary states of health, as well as to craft and shape their personal destinies by changing the luminous energy field" (Villoldo 2008, xiii).

To achieve these changes, they developed and followed four insights. Each of the insights, as in mythologies, is represented by a different animal (Villoldo 2008):

Insight 1: The Way of the Hero

Practices: Nonjudgment, Nonsuffering, Nonattachment, Beauty.

Represented by the serpent: this is the instinctual level. We see, touch, and smell an object knowing that it is physically present. We seek physical solutions to a problem: trade in a car, change a job, have an affair. We are aware of our physical body, but not cognizant of our mental, creative, and spiritual selves.

Insight 2: The Way of the Luminous Warrior

Practices: Fearlessness, Nondoing, Certainty, Nonengagement.

Represented by the jaguar: we realized that our experiences are influenced by our thoughts and our beliefs. A single insight can allow us to break free from our negative feelings or an old way of doing things that held us back. We have emotions: the capacity to love, to feel intimate, caring, and compassion.

Insight 3: The Way of the Seer

Practices: Beginner's Mind, Living Consequently, Transparency, Integrity.

Represented by the hummingbird: we sense that all of our experiences are part of our epic journey of growth and healing;

we find solutions to our problems at the soul level that cannot be resolved with the mind; thought. Visualizing is much more powerful than just reciting affirmations.

Insight 4: the Way of the Sage

Practices: Mastering Time, Owning Your Projections, No-Mind, Indigenous Alchemy.

Represented by the eagle: We are able to see both the entire picture and a tiny piece of it at the same time. When we face a difficulty, the closer we can get to the spirit level the less energy we need to bring about change.

Accordingly, both Aby Warburg and Walter may have overly adhered to the Jaguar level, in the words of Villoldo, "I think, therefore I am." In other words, they may have identified with their thoughts. Even so, they had personal qualities of the Hummingbird level, such as integrity; one is reluctant to judge, especially as regards the level of the Eagle.

The Laika realized that the universe always mirrors back to us the conditions of our dreaming. For instance, Walter at the end of his life, contrary to reality, became mired in despair, believing he no longer was able to be an effective professor. Therefore, he could not escape the dark reality created by fear. In his suicide note to Elly, Walter wrote, "I am at the end. For it appears to me now that I cannot deal with more trouble and worry than joy. Therefore, it seems that the time has come to disappear, even if it is difficult." In Villoldo's words, "Whatever scares us the most will be waiting for us around the corner . . . Fearfulness holds us back from growing and keeps us repeating our lessons through suffering and trauma instead of through the experience of our own radiance" (Villoldo 2008, 92). On the other hand, if we experience abundance, are grateful for what we have right now, we will actually have abundance. These can be any dreams that we may have: wealth, the joy of living, deep friendships. Villoldo wrote (2008, 135), "We can achieve anything we want by truly believing the dream we'd like to experience and following the way of the seer. We do this through the practice of beginner's mind, living consequently, transparency, and integrity." This, in other words, is called *the power of attraction.*

In August 1933, As the Nazis are rolling into power following the hopeful years of the Weimar Republic, Walter learns, while still in Bavaria, that, per order of the Nazis, all *non-Aryan* professors are being denied access and authority to teach at any German university. This decree naturally affects not only the scholars at the university but also the entire circle of intellectuals connected with the Warburg Library. By this time his professor Ernst Cassirer has left for England, where he had secured a position at Oxford. Walter's close friend from the Odenwaldschule, Raymond Klibansky, also has received a position at Oxford. By 1934, the Warburg Library leaves Hamburg for London. Walter helps pack many boxes of books and documents that are shipped to the library's new location in London's South Kensington section. However, Walter is denied the opportunity to join Gertrude Bing and Fritz Saxl in following the library to London. He is forced to stay behind in Hamburg. Gertrude Bing writes to Edith Geheeb that, though Walter is a great scholar, his psychological state of mind is too unstable for him to be brought along. She confides in Edith that, since she had taken care of Aby Warburg who was mentally unstable and depressed, at times institutionalized, she simply didn't have the energy to look after Walter as well. She mentions also that the British foundation that is helping to establish the new Warburg Institute in London by paying salaries, wants the Institute to hire British citizens, rather than bring all of their own people from Germany. Walter feels betrayed and abandoned as doors are rapidly closing behind him. In frustration, as depression takes over, he further procrastinates on his doctoral thesis.

During his trip to Germany in spring 2005, David asks Professor Joist Grolle, Walter's biographer, about his father's mental health. "Your father was very gifted; he was really a genius. You realize that brilliant minds are often emotionally unstable," Grolle explains.

"Do you know what the diagnosis of his condition was?" David is eager to know.

"No, I really do not know. You see, in those early days of psychology and psychiatry, the knowledge was not as advanced as it is today. It could be that in today's terms he would be considered bipolar." Professor Grolle continues to explain that Walter completed his best work under pressure. Therefore, had Ernst Cassirer given him specific topics and deadlines by which to complete his assignments, he might well have finished his doctoral thesis. Fritz Saxl made the same mistake by sending Walter to Bavaria on a scholarship to write his thesis in the quiet of a farm. He gave him no benchmarks and deadlines.

"Your father's best works were completed under tight deadlines. These included three days to prepare the memorial speech upon Aby

Warburg's death, as well as the memorial speech for Ernst Cassirer three days following his death. He completed his report on Dachau for the British government by the deadline that was established. Also, while your father was a professor at Bowdoin College, he had to complete his chapel talks on time—brilliant essays they were" (See Appendix B). As much as David feels relieved to hear Professor Grolle's kind and insightful interpretation, he wishes his father had received the help he needed to structure his life.

Fifty-one years earlier on a rainy, cold, early Sunday afternoon in May 1954, David's mother enters his room. He is playing with his Lionel electric train. "I have something exciting to tell you. Daddy has been given a year's leave, called a sabbatical, from his teaching job. In July we are all going to take a steamship to London where we will live and where Daddy will work at a library." Before his mother can finish, David bursts into tears: "What will happen to Beagy (the family's pet beagle)?"

"We'll ask Miss Packard. I'm sure she'll take Beagy for the year. He'll love to be at her big farm. I'm sure he'll get along very well with her Scottish terrier. She invited us for tea this afternoon, you remember. We can even ask her then."

By mid July, Beagy is happily settled at his new house, and the family's Brunswick home has been rented for the year to a visiting professor. Walter's colleague, Professor Pols, drives the threesome to the Portland terminal of the Grand Trunk Railroad to catch the slow train to Montreal. In Montreal, they board the Cunard Line's *Samaria* on its final cross-Atlantic voyage—seven days at sea. The family is thrilled to see icebergs in the Gulf of St. Lawrence. Mornings, David helps the chief deckhand to set up deck chairs and put out blankets; in the evenings he helps replace both. For his help, the deckhand gives him a pen with a tiny image of the *Samaria* floating in a bubble.

Two days into the crossing, David's father develops an ugly skin ailment on his hands that the ship's doctor bandages with white gauze. Walter remains in his cabin, probably because he feels embarrassed to sit with his family and others at the dining table. Nor does he come out on deck to sit on deck chairs or stand by the ship's railings to take in the sea breeze and watch the sky and the foaming trail created by the steamer's big propellers.

From that moment on, David recalls that his father changed. The frequency of his bouts with anxiety, tension, and despondency become more frequent, severe, and longer. David learns later from his mother that the skin rash had to do with anxiety. Undoubtedly, his father fears that as the Warburg Institute's door closed on him once before, it might this time open only partially, or maybe not all.

His anxiety has much to do with the enormous task he is to undertake at the Warburg Institute. Gertrude Bing has invited him to work on Warburg's *Nachlass*, his uncompleted works for which he received grants from the American Philosophical Society in Philadelphia and from the British Society of Learning. Walter is worried whether he will be able to complete the challenge successfully. After all, he has less than a year's time to complete this project. In addition, tensions exist between Bing and Ernst Gombrich, an art historian, who has been working at the Institute since 1936. The conflict is due to Gombrich's interpretation of Warburg, whom he had never met or worked with directly, as had Bing and Saxl.

Bing meets the three Solmitzes at London's Waterloo Station, to which the boat train from Southampton has brought them. She brings them in her new green Morris Minor to her neat red brick home in Dulwich. They stay there for about ten days before heading to the Berner Oberland in the Swiss Alps to visit Walter's mentors, Paulus and Edith Geheeb, directing their new school, the Ecole d'Humanité.

During this visit, Walter meets with a former teacher of his, Frau von Keller, from Geheeb's former school, the Odenwaldschule. He describes to her his project at the Warburg Institute: to prepare for publication fragments of Aby Warburg's work on expressive psychology. He is also expected to do preparatory work on Warburg's *Mnemosyne Picture Atlas.* The Atlas explores the history and psychological function of expressive forms in antiquity that remained constant throughout the centuries in spite of variations. Walter explains that perhaps his most daunting task will be to provide detailed explanations to the manuscripts. For instance, he will have to demonstrate how these writings relate Warburg's teaching of solid forms of expression, not only to his discovery of archetypes on which they are based, but also to those archetypes from which they are distinguished. Furthermore, he needs to relate these to Warburg's absorption with the history of astrology.

Frau von Keller responds enthusiastically to Walter's description of his project, suggesting that he meet with C. G. Jung to explore similarities and differences in Warburg's and Jung's work, and to discuss how Jung might be able to oversee and further develop the Warburg Institute's efforts.

Walter, in a letter to Jung, humbly expresses Frau von Keller's excitement for Walter to explore his questions and concerns with Jung. "I am here at the Ecole d'Humanité until the 2nd of September and can easily come to Zurich," he writes. "Should you, however, really feel that you could make a little time available to me, I would be very grateful. Then you could write to me the day and time at my above address. P.S. I can easily imagine that this moment may not be convenient for you."

On August 24, Jung writes back that he could meet with Walter on Friday, August 27, at 5:00 p.m. at his home in Küsnacht. He signs, "with the highest respect, your devoted C. G. Jung."

David never learned the result of their meeting.

On returning to London, the family again stays with Bing. As Walter begins his work at the Warburg Institute, Elly and David begin looking for a school for the eleven-year-old. In Rohampton they find Ibstock Place School, a Friedrich Froebel school for David to attend, across from a teacher's college based on Froebel's educational theories. In nearby Putney, they find a two-room flat in a modern apartment building.

As Walter begins to tackle his project, he realizes it is even more complex than he dared imagine. To a friend he writes, "The work is fascinating, but enormously difficult—for 1001 reasons."

Although Bing remains encouraging and supportive, Gombrich is critical of Walter's interpretation of Warburg. As acting director, Bing worries who her successor will be and how the institute will evolve. Also, during that winter Paul Geheeb becomes seriously ill, fostering in Walter fears that Geheeb, his surrogate father, will soon die.

David is aware of the deep depression that overcomes his father that winter in London. When he returns home from school, he takes his father in: His tall, thin body is slightly stooped. Sad, brown eyes are drawn toward the floor. His jowls are drooping. He stands motionless looking toward his bed in the tiny linoleum-floored living room of the two-room flat on the fifth floor of Harwood Courts on Upper Richmond Road in Putney. He doesn't talk. He lights a cigarette and continues to stare at the small twin bed that on rare occasions he shares with Mummy. She sleeps in the bedroom with David, her bed next to his, separated by a nightstand with a light on it, so she can read herself to sleep. Daddy's emaciated skin, his fingers stained brownish black from years of intense cigarette smoking, all blend into the gloomy atmosphere of a gray day, amidst mildewed and smoke-stained brick buildings, brick-tiled roofs, brick chimneys and smokestacks, and high walled-in gardens protecting plots of remaining flowers and vegetables.

David sports his only clothes, his school uniform, his gray shirt open at the collar. Thank goodness, he does not have to wear a tie at home, as he does at school. His green blazer, adorned with the gray insignia and inscription of Ibstock Place School, is hanging in the closet. On the shelf above is the little gray and green cap that he must wear to school. He is wearing those doggone itchy gray flannel shorts and knee-high stockings. The hard, brown leather shoes are less than comfortable. Walking like a duck, toeing out, the hard leather heel occasionally slips up, rubbing his anklebone, causing bloody stains on his stockings.

The following day, Saturday, David looks sadly at his father. He sees the tenseness in his shoulders as he strikes a match to light another cigarette. Enshrouded in a haze of smoke, father and son become closely enmeshed, yet, as if in a fog, they seem further apart. Together in the cloud of smoke, David asks, "Daddy, do you want to go for a walk with me?"

Walter responds, "Yes. I'll tell Mummy, we are going for a walk."

"Where are you going?" she asks. She glances toward Walter.

Still looking toward the bed and absorbed in thought, he quietly suggests, "To the Thames."

David is excited about the idea—to walk with him along the river. Father and son wait momentarily on the other side of Upper Richmond Road for the 37 bus. As this is a short ride, they don't bother to go to the upper level of the double-decker. Nor is Walter in the mood to wind his way up the narrow stairs and bend his way to the front. The bus is pretty empty, so they take the front seat opposite the driver. David likes to look out the windshield while pretending to drive the bus.

David looks forward to changing buses for the 72 to Hammersmith. He wants to tell his father of the scary experience he had recently when he took the 72 home from school and forgot to get off at the stop where he could catch the 37 home. It was only after the bus was well into a broad heath that he realized he had gone too far. Being in a heath seemed like nowhere. Not knowing where he was, he got off and crossed the street to take another 72 back and the 37 home. When David tells him the story, Walter seems uninterested, drifting into his mysterious thoughts. David wonders what he worries about. Is he thinking about Elly, about his work? He experiences disappointment, yet he knows his father is sick. He is surely suffering.

Luckily, the bus arrives shortly at the Hammersmith Bridge. The two get off. They needn't cross the bridge, simply head down the slight embankment onto the wide, gravel path. The river flows toward the sea while the duo heads upstream. The path is graced by bare, gray poplar trees blending into the overcast afternoon light. Walter walks slowly. Walking at a snail's pace, too, David becomes impatient. He wants to see what it is like around the next bend. He hopes they can walk all the way to Hampton Court. During the entire walk, father and son don't speak. David wants his father to call him "Munky," after which Walter always puts his arm and hand over his shoulder. He wants him to react to the scenery as he did when they walked together in Brunswick, even though there are no flowers here to bring home to Elly. Somehow David feels his sorrow meshes with the depressed mood of London ten years after the end of World War II.

Walking aside the brownish-gray river as it drifts toward London and the sea, David is lonely. He misses his father. He worries whether he will ever be the same life-loving father who used to take him for walks in the woods, on bicycle trips to nearby Maquoit Bay, and sledding on the hill near the Dionne farm in winter. At this slow pace, he wonders whether they will ever find a bridge to cross so they can take a bus home.

At last, David spots a man whose boat is attached to a cable that crosses the Thames. He immediately announces, with considerable excitement, "A ferry!"

Walter suggests they take the boat. Both climb aboard. The man standing with a long oar toward the back of the boat guides it along the wire. Walter doesn't speak a word. Normally, he would chat with the ferry operator, but not this time. They walk a while until they come to a bus stop, find a bus that takes them back to Hammersmith, where they board the 72 and later the 37 for home.

Monday is a long day as usual at school. David is not happy here except when eating the thick custard sauce that Miss Blitheberry in the kitchen prepares for the noontime meal. He also is fond of his primary teacher, Miss Akester. A young woman, she arrives daily at school on her big motorcycle. Taking David under her wing, she is patient when he has difficulty with math. She appreciates his essays, and thrills him with lively anecdotes about Queen Elizabeth I and Mary Queen of Scots.

Having to play soccer on a muddy field in the cold November dampness is misery. David hates soccer. For that matter, he loathes all sports. He is afraid of the ball, just as some people are afraid of dogs. He fears being kicked in the shin—accidentally, of course—by the heavy-cleated shoes of boys eager to win the game. Mr. Waterford, the coach, urges David to get into the game. Instead he tries to escape to the sidelines. Finally, Mr. Waterford insists that David be the goalie.

Naturally, when the ball comes towards his goal, he quickly steps aside, allowing the opposing team to score.

Calisthenics, coached by Mr. Mallory, the Latin teacher, at the tennis court is equally painful. David is poorly coordinated, and Mr. Mallory in frustration orders him to stand at the fence to watch for monkeys. "With people like you," he complains, "England didn't need the help of your country to defeat Germany."

Then there comes the day that he gets in trouble. He is caught throwing apples in the orchard at Mary, a boarding student supposedly from America, who refuses to admit to him that she is American. Being caught red-handed, David is sent to Miss Priestman, the headmistress. He waits on the wooden bench in front of her office door until she calls him in. Sitting behind her desk with folded hands while he stands terrified before her, she asks him why he threw apples at Mary. Before he can answer, she expresses disappointment, reprimands, and orders him to memorize the hymn "Faith of Our Fathers Living Still." Before he is allowed to return to classes the next day, David has to recite the poem to her.

Riding the 37 bus home, David's thoughts drift between freezing on the soccer field to wondering why it is important for an eleven-year-old American to learn about British history, to his father who seems excessively distraught and sad. At the same time, he find's Walter's tension and furtive look to be obnoxious. This is not the way his father, or, for that matter, any father should be. *Why are you such a damn tense bug?* He mulls with frustration. *Why do you tear up pieces of paper, stuff them into your mouth, and chew them with intensity between smoking one cigarette after another? Why can't you act normally? Why can't you hold your head up and look at me? Are you really sick? You're just plain weird these days. What will you be like when I get home? A tense bug, of course. And Mummy will be calm and distant.*

Disembarking from the bus, David enters their apartment building with a combined feeling of apprehension and joy—the fear of telling his parents about his transgression at school, but the joy of coming home, relief of getting away from that awful British school, and the thrill of having his toy trucks and buses with which to play. Two steps at a time he dashes up five flights of stairs. Throwing open the door to their flat, he expects to see his father either lethargically bent over at the table or sitting at the edge of his bed smoking a cigarette. But he isn't there. *Where is Daddy?* he wonders. His mother barely cracks a smile as she greets him, rising from one of the small chairs.

"Where's Daddy?" David asks anxiously before even thinking of taking off his dark-blue raincoat.

"I took him to the hospital this morning," Elly quietly replies with little emotion. "The doctor thinks he will be better off at the hospital for a few days."

David says nothing as Elly heads toward the kitchenette to prepare his afternoon snack. According to his routine, he takes off his coat, places it over the back of a chair and heads into the bedroom to remove his uniform. Looking forward to his snack, though not eager to taste the warm canned grapefruit juice, he returns to the tiny sitting room. Elly pulls up a chair at the table's end, asks David about his day.

"OK," he answers without feeling. Rather than recalling another unpleasant day at school, his mind is preoccupied with telling his mother about his misbehavior. He'd rather be playing among his toys. Elly continues to sit by David at the table as he gulps down the juice and eats a slice of Hovis bread with unsalted butter; every morning she buys a loaf at the bakery. Finally, he breaks the news to her that he has to memorize a hymn for getting in trouble at school. Maybe because she is so worried about Walter, she merely reminds David that he had better learn the hymn before he goes to bed.

Rising from the table, he goes to the bedroom, takes the box with his toys, and removes his new Matchbox brand London bus, as well as a small Dinky Toy locomotive with two passenger cars. Kneeling at first and then lying on the brown linoleum that covers the cold, hard floor, David imagines he is driving a route 37 red double-decker. Since the traffic is light and the bus is therefore early, he creates the putter of a slowly moving bus. The driver will halt at the request stop at Harwood Courts on seeing the outstretched arm of a schoolboy in a navy blue trench coat, standing with his mother. On boarding the bus, mother and child sit on the dark-red-and-green upholstered bench directly by the open door. The bus heads down the road toward Putney. The driver will let them off at the Putney Underground station where they will catch a train to Earl's Court to visit the boy's father in the hospital.

David now takes the two passenger cars without the locomotive. Placing them on the floor, he pretends that they are a short Underground train. He pushes the cars slowly into the station. After the boy and his mother embark, David imagines that the automatic doors of the car close and the train slowly moves out of the station. He makes the sound of the wheels—tick-tick, tick-tick—as they move along the tracks. The patter becomes faster as the train picks up speed, but changes tone to a low tuck-tuck, tuck-tuck as the carriages cross the bridge over the Thames River heading for South Brompton, Earl's Court, and beyond.

David wonders what Walter has been doing at the Warburg Institute. He thinks it has something to do with art history. He wonders whether he stops to put a few pence into the ragged hat of the one-legged artist who makes chalk pictures on the sidewalk. Did that man lose his leg in the war? David wonders if his father experienced the war. After all, he came to London from Germany before coming to America.

David thinks of the watercolor painting he recently completed that Elly likes so much. It is painted primarily with dark bluish gray—gray lines intertwined with black and white. From amidst the bombed ruins, the huge dome of St. Paul's rises. Driving past the ruins and St. Paul's is a red London double-decker. He wonders why his father always seems particularly sad when they see bombed ruins. Why do the little yellow flowers that grow amidst the ruins make David feel sad?

David recollects taking the Wimbledon Underground line from Putney across the Thames toward South Kensington, where Walter works at the Warburg Institute. A few stops beyond West Brompton, the train goes underground. The West Brompton station, an older yellowish-gray structure amidst bombed ruins, in a sort of deep concrete channel with railway yards on the left, impresses him deeply. The smoke and grit from a grimy black World War II shunting locomotive and all the coal cars it is switching add to the desolateness of the scene. Yet, an elderly stationmaster in navy blue uniform and cap can be seen watering the yellow and purple flowers planted in small circular gardens on the far ends of the platform. Pansies they may well be. This sight always spreads a ray of hope and brilliance amidst the dreary setting. David likes to imagine that his father still has that ray of hope within him, that radiance he used to experience on their Sunday morning walks less than a year ago in Brunswick.

When they return from England in 1956, Walter has more frequent and severe episodes of depression. Finally, Elly locates a private sanatorium, Baldpate, in Georgetown, Massachusetts. Walter has to take several leaves of absence from his teaching, each lasting about three weeks, for psychiatric treatment. Although he finds the elderly German psychiatrist, Dr. Schlomer—distant relative of his Elly's—understanding, he dreads the electroshock treatments that he has to undergo. Each time he feels his brain has been damaged, injury that will never heal. Although for a short time after each treatment, his spirits seem reasonably good, yet he quickly sinks back into depression.

In 1959, just four years after Walter's sabbatical at the Warburg Institute, Gombrich replaces Bing as its director. Bing, who is 67 at the time, dies five years later at her London home in 1964.

At Baldpate, information regarding the difficulties Walter encountered at the Warburg Institute in London are revealed by Walter's psychiatrist, Dr. George Schlomer:

> While in England he had "dreams of glory." At first there was some friction with a Viennese man [above mentioned] who had worked on Mr. Warburg's papers, and who was afraid that the patient's activities would interfere with his work. The patient himself was torn between his understanding and love for Mr. Warburg, and his lack of expert knowledge on the Renaissance. This created a great deal of tension, partly activated by his feeling of insecurity at Bowdoin College. At the same time Mr. Solmitz remembers that Mr. Warburg had mentioned to him, while he was still a young student, that he would like him to be his successor. The director of the Institute [Fritz Saxl] had died, and [the] patient dreamed of becoming successor to this Director, which did not materialize.

In a phone conversation with Ed Pols, Walter's colleague, department chair and close friend, Ed explains to David that for Walter to start a new semester was particularly difficult. He experiences a great deal of stress. For instance, the day before classes are to begin, he has a stack of books on his desk three feet high. Pages of these books are marked with little pieces of torn paper. He follows the same procedure for courses that he has taught many times before. Although Ed likes to be over-prepared for his courses, he easily understands that for Walter to teach in a language that he learned later in life is challenging.

Following Walter's death in 1962, Ed writes in an affidavit:

> During the period of 1955–1956, I saw a great deal of him [Walter], since the question of his transfer to the Department of Philosophy was then under discussion—he had a psychic disturbance of the sort usually described by the layman as a nervous breakdown. He was quite unable to teach or indeed to carry on any of his college duties. He had to spend considerable time in a nursing home, was under constant psychiatric care, and was, in fact, completely incapacitated. The financial drain upon

his resources was considerable. The whole of the academic year 1955–56 he was on sick leave from his duties at the college.

In the academic year 1956–57 he returned to his duties, this time as a full-time member of the Department of Philosophy. He seemed stronger and it was hoped that, work wholly in philosophy being more congenial to him than work in German, he might now manage to settle down and do not only the good teaching that was always characteristic of him when he was well, but also the philosophic writing that all who knew him were convinced he could carry out successfully.

It was, however, always obvious in the years in which we were so closely associated that his difficulties persisted in some measure. This was especially clear during times of some strain, e.g. examination periods, when one could see that it was only with an enormous expenditure of nervous energy that he was able to complete his tasks by the required time. In the last year of his life these symptoms gave way to more extreme examples of psychic difficulties. Early in the fall of 1961, for instance, it became clear that his teaching was deteriorating in the sense that matters he had once found it easy to express with force and elegance, he could now only enunciate in a most torturous and strained way. It soon became evident that a temporary withdrawal from teaching was necessary, and he retired [once again] to a clinic in Georgetown, Massachusetts. For a while I assumed his duties, but as it appeared he would be absent for some time, a substitute was finally appointed—Dr. Jay Bachrach—who came to us twice a week from a neighboring college. Mr. Solmitz made a partial recovery and returned after about a month, but during the rest of the time (i.e. until February 1962) he had many crises, and needed frequent help, especially with the preparation and reading of examinations. Qualitatively his work was markedly below that of his good years. There were several short visits to the clinic during that period.

The Bowdoin College physician, Daniel Hanley, writes in a similar affidavit in 1962:

In the fall of 1946 I first became acquainted with Walter Solmitz, and was his physician from that time until his death on August 23, 1962. During that time Walter Solmitz was never in full good health. His main difficulty throughout was manifested by extreme

> anxiety and varying degrees of depression. This combination of symptoms produced a disability so marked that at times he was forced to give up his teaching and to be hospitalized. Over the years, the periods of hospitalization became more frequent, lasted longer, and appeared to be less effective . . .
>
> In the period between hospitalizations, Walter Solmitz was able to teach but even at these times of his life he was almost never able to carry a full teaching load . . .
>
> In my opinion, Walter Solmitz's disability during the years I have known him was such that he functioned at about 30% normal efficiency, he was, in other words, more than 50% incapacitated during the years I knew him. His disability was, of course, worse during the later years.
>
> During these years Walter Solmitz's kind and pleasant manner made for him many friends on the faculty and college administration. These friends took up the extra burden of his duties when he was unable to do so. At times Walter Solmitz did meet all of his classes and was a most effective teacher. At other times his emotional condition reduced his efficiency to near zero.
>
> Walter Solmitz was a sensitive man and was more easily upset than others. In his days of depression simple items like the correcting of exam papers or the assigning of a grade to a student presented for him insurmountable decisions.
>
> It is my considered opinion Walter Solmitz's difficulties were the result of his treatment in the concentration camp when he was in Germany.

Dr. Patrick Quirk, a psychiatrist at the Georgetown, Massachusetts, hospital where Walter is a patient comes to the same conclusions as Walter's Bowdoin physician. On January 10, 1963, he writes:

> Walter Solmitz had overwhelming feelings of inadequacy and guilt, he could not understand why he escaped the fate that befell so many others of his associates who were in the concentration camps with him. Because of his feelings of inadequacy, he always had a great difficulty in judging others. This caused him to postpone even giving grades to his students, and led him to his having difficulties with the authorities at Bowdoin College.

Years later as David recalls his father's illness in London, his inability to return to work immediately on returning because of another bout with depression, he is reminded of Jill Conway, former president of Smith College, when she realized in *True North: A Memoir* that she had to hospitalize her husband due to his severe depression. David wishes that his mother had had the support that Jill had from her German housekeeper, who fought in the resistance against the Nazis, and the close friends they had developed in Toronto. However, growing up between two wars, the Great Depression, and her father's despair, Elly has learned to be independent and tough, as had Jill Conway.

> Now I had learned all over again the lesson I'd been taught so bitterly during the five-year drought on Coorain, my outback Australian home: Endurance is the great virtue when nature goes awry. If one only knows to wait, nature, of which we are so strangely both an integral part and a distant consciousness, will renew itself. (Conway, 1994, 132)

Every time Walter was committed to the hospital, Elly visited him without fail. On such occasions, she sent David to friends in the countryside, an experience he enjoyed. He recalls one time, when she was suffering from severe back pain. In spite of her discomfort, she headed out during a harsh New England snowstorm, leaving very early in the morning and reaching Georgetown in the late afternoon—a drive that normally took her two and a half hours. During these years, Elly worked as a secretary for Bowdoin's government and history departments. Later she typed a book on chemistry being written by Bowdoin's president at the time.

The emotional strain of Walter's worsening illness on Elly became evident as she lost almost all of her hair and had to purchase a wig. She also developed psoriasis over much of her body. Nevertheless, she remained undaunted in support of her husband. Like Jill Conway, she realized early on:

> In time, I was to come to a chastened recognition that there was nothing I could do to help avert what was to be a chronic condition. That I could be a companion but never a cure, to someone I loved so much, was to be the discovery that marked my real growing up. (103)

9

Shaped by Deep Sorrow

As a child, David seems to adopt his father's horrific experiences in Germany as his own fears. On Sunday mornings, David and his father walk nearly one mile to Morton's Newsstand, just across the railroad tracks at the corner of Maine and Depot Streets. After they pick up the *Sunday New York Times* and pay Mr. Morton, they walk home.

On this particular Sunday, they are enjoying the balmy sunny weather as they cheerfully head back up Maine Street. Hearing the groaning of what sounds like heavy trucks and tractors, David looks back. Huge green tanks with their guns pointing straight ahead are rumbling up Maine Street.

"Look, Daddy!" David exclaims. Walter turns, face whitening and shoulders drooping. David grabs his father's hand. He can sense his father is shaken. David is afraid. His father, who tightly holds his hand, doesn't utter a word. The tanks growl past, the leader of the pack followed by the other six, turns onto McKeen Street.

"Munky, don't be afraid," his father finally says. "See, they are heading toward the armory that is behind the high school."

Father and son continue their walk home, shaken by the experience, yet feeling particularly bonded. As usual, they stop at Higgins's little grocery store to buy a pint of three-flavored ice cream: vanilla, chocolate and strawberry, their regular Sunday dessert.

Walter comes home early, just before noon. In fact, he will not go back to his office this afternoon. The academic year is over; he has just handed in his grades—a moment for relief celebration.

David hears his voice gently calling, "Munky," his affectionate nickname for him. His father seems happy, not the stern teacher smoking his Herbert Tareyton cigarette and drinking black coffee from his thermos bottle while trying to explain mathematical word problems to his son.

"Munky," David hears again, as Walter suggests, "It's such a beautiful afternoon, let's go to the ocean. We can take the car."

David is delighted; so much easier than going by bike.

"Come on," Walter says, "put on your sneakers, and we'll be off."

Walter has already shed the Harris Tweed jacket that he wears during all seasons. He puts on an old pair of gray pants and a worn-out, cream-colored dress shirt, the sleeves of which he rolls up.

They clamber into their black, four-door 1948 Chevy. Elly, who stays behind, really doesn't like the car. It used to be a taxi; she finds it heavy and hard to steer. But Walter doesn't seem to care. David actually likes the uniquely stagnant smell of cigarette smoke that only comes in taxis.

"How about going to Simpson's Point?" Walter asks.

David's heart sinks into his stomach. "Okay," he reluctantly replies, not wanting or even daring to contradict his father. Sure, he likes Simpson's Point, especially where the road gets narrow, and he can look down over the steep embankment to the water below. However, seeing the remains of two burned buildings at the point bothers him.

Just as father and son enter the Simpsons Point Road from Mere Point Road, the burnt remains of a small house come into view, upsetting David. As they near the junction of the two roads he closes his eyes. On passing, he opens them to a squint, as he is still curious to see whether the house is still there. It is. He begins to fantasize what it must be like when a forest fire takes over a whole neighborhood or town. He has never seen such a thing, though he has heard about the great fire of 1936 that burned woods not far from their house.

David is sure that there is something more to his fear than he understands. It may stem from his father's experiences; however, Walter rarely, and only impersonally, mentions what happens in war, when bombs are dropped on buildings, fires rage, structures crumble, and people perish. Never does he reveal a single event from his own wartime experiences.

As they arrive at Simpson's Point, barely three miles from their home, the gray, burnt remains of the old wooden inn greet them. David is scared. Each time he and his parents come here, these burnt remnants of the once glorious hotel makes him sad, even worried. The now light-gray, charred wood, fallen timbers and boards, a partially standing wall give him the creeps. He doesn't know why, but wonders: *Am I afraid I might find the skeletons of people who were in the inn when the fire broke out? Maybe. I never thought of my fear in this way. I guess I hate to see anything violently destroyed.* Fire leaves scars reminding him of something terrible that happened. In this case a once-thriving hotel, filled with people who enjoyed their vacation by the ocean, has succumbed. An entire era has disappeared forever.

Walter asks him why he is so quiet. Hesitatingly, David responds that he doesn't like to be around burned-out buildings. They make him uncomfortable. His father takes his hand and suggests they go up to the old hotel to take a peek around. Maybe this will help him be less afraid, Walter explains.

David holds his father's hand tightly, as they walk across the lawn, up a slight slope to the remnants of the inn. As they get closer, he loosens his grip on his father's hand, and his fear begins to subside. Looking closely at the charred wood, he notices that it appears more gray than black, since the rains and snow, sun and wind, over the years have softened the forms scorched and disfigured by the fire. The floor itself shows no signs of the raging blaze, just bleached wooden planks with broken pieces of plaster scattered about from the small portion of standing wall. Other pieces of paled wood from the now caved-in structure show only faint scars of the terrible fire.

David feels nearly at peace with himself and with the remains of this once stately inn. He no longer experiences as much fear as he looks out on Middle Bay, watching the tide ebb while the first herons land on the mudflats to catch their afternoon meal. He imagines that where he is standing once a large dining room was located. People would sit at table with white tablecloths, fabric napkins, wine glasses, and baskets of hot rolls, waiting for their meals as they looked out onto the calm waters of the bay and small islands in the distance. On the lawn, just in front, he imagines children playing croquet. He even imagines a white steamship arriving from Portland bearing passengers and mail to the Simpson's Point dock just below the hotel.

The faded, charred, and scorched remains of the fire, the bleached floorboards and caved-in walls remain subconsciously imprinted into David's being. They represent experiences, unknown to him, that his parents began to endure as small children growing up in Germany, as World War I was raging. They represent members of his family and his parents' friends who never made it out of Germany, who perished at the hands of the Nazis. Since he has never experienced the agony his parents experienced, the burnt ruins have become a symbolic expression of his childhood fear of becoming acquainted with and re-experiencing their torturous suffering.

Several years pass before father and son return to Simpson's Point. The burnt house at the corner of the Mere Point Road and the Simpsons Point Road has been rebuilt. It is a small cape painted light gray with white trim. David is even more excited to see Simpson's Point again, this time without fear, even if the remains of the old inn are still there.

As the two pass the steep embankment on their left, David glances up at the spot where the old hotel used to be. In its place stands a brown wooden ranch surrounded by No Trespassing signs on every tree. As they park the car, get out, and head towards the water's edge where clam diggers used to park their trucks, they hear the deep, raspy voice of a woman. "Get off my property! Get off my property!" she yells again and again, her petulant screech coming closer toward father and son.

As David looks up toward the house, he sees a slender, middle-aged woman with graying hair clad in dark slacks and an olive green blouse staggering toward them. In her left hand, she is balancing a glass of whiskey, in her right, a rifle haphazardly points toward father and son.

David is overwhelmed by sadness, not fear, as his father and he realize that they must head back to their car. This once beautiful spot, spoiled for him in his childhood as it seemed haunted by the ghosts of a raging fire, has now become inaccessible to him in another real way.

Walter, with his arm over David's shoulder, and David with lowered head, slowly retreat to their car. The mutterings of the gun-toting woman fade as she returns to her house. They scramble silently into the car, turn around, and head for home, leaving the natural beauty of Simpson's Point to a day when maybe they both can finally come back, fully able to enjoy its majestic splendor and serenity. Then a gentle breeze will caress their faces while they gaze upon the blue water of Middle Bay. They will look through the silvery leaves of poplars, the robust leaves of maples, onto small, tree-covered islands in the distance and the orange-and-brown seaweed-covered rocks on the opposite shore bordered by white birch, poplar, maple, oak, pine, and fir trees in their summer glory.

On an earlier occasion, when David was about eight, he recalls swinging in his yard—swinging higher and higher as his red wooden swing rocks rhythmically. A gentle breeze flows through his brown curly hair; his blue eyes gaze upwards at the sky watching white and pink puffy clouds changing shape. Sometimes the formations remind him of wild animals—a bear, a lion, a tiger. Sometimes they appear like mountains, causing him to dream of climbing onto snow-covered peaks with his father. On occasion, they look like maps, such as Italy's boot stretching into the Mediterranean, or England, or South America. As he sees these images, he wonders what it must be like in those distant places.

He thinks of his parents who emigrated from Germany. *Was their country like this? Did his parents have swings in their backyards? Do all Germans wear* Baskenmützen *(Basque berets) like his parents do? Do they ride bicycles with thin tires to work like his father does? Do boys in Germany his age have to wear shorts?* His mother wants him to wear shorts, but he hates them. Even though it is a warm, early summer day, he still wears long pants, dark-blue ones, because his mother thinks that color is appropriate for him—they match his blue eyes. He likes the feel of the loose-fitting material opening up at his feet when he stretches his legs to reach higher and higher toward the sky, allowing the breeze to creep up his legs. He imagines he is in an airplane flying high above the earth with the wind whizzing by on either side of the silver plane.

He prefers swinging facing the field and woods behind his house, rather than looking toward the street. Gazing at the field that has grown over with wild blackberry bushes and milkweed intrigues him. He loves to watch the solitary old apple tree, bent and bowed with age, its gray bark deeply wrinkled and scarred from years of neglect. In the fall, he feels saddened when yellow and brown apples scarred with black spots drop to the ground where they rot. He wishes there were deer that would come to eat the apples, but deer no longer come close to town.

Behind the old apple trees are two sheds that have been neglected for years. Their roofs have pretty much caved in; the side wall of the larger shed is bulging outward. The smaller one, he believes, was once a chicken coop. Directly behind the sheds is the edge of the woods. Stately pines and majestic firs grace aging maples. The maples' massive trunks and broad branches are gnarled like withered faces of old men. In the fall, David takes in their display of brilliant orange, warm yellow, and deep red, reminding him of the male peacock, who struts about pompously with flamboyant tail feathers.

Behind the trees, the ground slopes steeply to a small marsh and tiny stream. A narrow path just beyond the apple tree leads into the gully, at the bottom of which weathered wooden boards still make crossing possible without soaking one's feet. At the far side of this narrow chasm is an abandoned spring marked by a wide pipe installed in the swamp. David likes to go down to the spring because it is peaceful and refreshing.

Large, broad-leaved skunk cabbages appear lush and healthy next to graceful ferns fed by the spring's lucid water and the rich black earth. Early in the spring, he clambers down the slope to pick dark red trillium, more commonly known as Stinking Benjamin, and, if he's lucky, he finds a painted trillium with white petals and a red center that he happily brings home to give to his mother.

Even though the field hasn't been mowed, plowed, and reseeded for years, blades of fresh green sprout forth amongst the tufts of unkempt yellowed grass burned by the hot sun of past summers. David recalls the following incident that occurred when he was about eight, early on a fall morning.

As he is in the bathroom getting ready for school, he hears the throbbing sound of a tractor. Standing at the only window, he presses his nose to the glass to look toward the field and the woods. To his dismay, a small John Deere crawler tractor is pulling a wooden skid across the field. Wild thoughts flood his mind: *Is the operator going to bulldoze a road across my precious field? Will the woods be cut down so that houses will be built there? No! No! They can't do this to my field and woods. Why didn't Daddy buy the field from the Bryants as he had said he would?* David remembers his father having talked to all the neighbors, encouraging each to buy a swath that abuts their house lot, after he realized he couldn't afford to buy the whole field himself.

David begins to feel anger toward the neighbors. *Why don't they care? Why did they let Daddy down? It's not fair. It's just not fair.* Everything he cherishes rushes before his eyes: the old apple tree, the field, the woods, even the old dilapidated sheds. He believes he will be seeing these for the last time—the birds he loves to watch and hear: the crows, the blue jays, robins, an occasional gold finch or blue bird, a rare cardinal, and even occasionally a Baltimore oriole. Their homes will be destroyed forever just as he feels his life will never be the same.

David runs out of the bathroom across the hall, shoving open the door to his father's bedroom and study. "Daddy, Daddy," he calls. "Come quickly!"

His father, noticing his son's voice resonating with terror, rushes out of his bedroom. Cigarette already in hand, clad in his gray pajamas, he follows him into the bathroom.

"Look!" David cries in desperation as he points to the window.

Walter stops as he enters the bathroom, then walks slowly to the window, fearing that something terrible has happened. Even though the puttering of the crawler appears to have become louder, he barely seems to notice the sound. After looking outside, he turns silently and solemnly to his son, his brown eyes gazing down with such sadness that tears begin to roll out of David's eyes, spilling onto his cheeks. Without uttering a word, Walter puts his right hand on his son's left shoulder. David immediately senses that his father is deeply saddened by the scene. The field, the old apple tree, the woods they both so much love are going to change forever.

As father and son stand in silence, Walter smells hot black coffee and oatmeal wafting into the bathroom. He gently beckons to David to head downstairs for breakfast. Elly has already placed David's blue-and-gray ceramic mug filled with warm milk, a small glass of orange juice, and a bowl of piping hot porridge at his place on the table. He sits in the middle, his parents on either side of the kitchen table. As all three sit down to breakfast, Walter assures David that on returning from school in the afternoon, both will go into the woods together to examine the damage and to try to determine exactly what is going on.

Upon coming home from school, David reads the note on the banister: "Wake me up at 3:00—Daddy."

Knowing it will only be a short while before it is time for him to wake up his father, he rushes through the kitchen to look out the window, imagining the worst. He worries that there no longer will be a single tree standing, tree trunks and branches strewn across the field where once lush green leaves, which used to flutter in the breeze, will be lying limp. He pictures the big trees that sway gently in the wind, as if they are dancing and embracing one another, now lying prostrate on the ground, viciously cut off at the base, destroyed forever. As he stands at the kitchen sink, anxiously gazing through the glass, he is relieved that the trees are still standing, the scene largely unchanged. What he does notice are two well-worn tracks through the field, in which the grass has been flattened into the ground. Looking toward the far end of the field by the woods, he spots the small green crawler emerging from among the trees—actually coming from the path that he, his father, and his friend Peter often walk.

Waiting impatiently to awaken his father from his nap, David continues to scrutinize the scene from the kitchen window. The tractor is coming closer and closer along the trail that leads from the woods. He observes that the crawler is dragging the trunk of a single, huge pine. Finally, glancing again at the clock, he realizes it is time to awaken his father. Scurrying upstairs, he taps gently on Walter's door. "*Komm hinein*," his father murmurs in German. As David enters the room, Walter lifts his head from his pillow smiling gently at him. "Are you ready to go to the woods?" he asks calmly.

"Yes," he replies anxiously as his father gets up quickly, tightens his belt, and slips on brown Oxfords before following his son downstairs and out the front door.

Walking behind the house, they cross the backyard into the field. David's anxiety intensifies. Walter grabs his hand, holding it tightly while surveying the first signs of damage—the packed grass, through which some brown dirt appears to have been scoured from beneath the sod by the crawler's metal cleats. As they reach the newly worn track, the tractor dragging the fallen pine is well on its way to Maine Street. David spots the driver's back, his grease-stained, dark-blue Dickies brand shirt, curls of graying, brown hair sticking out from the back of his forest-green cap.

As Walter and David head in the opposite direction of the crawler, David looks apprehensively toward the entrance to the woods from whence the tractor emerged. Nothing seems terribly changed. Yet, as father and son approach the path they have so often followed, David is stricken with sadness. He sees the leaves of anemones, wintergreen, ferns, and young trees crushed beneath the tractor's treads and further smashed by the sledge and the logs that have been hauled out by the small but powerful crawler. As the two stroll further into the woods, they spot an opening amongst the trees through which the late afternoon sun spreads a warm yellow glow onto the gray-brown bark of a small stand of maples, sending its rays directly on the bleeding stump of a once magnificent pine. The trunk of the tree has already been hauled away, but its branches are strewn chaotically, some reaching across the path, making it nearly impossible for them to walk further.

"It could be worse," Walter says as he turns around to head homeward, still tightly holding his David's hand. "You know," he continues, "even if they take out more trees, others will grow back." Feeling relieved by his father's words, David lessens his grip on his father's hand. "Later, when you are an older man, you will come back and hardly notice that anything has ever happened," Walter persists, slowly glancing from David to the beautiful trees still standing in front of him. "The branches that we see scattered all over the place," he explains, "will have rotted, creating good, fertile soil. Maybe you will spot the rotten remains of an old tree stump, but that will be all. New, strong trees, aided by the sunlight, will grow up. Possibly, the field that we so much love will grow up into a forest itself. You will walk through these woods remembering this day, pleased to see how nature is able to take care of the damage caused by man."

As the days pass, during clear crisp autumn days, in the warmth of the spring sun, on hot muggy summer afternoons, David continues to swing. He has never forgotten his shock from the day that the green crawler tractor traversed this special field heading into the woods to cut trees. Apparently, the Bryants, needing some money, sold the stately pine and proud fir for lumber.

Now as a man in his early sixties, he is awakened from a nightmare. Crews of men with chainsaws have cut all the trees behind his home at 10 Bowdoin Street. A huge, yellow skidder has been hauling them away. Bulldozers plow through the field, creating a wide swath, and then spread gravel hauled in by big ten-wheeled dump trucks. Soon the new road will be paved. Already the cement foundations are being poured, onto which row houses will be built where the two old sheds once stood, graced by huge maple, pine, and fir.

Some days after the dream, David drives through the cold, snow-covered landscape to his old home in Brunswick. His family's house at 10 Bowdoin Street is still there, only it is larger, with an addition in the back and a new garage. The blue spruce that he planted on the front lawn at the corner of the driveway has become a huge, sprawling tree. The red swing that he enjoyed so much as a child has disappeared. The field behind the house has grown up into young woods, as his father had predicted. Yet hidden among the saplings and larger trees, although its largest limbs have broken and fallen to the ground, the old apple tree remains.

A few houses down from his own on Bowdoin Street, David is sitting together with his friend Sky on the railing of his porch. Facing the Stubbs' house, they watch Mrs. Stubbs come out of the side entrance. Standing in her driveway, this short, rather heavyset woman wearing a smock with a floral print is calling her two boys, "Skippa, Raunnie; Skippa, Raunnie!"

Amused by her nasal drawl accented by a Franco-American twang, like a parrot, David echoes her call loud enough for her to hear. She looks up at the two boys who laugh, poking each other in a friendly jest.

On returning home a short while later, David notices that his parents seem unhappy. His father, who has been sitting at the kitchen table, slowly rises. Without his saying a word, his sad, stern eyes pierce his son's with their disappointment. "Mrs. Stubbs called—" he says quietly, causing David to feel immediate guilt. He appears so large to his son, who feels so small. David remains speechless. "Do you know why?"

What else can he say but yes. It never occurred to David that this simple, coarse woman would tell on him. Only now does it dawn on him that his actions were wrong.

"Sit in the bathroom," Walter says solemnly and quietly, gesturing slightly toward the upstairs. Like a dog with its tail between its legs, David quickly climbs the stairs, walks into the bathroom and shuts the door. He sits on a large ornate oak dining-room chair that his mother had painted light gray. Although the summer sun shines warmly from a bright blue sky filled with pink and white puffy clouds, he dares not look out the window onto the yard, at his red swing, the field with the old apple tree and the woods behind. Instead, he sits still, looking at the floor, anxiously awaiting his father's arrival. Time drags. At last, he hears his father's steps slowly coming up the stairs. Before he arrives, David pictures a tall figure opening the bathroom door, standing with bowed shoulders in the opening, looking at him with great disappointment. David worries what he might have to say to him. At the very least, he will have to admit his transgression. On entering the bathroom, his father quietly shuts the door as he approaches his son. Softly he asks, "What did you do?"

Taking a deep breath, David explains "I, I, ah, imitated Mrs. Stubbs as she was calling her boys for lunch."

"You imitated her? Could you be specific?" he asks politely.

"Well, ah, you know, I imitated her calling her boys."

"You mean, you were mocking her?"

"Yes," David replies with lowered head. A tear runs down his cheek. Another drops onto the floor.

"Do you think she appreciated you mocking her?" Walter asks.

"I didn't mean any harm," David replies.

"How would you feel if somebody mocks you?" his father wants to know.

"Badly," he can barely utter.

"Would you do this all by yourself?"

"No."

"Then why did you do this with a friend?"

"I don't know."

"Really? You don't feel stronger when you and your friend do the same thing—attacking another person? Is there any difference when a whole group of people attack a smaller group, like white people attacking the Negroes?"

David shrinks in his chair, wishing he could disappear. He can't bear to look into his father's distressed eyes.

Turning from him, Walter slowly opens the door. Leaving it ajar, he methodically walks downstairs. Knowing that dinner is waiting for him, David has no choice but to follow, taking his seat at the center of the table at which his father has already sat down. Elly brings forth the food from the stove: baked potatoes, a roasted chicken, and frozen green beans. The three eat in abject silence. David dares not look up at his father's ashen gray face, fearing his solemn expression of disappointment with him.

On another occasion, Walter walks briskly toward David and his friend Peter where they are kneeling on the side of their street under a huge maple tree just a few yards from their homes. Even before reaching them, David senses his father's frustration and pain. David's heart sinks into his stomach. With one gentle gesture of his hand, Walter signals to his son to come home. As David timidly walks toward him, Peter scurries to his house. Walter firmly but quietly directs him to go to his room. David knows this is a serious matter.

Ascending the stairs, David heads for his room, closes the door behind, takes off his shoes, and sits cross-legged on his bed. *How can I own up to what I just did?* he asks himself. He and Peter have been throwing pebbles at the boy they call TTX—their neighbor Frank, who is retarded due to a so-called water head at birth. *Daddy must have seen us. Of course, he'll ask why we did what we did. I can't explain to Daddy that we found one of my trucks in a pothole covered with patching tar right by TTX's house on Maine Street. Would Daddy believe me if I were to tell him that TTX had ruined the Dinky Toy Bedford garbage truck that Uncle John sent me from England for Christmas? No, he'll ask whether I have proof. I don't, but Peter and I guess TTX did it. So we threw pebbles at him when we saw him coming by.*

After what appears like eternity, Walter enters the room, sits next to David on his bed, and turns toward him to look directly into his eyes. David knows he isn't just disappointed at him this time, but hurt and angry that his son could be so insensitive as to throw pebbles at a poor retarded kid.

Father and son look at each other, eye to eye. David feels his father's penetrating scowl is going to destroy him. He is terrified. Walter finally asks, "Do you understand what you have just done, David?" Only when he is terribly upset with his son does he call him by his given name. At all other times he fondly calls him Munky or Munk.

"Yes," David shyly says, taking his eyes away from his father's. What else can he say? After all, he feels frightfully guilty.

"How do you think Frank must feel when two normal boys to whom he looks up, throw stones at him?" Walter enunciates every syllable.

"Awful," David replies.

"Awful is all you can say?" he asks with an especially stern expression and forceful tone. "Two of you ganging up on a poor, helpless boy are more than awful," he continues as tears begin to trickle from David eyes.

"Well," David sobs, "we found our truck, the Dinky toy that Uncle John—" His father won't let him finish.

"Your reason is not pertinent. There is nothing that you can ever say that can justify what you have just done," he reprimands.

Walter gradually stands up, looks at David with an ashen gray face and deathly sad eyes. He turns toward the door, opens it, walks out, and promptly closes it behind him.

What does he want me to do now? David wonders. *Obviously, I can't leave my room. Do I have to wait until he comes again? I don't dare to leave my room, but I don't think he'll be back. I'll wait a while. At least Mummy will call me in a couple of hours when it's suppertime.*

David understands the connections among all these memories. The military tanks rumbling along upper Maine Street, his fear of burnt ruins, the destruction of the forest behind his childhood home—these all reflect a deep bonding to his father, as do Walter's grave disappointment at his son's transgressions. David knows his father is a man whose acute suffering, penetrating insight, and vast wisdom caused him to develop profound compassion for all living things, especially those who are victimized. He knows that Walter never had the opportunity to bond with his own father. In spite of Walter's ill health, David feels his father's unwavering deep love for him.

10

Middle Bay: The Artist Within

DAVID, NOW IN HIS EARLY SIXTIES, HAS returned to his hometown of Brunswick for the day, to one of his favorite spots by the sea. Pennellville, within three miles of his childhood home, is located on Middle Bay, a short distance to Simpson's Point. Never did he return to the site of the burnt ruins of the hotel at Simpson's Point that eventually became the modern home of the gun-toting woman. At this moment he is sitting cross-legged on a little grassy mound, beneath an aged oak tree. David looks onto Middle Bay through the tree's rustling green leaves. As the tide is receding over the shallow mudflats, the rust-colored seaweed that covers the rocks and the remaining posts of the slips of the Pennell Family Boatyard appears. During the 19th century and into the early years of the 20th century, the Pennells built and launched sloops here at Pennellville that traveled up and down the East Coast, crisscrossed the Atlantic to Europe, and actively partook in the China trade.

As the tide continues to recede, little pools of seawater in the gray mud reflect puffy, billowing clouds in a blue sky. A few great blue herons glide down from the east onto the mudflats, where they fish for their meal. Looking directly across the bay, about a mile away, varied coniferous and deciduous trees are reflected in the still water, a cobalt blue splashed with broad swipes of Prussian blue and Payne's gray where the ebb tide has not yet reached. David looks westward where the sharp, tough Indian yellow marsh grass grows out of the mud. There a long, slender ledge of light-gray rock etched with deep crevices stemming from the last ice age stretches toward a little island that is accessible only at low tide. The rocks are littered with broken quahog, clam, and mussel shells dropped by seagulls in their attempts to obtain the meat inside. As the farthest rocks, covered with sepia-tinted seaweed, extend into the mud flats less than a hundred yards away, the tiny rocky island rises, graced by a handful of small, bent, windswept spruce.

David remembers his thirteenth birthday on June 2, 1956. At his mother's suggestion, they take their painting gear and head off to Pennellville. Into an old dark-blue cloth shopping bag, a remnant from Germany, she puts her box of tube watercolor paints in which she also carries her brushes, and a #2 pencil. David follows suit. Filling two instant-coffee jars with water, they fasten the covers tightly. Sliding their paint boxes to the side, they slip in the two water jars. Elly carries the bag, and David the two watercolor pads on which they'll paint. She opens the door to their whitish-gray, two-door 1952 Plymouth Cranbrook sedan, pushing the driver's seat forward in order to deposit their materials on the back seat.

The drive to Pennellville is three miles from their house at 10 Bowdoin Street, the last street in town just off upper Maine Street. Heading toward Mere Point, they bear left onto the Middle Bay Road, a gravel road. They pass through woods until they reach a field. Here, in the middle of this pastureland, they turn right. On their left stands a sprawling Greek revival farmhouse, behind which there is a long, multistoried chicken barn. A quarter of a mile further on the left, another smaller, square, white, two-story farmhouse appears, and just beyond that, on a little knoll, a yellow cape, the original home of the Pennells, now the home of David's family friends, the Packards. Closer to the bay, set far off from both sides of the narrow road, are several impressive captain's houses. The early 1800s estate that remains in the Pennell family has a cupola in which the captain's wife would sit looking out to sea, hoping to spot her husband coming home on his long journey from such faraway places as China.

After his mother parks the car in the little turnaround, they gather their painting gear. They climb down the narrow path to the shore and walk along the thick grass over a few rocks. Before reaching the slender ledge, they step back to settle on a little grassy mound beneath an aging oak tree. Unpacking their brushes, paints, and water, they place these amidst the soft marsh heather for easy access.

Elly teaches David to make a quick, light sketch of the scene he chooses to paint. Like her, he has chosen the little island. The tide being low, the island appears closer than at high tide. "As you think about composing the picture, the main focus, the little island, must be large," Elly explains, as she looks at his rough sketch.

David redoes his first attempt. He enlarges the island, bringing it closer to the foreground. He does not forget that the outcrop of ledge covered in part by seaweed must remain prominently in the foreground, and that a distant island in the background helps to create a well-organized and balanced composition.

As they begin to bring out their paints, Elly gently reminds her son, "Look how blue the sky is, and those pink, billowy clouds floating so gently above the island. Let's paint the sky first with a wash, making sure we blend in the various colors of clouds and sky. Remember that when we paint the water at the end, it should blend on the horizon right into the sky."

"Which brush do you think I should use?"

"I like to use my one-inch. With a wide brush, you will feel more relaxed and thus are better able to capture the transparency of the scene. It should appear light, lively, and still have brilliance."

Once the sky is completed, mother and son focus on the island itself. David begins by painting the little island's iconic rock. It appears more yellow than gray in the late morning light. Browns and grays help to distinguish its rough features. His next step is to make a few bold strokes of short, somewhat stubby lines. Using a mixture of brown and gray with the wide tip of the brush, he tries to represent the scraggly trunks of the windswept trees. Filling in the needles with a few wide strokes of dark green into which he melts some warm yellow, he tries to reflect the bright sun on these lonely but close-knit trees. With a blue-green wash, he places a distant island in the background. The climax of his effort is now at hand. He mixes up a variety of blues, brown, gray, and yellow, so that the mudflats in the foreground appear to sparkle in the sun. The muck seems dark and quiet in the shade. The tone changes to a lighter, bluer gray as the mud extends into the sun-filled bay. With the rising tide reaching and gradually covering the mudflats, the gray turns into various shades of blue that eventually blend on the horizon and into the sky.

On completing his painting, David cleans up his palette and brushes, and packs these back into the bag. While his mother is finishing her painting, he heads off to the water's edge to find horseshoe crabs milling about in the muddy brine. When Elly finishes, she looks at his picture. "It's lovely," she says. "Now, what could you have done better? Look carefully."

"The island looks a little stiff, doesn't it? And the foreground, although it does seem to blend in with the rest of the picture, looks too muddy."

"Good observation. Now what can you do to make it better?"

"Don't try to be so careful, just let the brush and watery paint flow like you did?"

"Yes."

"But how then do I avoid making the picture muddy?"

"You know the answer to that."

"Don't go over the part you have already painted. If you do, you must use a translucent color."

"That's right. With watercolors you can only paint once. It's almost impossible to make corrections. That's part of the fun and beauty of watercolor painting."

David appreciates his mother's feedback. Through her faith and confidence in him, she encourages him to do better the next time. He feels happy and close to his mother.

They leave, looking back at Middle Bay as the rising tide begins to lap against the shore, and the blue, oh-so blue, water that Elly loves is glistening in the sun.

As they head for home, Elly suggests that they stop at Warming's Market to see whether there are any fresh native strawberries they can savor for lunch. He likes the idea. After all, his mother knows how much he enjoys strawberries.

Immediately upon their return home, they lean their pictures on the sofa. When David's father comes downstairs for one-o'clock lunch, he will see their paintings. David looks forward to that moment, when, from amidst the smoky odor of his breath and clothes, he praises his picture, "Munky, that is beautiful. I feel I am there with you."

Although Elly taught him to paint with watercolors, she never painted with oils nor introduced him to that medium. "I love watercolors," she once explained to him. "On the one hand, one is so free with watercolors. One feels the natural beauty of the sky and water as one's wet brush glides over the paper to create sky with wispy clouds of summer. The translucent sunlight even brings out lightness to the Prussian-blue sea."

As much as his mother loves Brunswick, the nearby ocean, the gently rolling countryside of woods and fields, as well as lectures and concerts at Bowdoin, she is a city girl. She grew up in Hamburg, attended her schooling there, made lifelong friendships, and met Walter in that city on the Elbe River. She also misses Cambridge and her friends there. After all, Cambridge was her and Walter's first home in the United States. Their close friends, refugees from Germany, the Alexanders, also lived in Cambridge before moving to Belmont, a ten-minute ride from Cambridge by bus. Each year she and David visit the Alexanders, sometimes during the Christmas or February vacation, but most often during April break.

While at the Alexanders', Elly and David take the Red Line subway from Harvard Square to Park Street. On occasion, especially in spring, they walk through Boston Common to the Public Gardens for a ride on the Swan Boats. More often, however, they change at Park Street to the Green Line to Boston's Museum of Fine Arts. Elly introduces David to her favorite artists, who have become his favorites as well: Rembrandt, Turner, Van Gogh, Monet, Manet, Degas, and Cézanne. As they look at Rembrandt's dark brown and black painting of an elderly, well-to-do gentleman with a white collar, Elly likes to say, "Follow me." Walking from one side of the painting to the other, she comments, "See, he is always looking at you! Isn't that impressive?"

As they approach a Turner painting, she becomes excited. "Look how the sun penetrates the clouds, creating a warm glow on the stormy ocean. Turner always has such a wonderful feeling for light and warmth, in spite of the gruesomeness of the shipwreck scene."

Proceeding to the Impressionists, she routinely remarks, "Oh, how lovely," as she observes the landscapes by Monet. They are "so gentle in his use of color, yet so brilliant. Don't you feel the warmth of the summer day by the sea?" And on to Van Gogh: "I love his strong, wild, passionate, yet controlled brush strokes."

When David is nine, Elly finds a cottage for the Alexanders, the Sea Crest, at Small Point, within forty-five minutes of Brunswick. She is so delighted to have found this isolated, early-1800s fisherman's house on a knoll overlooking a tiny sandy beach, a jagged, rocky coast, and a small barren peninsula that juts into the open sea, that she rents it for a week for her own family. Daily she and David paint the scenery. David particularly enjoys painting the little rock-bound peninsula covered with grass, low bayberry bushes, and bold rocky outcrops. Sometimes they sit on the unmown grass in front of the house or they carry their art supplies to the little beach.

Two years later David and his parents spend his eleventh year in London. Elly enjoys taking him the Tate Gallery at Trafalgar Square. There, too, they admire Rembrandt, Turner, and the Impressionists. David's father introduces him to the British Museum's ancient Egyptian, Greek, and Roman sculpture, and the Rosetta stone. David finds the galleries filled with stone sculptures particularly cold. He is much more attracted to the warmth of paintings of landscapes and scenes with people. During that year he continues to paint with watercolors. He enjoys painting the untamed landscape of Richmond Park, where deer roam freely, as well as the daffodils and other spring flowers in manicured parks, like Hampton Court. He is also particularly taken by the gray bleakness of London and by the bombed ruins nearly ten years after the end of World War II.

One of his watercolors, done entirely in gray except for a red double-decker bus, shows gloomy streets with St. Paul's Cathedral in the background. Another, using the same idea of gray, represents bright yellow flowers amidst bombed ruins, with St. Paul's as the backdrop.

Taking the underground from Putney, where he lives, to South Kensington, where his father works at the Warburg Institute, David is particularly taken by the West Brompton station. In an area where the tunnel had not been rebuilt, and a grimy wartime steam locomotive is switching freight cars in the rail yard beyond, lies a small flower garden tended by the stationmaster. This image becomes the subject of several of his watercolors. His gray paintings of postwar London represent the sorrow he feels in being reminded of his parents' own wartime suffering. Yet, thanks to his mother, he has learned to express these feelings in his art.

Although Elly is never able to make a career as a professional artist as she had hoped, she enjoys painting as hobby. While living in Brunswick, she exhibits her work at several local art shows. Returning to Cambridge following Walter's death, she takes art courses through Harvard's adult education program. These include figure-drawing classes, sketching models, and modern sculpture, using paperclips, staples, and thumbtacks. Developing a close friendship with a Japanese potter, she takes courses in Chinese calligraphy and ink brush painting. Only when she moves back to the Brunswick area in her early eighties, does she gradually give up painting.

As David reaches his mid sixties, he returns to watercolor painting. For the first time, he takes watercolor lessons with an artist who lives nestled on the side of a hill deep in the Maine countryside. For his continued love for painting and the pleasure he gains in visiting galleries, he can only thank his mother.

11

Lured to a European Classic

ON A LATE AUGUST DAY IN 1965, with watercolor pad on his lap, a box of paints and jar of water at his side, and a one-inch brush in his hand, David is sitting on the lawn of the Ecole d'Humanité, high in the Berner Oberland of Switzerland. He is painting a gentle, grassy mountain, the Planplatten, that he climbed as an eleven-year-old boy when visiting the school with his parents during Walter's sabbatical in August 1954. Beyond the mountain rise rugged, snow-covered Alps. As he paints this scene, fond memories arise of him and his mother painting by the Maine coast. He also feels her love and insight.

After his graduation from college in June of 1965, Elly suggests that David spend a year at the Ecole d'Humanité, the former Odenwaldschule that his father had attended when it was still in Germany. Edith, the wife of the founder, is still living at the school, although she has retired from her role as director. Knowing that David has no idea what he wants to do with his life, Elly believes he needs a break from the recent particularly difficult years they have had together in Brunswick. Now that David has graduated from college, she is going to sell the house in which she and Walter raised him, to move back to Cambridge, where she will work at Harvard University's Fogg Museum. In Switzerland with Edith and her husband Paulus, who so loved Walter, Elly feels David will be in good hands. Maybe, she thinks, he will use the experience of teaching at this idealistic school as an opportunity to find out whether teaching is what he really wants to do.

On the fourth morning since his arrival at the Ecole d'Humanité, David attends the first teachers' meeting of the school year. He is sitting at one of the several tables arranged in a semicircle looking out large windows across the deep valley, the Haslital, below. He is enthralled to see the snow-covered peaks of the *Mönch*, *Eiger*, *Jungfrau*, and *Wetterhorn* glistening in the morning sun of late summer. They seem so close—as if they were merely a mile or so away. Hearing the door open, he turns to watch a young woman in a black dress enter the room—late. Shoulder-length, dark-brown hair pushed behind her ears frames gray-blue eyes on a pimply face. Self-conscious, she looks toward the floor.

Getting to know her, he soon learns that Esther Bircher is an artistic child prodigy. She is also a talented pianist. A creative yet disciplined teacher, adored by her students, she cultivates the arts with small children while exploring literature through pantomime, dance, and other forms of movement.

David feels comfortable with her. After all, she is European—though not Jewish—and reflects the heritage his parents inherited and handed down to him. She comes from a family that has been devoted to humanity. Her melancholy persona attracts him; she seems mysterious, creative, and a loner like himself. Her grandfather, Dr. Max Bircher-Benner, founded the Bircher-Benner Clinic in Zurich, that focuses on natural foods to nurture both physical and spiritual health.

Only toward the end of the school year does their friendship begin to flourish. In spite of his inability to teach effectively and control students, the school director, Armin Luethi, kindly allows David to spend a second year at the Ecole. Esther helps him develop his history classes into lessons to which his students can relate. She also assists him prepare his case for conscientious objection, so that he will be able to do alternative service instead of being drafted into the Vietnam War. To this end, Esther introduces him to the work of the German educator Rudolf Dreikurs, to whom she and David refer in his application. He familiarizes Esther with the

Esther Bircher-Solmitz, Mercer, Maine

works of his intellectual mentors Ralph Waldo Emerson and Henry David Thoreau, and with William James' essay *The Moral Equivalent of War*—given him by his father—all of which influence their thinking as they draft his petition.

As Esther and David become closer, to his dismay his mother decides to visit him at the Ecole d'Humanité at the beginning of the summer vacation. Together the two of them will travel to Paris and Amsterdam. Although mother and son have been corresponding regularly by mail throughout the year, David is surprised by her firm announcement of her intention to visit. Especially since he has a girlfriend with whom he wants to spend the summer, at age twenty-three he has no desire to travel together with his mother. Of course, he doesn't take into consideration that it was Elly's idea that he go to Switzerland in the first place, and that she made all the arrangements and paid for the trip.

Prior to Elly's arrival, Edith Geheeb calls David to her living quarters on the second floor of the school's main building, *das Haupthaus*, a large wooden chalet.

"I understand that you and Esther are spending much time together, yes?" she asks.

"Yes," David replies, feeling uncomfortable in the presence of this strong, elderly woman.

"My dear, you need to be very careful with Esther. A long-term relationship and the possibility of marriage will not be good for you."

David feels faint. He reels with anxiety and holds back anger. *What right does this old woman have to interfere in my life?* He remains mute.

"You see, Esther is melancholy person. You are attracted to her because she reminds you of our dear Walter. You need to be with someone who is more cheerful. She will drag you down."

With slumped shoulders and eyes glued to the floor, he leaves Edith's room, trying to ignore her advice. So what, he thinks, if Esther is like his father?

On his mother's arrival, he introduces Esther to her. As she seems cool and unimpressed with Esther, he withdraws into disappointment and anger. *Is she in cahoots with Edith* he wonders? That night, Esther and he spend much of the night together before Elly and David depart the following morning on their trip.

In Paris, they visit with distant relatives of the Solmitz family. In spite of his reservations, David enjoys his time with his mother visiting the cathedrals of Notre Dame and Chartres.

From Amsterdam, where Elly immediately leaves for Denmark,

David hitchhikes to the North Sea. On the beach, he paints with his watercolors, sleeps at a youth hostel, and hitchhikes the next day to Friesland. There he stays with a Dutch family, whose daughter is a *Mithelferin*, staff member, at the Ecole d'Humanité. What an experience to be hosted by a local working-class family! The meals—a breakfast of bread with banana slices and chocolate sprinkles and a lunch of horsemeat sandwiches—delight him. Cycling to and then walking along the dykes gives him more of a feeling for this flat land that so easily could be flooded by the sea, should these earthen walls break. From the little village of Metslawier, he hitchhikes to the German border, whence he takes a train to Hamburg.

In Hamburg he stays with his father's friend, Professor Koelln. David has no interest in seeing the street and house in which his mother grew up, nor the university where his father and Fritz had first met. He is, however, curious to see the street near the harbor that is lined with legal prostitutes. Following a few days in Hamburg, he eagerly heads by train back to the Ecole d'Humanité to be together with Esther.

In December, David announces to his mother that by late summer he will be a father. Somewhat embarrassed and ashamed, David also relishes a certain pride: *I am a stud,* he thinks. Elly writes back immediately without the criticism that he is expecting. Rather, she asks when they will marry and tells him that she has already begun planning to come for the wedding. David tells her that he wants a simple marriage before a justice of the peace without any ceremony, just as his parents had when they wed in Germany on July 1, 1936.

Years later Elly tells David that she and Walter had no choice but to have a simple wedding due to the rise of Nazism.

Following David and Esther's "private" March wedding, Esther's parents host a large party for the young couple, to which they invite Elly.

As David continues to write frequent letters to Elly and sends her postcards from his travels, Esther writes her lengthy, detailed letters as well. Elly appreciates Esther's thoughtful letters, always responding with warmth. She is developing genuine fondness toward her.

Since midwinter the couple have been living with Esther's parents near Zurich. David has quit his job at the Ecole. Although his teaching has improved significantly due to Esther's help, the director of the school seems relieved to let him go. Not only have Esther and David been shacking up at the school, her pregnancy has become obvious.

During this time, David develops a close relationship with Esther's father. This kind man in his early sixties becomes a surrogate for David's father, who had died a few years before. Shortly after Esther introduces David to her parents in early December 1966, Ralph Bircher writes to him in English.

> My dear David,
>
> I understand we are not going to see you before your vacation trip to France, but only afterwards. So I send you my little gift herewith. It is a book about naïve art. I found it charming and hope you will enjoy it too.
>
> We wish you heaps of luck and happiness. I'm sure you will do your best to make my Esther happy and that she may unfold the riches lying in her, and hope she will do the same with you.
>
> I liked you instantly and am anxious to learn more about you and get really acquainted with you.
>
> Yours with love,
>
> Ralph Bircher

David and Ralph are able to share their most personal thoughts, an experience David rarely had with his own father. Dr. Bircher is the theoretical director of the Bircher-Benner Clinic that his father had founded and directed. As the years pass, Ralph publishes several of David's essays on education in his monthly journal *Der Wendepunkt* (The Turning-Point). As both David and his father-in-law are interested in alternative lifestyles, they travel together to spend a few days at a tiny abandoned mountain village in the Tessin, the Italian part of Switzerland, to visit young hippies who have established a commune there.

In June 1967, Esther and David sail from Rotterdam to America on the final voyage of the *Nieuw Amsterdam.* Elly meets them at the pier in New York. On the way to Cambridge, they stop for lunch at a Howard Johnson's restaurant. Esther finds the artificially colored green peas revolting, as well as the rubbery hamburger patty and instant mashed potatoes. What a disappointing beginning for Esther!

Shortly after their arrival, they celebrate Esther's July 25th birthday. At Elly's suggestion, he buys her *The Joy of Cooking* and inscribes it *for many years of joyous cooking.* David can't comprehend why Esther seems humiliated by his birthday gift.

Although David doesn't have any specific plans as to how he will support his new family, it never occurs to him to remain in Switzerland. Nor does he ever ask Esther about her feelings in coming to "his" country, meaning of course the state of Maine. Although he has saved enough money for the trip back home, Esther's parents and Elly help the young couple with additional costs. David takes it for granted that Esther and he can stay with Elly in her Cambridge apartment until their baby is born and he has found a job. During this time Elly is working full-time as a secretary for Professor Landes of Harvard's history department, translating German for him and typing his books.

David finally figures he will try to get a job with the antipoverty project he had started during his senior year as a Bowdoin student. By now it is a federally-funded project operated by the Office of Economic Opportunity. Should he fail to find a job through this avenue, there is a teacher shortage in Maine—he surely could find a high-school teaching post there. After all, he imagines public school students must be better behaved than those in an alternative boarding school like the Ecole d'Humanité.

On August 1, 1967, Swiss Independence Day, David and Esther's son Oliver is born. On returning home from the hospital, David receives a phone call from none other than Jane, a former girlfriend, who happens to be in Cambridge. He invites her over to meet his family, picking her up at Harvard Square. She seems uninterested in his wife and newborn son. After Jane's departure, Esther is furious with him. "How could you invite your former girlfriend over at this time? What's wrong with you?" David believes there is no need for Esther to feel angry or even jealous because the feelings he once had toward Jane as a high-school student and college freshman have long since dissipated.

Esther and Elly take care of Oliver—not only when David is on the road seeking employment, but also when he is at home. Elly immediately develops a close bond with Oliver, falling in love with him. David doesn't mind that his mother is more involved with his son's life than he is; he has other things on his mind: finding a job, a place to live and a car to drive.

He experiences no sensations of guilt or humility for being penniless and living off his mother—amazing for a person who usually seems to be obsessed by pangs of unnecessary guilt. Only later does he realize that his mother's fondness for Oliver is transference of her own love for him. After all, he has disappointed her greatly. Their once close relationship has become quite distant. In reality, he is not only relying on her, but also using her to take care of his new family and himself, at least until they are settled.

David finally lands a job as a community worker with the antipoverty project he started before leaving for Switzerland. The new family of three moves to the village of Topsham, directly across the river from his hometown. Esther is clearly not happy in their new life together, but she and David do not talk about her concerns and her fears at all. She feels alone and alienated in America. Her family and friends are in Switzerland. She no longer has a career as teacher. She doesn't have a piano on which to continue to practice. After all, she is an accomplished pianist. Furthermore, she has an unplanned baby for which she takes nearly full responsibility. David feels that in his role as the man of the family, he is solely responsible as the family breadwinner.

During their first months of living in their small, second-floor apartment in Topsham, he fails to understand why Esther isn't overjoyed when he surprises her by coming home with a newly purchased ironing board. Believing this to be a thoughtful present, he obviously hasn't learned from the cookbook experience that Esther does not relish the domestic role he has placed her in. Nor can he understand why she resents his buying an ice-cream cone for a client of his, an attractive young woman and single mother with whom he is working on developing a cookbook for low-income families.

Years later, David begins to understand Esther's feelings. He is a late developer, an immature young man not yet ready to be a husband and a father. In a way, he is following in his mother's footsteps. She grew up in a culture and a time when wives were expected to serve their husbands. However, in own her marriage she was the more practical and tenacious partner. Maybe because she realized that she had to take care of and advocate for her husband, a man she truly did love and admire, she subjugated any frustration and anger she may have felt toward him by instead idolizing him and placing him on pedestal.

Having grown up with this dynamic between his parents, David expects at least subconsciously that Esther will treat him the same way. As Esther perceives that he is using his mother as a model in regards to his expectations for a wife, tensions arise between them. Furthermore, David is still his mother's sheltered little boy who submits to her suggestions. Rather than listening to Esther on how to raise Oliver, he pays more attention to Elly: *Mummy always knows best.* While they are living with her in Cambridge, for instance, she gives the couple a book on childcare by a well-known pediatrician, Barry Brazelton, and sets up an appointment with the doctor for Oliver to be checked and for the couple to gain advice on child rearing. Both Esther and David find Dr. Brazelton rather cold and uninterested in Oliver and themselves. Later, when it appears that Oliver has a lazy eye, Elly arranges for the couple to travel down from Maine to see her ophthalmologist in Cambridge, the son of Jewish refugees. He eventually does surgery on Oliver's eye at Boston's Eye and Ear Infirmary.

Over the years, Esther and David slowly learn to communicate better with each other. She joins a women's group and he a men's group. These experiences help David to listen more attentively and compassionately to Esther. Yet, whenever Elly visits, he feels as if he is still a child under her control and becomes tense and irritable. Esther is annoyed at his passivity, sheepishness, irritability, and distance from her. As a result, his mother's visits are spoiled by tensions among the three of them.

At the same time, David resents that Elly constantly talks with pride about her friends at Harvard, all cultured people who are interesting and interested in scholarly thought, who appreciate art and music. David believes that his mother views him as nonintellectual and uncultured. He rationalizes that in her eyes he is inferior to her Harvard friends, yet he also feels guilty for letting his mother down. After all, he did poorly in college. He never will become a great scholar and wise humanist like his father, nor as well-cultured as her Harvard friends. Instead, he has become a lowly high-school teacher who has difficulty disciplining his students in a small rural, central Maine mill town.

When Esther and David decide to join others in starting an alternative school—part of the free school movement of the late sixties—for Oliver to attend, Elly supports their efforts. She likes the teacher whom they hire and is pleased that Oliver is happy at school, a far cry from her own schooling experience. Having settled in central Maine, where David teaches high school, Esther and he develop friendships among the hippie culture, city folk their age who have forsaken the metropolis to live off the land. Elly looks down on this counterculture folk. Even though they are college educated, she cannot understand why they have alienated themselves from the vibrant society that she enjoys in Cambridge. "I have nothing in common with these people. There is nothing we can talk about," she laments. Although she understands their motives in giving up the comforts and convenience of an urban lifestyle for simpler ways, she dislikes their torn and dirty jeans, soiled plaid flannel shirts, and "unwashed bodies" as well as their "unkempt" hair.

Esther doesn't continue her drawing and painting in Maine, blaming her father for having pushed her art talent during her childhood too much. Instead, she devotes her creative energy to playing the piano. Her father has her upright piano sent from Switzerland to their first apartment in Topsham, Maine. Ropes and pulleys were needed to lift the piano through a large window of the upstairs apartment located in the back of a mid-1800s farmhouse.

Only seven years later, after the young family moves into an abandoned 1820 farmhouse on 148 acres in Norridgewock, Maine, that they restore according to Esther's detailed design, does she finally find the time and joy to play the piano. She purchases a baby grand piano on which she practices several hours daily. Together with a pediatric surgeon who is a cellist, and a flutist from a nearby college, she forms a trio, the Belgrade Chamber Players. The group quickly gains recognition as top-rated classical musicians. David is envious that Esther appears to be devoting more and more of her time and energy to her music and less to Oliver and Ruben, their younger son, and himself. Then, on May 14, 1977, on the afternoon before the day she is to give a recital on a harpsichord that she had commissioned from a local artisan, she is killed in a head-on car crash. She was on her way to her lesbian lover, who was also from the Canton of Zurich in Switzerland. Ruben is thrown from her car, his head landing on the black asphalt.

12

Tomorrow's Wedding

EIGHT MONTHS AFTER THE ACCIDENT, IN THE early evening of February 19, 1978, sitting next to her on the side of their bed, David laments: "I can't go on with this. I want to cancel tomorrow's wedding."

She remains emotionless.

"I just don't think I am ready to get married again."

She says nothing.

David continues, "I can cancel those we invited." Her passivity aggravates his rage; his blood seethes and curdles in his veins. He throws his arms in the air, sighs, not daring to actually say the words: "It's over."

David remembers May 14, 1977, a clear, cool, blustery afternoon. Esther left with Ruben an hour or so ago on her way to visit Christina, her lover. Like Esther, Christina grew up in Switzerland. In fact, she was raised directly across Lake Zurich from the little town of Erlenbach where Esther lived with her parents, sister, and two brothers.

Lately, their lesbian relationship has become tenuous, as Christina has grown increasingly dependent on her husband. Christina had undergone a kidney transplant that past winter; now back at home, Charles, her husband, routinely hooks her up to the dialysis machine to carry out the procedure to purify her blood.

David and Oliver remain at their 1820 farm atop Wilder Hill, cleaning the yard for tomorrow, Sunday, when Esther is to give a dedication concert for the harpsichord she had commissioned. Oliver, age nine, is accompanied by Craig and Scholl, family friends who are preparing a garden on land belonging to Esther and David. As a dark-blue police car pulls into the farm's crescent driveway, Oliver comes over to David. "Did Shane bite somebody again?" he asks, speaking of the big white dog they adopted from a couple who left the area. "Did he steal the Wilders' chickens again?"

A young officer gets out of the car. Walking slowly with head lowered to where David and Oliver are standing with Shane nearby, the officer says, barely audibly, "You are Mr. Solmitz?"

"Yes," David replies.

"I, ah, have bad news . . ." he says as thoughts run through David's mind. *What did Shane do now? Will we have to put him to sleep?* "Your wife was killed in a car crash near Farmington."

Oliver throws himself prostrate onto the ground.

"And your son has been transported to the Lewiston hospital."

Craig and Scholl, witnessing the scene from a slight distance, run over. Scholl grabs Oliver, hugging him, while Craig gently caresses his head and back. As the officer departs, Scholl, holding Oliver tightly, tells David that she and Craig will take Oliver to their tiny home so that David can take care of whatever needs to be done.

David immediately calls the Lewiston hospital. His call is transferred to Dr. Swengel, the neurosurgeon, who has already drilled burr holes in Ruben's skull to relieve pressure from his swelling brain.

"Your son is in a coma."

"What happened?"

"He was thrown from the car and landed on his head."

"Will he survive?"

"That I can't say."

"What are his chances for recovery?"

"Slim."

"Maybe it is best that you pull the plug."

"No, that I cannot do." The doctor hangs up.

Earlier that cold, gray February afternoon, David and his girlfriend Sally have been baking their three-layered, white wedding cake with white frosting—three heart-shaped cakes with the smallest at the top. As they are mixing the batter, David recalls the evolution of his cowardly betrayal of Oliver.

He had been visiting Ruben every day at the Lewiston hospital, over an hour's drive each way. There he developed a friendship with Sally, an intensive care unit nurse who lovingly had taken care of Ruben. She even knit him booties. As the spring progressed into early and then mid summer, she invited David and Oliver to visit her, her three-year-old son, and her mother at the cottage they rent on Swans Island, off the Maine coast. He had fantasized that eventually he and she would buy a little cottage by the sea on this island inhabited by generations of fishing folk. Marrying a native Mainer, whose family for generations grew up on this island, and who can trace her roots back to the *Mayflower*, appealed to David. He was keenly aware and saddened that he and his family were rootless.

As he thinks guiltily about his behavior toward Oliver, his memory trickles back to Margaret, one of his sophomores at Madison High School, Madison, Maine. She is without a doubt one of his best students, and her older sister, Elizabeth, had been valedictorian of her class. Margaret once told David that her parents were divorced. It was now hard for her to go home. Why? he wants to know.

"You see, my dad took me on this trip I thought was just for him and me. But it turned out we went to see his new girlfriend," she explained matter-of-factly.

"Yes," David responded, feeling a little shaken. "You felt betrayed. You must be terribly hurt." He wondered at the time how a father can be so cruel to his daughter. But now he begins to understand.

Ruben (left) and Oliver Solmitz, summer 1974, Norridgewock, Maine

On a warm mid-June day, about a month after the accident, he suggests to Oliver that tomorrow they go on a camping trip to Swans Island.

"We'll take the car to Bass Harbor, where we'll board the ferry, car and all, for the trip to the island," he explains to Oliver. "It's about an hour's ride across Penobscot Bay."

Oliver likes the idea. He is a rather shy boy, a loner, who loves the outdoors. His straight, sand-colored hair reaches to the nape of his neck. Due to a lazy eye, he wears brown-rimmed glasses. Beneath the black suspenders that hold up his jeans, he sports a light-blue T-shirt. He also has on his favorite shoes, well-worn work boots that he regularly treats with mink oil.

"Shall we take our watercolors along," David suggests, "so we can paint the rugged scenery of the island? We can also hike along the cliffs and hopefully find a grassy knoll overlooking the sea."

With a faint smile, Oliver expresses his approval and excitement.

They pack some food, their tent, and their sleeping bags into their metallic-blue 1973 Plymouth van. Early in the morning, following a hearty breakfast of oatmeal, they depart for Bass Harbor to catch the 10:00 a.m. ferry.

Although Oliver rarely speaks, both enjoy the drive together. Silently, they absorb the beauty of the wild blue, purple, and pink lupines growing along the roadside and spreading deep into lush summer fields. Puffy clouds passing silently yet quickly cast dark shadows on the fields and woods below. Just before crossing the long, green suspension bridge high over the Penobscot River, they stop in Knox to admire the bridge, a graceful engineering marvel constructed in the 1930s.

Arriving at Bass Harbor, they purchase their tickets and drive onto the dock to await their turn to drive aboard the ferry. On embarking, they clamber out of their van, climb the narrow, steep steps to the ship's bridge where they peek through the open door to watch the captain maneuver the ferry away from the dock and out of the harbor on their way to the island. They gaze at the sea below as the ship plows through gentle swells of Prussian-blue velvet. They spot lobster boats close to the shore and trawlers, as they advance toward the open sea. A sloop under full sail, which surely belongs to a summer resident, overtakes them. Islands seem to pass by as if their ferry were not moving.

They disembark on Swans Island and proceed down the main road looking for a little road that might take them to a picturesque spot where they can have a picnic lunch and paint the scenery. Finding a rocky ledge overlooking the open sea, parking the van as close to the side of the narrow road as possible, they grab their insulated lunch bag as well as their paints, water, and paper. They find a perfect spot on the rocks on which to settle. After munching on tuna-fish sandwiches and apples and each relishing a Hershey chocolate bar for dessert, they settle down to paint. Both of them concentrate on the rock-bound coast, the dark spruce trees growing tall and straight from the shallow soil above the ledges overlooking a calm sea and distant islands. David observes Oliver, who dips his brush into his jar of water and then skillfully mixes various shades of green before making broad strokes on the blank white pad to bring spruce trees to life. Upon completing their pictures and standing each up against a small rock to admire their masterpieces, David breaks the news to Oliver:

"You know Sally," he says without looking Oliver in the eye, "the nurse caring for Ruben?"

"Yeah," he replies without interest.

"Well, she, her three-year-old son, and her mother are spending a few days on the island. Is it OK if we stop by to visit them?"

What can Oliver say? His face drops. That should have been enough for David to say to him, "No, we won't visit them." But he has already made arrangements to visit her. Hell, he is lonely. He desperately wants a woman. Ah, but Sally isn't just any woman. She's the one who crocheted little booties for Ruben as if she were his mother—

Ignoring Oliver's sad face and blocking his own feelings of guilt, David walks with his son back to the van. Oliver trudges behind with lowered head, his shoes scuffing on the loose gravel. Once in the van, they drive back to the main road to look for the little roadway that leads to the cottage that Sally and her mother are renting.

As they slowly drive along the only major tarred road of the island, David carefully looks to the left for the narrow, dirt way with two tracks divided by a hump of grass that will take them to the cottage. He finally spots the trail-like road amidst a grove of stately evergreen trees. Cautiously, he meanders through the serene forest, between the moss-covered rocks, the soft bed of fallen needles covering rich, black earth, and the tall firs and spruce hovering over them. Within moments the tunnel of trees opens up to a view of a grassy perimeter bordering a rocky beach, beyond which the gently rolling sea fades into a cloudless sky.

As the leave the woods, a cottage of weathered, gray cedar shakes and turquoise trim appears on their right. It is nestled on a grassy patch

Justin Solmitz

backed by a forest of healthy conifers and facing a small rocky beach, beyond which the sea lolls peacefully.

Hearing their van pull up, Justin, a stocky three-year-old with blonde hair falling into his eyes, bounces out of the cottage, letting the wooden frame screen door slam behind him. Running to David and Oliver's car, he shouts a happy "Hi."

They climb out—David from the driver's seat and Oliver from the two-hinged doors on the passenger side of the van. As Justin quickly leads them to the cottage, Oliver keeps a remote distance from David, though in no way leaving sight of him and never more than five paces away.

Although Oliver does follow David into the house, Justin almost immediately grabs his hand urging him down to the rocky beach. Before reluctantly trailing Justin out of the door, Oliver takes one quick glance over his shoulder at David as if to say, "You are betraying me."

Following an introduction to Sally's mother and a little small talk, Sally and David decide to take the boys to the head of the island. Here, a few feet back from steep cliffs that rise high above the sea, a white lighthouse still focuses its bright beam as it has for over a hundred years, warning ships of the dangerous rocky outcrops and sharp, knifelike ledges. Justin, who is the first to spring out of the van, runs toward the cliffs, scaring both Sally and David.

Imagining that Sally and he might someday be living together, David is quick to firmly warn Justin that, not only is such wild behavior dangerous, it is also unacceptable. The entire time Oliver keeps a safe distance, not just from the cliffs, but also from Sally and David.

After returning to the cottage for a simple supper, Sally directs the duo to a lovely, protected spot at the edge of a wood overlooking a peaceful bay with the open sea in the distance. She reminds David that camping on the island is forbidden; however, she assures him that they won't be discovered.

As David and Oliver begin to take the tent out of its bag, unfold it, and string the poles together, Oliver comes to life. He takes charge of the entire operation, giving David directions primarily with non-verbal cues. David promises him that they will be alone for the night and for the next day as well. They will travel around the island, walk along the ledges before taking the ferry home.

Thirty years later, David recalls his feelings regarding Margaret's father's betrayal of her, and wonders how he could possibly have been so self-centered and selfish as to think only for himself and not of Oliver. In fact, it has taken nearly that long for the two to become close again. In the meantime, Oliver married and fathered two sons. Now divorced, he remains dedicated and intensely involved in raising his boys. Although he continues to be attracted to the opposite sex, he remains mistrustful of women. No wonder: he lost his mother twice—first she favored his younger brother, Ruben, and then she was killed in a car crash. David, of course, feels guilty for betraying Oliver by marrying Sally. Oliver and Sally never got along.

On that evening in February 1978, David debates with himself as to how he can make his difficult announcement. He wonders why he ever proposed to Sally. Following the accident, he wanted to carry on his life as if nothing had happened. He knew then and he knows now that it was both irrational and wrong to jump so quickly following a life-changing disaster into a new relationship. Elly had made that clear to him, and ever since he was a child, Elly had warned him when he might be doing wrong. On his acknowledging a mistake to Elly, she would say, *Mummy knows.*

He feels guilty for giving in to Sally's request to not invite his mother to the wedding. He knows his decision is hurting her terribly. It was Elly who took David and his pregnant wife Esther into her home when he returned to the United States in July 1967 without a job or a home. From the moment Oliver was born, Elly developed a close and lasting bond with him. It was Elly who took loving care of Oliver and his mother when David was job hunting in Maine. It was Elly who helped the young couple to get onto their feet financially.

Yet Elly and Sally dislike each other from the very beginning. When Elly visits some weeks after the accident, she is surprised to find a new woman and her son staying at the house. David hadn't even told his mother that the two would be there. God forbid, they even spend the night. To her, particularly at this point, caring for Oliver is of most importance: "After all, he has lost his mother. And now you are involved with another woman. You surely will find a better woman." She complains that "his friend" is uneducated, not intellectual, and therefore uninterested in the world of ideas. She adds, "This woman is using you. You are financially secure, own your home. She knows you will be a good father to her wild three-year-old." As much as David is upset and angry at his mother for interfering in his newfound relationship, he knows she is once again right.

He also feels guilty toward Oliver, who had broken his legs a few days before the wedding while on a school-organized ski trip. Sally has never taken a liking to him, shows no sympathy following his accident. Although Oliver never complains as he limps about on crutches, he seems to get on her nerves. She doesn't treat him as a mother would. David wishes she would pamper Oliver as Elly had when, as a child, he was sick, for instance with the mumps, measles, and the flu. If he kicks Sally out, at least Oliver will be happy. At least he'll have his Dad back.

Obsessed by guilt, David can't kick Sally out, not with her cute, blonde, blue-eyed, good-natured and hyperactive three-year-old son. Justin has bonded nicely with Oliver, and David has promised to adopt him. David worries how Justin would take the emotional blow. He would be badly hurt.

He wonders how in complete sincerity he could design their wedding rings—two golden bands, each with a single continuous evergreen branch. Does he really intend that their life together will remain evergreen until separated by death? The design of their wedding announcement that he created, a linoleum cut of the ring design, bears the same message. He also wrote their marriage contract, that focuses on open and honest communication to assure an evergreen life together:

Always show each other affection—be it a gentle touch, a friendly look into each other's eyes.

Express appreciation of the other person—notice when he/she has done something, crocheted, painted a picture, done a chore about the house such as tidying up a room.

Be constantly aware of the other's feelings and be able to respond adequately to them.

Listen carefully and empathetically—as to the details of one's day, be it at home or at work and be especially careful to be able to let the other fully release all pent-up feelings.

Never withdraw—when one withdraws, the other should reach out with a little affection, a hug, at the least a gentle stroke.

Encourage the other to express fully what is bothering her/him.

When disturbed by the other person, tell her/him; however, tactfully and at an appropriate time/place, i.e. not when the other is anxious. But never let the irritation go un-passed; the earlier it can be dealt with, the easier it can be resolved.

When angry or uptight, express the feelings. Leave discussion of the problems to a time when cooled off. To release tension go for a walk, pound a pillow, write into one's journal. When able to talk, find out the reasons for the anger and attempt to achieve a solution agreeable to both.

Have lots of fun with each other—joke (but not sarcastically), wrestle, go out of doors frequently, walk, ski, swim, read together, often do light and lively things.

Respect and appreciate each other's independence and give each other support in such areas as work, special projects, hobbies, and individual friendships.

Be able to take time for oneself—either time one needs alone or time and attention one needs from the other.

Encourage expression of children's emotions appropriate to the situation, respect their needs and feelings, further participation in daily activities of the family, and partake in frequent family activities.

David feels irritated and frustrated that Sally makes no suggestions for changes to *his* document. She accepts it passively.

By the time the cake is baked and decorated, the boys fed and sent to bed, the evening passes quickly. He has to make his decision.

He imagines what may happen when his old friend, Maurice Cobb, a Unitarian minister, will raise the question: *Will you willingly marry her?* At that moment will he be able to announce to everybody's dismay a firm "*no*?" A flurry of gasps would erupt. People who have stood silently would begin to move uneasily. Would Sally's mother's and sister's mouths drop before they can let loose their anger? Would his friends lose respect for him? Would each take their gifts and cards of congratulations and warm wishes back with them? Certainly, he wouldn't want to keep them.

David also recognizes he needs Sally. Without her, how would the two boys get back and forth to the New Day School, the alternative "free" school Esther, he, and several others had created—a forty-minute drive one way? She is committed to driving them in the mornings, he to picking them up after he finishes his teaching day in Madison.

If Ruben is to get better, he needs round-the-clock care by a nurse. David remembers how touched he was to see that Sally had knitted booties for Ruben within days of his arrival into the hospital's intensive care unit. She had been on duty in the ICU when Ruben was transferred there comatose that afternoon in May.

David recalls his gratitude to Sally, when, on a dark early December Friday, as winter is approaching, they bring Ruben home for the weekend. He is unable to walk, has to be carried, is spastic, and cannot communicate either verbally or with bodily gestures. This is not the lively, intelligent, outgoing five-year-old who had begun to read with pleasure, enjoyed being with friends, and was adored by classmates and teachers alike at the New Day School.

On a typically raw morning later that month, David and Sally pick up Ruben at Clearview Pediatric Center in nearby Fairfield to bring him to the rehabilitation institute in Newton, Massachusetts. They have prepared the back seat of David's VW Golf (for which he has traded his Plymouth van) for Ruben with pillows and blankets. He is properly supported and able to look out the car windows.

Upon their arrival at the dirtied yellow-brick facility with painted concrete floors, the social worker to whom they are assigned is cold and discouraging. If Ruben doesn't make significant progress in six weeks, he will be sent back to Clearview. David feels helpless. Why didn't the doctor pull the plug as he had requested? No matter how much loving care he will receive, Ruben will suffer until he dies. At least, Sally will be there to care for him. What a relief.

Days before the wedding, David receives a letter followed up by a phone call explaining that Ruben is not making sufficient progress. Sally and he will have to come to Newton to pick Ruben up and return him to Clearview. The diagnosis is *no change.* "We must direct our efforts to those children who will improve," the same social worker explains to David and Sally. David feels angry, dejected, and rejected. The threesome leaves the Institute for the trip back to Maine.

At a roadside restaurant along Route 1 in Danvers, they stop for lunch. Carrying Ruben into the restaurant brings curious stares and frowns from customers and wait staff. David wants to scream: "Don't stare! Do you know how that makes him feel? Lay off!"

He controls his rage and sorrow, as he watches Sally patiently and with a gentle smile feed Ruben one French fry at a time. He drools as he tries to chew the greasy, deep-fired potato dipped into ketchup. After leaving him at Clearview Pediatric Center, David realizes the only way he can care for Ruben in his home is to have Sally there for him round the clock.

Sitting on the bed, David feels time running out. Sally sits without saying a word. He is restless, frantic, yet quiet. Yes, he expressed regrets in his journal over initiating marriage. However, he did invite Sally and her three-year-old son to move in with him and Oliver less than four months after the crash; therefore, marrying her is the *right* thing to do. He apologizes to Sally. The wedding is on. The day after the marriage ceremony, Sally and David take a short honeymoon to New York City, while Sally's mother looks after Justin and Oliver.

During the next months both David and Sally frequently visit Ruben at Clearview. On occasion they bring him home for a weekend. Lovingly, she cares for him. By May he is able with some difficulty to pedal a low-riding plastic tricycle. Although he still cannot talk, he is making progress. David and Sally have a PET (Pupil Evaluation Team) meeting with the superintendent of the local school district. The school is willing to provide specialized training for him. David finally begins to feel some hope for Ruben, though he is sadly aware that he never will be a normal child again, never to become the promising individual into which he appeared to be developing so well.

Then, on the afternoon of May 31, 1978, he receives a phone call from Clearview. "Your son has been transported to Thayer Hospital. He experienced heatstroke while outside in the sun at our swimming pool."

Later that night, he and his wife are awakened by the phone. Reaching for the receiver, he sleepily says hello.

"This is the nurse at Thayer Hospital's ICU. Your son aspirated. He passed away about 11:00."

"He what?"

"He died."

"How is that possible?"

"We kept him in our isolation unit. This happened suddenly."

David, Sally, Oliver, and Justin bury Ruben next to his mother beneath a huge, ancient pine in the little old family graveyard behind their 1820 farm. As was done for Esther, the three travel to the old slate quarry in Monson, where they find a piece of slate. They bring the stone to an engraver located in South Portland. He is the last craftsman in Maine who still engraves by hand with a hammer and chisel. A quote from *Curious George* is inscribed on the stone.

Within three weeks Sally announces to David that she is pregnant. How could that be? She is on the pill. They never discussed the possibility of having a child. He is not ready to raise another child from birth. Now Ruben is gone. He could be free. He feels trapped, distant from her, and angry with himself for not having said *no* when he had the chance.

Driven by fear, a guilt complex, fantasy for freedom, and cowardice, David seems unable to take charge of his life. The freedom for which he yearns is out of reach. Tensions between David, his wife, and his mother intensify. Both his mother and he favor Oliver.

David always has felt close to Oliver, who has similar likes and dislikes to his own. Ever since Oliver was a toddler, father and son built roads in the sand with toy construction vehicles, just as David had during his childhood. When Oliver was three, they moved from an apartment in Madison, Maine, where David was teaching high school, to tiny Mercer village. There David and Esther bought a deteriorating 1830s Greek revival house atop a little knoll by the mill pond. Oliver enjoyed being alone outside. Walking in the woods with David, feeling soft moss with his hands, helping his father prepare the soil and plant a vegetable garden gave him pleasure. By age six he was helping farmer James next door shoveling cow manure from the gutter in his barn. That summer he helped David dismantle a rotting shed attached to the house. When Oliver was seven, David and Esther sold their Mercer homestead for the farm on top of Wilder Hill in nearby Norridgewock. By this time Oliver enjoyed drawing scenes of nature and later of his horse. He was quiet, a loner, more like his dad. Ruben on the other hand was quick, sharp-witted, energetic, and quite social.

Sally resents the fact that David and Elly favor Oliver over Justin. Naturally, this draws Oliver closer to his father. David refuses to acknowledge his favoritism to Oliver.

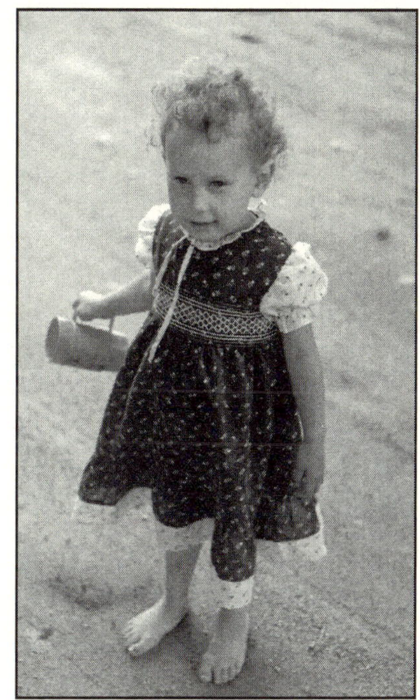

SONNET SOLMITZ

Sally insists that Elly treat their children equally. She becomes furious when Elly signs frequent letters to Oliver "with all my love" while sending postcards to Sally's son and later to their daughter Sonnet, born in January 1979, only "love." She begrudges Elly for inviting Oliver to her home in Cambridge several times a year and not inviting her son Justin.

David feels caught in the middle. He feels obligated to support his wife. Yet he feels guilty letting his mother down. Adding to his guilt, Elly reminds him of a Chinese saying: *When a son marries, he abandons his mother.* This is exactly what he has done. And, to a certain extent, he has also abandoned his son. As much as he favors Oliver, he fails to defend him against his stepmother's wrath. In fact, he now supports Sally in preventing him from continuing to see his only grandmother. At the same time, David consciously tries to accept and treat each of his three children equally.

As tensions escalate between Sally, Elly, and David, David initiates an ugly and hurtful exchange of letters and phone calls with his mother. Beginning in early November of 1977, he writes a letter to his mother concerning:

> The tensions that exist between us. They have caused both of us to be badly hurt by each other. I tried to understand your concerns: that I made a wrong decision to live with a young woman so soon who has a child of her own; that Oliver after losing his mother

needs a father more than ever; that he is not getting that attention because of my relationship with S. and another child in the house. *Yes, Mummy knows.*

He then defends his new wife.

You should understand Sally's feelings, too. She moved up here just a few days before you came for the Labor Day weekend. She immediately felt that you found it hard to accept the fact that she was living here, that you, who never felt you could marry after Daddy's death, now had a son who has taken a woman and child into Esther's home so shortly after Esther died. You hadn't had time to deal with just one other major disaster in your life before this change occurred. This made her feel uneasy and also be on the defensive. The fact that you found J. difficult and did not want to have him on a particular afternoon made her feel rejected. She has been hurt many times before, and this was simply another hurt on top of the others, another feeling of rejection. This finally came to a climax at our last visit with you in Cambridge just prior to your departure for England.

Tensions intensify so that in May, 1978, Elly makes an appointment to meet with a psychologist in Waterville to whom David and Sally are bringing Oliver for counseling. On May 19, David writes angrily:

Dear Mother,

Oliver's psychologist told me today that you met with him. Again you interfered in our lives. Again you tactlessly interfered behind our backs. If you are *really* concerned about reconciling our differences, you finally blew it now. What gives you the audacity to interfere so destructively in our lives? As of now, until further notice, relations between you and my entire family are severed. You may NOT see Ruben this summer. You may NOT telephone at our home at all. If necessary, I am prepared to take legal action.

David

On May 22, 1978, Elly writes back:

You are not yourself. You used to be kind and sensitive. Now you are cruel and vicious. You are sick. You are not the way you

> used to be. If Walter, your father, knew what kind of son you had become, he would be terribly unhappy. All of this is your fault. I wanted to be friends with Sally. She didn't want me at your wedding. I sent you a wedding present. You didn't even acknowledge it. You twist around everything I say. That is so clear through your letter. You need help.

She is right, but, alas, David doesn't realize her wisdom at the time. Although he and she continue to communicate and to see each other, resentment and anger are still on the front burner. Yet, Elly always ends her letters on a positive note even when, for instance, she asks, "Who is more hurt, you or I?"

> Spring is here in all its glory. Landes [the professor for whom she worked at Harvard] is in Zurich and I am at ease and can do things I have to and want to do . . . Maybe I could do something with Justin on Saturday and with Oliver on Sunday. If you want to see me, needless to say, I'd be happy, but I leave it to you.
>
> My best to you all,
>
> Mother

As David reads carbon copies of these letters many years later, tears come to his eyes. How could he have been so cruel? Why did he keep this file? Was he paranoid? Well, maybe. Elly had always kept a tight paper trail—gathering and keeping documents—a necessity for her and Walter to escape from Germany. Perhaps he learned this habit from her. Of course, Germans, especially the Nazis, were known to have been precise keepers of records.

David documented phone calls and retained letters to and from his mother, should it be necessary to defend and even excuse his actions toward her. He refused to admit to himself that *Mummy might be right.* Therefore, he even kept letters that he sent to Nellie, a close family friend originally from Braunschweig, whom he asked to act as a mediator for them. He did not then realize that in this instance, he had preserved an accurate record of his own viciousness.

Was he also driven by fear? Fear of women? Fear of rejection? Maybe. Anyway, as he was submissive to his mother, he was acquiescent to his wife. Therefore, in the process of avoiding rejection, and always demanding acceptance, he was destroying his relationship with his mother and distancing himself emotionally from his wife.

In a letter to David written October 13, 1980, on yellow, lined paper, Elly confirms her loneliness, the pain that her only child has brought to her, her incredible strength, honesty, and wisdom:

> I'm 70 years old and seem to be able to cope with life—overcoming to some degree Walter's illness and death, Esther's and Ruben's and my parents' tragic death in Theresienstadt. The pain always lurks in the back of my mind, and the loneliness is great. The loneliness is increased by my estrangement with my only son David. What went wrong? Where am I to blame?
>
> We have always been close. Maybe Walter's illness brought us closer. After Walter's death when David came back to Brunswick and went to Bowdoin, his concern about me seemed great. I didn't want to have a 19-year-old son feel so responsible for his mother, and I made it a point that he should have all the freedom he could, hardly ever going out with him to concerts, plays etc. Also, it was I who suggested out of this concern that David should be entirely on his own, and it was also my suggestion for him to go to Switzerland to teach. A cousin of mine said, "If he'll go to Switzerland, you must expect that he'll marry a European girl." He did—I liked Esther very much and later learned to love her. There were the usual misunderstandings between daughter-in-law and mother-in-law. Here Walter would have been a tremendous help—I've always been very grateful that she wanted a good relationship with me and their children. O. was born soon after they came back from Switzerland and stayed with me. It has been a very close relationship from the beginning. Ruben was a bit more difficult to reach, but when he was here alone with me it became an absolutely lovely relationship.
>
> I do mourn Esther and Ruben. That is probably one of the many reasons for David's resentment for the last years of their marriage had been difficult. The other, or one of the others, seems to be a tremendous feeling of intellectual insecurity, so that whatever I may say will be held against me as a criticism. When I've been talking about my job at Harvard, which interested me, and, since I worked full-time, played a major role in my life, it was construed that I had wanted David to be at Harvard and that he failed me. Nothing could have been further from my mind and also Walter's. Walter would have been quite happy if David

had become a gardener, which he often had wished for himself. David, however, felt that Walter didn't mean it.

The main source of resentment now, however, is S.

Surely, I was taken aback when I came to visit, not yet three months after Esther's death, and found S. there without being told beforehand. At a second visit, I said to H "that I'd like to be her friend." Then I was told later "I didn't mean it."

Our backgrounds and upbringing are very different. Mine still German "don't show your feelings, and don't ever gush!" and there is also, of course, the generation gap.

I've tried hard to overcome these obstacles without success.

Now that my life is running at a more even flow it could be very pleasant with a good relationship with my family. The thing that makes me deeply unhappy and gives me sleepless nights is that my relationship with Oliver is being strategically destroyed. I've always loved Oliver. We have similar interests—drawing, music—and Oliver is attached to me. He is treated as a pawn now, which, I'm sure, does him some harm, too.

What to do? I don't know.

S. seems to make come true everything she said to me when they stayed with me three years ago:

"Oliver is *my* son now."

"It's *my* house now and I don't want you to come there."

"When you are old and sick and need help, I won't raise a finger for you."

What kind of a person can say things like this?

Mummy knows! What incredible insight and understanding she had.

Yet when a sliver of hope appears, it is quickly destroyed. For Elly's 75th birthday, August 10, 1985, David and Sally host a party at their farm in Norridgewock. Old friends from Bowdoin and David's only relatives travel from the Boston area to join them. Sally is hurt, claiming Elly ignores her and apparently doesn't thank her.

On the following morning, Sally insists that she, David, the two boys, and their six-year-old daughter, Sonnet, leave Elly behind. With their children, they will spend the day at Rangeley Lake. Elly will have to cut short her visit with her family. Feeling guilty in turning against his mother by supporting Sally, David nevertheless gives in to Sally's wish without hesitation.

As they drive off, he turns around to see his mother looking after them. She stands in the semicircular driveway. Her stature is erect; her face is ashen, almost ghostlike. She must be crying deep inside; her struggle through life would never allow her to show her pain.

No matter how badly David behaves, Elly always remains generous to him and his family. She helps pay for his trip to China in 1992 to teach English, for which he received sabbatical leave from his high-school teaching position. Of course, this is his way to flee from Sally. There, in the late autumn of that year he meets Jing, a fellow English teacher at Shantou University in Guangdong Province.

13

The China Connection

HOW IS IT POSSIBLE THAT JING AND I came together? David wonders. It is a late January afternoon in 1993. Jing and David sit together on the wooden two-seater in his sixth-floor apartment of the foreigners' quarters at Shantou University, Shantou, Guangdong Province, China. She is a very popular English teacher at the university, an outstanding ballroom dancer, a prize-winning soprano. *No way, not for me. Popular people are superficial. They make me feel like a child.* When Katie Wyman, president of his senior high-school class, placed her hand on David's shoulder, saying with a smile, "Hi Dave," he shuddered. *Don't play games with me*, he thought. *I'm not like you and your group.*

How can I feel comfortable with a popular woman twenty years my junior? I only gravitate toward girls for whom my rescue pattern is activated. It surely can't be set in motion if she is popular. And yet, David's pattern—his attraction to women in need of rescue—is ignited when Jing describes standing above the university's reservoir the evening before. Behind a veil of haze, a brilliant orange sun is setting in back of craggy knolls that surround the reservoir. Reflections of dry, yellowish-green trees jut forth among boulders that appear black in the placid water. Not even a solitary ripple drifts onto the sepia-toned mud of the tarn, bordered in the twilight by tall, eerie grasses. The air is still and heavy, showing no sign of even the slightest breeze. As she stands on the low, stone and concrete wall of the reservoir, the bright illumination of the sun on her face fades, as it slips behind the hills, her silhouette black against the remaining light.

Like a candle's last flicker before being extinguished, she sees shadows of her childhood dancing. In elementary school, she was selected to be a member of an esteemed dance troupe of about twelve. The dancers frequently were called out of their classrooms to rehearse. They were even sent to studios for professional training to learn already choreographed revolutionary songs representing the political ideology of the Cultural Revolution in China, from 1966 to 1976.

Jing age 5 with her parents, 1968

Not only was every artwork—drawing or painting, poem, song, play, or dance—required to have a political message, even their personal diaries were required to demonstrate their political loyalty. For example, in her diary she might say, "When I was tired of doing my homework, Mao's (Mao Tse Tung) words came to mind," which she then quoted.

Peering into the dark water of the tarn, Jing recalls dropping a wooden bucket attached to a long rope into the depths of the communal well. Feeling the coolness of the evening air following a stifling, muggy day, she recalls the chill of the morning as she hauls water for breakfast tea and rice porridge with pickled bok choy. Filling two wooden buckets, she heads back to the compound at which she and her parents share two tiny rooms. Entering, she sees standing in the middle of the room the solitary table that her parents brought with them from Shanghai on learning that they were to be sent to the countryside. During the Cultural Revolution, all people who had the slightest affiliation with the bourgeoisie were sent among the proletariat to become reeducated.

Jing age 5

Jing recalls her grandfather standing tall and straight by the door of the large house in Shanghai where she lived with her grandparents for several years while her parents labored for the Communist Party in the countryside. The Communists have subdivided the house into several units. Her grandfather's dark eyes are saddened by the departure of his beloved granddaughter as she leaves to join her parents in the countryside. She takes a quick glance back as she heads through worn, wooden double doors.

Now from the stillness of the tarn, she imagines her arm and hand reaching up for her tall grandfather to grasp. With firm but tender grip, he leads her through the fresh early morning air to a nearby park. Here

Jing's mother in Beijing in her early twenties

among the others gathered for their daily Tai Chi ritual, he teaches his granddaughter the gentle movements of his meditative practice. As the rising sun paints bright patterns on the broad leaves of old, wrinkled trees in the park, she feels a soulful bonding with her grandfather. Recalling the movements that stretch her body and mind, she feels the softness of the evening air and the chill that rises from the reservoir. She experiences the cool air that filled her lungs and the warm air she exhaled while doing Tai Chi. On returning home, she is intrigued as her grandfather meditates for hours, sitting erect and cross-legged on the wooden plank that is his bed. During this time, she develops a close spiritual relationship with her grandfather that starts her on her own mystical journey—a journey that is impeded for many years by Mao Tse Tung's tumultuous political era.

While the evening darkness envelops the reservoir and the surrounding hillocks, large boulders appear lighter than the cracks and indentations in the rock formation that are now pitch black. These imposing rock formations remind Jing of two barricades she had to overcome to reach her little home in the countryside. Upon arriving at the wooden door encased in the brick wall surrounding her compound, she encounters several children blocking her entry. Yelling at her, "dirty bourgeois bitch," two boys grab her and shove her against the doorframe. They kick her in the shins and stomach. Finally released from their grip, she steps through the second entrance into her home. Hearing her mother screaming insults at her father, she quietly steals into the room, trying to avoid the tantrum.

Angered by her secretive entry, her mother grabs Jing by the hair, slaps her face, and kicks her shins already sore from previous beatings. Screaming, her mother demands an apology for her daughter's lack of respect for failing to greet her parents upon returning from school.

Her mother's rage and beating intensifies as her daughter steadfastly refuses to shed a tear. Her father, who initially stands silently in the background, joins in the action to support his wife. As the beating subsides, the girl slinks toward her bed at the far end of the little room. It rests next to the wall at a right angle to her parents' bed.

Recoiling from memories of such incidents, Jing remembers standing next to the principal's son in her middle school's yard. All children and teachers are gathered here, where a temporary wooden platform has been constructed. The door to the school bursts open from the inside. Several boys wearing red scarves force their principal out of the door. Grabbing his arms, tugging him forward while others shove from behind, they thrust him onto the platform. Placing a dunce cap on his head and a big wooden placard strung with wire around his neck, they denounce him as a counterrevolutionary. The young boys shriek at him, demanding that he admit his betrayal to the revolutionary cause, as they mercilessly kick him in the stomach, punch, and slug him.

That David, an American, meets Jing in China is no accident. Nor is it mere coincidence that on an excursion to China, his mother is on the first tour boat to visit Shantou in many years.

As a small child, David's parents gave him a children's book by Yui Shufang, *Chinese Children at Play*, published in England in 1939. He loved the stories and the delicate, colorful pictures of children kicking the hacky sack, swinging and skipping, playing the lion game. Of course, at that time he didn't know that the author of this book had fled China for England, due to the Japanese invasion of his fatherland. Nor was he aware that this author longed for Westerners to understand the beauty and depth of Chinese culture. In the introduction to his book, Yui Shufang wrote:

> The great wise man, Confucius, who lived five hundred years before Christ, taught that every man should be filial and benevolent if he did not want to bring shame upon himself. We youngsters, therefore, were brought up to see no difference between black people and yellow people or people of any other color. So you see we were taught much of the same principles of kindness to others as you. (Shufang 1939)

At the age of four, accompanying Elly to the grocery store, David asks her on seeing a Chinese man wearing flip-flops, "Why is the big toe of Chinese people separate from the rest of their foot?" At about age six, when his parents are invited to dinner by a guest professor from China, he accompanies them. He is fascinated by the use of chopsticks and the manner in which everybody dips their sticks into dishes set in the middle of the table.

Several years later, Mrs. Pennell gives David a tour of their Pennellville home located on Middle Bay, the very cove where David and his mother used to paint the scenery with watercolors. From the early to late 1800s, the family built and sailed ships from the family shipyard here. Not only does he admire the meticulously handcrafted models of sailing ships in the house, he is amazed at the bright-red wallpaper with a black *bagua* design (offering good energy and fortune) decorating the parlor of their home. He is told it was brought back from one of their trips to China in the mid 1800s.

During his third year in high school, David and three friends establish a political discussion group. Their first topic is whether China should be admitted to the United Nations. Of course, he favors acceptance.

For the summer of 1989, he receives a Fulbright scholarship to tour China with other teachers from throughout the United States. To his disappointment, the trip is postponed for a year due to the early-June Tiananmen Square uprising. Finally, in 1990, when he actually arrives in China with the Fulbright group, halfway through the trip he falls, tears a knee ligament, which, against his will, causes the Chinese authorities and the U.S. embassy to send him home. At this point, he swears that within two years he will return to China to teach for a year. Finally, after twenty-eight years of teaching at the small-town high school in Madison, Maine, he is the first teacher there to ever take a sabbatical year's leave. He will teach English at a new university in southern China.

While David is teaching at Shantou University, Elly is reluctantly accepting aging at a retirement community. She has been living at the Highlands in Topsham, directly across the river from Brunswick, for the past two years. As she is sitting at the dinner table with her elderly acquaintances on a cold, snowy February evening, one woman tells of a forthcoming escorted trip to China.

"The small tour boat leaves Shanghai, travels up the Yangtze River, returns via Shanghai, follows the coast to Shantou, and concludes the excursion in Hong Kong," her friend explains.

"Did I hear you say Shantou?" Elly asks.

"Yes," her friend replies, a little bewildered. "Why?"

"That's where my son is teaching," she replies.

"Maybe we can go together and you you'll have a chance to see him," her friend replies.

"Did you say when the trip will take place?"

"Late May to early June."

Becoming more interested, Elly asks, "Do you happen to have the itinerary?"

"Yes. Why don't you come by my room after dinner?"

Elly is excited about the prospect of getting a glimpse of China. She fantasizes about meeting her son in this distant land. Already several years ago she visited her friend, Akiku, a potter in Japan—a visit of which she has fond memories. After supper, she joins her friend in her room. Sitting on a sleek Scandinavian sofa, she sips coffee as her friend finds the trip itinerary in her desk. Upon reading the itinerary, Elly becomes very excited.

"The boat will stop in Shantou for a few hours on June 2nd. That's my son's 50th birthday!" she exclaims.

"That's meant to be," her friend replies joyfully.

"We'll travel together," Elly says dropping her usual reserved air.

June 2, 1993, turns out to be a warm, sunny day. David and Jing, for whom he has already initiated the divorce process from his wife, Sally, board the bus from the university to the city's port. They arrive as the tour boat, a small, elegant, coastal steamer, glides into its berth. Looking up, David catches his mother's eye as she stands amongst others at the ship's railing. She is dressed in her usual beige skirt, a white blouse with yellow stripes, and an amber necklace. Catching sight of each other, both smile broadly. With the gangplank finally lowered, David's eighty-two-year-old mother proudly descends onto land. The two kiss and hug warmly, shedding years of strained relations. Left behind, also, are David's wild mop of hair and bushy beard.

Standing next to her son is a beautiful Chinese woman twenty years his junior. Both Elly and David are enraptured by her graceful, light,

Jing, Elly, David in Shantou, China, June 2, 1993

and lively appearance. Her dancing brown eyes and shiny black hair bound in a loose ponytail match the flowing floral pattern on the white background of her dress. Having experienced a hostile relationship with David and Sally, Elly is delighted to be welcomed graciously in fluent English by this utterly charming young professor.

"How has your trip been?" David asks.

"Lovely," she replies enthusiastically.

"Do you enjoy the other people on the ship?" Jing asks.

"There are lots of Germans on the boat," she replies matter-of-factly.

"So you could speak German with them?" Jing asks.

Elly's face instantly darkens. "Never!" she hisses through clenched teeth, demonstrating her deep pain, hatred, and suspicion of Germans.

To change the subject, Jing quickly asks about her trip down the Yangtze River.

"The trip was beautiful—such a big river! We passed through lovely countryside, big cities, and so many boats—big ships, barges carrying wood and gravel, and little skiffs."

"Jing has traveled many times along this river," David explains.

"Oh, really?" Elly remarks with interest.

"As a child during summer vacation, I often took the boat to visit my grandparents in Shanghai. My parents, like all people of the bourgeoisie, were sent to work in the countryside during the Cultural Revolution. Since there were no roads to this town, everybody had to travel by the river."

"Those must have been hard days," his mother says empathetically.

"Yes, they were. At age ten, my parents brought me at 1:00 a.m. to the dock to await the ship. As they had to work, I had to travel alone one whole day and another night until we arrived early afternoon in Shanghai. My parents purchased my ticket and asked a trustworthy-looking soul to keep an eye on their daughter. When there was no space on the huge overcrowded ship—for each of its many cabins had fourteen berths—like others I rented a bamboo mat and blanket to sleep on the deck."

"That's amazing to travel alone at that age. Tell me more about your family." Elly asks with interest.

"I was born in Shanghai in January of 1963, when a difficult period was coming to an end and another period of hardship was beginning. As the brotherhood between the Soviet Union and China broke up in 1961, the Soviets suddenly withdrew their engineers and other experts, abandoning all projects that had been started. The result was a three-year period of starvation. We were, like all families, very poor. We had a two-room dwelling in a compound of homes. Like the others, we had no running water, no toilet. We had to haul water from the well, wash our laundry by hand at the well—"

Over the course of Elly's visit, Jing shares the stories of her past that have so intrigued David. She explains how her parents met in Beijing where they both were studying Russian. Her mother wanted to become a Russian teacher; her father had left home at age seventeen, following the arrest, imprisonment and murder of his father, mayor of a small town, at the hands of the Communists. As one of twelve children, he had to fend for himself. He headed north from his native southern province of Guangxi, seeking employment and education. Landing in Tanjing near Beijing, he did administrative work at an architectural school. Even though he was not gifted in learning foreign languages, the school sent him to Beijing to learn Russian.

Before her parents had a chance to earn their bachelor's degrees, the Sino-Soviet relationship disbanded. Both were sent to Anhui province along the Yangtze River. At least at that time, engaged couples were still permitted to be sent together to the same area. There the Communist Party demanded that Jing's mother study dairy science, for which she had little interest. As her father was an outstanding calligrapher, he was assigned to copy Mao's slogans with brush and ink, and essays on big sheets of paper, *Da Zi Baos*, that were pasted on walls throughout the city. He was glad to have this job as he did not have to talk with anybody. He never learned Mandarin; therefore when he spoke, it was with a strong accent, and he lived in constant fear that he would be misunderstood and sent to prison. Out of fear he did not contact his family for many years, as they were seen as enemies of the Communist Revolution. Only after two decades did he venture home for a visit. Jing, who was fifteen at the time, and her mother accompanied him.

Elly is fascinated by Jing's recounting of her history. "I'm so glad I had the opportunity to travel on the same river you did, Jing. I feel all the more bonded to you. I'm only sorry you had to endure such a difficult childhood. The Cultural Revolution I understand had similarities to the difficult times I encountered in my motherland."

"David has told me about your terrible experiences during the Nazi era," Jing sympathizes.

"I really didn't want to mention this, but when our plane landed in Shanghai, our trip was delayed by several hours as gun-toting soldiers interrogated each passenger and searched our luggage meticulously. This brought back terrible memories of leaving Germany. These soldiers were stern and coarse. They treated us roughly, as had the Nazis some fifty years earlier at the airport in Munich, as we were trying to get on our flight out of Germany. We were so lucky then that the plane was delayed because of ice on its wings. This time I hoped that we would be released, and I would be reunited with my son."

Elly's eyes that moments ago appeared bright and sparkling now have become gray again. She lowers her head as memories flash across her mind. She has just accompanied her husband to the SS headquarters in Munich, as required by his arresting officers. She watches him disappear along a dark corridor strewn with broken beer bottles. Soldiers are yelling at detainees. She hears a piercing scream of pain resound from behind closed doors. Her mind drifts between waiting in the dimly lit hall at Shanghai terminal and being interrogated at the Munich airport by callous soldiers. Glancing at her watch, she sees the time for their flight out of Germany has elapsed. So close to have been able to escape from Germany, she becomes dejected. She fears that she and her husband will never be able to leave Germany, that they both will die at the hands of the Nazis.

Following lunch in the city, David, Jing, and Elly take a taxi back to the university. Sitting next to Jing in the back seat of the taxi, Elly takes Jing's hand: "I like you," she says with much joy and kindness.

Walking past the little market at which David buys fresh vegetables and meat daily, they head to his apartment. David is pleased to see his mother climb the six flights of stairs with remarkable ease for her age. Jing prepares hot tea that Elly enjoys. Soon they are joined by a mutual colleague who is fluent in English. Together they take a tour of the lush campus: a park with a pond, little bridges, and arborways. Although exhausted by now, David's mother expresses her enthusiasm for the modern architecture, the white stucco buildings with red tile roofs.

It is no coincidence that David finds himself drawn to a woman who as a child endured torment during the Cultural Revolution in much the same way David's parents suffered during the Nazi Holocaust. David, who never experienced totalitarian rule, yearns to understand these hardships experienced by those he loves, and so becomes the unifying element between two people of different generations from different lands who were persecuted at the hands of dictators. Indeed, the bond that develops among Jing, Elly, and David, fostering a rewarding relationship for all three, is deliberate.

Sensing that Jing is like a tightly closed bud protected by its leaves as a defending shield, David envisions how this youthful bud will unfold and blossom in America. He imagines her in many scenarios, such as a national television anchor, an opera singer at Lincoln Center, a prominent businesswoman breaking the glass ceiling, a graceful dancer in the tradition of Martha Graham.

Then there are times he is standing on his sixth-floor balcony with arms gesticulating wildly. He calls out to Jing passing below, demanding that she come upstairs; she shouldn't; yes, she must. She needs to prepare for her courses at his apartment, not at her home. She may not hang out with her student, who introduced her to David.

How can Jing ever think of joining this fifty-year-old, a klutz, a humorless man from a distant land, in his isolation in a rural Maine mill town? How can she conceivably deal with his back-and-forth antics? She has never had a yearning to leave her motherland. While in college, she showed no interest in the TOEFL test that her fellow students took to prove their English proficiency and to allow them to study and work abroad. Yet she seems captivated by his unyielding optimism and hope, maybe even his naïveté.

David's sabbatical ends in a few months. What should they do? They'd like to settle in Zhuhai in southern China. But David has a teenage daughter and an aging mother at home in the States. If they settle down first in China, Jing wonders whether it might be harder at a later time to return to America. After all, David will have broken his contract with the school. Living in Maine and returning to China at a later time might be easier. David feels that for Jing, an English professor, living for a while in the United States would be valuable. Jing wonders what she will do in America. She feels she has no skills other than teaching English, which would be of no use there. She has no interest in being a housewife. David will have little money. Since he feels guilty divorcing Sally, he lets her keep the house they built. All he will get are his books, his few tools, and his car. He'll have to pay child support for his fifteen-year-old daughter, Sonnet. With no clearer indication of how they will manage, Jing relies on her intuition that their being together is meant to be.

Jing receives a thirty-day visa without any difficulty. The American consul is impressed by her grasp and fluency in English. When Jing arrives at Chicago's airport for transferring planes to Portland, Maine, she experiences no sense of loss or longing for her motherland.

David has arranged with an attorney in the small, Maine mill town where he teaches to advocate for her, so that the two of them can start an import-export business. Of course, neither of the two has any business experience or actual interest in business. East meets West on December 18, 1993. On a little bridge over a frozen stream deep in the woods of his 600-acre farm, their attorney friend performs their marriage.

In the United States, Jing reconnects with the spirituality of her childhood, from which she has disassociated. She continues to be blessed by the spirit of her grandfather, whose inner peace and beauty she cherishes with great fondness. Jing's bud gradually begins to peek out of its protective shell. Slowly her petals unfold, as the richness of the flower radiates the inner depth of a spiritual being. Tender feelings—love for the beauty, peace of mind, harmony and balance from which she had to detach in order to survive a childhood in a highly controlled revolutionary society—gradually come to life again.

During her early years in this country, Jing earns her master's degree in psychology from Goddard College in Vermont, a progressive school that fosters self-directed study. Under her guidance, David follows in her footsteps to also gain a master's degree from Goddard. For the first time, his democratic approach to teaching is appreciated by both his professors and fellow students. Under her influence, in 1999, after thirty tumultuous years of teaching at rural Madison High School, he retires. Within two years he is teaching again part-time—English and sociology at a small business college in Waterville; Jing introduces him to Natalie Goldberg's approach to writing from the heart and to the practice of mindfulness as taught by Jon Kabat-Zinn. At the end of his sixth year he retires again, only to take up teaching at a community college two years later.

David learns that relatives of his have a Chinese connection. On the same day, Crystal Night, November 9–10, 1938, that David's father was arrested and sent to Dachau, the father of Curt Frankenstein was apprehended. (Curt later married Renate Solmitz. Her father, Werner, was David's father's cousin). Curt, aged sixteen, together with his fourteen-year-old brother, witnessed as a car with four SS men approach their home in Halle on the Saale River. The soldiers jumped out of the long black car, stormed up to their door, forced their way into the house, demanding that Mr. Frankenstein appear immediately. As Curt, his younger brother, and their mother stood horrified, Mr. Frankenstein appeared from another room. Before he had a chance to utter a word, the soldiers rushed toward him, grabbed him, and forced him out the door into the waiting car. He was sent to the concentration camp at Sachsenhausen.

Although Curt's father was Jewish, he was agnostic and had married a Protestant. That made no difference to the Nazis. In their eyes, he was a full-blooded Jew who was vile enough to marry a Protestant woman. Foreseeing problems for Jewish children, Curt's mother had made sure her sons would be baptized. At age eleven, Curt officially became a Christian. As mandated by Nazi rule, all public-school students took two hours a week of religious instruction. Since Protestant and Catholic classes were separated, enrolling in the Protestant class made the process easier for Curt and his brother to be baptized into the Protestant faith.

The Frankensteins were considered a family of businessmen. Curt's father followed in his dad's footsteps as a milliner. As that business fell into bad times, he tried his hand at selling jewelry and watches. This business also turned out to be unsuccessful. However, Curt's younger brother did try his hand as an apprentice to a watchmaker until separated from his mother by the Nazis.

During the First World War, Curt's father fought on the front lines as a member of the Verband Jüdischer Soldaten (Federation of Jewish Soldiers). In part because of his prior service to the Kaiser, he was released from Sachsenhausen in early January of 1939. Although he returned home very ill, he had to leave Germany immediately or face repeated arrest and incarceration. On his release from Sachsenhausen, he learned that he could get permission to go to Shanghai, China, the only place in the world for which no visa was required. The government in power at the time, headed by Wang Jingwei, was one of several puppet states of the Japanese Empire in China. Since Wang Jingwei negotiated and cooperated with the Japanese occupation of Shanghai, the visa requirement to the international settlement of Shanghai had been rescinded.

Knowing that Curt's father was soon to leave for China, his mother acknowledged it would be best for her elder son also to seek sanctuary there. She purchased a one-way fare from the shipping company Hapag-Lloyd for Curt to sail from Trieste to Shanghai. As his father had left several weeks earlier from Bremen, Curt and his mother believed that he would arrive in Shanghai before Curt. However, that was not the case. The ship on which his father traveled, organized by the Nazis for concentration camp inmates, took the long route to China via the Cape of Good Hope. In spite of the fact that the transport was funded by money confiscated from Jews, the Nazis didn't want to pay the British fee to take the shorter route through the Suez Canal. Therefore, it took many weeks for the overcrowded ship, built for three hundred passengers but carrying six hundred, to arrive in Shanghai. During the voyage, his father's condition worsened. The food was scanty and awful.

Many prisoners became seriously ill. Those who died were thrown overboard.

Although Curt had to travel alone, his mother assured him that she and his younger brother would follow. As she was suffering from thrombosis on her leg that wasn't healing, her doctor advised her to remain in Germany. However, by the time she had recovered sufficiently to travel, Hitler had already invaded Poland. Since the war had started, she was no longer permitted to leave the country. Worried and depressed, she had no choice but to remain at home. At least, for the time being, she had the comfort of her younger son.

The ship on which young Curt traveled stopped at Alexandria, Bombay, and Hong Kong before arriving in Shanghai. With ten German marks (approximately $4 in today's money) in his pocket, the maximum the Nazis allowed him to bring, Curt felt destitute and frightened as his ship sailed out of Trieste harbor. Having no knowledge of Chinese, no idea where he would live, especially since he had so little money, he tried to bury his fears in order to focus on survival.

When the ship finally arrived in Japanese-occupied Shanghai, he found his way to the city's Jewish community of Hongkew. Using the little English he knew from his school days in Halle, he was able to get directions to a refugee camp for Jews located in some abandoned buildings. These had actually been hit by Japanese bombs and rebuilt by Jews. Imagining he would find his father waiting for him there, Curt looked everywhere without success. The boy naturally was worried. Was his father's ship attacked on the high seas? Was he arrested? Did the ship sink and did he drown with it? Of course, at the time, Curt didn't know that his father's trip taking him around the Cape was the long route to China. Only many weeks later, to Curt's surprise and gratitude, did his father arrive—safe, but exhausted and ill.

Young Curt felt uncomfortable with the older men who lingered around the camp, immersing themselves into the two Jewish communities: the Sephardic and Ashkenazi. As many were entrenched in their Jewish orthodoxy, they seemed to have no desire to try to embark on a new life in Shanghai. The Sephardic community had already been in existence for nearly a hundred years. Some of the most well-known businessmen and individuals on the Shanghai social roster were from this community. The more recently arrived Ashkenazi Jews, who came largely from Russia, were never a match to the commercial success of the Sephardic.

Curt, now seventeen, realized he must get out of confinement at the camp. Fortunately, he met and was inspired by another refugee, a painter who sold his works to Chinese officials and other Chinese who liked European-style paintings. Although Curt had no training as an artist, he had enjoyed painting as a boy. He saw his chance to break out on his own. Discovering that the little money he had from Germany would go a long way in China, he purchased the necessary supplies and began to paint realistic, European-style paintings—a kind of commercial art. He would set up his easel on the busy streets, painting street scenes, hoping wealthy passersby would purchase his detailed, almost photographic pictures. He would also, like his friend, approach the offices of Chinese officials, who on rare occasion did buy his work. Curt's youth and anonymity were not impediments; he quickly discovered that the appearance of the paintings was more important to his buyers than the artist's name. However, he barely survived on the pittance he made from his work. He lived from hand to mouth, very poor—a homeless person, as he would later describe his existence during these years. For a little while, he had a bed in the workshop of the artist whom he had met at the camp. At one point, he shared a room with a Jewish refugee who repaired typewriters. Later, a Chinese family allowed him to live in an unheated spare room in their house.

Following the war, American naval ships docked in Shanghai. Curt would bring his paints and easel to the harbor to paint the Allied ships in port, hoping that ships' officers would take an interest in his art. His luck came when he sold a painting of the American hospital ship *Repose* to a doctor on the ship. The doctor was so impressed that he arranged an affidavit to bring Curt to the United States.

In May of 1947, Curt left Shanghai for America. On arriving in Chicago, he received a scholarship to attend the American Academy of Art there. The realistic manner that he had cultivated as a street artist in Shanghai developed into his super-real style. For his art that portrayed deeper, more mystical meaning than a straightforward realistic painting, Curt Frankenstein became a well-known artist in the United States and abroad. At a gallery in Chicago where he exhibited his painting, the landlord invited him to a party. There he met the woman he would marry, Renate Solmitz, the German-born daughter of Werner Solmitz who had become a pediatrician in Chicago.

In trying to comprehend these various connections from faraway China, David is encouraged by Jing to explore the meaning of life. As Jing shares her insights from her own spiritual practice, David gains understanding of human connections. In November 2007, at a writing workshop in Rowe, Massachusetts, led by Deena Metzger, David participates in a small group discussion, listening to a ferryboat captain tell of an experience she had during the previous night. "My arm has died. It is dark, pitch dark, and still. I know my arm is there. I move and feel it. Yet its cells are dead. I fear that death will spread across my chest."

"What images come up?" David asks.

"It makes me think of my father who is in the hospital. We would like to take him home, but the hospital staff says no. When he gets a little better, we may look after him at home."

The small discussion groups break up, and they return to the larger group; later that afternoon she learns that her father has died during the night. David realizes that when the ferryboat captain felt that her arm had died, she was experiencing the actual death of her father. A spiritual and cosmic connection of which we are consciously unaware is evident. That this experience happened to a ferryboat captain calls to mind ancient Greek mythology, in which the souls of the dead on their journey from the world of the living are ferried across the sacred River Styx. It is such cosmic connections that help David realize that what appears to be coincidental does not happen by chance.

For David, the image of the ferry represents his bridging the gap between two worlds: the Nazi Holocaust under which his parents suffered and the cruelty of the Cultural Revolution that Jing endured. A ferryboat captain also brought Elly to Shanghai and guided her along the Yangtze River on which Jing traveled in her youth. David's feeling of connection to China since early childhood, his bonding again with his mother there, the experience of Curt having come to the United States via Shanghai and marrying the niece of the son's father, and Jing's transference of her cloistered spiritual development in China to its blossoming in the United States reflect the crosscurrents of experience that unite us all. The ferry is therefore the unifying symbol, one that brings together the many interrelated components of our expansive yet ever-shrinking world.

14

Like Father, Like Son

As he reads a chapel talk Walter delivered at Bowdoin College in 1948, David realizes that, like his father, he is burdened with guilt. Walter's propensity to engage in passionate correspondence in defense of democracy under fire from Senator Joe McCarthy arose from his painful experiences during the rise of Nazism. In turn, Walter influenced David's zeal to become a social activist and innovative teacher.

> It has happened to me. I am going to make a confession to you, with somewhat mixed feelings. I am following the urge to make a confession—that urge which is characteristic of a person who feels guilt: at the same time, I am somewhat embarrassed because the story reveals me as somewhat of a coward. (Solmitz 1948)

In his chapel talk, David's father admits to feeling guilty—in public. He goes on to discuss an incident from the previous year, when his son was four years old.

> One afternoon last fall I was at the railroad station with my little boy, whose favorite place is the railroad station. We watched the diesel train, and went along it on this side of the train, i.e. not on the side where the passengers wait and get in and off the train, but, so to speak, on the backside. Suddenly my boy drew my attention to a man who was sitting in some corner of the diesel engine; and when I looked up, the man shouted something which I did not get at once; he shouted again, and asked how far it was from here to Portland. I called back that it was about forty minutes; apparently, he did not get me, and asked again. This time, I did not answer, but dragged my boy away, drawing his attention

> to some thing or other of the train. I did not tell anybody about it. What would you have done? The man obviously was a veteran, to judge from his clothing. He was a colored man. (Solmitz 1948)

Walter went on to explain the conflict and guilt he experienced as a law-abiding citizen for failing to inform the stationmaster of this man. He wondered whether this person might be a criminal escaped from prison. He feared that he simply lacked presence of mind, was a coward, or didn't know what to do.

> Perhaps I wanted, in the presence of the child, to avoid the excitement that would come with the denunciation. I acted somehow as if he had not seen anything, or as if I considered what we had seen was very unimportant and uninteresting. This strategy of mine, however, has proved very unsuccessful indeed. He has kept asking me about that man sitting in the corner of the engine for a long time, and after a long break, he came up with this question only the other day; there must have been something uncanny in this experience since it has kept his imagination busy, and made him, at one time, see a man sitting in the corner of a church door where there was no man at all, but where only the shadows combined with the snow had perhaps formed some unusual figures. (Solmitz 1948)

As much as David loved trains and still does, he does not remember this incident. His father raises the question to his audience at this chapel talk, reflecting his mindset of guilt from his past: What would *you* have done in this situation? During the late 1940s hobos traveled on the freight trains. In the Bowdoin Pines directly behind the president's house, hobos camped by the tracks where two rail lines diverged, one to Rockland by the sea, the other north to Bangor. As David does have sympathy for the homeless, should such an incident happen to him today, he might respond as his father did. However, like many others he has become increasingly mistrustful of strangers; he might not answer the man. If this person is a veteran, he might very well be suffering from post-traumatic stress disorder. To whom could he report such a person? The police? That probably would not be helpful to the person. As he thinks of these alternatives, David encounters the feelings of cowardice to which his father refers.

Like many children of Holocaust survivors, David has adopted a form of survivor's guilt that Helen Epstein discusses in her book, *Children of the Holocaust.* He subconsciously feels guilty for his parents' suffering while he in contrast has been raised within an accepting environment in an affluent society of a relatively tolerant nation. Epstein explains that for survivors the concentration camp "became a badge of courage rather than degradation. It became 'an untouchable standard of fortitude'" (Epstein 1979, 11).

As Walter had been an outcast in his fatherland and felt alienated in his adopted land, David realizes that these experiences helped foster his father's humanity. Feeling estranged from mainstream society has also caused David to adopt a pattern of alienation. Furthermore, he is impressed by and identifies with his father's compassion for the underprivileged.

In spite of being a great scholar, Walter reflected the humility of his professor Ernst Cassirer with his students as well as with anybody with whom he came in contact. He felt special empathy for the less fortunate people in the community—the less privileged, the social outcasts.

For instance, as he often worked at his office into the early hours of the morning, he welcomed the college night watchman on his campus rounds to join him in lukewarm coffee from his thermos. Years later, David happens upon this sad, thin man. Mr. Moody relates, "Late nights when I saw the light on in Professor Solmitz's office, I would go up the stairs of Adams Hall and gently knock on his door. You know, I didn't want to disturb him. He always answered 'come in,' in his strong accent. He put his burning cigarette down and poured me coffee. I never asked for it. He was right there, looking at me with such kind eyes. I felt his love. Each time I left, I was grateful to your father."

David recalls that on a hot summer day two highway department workers are patching potholes in front of their house. Walter approaches them. Beckoning, he says, "*Kommt*, into the shade of the porch. I bring you lemonade." The men, hot and sweaty, gratefully accept. They thank him warmly.

On another occasion, David is riding on the metal bar of his father's bicycle. On warm summer afternoons, father and son take the three-mile ride to Maquoit Bay. When the tide is low, the mudflats reach nearly a mile to the water's edge. Walter stops to chat with clam diggers who carry their heavy baskets through the thick muck to the shore. They enjoy talking with him about their work, the weather, and the low pay for their tough labor. Before ascending the sandy hill heading back from the bay, Walter and David regularly stop to chat with an elderly couple living in a tiny tarpaper shack. On this trip, the tall, slender man, wrinkled and bent from years of toiling in the mudflats, tells them that his wife is ill.

"She ain't been well for some time now."

"I'm so sorry," David's father says. "From what is she suffering?"

"She can't get outta bed; she's that weak."

"What does the doctor say?"

"What's the point of gettin' a doctor. They don't come out he-ah. And anyways, we ain't got the cash to pay."

"That can't be."

"Well, ya know life comes an' goes. We've had a good life together, but it's been tough."

David is intuitively aware that his father takes on the suffering of this elderly couple. Walter's face becomes ashen. His dark eyes bow towards the ground. He seems helpless. As father and son leave the couple behind, they head homeward. Walter is silent. Gradually as he cycles his spirits brighten. Father and son are bonded. Both experience a warm breeze that pushes them ahead. They relish the scent of sweet fern growing aside the road. Walter undoubtedly acknowledges gratitude and becomes tranquil.

As the only child of immigrants in a small Maine town in the late 1940s and early 1950s, David feels awkward among his peers. David is particularly uncomfortable with the children of other college professors. They seem at ease, are top of the class, and dress better than the other kids. Instead of associating with these children, he hangs out and is at ease with the children from Moodyville, a community of little shacks, dirt streets, and open sewers, owned by an illiterate "honey dipper" (septic tank cleaner), Dan Moody. Even the school bus that brings children from Moodyville to Longfellow School is the school system's oldest. It is short, more orange in comparison to all the sleek yellow buses. David befriends Jerry, whose little hovel, to his surprise, has a dirt floor. His friend George lives in similar circumstances.

At school he likes to hang around with a few girls who are from low-income families. He is particularly attracted to Maimi, one of many children in a poor clam digger's family from Maquoit Bay. When David and his father cycle past their shack, he hopes to see her, but never does. She has sad dark eyes, wears shabby clothes. He also enjoys the presence of Patty and Gloria. In winter, he likes to help the three girls put on their boots.

During recess, David wants to swing on the swings. But they are on the girls' side of the segregated playground. He doesn't like to play with the other boys. They like to play ball; he is afraid of being hit by a ball. They like to roughhouse; he likes to be quiet. Rather, David stands at the edge of the playground by a solitary tree. Using his foot as the blade of a bulldozer or road grader, he imagines he is constructing roads. Ray, a retarded boy, who drools, limps, and has the use of only one arm, often accompanies him.

According to Helen Epstein, David is transferring his pattern of survivor's guilt and alienation in befriending the children of the poor, and developing passion for girls who appear sad and suffering. He secretly wants to become their saviors. During his high-school years he becomes attracted to a lonely, sad, highly intelligent girl who plays the flute beautifully. Poor Jane, he romanticizes, her parents had to get married because her mother had become pregnant. They have long since divorced. *Can you imagine*, David thinks, *a mother telling her child: You are not wanted.* And her father broke her nose in a fit of rage. Poor Jane! He fantasizes that should she become pregnant, he will take care of her forever. She will become a professional flutist instead of following her mother's desire that she become a doctor.

Elly doesn't care for Jane: "She's using you. Look, you take her to the Bowdoin Union for hot chocolate. That is her way to get to know Bowdoin students." (At that time Bowdoin was still an all men's college.) Of course, his mother is correct, but his father particularly understands David's motives. In a letter to David, now a freshman at the University of Maine, he writes,

> What Jane really needs is affection and security. Perhaps—perhaps—you can be of *some* assistance to her by helping her find the way to some of it. Her longing for both is so important because she has had so little of either. And now she believes or dreams that one could "get" or "have" both, affection and security, once and for all. She'll have to learn that one has to win (or try to win and gain) them again and again—*and* again. Just as one cannot have food once and for all—but has to eat (and work for one's food) every day.
>
> She still dreams of *the* man who will provide both affection and security for her. I do not think that you are the man who can give her that now—and frankly (quite frankly) I do not think that she would consider you that man. And I think you are quite right in feeling that any "small doses" will be of no help. You can help her by giving her what *you* can be for her: an understanding,

> cheerful, and intelligent friend with whom she can talk: and in talking she can become clearer in her own mind, and find out what it is that she really wants: i.e. *NOT* what she would like or wish to "happen"—but what she really and sincerely wants—and what she wants to do for it. (Solmitz 1961)

Walter was speaking from experience. As a young man, he, too, felt that he could be the savior of Anne Cassirer, with whom he fell in love. His reaction to her in a letter he sent to Edith Geheeb seems similar to his son's relationship with Jane: "As Anne has a leaning toward tragedy, she is on a path that bodes disaster, but perhaps can be changed. Tragedy is certainly not a misfortune. It is better that a person has a tragic fate than no fate at all. However, I am not so certain whether Anne is able to withstand such a fate" (Grolle 1994, 21).

The summer of 1962, following his sophomore year at Bowdoin and his father's death, David is accepted by the American Friends Service Committee (AFSC) to participate in a work project with a group of college students at a state hospital for the mentally retarded in tiny Woodward, Iowa. Against the advice of his mother, relatives, and friends, who all believe he is punishing himself for his father's death, he accepts the opportunity. As an orderly, he and one full-time employee take care of 78 men—some who are severely mentally retarded, while others are juvenile delinquents. Often David works double eight-hour shifts, cleaning soiled invalids, changing bed sheets, and washing floors.

When he is not attending to his various duties, he draws pictures with some of the boys, sings with them, and reads their writings. One young man, Harold, wrote:

How a Son Thinks About His Mother Inngeborn Louisa Kinsedahl

She doesn't give her son a chance at life.
What does he have to prove to his mother?
Why does he have to live in strife?
There is so much in his future as planned.
It takes a good son to become a good man.
At the age of 32 I had to find out what kind of man was he.
I have never seen my Dad, but I bet you he was glad.
All my life I never saw my Dad but I found out he was in the pen.
I didn't know why he went to the pen.
Once more I found out why he went in,

For bad checks he has made.
I know my mother was too ashamed to tell me
Tho' my Dad died in the pen for not telling me the truth my mother
sinned.
As a baby I was on a farm and
I've never seen my Dad since I was born.
The rest of my life I won't ever be glad
For what I found out about my Dad.
I guess that I will never know
Because the truth will hurt her so.
Maybe she wishes that I was dead
Because she thinks I'm off in the head.
When a baby plays with a toy,
She should prove her love just to her boy.
To my mother who feels so proud,
Who never thinks I am a man.
Just let me have a chance to work today.
This is all I have to say.
Just because you think I want to live off you and step-dad.
You let me work on the farm is all I ask
For two months or four until I can find a job.
You had a chance to make it on your own,
But never turn your back on your son.
Some day it will be too late than all you will think will be about hate.
It's the truth that doesn't hurt the one I love so well,
And it's here I have to stay.

(Loomis, 1963)

At the end of the summer, David writes a report to the administration in which he praises the orderlies with whom he worked on different shifts, but also expresses his concerns. These include a low annual pay of $2,800.00 these men earned, poor communication between employees and the administration, and the lack of job security (six employees were fired during the few weeks that he worked there). He writes,

> The employees work under constant fear of their superiors. Thus, they are unable to work to the best of their ability. There is a lack of help and training. Two attendants cannot effectively take care of a ward of seventy-plus patients. Being untrained in the basic necessities of nursing is not an asset to get more and

better work from the attendants. We don't even know about the medicines we give out. (Solmitz 1963)

Surely working at this institution reflects David's pattern of martyr as victim: he takes on a difficult and thankless job and writes a report in which he supports his fellow orderlies and is critical of the administration. His need to pity others and thus to save them from misery manifests itself in a friendship with one of his project's fellow participants. Betty is a mulatto from New Orleans. Holding hands as they walk through cornfields, she chides: "I hate the white race." Black and white together feels romantic. He can be her savior! So what if he is a non-practicing Jew and she is a devout Southern Baptist!

As if that summer were not enough to fulfill his martyrdom, the following summer David works at Pineland, Maine's institution for the mentally retarded. This time he does not belong to a project of concerned youth eager to contribute to the needs of the less fortunate. He is a lonely college student living at the E-Home, an old farmhouse at which employees live. The rather dilapidated place does not even have running hot water. For much of the summer he works at Cumberland Hall, where the most severely retarded are bedridden. The ward smells of urine and excrement. His job is to check on each patient. If he or she is soiled, he has to change diapers—in those days with bare hands. At meal times he props up these patients in order to spoon-feed them.

His only pleasure during the five weeks he is employed there are midday and evening meals in the cafeteria. Although the dining hall is segregated—orderlies in the front row, followed in the next by LPN nurses, then RNs, and finally doctors by the windows—he breaks the rule by occasionally sitting with the doctors. He is particularly attracted to a young Filipino physician, who invites him for tea at her little apartment on the hospital grounds. However, his coworkers criticize him openly, as well as speak disparagingly about him behind his back for his blatant disrespect of the status quo.

Like Walter, who passionately expressed his concerns regarding political trends that he saw as eroding America's democracy, David follows suit by becoming a social activist. His actions are influenced by his father's sense of humanity and experience of suffering in Nazi Germany, by his own pattern of martyr as victim, and by his desire to save the downtrodden from misery through the creation of practical and concrete projects.

As a college senior in the fall of 1964, while President Johnson's War on Poverty is underway, and having read Michael Harrington's *The Other America,* David starts Brunswick's first antipoverty project. This endeavor begins in the Moodyville section of Brunswick. The aim of the project is for high-school and college students, with the support of local merchants, to work with low-income folk to winterize their homes. By doing so, he hopes to generate greater awareness of poverty. To alleviate these dismal conditions, different socioeconomic groups in the community must work together.

Full of idealism, he wants the project to become the cornerstone by which the community can demonstrate that townspeople, without federal help, can handle one of the most pressing problems facing their community. The project is conducted not as charity but in the spirit of neighbors helping each other. When the community understands the reasons for poverty, they will become more active in seeking means to abate it.

Having worked on an AFSC project previously during his summers, David is well aware of the AFSCs throughout the nation. Therefore, he seeks their support in an advisory capacity. He approaches the newly-formed Turn Toward Peace chapter to enlist the aid of merchants to supply materials, as well as organizations and individuals to supply funds. The local branch of Turn Toward Peace consists of influential and concerned citizens in the community, including the editor of the local paper, a prominent local merchant in the oil and lumber business, a college professor and peace activist, and a Unitarian minister. A steering committee is formed, including members of the peace organization, the president of Bowdoin College's Student Council, an exchange student from Morehouse College, as well as several other college and high-school students.

Following the donation of materials, and financial support from local businesses and organizations, as well as the use of donated trucks for the day, student and adult teams visit families. They explain the project, seek their participation, and learn what needs to be done to winterize the family's home. A local carpenter offers his service as advisor for construction tasks. One of these is to build and install an indoor outhouse, another to abate the draftiness of a home, and a third to repair a crumbling porch. Other less complicated projects include installation of plastic as storm windows, and painting indoors and out.

Finally, the Saturday in mid November arrives when sixty volunteers—half of whom are Bowdoin College students and the other half students at Brunswick High School—come together to work on eight homes. Members of the participating families, including young children, work together with the students. Following a day of fulfilling work, a spaghetti supper is held for all involved. During the supper, plans are being made to continue the effort that has just begun. People from the low-income neighborhoods become actively involved with the planning committee.

Bordering the town's most obvious poverty pocket is a large tract of land, abandoned for many years, the Town Commons. The group decides to invite an AFSC summer project to build a playground on a five-acre corner of the wooded land for the children from Moodyville. A group of about twenty high-school students from all over the United States and Canada, plus counselors, join forces with children from the area. They clear brush and build picnic tables, a basketball court, and playground equipment. An editorial in the *Brunswick Record* on July 20, 1965, highlights the success of this venture and raises important questions for the future. According to its author, the success of the venture makes it clear that teenagers are capable of doing great works together in an organized, thoughtful, and harmonious manner.

> There were many reasons why the project could have failed. None of the twenty young persons who came to Brunswick had ever been here before; none of them had ever met each other before. Nor had they met their leader. None of these people is over 22. None under 16; most are in the 18-to-20-year bracket. None of them is experienced in the ways of the world, and much less in the professional techniques, which many might insist their project demands. And, as if inexperience and unfamiliarity were not enough, their organization is run by consensus of their group opinion. This means not one action can be taken until it is fully discussed before the entire body approves it. And this with teenagers! [Visitors who enter a small building near the common] will see preschool children being read to, being made enthusiastic about the act of learning, being encouraged, being shown, being taken to places they have never visited before. The young persons doing the reading and showing and teaching are AFSC teenagers, but they are doing what few adults in the community have had the time or inclination to do before. (Cole 1965)

The editorial concludes that the work that has begun must be continued. Brunswick High School students who volunteered for the summer project have indicated they will continue their efforts in the fall. However, the same editorial notes that "they need leadership, organization, and most of all the support from the town, the same sort of support which had been given to the AFSC project and more." The article's final words state that "the people of Brunswick have been shown what it takes to change a community. Now they must keep up the good work" (Cole 1965).

Over the next couple of years the Town Commons project falls into disrepair. It is severely vandalized and is never rebuilt. The community's recreation department never fulfills its promise to carry on the work that had been started there. Instead, the Brunswick Area Coordinating Committee is formed under the leadership of a local psychologist and others who were involved with AFSC summer project. This committee becomes the catalyst to prepare a lengthy application to the office of Economic Opportunity for federal funds to establish a Community Action Program (CAP).

Unfortunately, no low-income families are members of the committee. Only upon receipt of the grant is an attempt made to recruit low-income people and to encourage them to become actively involved. The new federal agency, instead of focusing on one community, handles eight towns in the region. Over the years, on the board of directors consisting mostly of professional people, there are a few token representatives of low-income families. The growth of the program is described in a 1994 letter from the organization's executive director at the time.

> The Community Action Program grew through a variety of transformations. By the end of the twentieth century it had become the Coastal Economic Development Center (CED). Currently it serves seven counties. It still helps low-income families and individuals by providing support and new opportunities necessary for their self-sufficiency and well-being. Each year our agency helps over 11,000 individuals in the mid-coast area by providing affordable housing, fuel assistance, nutritional assistance, Head Start, job training, and housing repair. We also have a successful youth community service program which allows us to assist many in the community using the volunteer services of the area youth. (Coastal Economic Development Center 1994)

Even before the initial summer program begins in 1965, David has graduated from college and is on his way to Switzerland to teach at the

Ecole d'Humanité, the former Odenwaldschule that his father attended years before. Returning to the States two years later, David takes a job as a community worker for what has become a federally-funded Community Action Program. Before a year is up, he is fired. Not only does he have no experience as an administrator, he is at odds with his supervisor because he believes he can learn a lot from the low-income people of whom he is "in charge" and from community leaders involved in the project. He disagrees with his supervisor's demands to follow an interpretation of Saul Alinsky's approach: organize the poor against the rich. Rather, he wants to continue the approach with which he started—the approach used before this venture became an agency of the Office of Economic Opportunity. Feeling discouraged, David returns to teaching.

15

The Educator: Transitioning from Father to Son

EVEN THOUGH TEACHING SEEMS LIKE THE ROUTE of least resistance for David to take, he is unconsciously following in the footsteps of his father, who also fell into teaching. Shortly after arriving in the small, rural, mill town of Madison, Maine, conflict arises between him and his administrators, because he wants to save his students from the tyranny of abusive administrators and unenlightened teachers. He believes that discipline should not focus on punitive measures, but rather center on developing the inner strength of each individual. Ways to do this range from developing methods that excite students about learning, to facilitating their development of respect for and a sense of responsibility to themselves and others. These aspects of discipline should help each student to become a self-actualized person, who has learned to think independently, to question authority, and to courageously stand up for the ideas and principles in which he or she believes.

As he holds fast to views that deviate from the mainstream, David finds it challenging to win the support of students and administrators who are neither familiar with nor willing to accept his manner of thinking. Eager to keep his position, he becomes obsessed with traditional classroom discipline, the key to his survival in the system. He has either to maintain proper decorum in the classroom or face the humiliation and financial hardship of being fired. After all, he has a wife and child to support, with another child on the way. Firmly believing himself both martyr and victim, he repeatedly perceives that the administration favors students he has disciplined rather than support him.

When students misbehave in his classroom, he feels as if he is the target of their frustrations. Standing in front of the classroom, he imagines they see him as their controlling father or some other authoritarian male figure with whom they have problems and toward whom they feel anger. He experiences a combination of anger, guilt, and empathy.

Nearly ten years after he begins teaching social studies at Madison High School, rowdiness among students becomes common throughout the school. On several occasions, cherry bombs are ignited in the bathrooms. Some kids come to school drugged. During the first week of September 1978, the superintendent of schools expands a paper trail that he had convened the previous winter with the intent to fire David. The superintendent resents having to deal with a controversy that brewed because a student complained about the foul language in Ron Kovic's *Born on the Fourth of July,* a book David chose in an effort to motivate his lower academic-track students. Nor does the superintendent appreciate a grant David submitted to purchase a potter's wheel and art supplies for his social studies classroom. However, in his attempt to fire David, the superintendent chooses to focus on David's apparent lack of discipline. In one letter he complains about David's inability to manage a study hall effectively:

> I was most distressed to hear from Mr. Y about problems which you and Miss R. experienced with the study hall situation on 9/7/78. As you are aware, we are very crowded this year and need the full support of all teachers to keep things under control. It is imperative that we can count on you to carry your weight in the monitoring process.
>
> If students see that they can get the better of you in a study hall, it is certain that they will try to take advantage of you during your classes as evidenced by the problem you have already had in your class this first week of school.
>
> We talked about "student control" problems last year and you assured me that you would take courses during the spring to improve in this area. I also made it clear that your continued employment depends upon your ability to control the students. (Hennigar 1978)

The superintendent's true colors seemed to shine brightly:

> Finally, I cannot help but feel your personal appearance, the appearance of the classroom and your philosophy of providing a democratic classroom contribute to the management problems

> that you are having with division A. It is imperative that you address these three areas seriously if true progress is to be made in student management. (Hennigar 1978)

In thinking about his own approach to teaching and his own struggles with insensitive administrators and unmotivated students, David remembers that his father often felt that some students took at least his introductory philosophy course because they felt it was an easy way to get an A. They didn't seem to appreciate that he was exploring ideas, exposing them to difficult concepts, trying to get them to question, to think. This becomes particularly evident to David when he reads a short story about his father by a Bowdoin student, R. D. Skillings, who took Walter's introductory to philosophy course. "What's True" (2002) could very well have been accurate.

> "One sentence of Spinoza is worthy of two weeks of contemplation," he would say. His classes took place in his dusty office around a table littered by books filled with overdue notices. He was probably not a good teacher. He sat among us, in no particular chair, shabby, brown and nondescript, a bent man with a beaked nose and circles under his eyes, chain-smoking and speaking English with grave embarrassments and wry chagrins, asking questions about Kant we could not answer, squinting to think, and then attempting to answer them himself. Now and then he set himself afire or lost his watch. He spent months correcting our examinations and returned them the following semester covered with comments. We didn't study much. Some took his courses because he gave only A's and B's, but he tried to teach us all.

Wow, David thinks, *I never realized how similar my father's and my approach to teaching appear to be. Neither of us is interested in grades. We've both had students who have taken advantage of us. So what?*

In order to learn more about his father's teaching, David writes to former students of his father. Frank Scmit, who wrote to David in 2002 from his home in California, further confirms the similarity between Walter's and David's teaching style.

> His teaching was unequaled in my seven years of higher education. In one stroke he strengthened my life and gave me

> confidence: I was unprepared for a test and instead of answering the question about what the philosopher had said, I wrote some of my own thoughts on the subject. It came back with this circled and the comment: "Mr. Scmit, it is clear that you have not read the material, but for this pearl of wisdom, I am giving you an A." (Scmit 2002)

Shortly thereafter, David comes across a paper written by Alice, one of his high-school students in 1996. Entitled "Life," it was assigned as a research paper for the high-school, college preparatory, United States History and English classes. Although Alice's paper was neither a research paper nor did it relate to United States history, David was so impressed by this sixteen-year-old student's insight, he gave her an A. On the other hand, her English teacher assigned her an F for failing to adhere to the prescribed instructions. To his surprise, his own comments remind him of what Frank Scmit expressed about his father's approach to teaching.

> Alice, this is an OUTSTANDING paper. It is beautifully written, coherent, compelling in its arguments. I cannot justify giving you a failing grade. I can easily defend the A that I give you because you wrote a very well thought through defense of your reasons why you couldn't do this paper. This paper represents incredible insight into yourself and others. It demonstrates to me that you are a student in the true sense of the word—asking questions and seeking answers! (Solmitz 1996)

Alice had concluded her essay:

> This is my paper. I know that I will probably receive a failing grade because it isn't long enough, it doesn't include footnotes, citations, or research. But I believe I researched a lot more than most people because I researched myself. So I will accept any grade I get with no argument, no problem, and a smile because I know what it took to write this paper and it took a lot of soul searching and admitting of uncontrollable faults, and getting in touch with me. I have done that. My work has satisfied me and I feel that is what is most important. (Gordon 1996)

As David reads Alice's paper eleven years after she wrote it, he is amazed that she reflects teachings of spiritual leaders who arrived at these realizations during years of meditative practice. He recalls that as a teacher in poverty-stricken rural Maine, then as well as now, his wish is to inspire and to motivate students to reach beyond the limitations of dysfunctional, low-income families in which many find themselves entrapped. Like his father, who felt passionately about those who were less fortunate and alienated, he becomes excited when such a student such as Alice shares her feelings and ideas.

As a teenager from a troubled family, Alice understood what John Welwood in his book *Perfect Love, Imperfect Relationships* (2002) refers to as the "wounded heart." He writes that when a child does not feel fully embraced or accepted in her family of origin, she becomes disconnected from love, fearful and mistrustful. The wound will affect her for the rest of her life. Alice expressed that wound succinctly.

> I am not looking for pity. I don't want it and won't take it. I just want you to know that—unlike you—I wasn't born behind a white picket fence. Our "fence" was torn down, had peeling paint, and was extremely dirty and worn. I am now trying to repair our "fence." But it has to be cleaned, sanded down, repainted with a strong paint that has a lifetime warranty. But it is a very long and extremely difficult process. (Gordon 1996)

As described by Welwood, absolute love, or the love of being, comes through us naturally when we fully open up—to another person, to ourselves, or to life. In relations to another, it manifests as selfless caring. In relation to ourselves, it shows up as inner confidence and self-acceptance that warms us from within. And in relation to life, it manifests as a sense of well-being, appreciation, and joie de vivre (Welwood 2002, 33).

Alice understood:

> Some people just don't know how to show love. I am one of them. I don't say that proudly or regretfully because either way it isn't my fault. When one isn't shown how to love they don't just wake up one day and say, "I think I will start to love today." . . . People aren't born knowing how to love. You are taught how to love just as you are taught how to ride a bike. You fall off and get hurt sometimes, but you always get back up and one day you

> finally learn how to ride that bike. After that it is like a second nature. Showing love—or even like—isn't hard, but also isn't easy when you have to teach yourself. You see, showing affection is a learned characteristic. And if you weren't taught, then you have to find the strength to surround yourself with a positive mindset and teach yourself to love. Someone had to break the chain of a loveless life because it passes down. Believe me, you can say all you want, "I'll never be like that," but you will if you can't love. (Gordon 1996)

Alice also clearly grasped a concept expressed by the German Buddhist nun, Ayya Khema, that we grow by understanding our experience. Khema has observed that we are all born with good and bad; therefore, it is pointless to condemn ourselves. We simply need to recognize these tendencies and encourage the good ones to flourish in order to counteract the bad ones. Alice also recognized the existence of both good and bad in each of us. She wrote:

> Love is not just in the "heart." It is in the soul . . . Love acknowledges the bad as well as the good. But the bad is looked upon as human nature and is dealt with that way . . . But knowing how to love doesn't mean overlooking the bad characteristics, it means learning about them, understanding them, and finding their good aspects. If you overlook bad things—ignore them—they will come back later and will cause many problems that probably won't be able to be overcome. But, as I stated, ignoring things doesn't make them go away. It just gives them time to fester and they only get worse. It's kind of like the stuff in the back of the fridge. Without the attention it needs, it will grow mold and once it has been spoiled, there is no reversal of the process. That is what happens to people. Some—because of lack of attention and love—become spoiled or no good. And people like that get "thrown away." Or if they are lucky, they get "shoved to the back of the fridge" to be dealt with later. They are the lucky ones because sometimes they can be saved before they "spoil." It takes a lot of work and knowing how to teach love and accept it. It is a different process, and a long one, but one that will better you as a person, and the people around you, in the long run. I am in the beginning of that process. Teaching myself how to love. I don't mean how to love my boyfriend or my friends or my

> family because it has to begin inside me. I have to love me before I can give it wholeheartedly or receive it. I won't lie—it is hard. But I know why I am so mean, why I don't show much remorse. (Gordon 1996)

David, who clearly is influenced by his father, understands that Walter's ideas on education began to evolve during his years as a student at the Odenwaldschule. In 1910 Paulus and Edith Geheeb established the Odenwaldschule along the principles of the great philosophers of the Age of Reason: liberty, equality, and brotherhood. Instead of a reciting a prayer before mealtimes, Paulus routinely quoted from such thinkers as Johann Wolfgang Goethe, Gotthold Ephraim Lessing, Friederich Schiller, and Wilhelm von Humboldt.

As a theological student at the University of Jena, Paulus became familiar with Johann Fichte (1762–1814). Fichte had in turn been impressed and influenced by the Swiss education reformer, Heinrich Pestalozzi, whose approach to teaching focused more on developing the child's entire personality than on acquiring information. Fichte tried to encourage Germans to establish thousands of schools similar to those of Pestalozzi, in which young people could learn to integrate their own needs with those of their communities and to fight for moral principles. Like Jean-Jacques Rousseau, Fichte also wanted children and youth to grow up close to and to develop appreciation and respect for nature. Rather than become materialistically inclined, he wanted students to develop idealistic attitudes that would raise Germany and the rest of Europe to the highest of moral conduct. He also believed that single-sex schools were unhealthy and that boarding schools should be coeducational. All of these beliefs influenced the founding of the Odenwaldschule.

Given the focus of Paulus's Odenwaldschule, it is no coincidence that Walter developed a passion for 18th-century philosophy. Furthermore, Walter's professor at the University of Hamburg, Ernst Cassirer, not only was a scholar of Kant and Goethe, but his entire approach to teaching reflected that of the 18th-century philosophers. David looked up to his father in a similar way to how his father had held his professor in awe. Unlike other professors, Cassirer did not use notes for his lectures. Walter was grateful to Cassirer for allowing his students to take part in the free development of his thought during a lecture. In his eulogy, Walter wrote, "One could not help but follow, with a sense of dramatic suspense, as he led from two conflicting views to their reconciliation, from a problem to its solution, from an apparent confusion to an intrinsic clarity" (Solmitz 1945).

Walter was deeply impressed that professor Cassirer encouraged his students to learn something sound and solid, in science or in history first, before concentrating on pure philosophy. Cassirer would say that one could not study philosophy, one could only study philosophically.

> [Cassirer] taught us not to judge any system of thought from our own point of view before having placed ourselves in the very center of that system itself first. This procedure was a natural consequence of his form of understanding in general, and it was perhaps founded ultimately in his comprehensive benevolence and his love for everything and everyone. He found that he understood anything only when he had discovered its peculiar truth and its peculiar good; and if he could not discover anything good, then we he would simply say that he did not understand it. He would not reject anything, but try to discover the point from which it was possible for him to agree. He would not easily say: "No." In this respect, he went to extremes. In the seminar, he would answer some objections by saying: "Yes, yes, that is quite right; but is it not just the other way round?" This kind of turn was a characteristic feature of his thought in general . . . Cassirer pointed out that it was precisely the most important German thinkers who had made it clear that the lasting ideas and ideals were not limited to and not exhausted by any one period or nation, but were transnational. He could be so flexible in his different approaches, because he was so absolutely firm at the bottom. (Solmitz 1945)

Eager to know more about his father's teaching style, David contacts some of Walter's former students, several of whom respond to his requests. Louis Asekoff, a friend of R. D. Skillings, observes some other aspects of Walter. Watching him "twisting the cigarette in his amber-colored finger tips," Louis noticed that Walter had a slight tremor. He also perceived that Walter seemed deeply haunted. At the same time he appeared to Louis to be very calm, always attentive, patient, and thoughtful. "He was the personification of goodness, of moral conscience. I was impressed by his moral weight, his deep suffering. He clearly was the paradigm of goodness and deep suffering" (Asekoff 2001).

Although both Skillings and Asekoff took the same survey course, From Plato to Kant, as sophomores, Asekoff has a somewhat different impression of the class.

> We spent the first three months of this semester course studying Plato's *Protagoras*. We often spent the entire hour on one sentence. After three months Walter suddenly remembered that we still had to cover Hume and others before we reached Kant. At last he jumped from Plato to Kant. Although he never followed or finished the syllabus, he always thought things through with us. He taught us that philosophy is a kind of thinking, of important issues that had to be engaged in. (Asekoff 2001)

Another student, Kent Spriggs, has this to say about Walter's teaching style.

> He had an infectious enthusiasm for communicating his knowledge of the great philosophers to us. For me his enthusiasm inspired me to work harder. (I was not a gifted student of philosophy.)
>
> One of the things he often said that stuck with me had to do with our not keeping up with the schedule of readings which he would pass out at the beginning of the term. He would say that he had intended to keep up with the schedule but that if he did not feel that we had adequately explored a given author's work (in accordance with the schedule), it would be wrong to move on until we had done so. It's almost as if his guiding us through the greats had a life of its own to which he was attuned but which he did not control.
>
> The following anecdote illustrates his humility and at the same time his wonderful way of encouraging us in our study. I remember vividly when we started Nietzsche, I tried to dive in and then accost him to convey my enthusiasm for the endeavor. I met him crossing the campus and said: "I've been reading Nietzsche and I think I am just beginning to get a sense of what he's saying." He replied, "I've been reading Nietzsche for 40 some years, and I, *too,* am just beginning to get a sense of what he's saying." From anyone else this would have been the biggest put-down, but there was not the slightest inkling of that in his response. It was his way of encouraging exploration, of

> conveying that he too was still a seeker. It is certainly reflective of his great humility. (Spriggs 2001)

Henry Martin, who now lives in Italy writing about contemporary visual arts as well as translating from Italian and German into English, writes in regard to those students. Henry's values were different from those students.

> I remember him as having had the reputation of being a fairly "easy" professor. So his courses were also chosen by people whose interest in them didn't go very deep. Bowdoin had "distribution" requirements. So even the students who were furthest away from the humanities had to pay them some lip service, or at least to sit through a course or two. More than anything else, your father seemed hurt by such students' lack of interest and attention. Hurt more than angered. Though I wouldn't say that he was free from anger. But that anger wasn't well directed. He didn't or couldn't use it as a tool. I imagine now that he may mainly have resented the system that sent those students to his classroom for reasons that assured real benefit to no one. (Martin 2001)

Like Louis and Kent, Henry expressed to David his admiration of Walter:

> I think your father helped me to become a seeker not by way of any particular questions he asked, but by way of seeing me clearly. Simply that. He had the power of the effective witness. Simply knowing or feeling that someone has seen you clearly can be enough to make you see yourself, and to make you understand the directions in which you have to move, or the ways in which you need to change. (Martin 2001)

Ben Ray also emphasizes Walter's concern for fostering an individual student's interest and enthusiasm about philosophy, rather than giving grades or following administrative guidelines. In a letter dated April 4, 2004, Ray writes:

> Strange as it may seem, I never took a formal course with your father in all four years at Bowdoin. I started out in philosophy with upper-level courses and never took the two-semester survey in the

> History of Philosophy survey that your dad taught. He spoke to me in the spring of my junior year, as we were working out my senior schedule, and insisted that I should not take his two survey courses the following years, even though they were mandatory for the major. These two courses, he said, were really too elementary for me—and that he would feel almost embarrassed if I were in the classroom. So he would simply enter the grade A each semester, so I would get credit for them (I had A's in almost all my other philosophy classes). I felt a little stunned by this "advice" and questioned him about it, so he rather patiently explained his syllabi for these two classes, and pointed out the readings—virtually all of which I had already done in other classes . . . The real joy was the two semesters of Major Meetings he held in his house with me and three other majors. Those readings and discussions were superb. Without having to take those two survey classes my senior year, I was also able to devote much more time to my honors thesis. (Ray 2004)

Finally, student Peter Anastas, in a September 1983 issue of the *Gloucester Daily Times*, wrote of Walter's teaching style:

> He didn't lecture so much as probe and question. Individual concepts or schools of thought were never merely digested to be fed back on exams or quizzes. What you got with Walter Solmitz was the actual, the living experience of philosophy. He didn't teach so much as philosophize right there in front of us, drawing us into the process in his Socratic manner . . . For those of us who wanted, indeed craved, the other—the philosophical encounter—it was never enough. And we lingered after class to talk and listen as he spun out a point in his thick Germanic English or we followed him to the student union for the black coffee that would revive us all at 9 or 9:30 on a cold Maine morning. (Anastas 1983a)

When David tries to read Walter's philosophical essays, such as his 1949 publication "Cassirer on Galileo: An Example of Cassirer's Way of Thought," he becomes lost. In reading a follow-up column by Peter Anastas in the September 22, 1983, edition of the *Gloucester Daily Times*, his awe and admiration for his father are further confirmed.

> In front of him as he prepared to begin class, a cigarette

> constantly between index and middle finger, he would have laid out the discussion in the original Greek. Relevant words or phrases would be chalked on the board in translated Greek. He would also have commentaries with him in German or French which he referred to freely, always translating the terms for us carefully and chalking them up so we could visualize and learn them. (Anastas, 1983b)

Walter's persona—his intelligence and his devotion to the life of philosophic inquiry—had a profound effect on both his students and on his son. Louis Asekoff expressed this succinctly.

> I was a day late in handing in my paper to him. I saw him coming down the path. I hid behind a tree. He would never raise his voice or express anger. He would just look at me with his deep, sad, penetrating eyes. That was much worse than if he were angry at me. I felt I had failed him. (Asekoff 2001)

In addition to his enthusiasm for philosophy and the life of a scholar, Walter encouraged a democratic environment in the Bowdoin College community. This is not surprising, considering his experience at the Odenwaldschule and his admiring and personal relationship with his professor Ernst Cassirer. In December of 1957, Walter wrote a letter to the *Bowdoin Orient*, the student newspaper. In the letter he expressed appreciation for the paternalist attitude of the previous president, Kenneth Sills, who, together with his wife, considered faculty and staff as their Bowdoin family; however, he focused primarily on the desire of the current generation of students to emphasize mutual responsibility, "which seems to go well with the idea of a family too." Therefore, applying the metaphor that everybody at Bowdoin is in the same boat, he argued that if a student sees an iceberg before an officer or a captain, he should report this to the officials. "He does not even have to go through channels to do so; and it does not have to be the case of clear and present danger either. Any clear and present view may well induce a student to do so, and, as I personally see it, he can be pretty sure that any serious suggestion on the student's part is not only warmly welcomed but invited urgently" (Solmitz 1957).

In the mid 90s, David, who has been teaching world history at Madison High School for nearly thirty years, is suddenly required to teach a new course called Government and Economics. He realizes that he can only make a course in American government relevant to his students by putting the principles of democracy into practice within the classroom.

One of his first efforts to create a greater sense of community is to address the grading system. He dislikes grades because they are not only a tool to maintain discipline, but a competitive practice by which the top students are rewarded with praise from both the school community and the community at large. Students who fail continue to be conditioned to believe they are stupid and do not deserve the recognition that high achievers receive.

As a public-school teacher, David has no choice but to give his students grades. Therefore, he devises a grading procedure to try to establish an environment whereby students may develop respect and appreciation for one another as well as for the teacher. He grades equally for class participation and for written work. It seems only fair to take into consideration that some individuals express themselves orally better than they do in writing. At the same time, he wants to be sensitive to those students who are shy in class and have a hard time speaking up. He establishes a point system by which each student has to earn three out of six in order to pass for the day. The remaining three points are cumulative in order to achieve a higher score. This method encourages students to attend class regularly. They are:

- 1 point for attendance—being in the classroom with all materials (books, pens, notebook) and ready to start class at the sound of the bell
- 1 point for attitude—respect for yourself and others (according to the policies agreed on as a class)
- 1 point for being prepared for class, trying to complete all work, working the entire period (reading, writing, oral participation)
- 1 point for average work
- 1 point for good work
- 1 point for excellent work

The average of these grades counts as 50 percent of the quarterly grade. The other 50 percent is based on essays and research projects. The research projects, which have to be on a subject that interests the individual student, are often presented orally. For these, David asks to see the student's written preparation, including notes, and a bibliography. On rare occasions, he does give an unannounced, thought-provoking quiz.

Essay quiz questions are developed to help both student and teacher see how well the student understands the concepts they are exploring and how effectively he or she is able to support a point of view with plenty of evidence.

In looking back, David sees that the establishment of this more democratic classroom system was an initial step on his journey to practicing compassion—no longer as a tolerant observer and social activist but in a more direct and personal way. Influenced and encouraged by his wife Jing, completing her degree in psychology at Goddard College, he enrolls in an MA program in education there. For the first time in his lengthy career as a teacher, he feels validated by his fellow students and professors. With an MA in hand and the publication of his book, *Schooling for Humanity: When Big Brother Isn't Watching* in 2001, he gradually realizes that he can trust his intuition, feel more confident and comfortable with himself and others. With Jing's support, he begins to develop the strength to break from old patterns and dare to explore other paths in life.

16

Creating a Democratic Classroom

By the fall of 1998, David is ready to jump into making his classroom as democratic as possible. After two and a half months of summer break, he returns to school full of enthusiasm, ready to implement ideas he has been developing over the summer. When his first class arrives, a middle-track group, one boy speaks up, "We hear this class is different—all you do is watch R-rated movies. You don't learn stuff."

David responds, "I'm so glad you raise this issue. In fact, this is really one of the issues I want to explore with you. That is, how do you learn best? How do you become a knowledgeable, mature, and wise person? Is this through direct experience, through books, through personal contact, or through a combination of these?" Therefore, he explains the need to address these questions, so that they can all work together: "I need to understand from where you come, and you should know my purpose for conducting the class the way I do." At this point, David introduces himself as a facilitator, one who supports all students individually throughout their learning process.

The students say they learn best through discussion, practical activities, and experience. "What about books?" David asks.

"No. They are boring. We don't learn from books," one student says. "We use them only to cheat on exams."

David responds, "Oh, isn't cheating a skill that you learn? So you are learning something? Practical experience?"

Three boys affectionately known as the Three Stooges have become a little disruptive, giggling, and even laughing aloud. David asks why they laugh.

"This ain't the way we're supposed to learn in school," one of the Three Stooges replies as he takes his shirt off.

"What message are you trying to tell us?" David asks.

Embarrassed, the boy quickly puts his shirt back on.

"Yeah," the first boy continues, "when the class is boring, I fall asleep. If I can't sleep, I become disruptive."

"So our discussion is boring?" David asks.

"No way. It's weird," he replies.

At this point, David suggests they get down to the business of what this class is all about, namely United States government. "To understand our government, we have to understand what democracy is and actually practice it in the classroom. Only in this way will you be able, I believe, to become willing and active participants in our school's policies and in our city, state, and country's government."

Following a brief presentation as to what democracy comprises, David explains how small groups in the class will work. Each will consist of a facilitator, a recorder, and a spokesperson. He emphasizes that the following rules must be followed in every group discussion.

1. Everyone belongs because you are here and for no other reason.
2. Only one person may speak at a time.
3. Before one person speaks again, all others must have the opportunity to speak.
4. Listen carefully to what each person says.
5. Respond directly to what each person has said.
6. Look at the person to whom you are talking.
7. Be open-minded to different points of view.
8. Back up your opinions with as much factual knowledge as possible.
9. No putdowns.
10. No foul or abusive language.

Then David hands out the first in-class written assignment that includes the following questions.

1. Define *freedom.*
2. Identify four (4) freedoms and identify at least two (2) responsibilities that accompany each freedom.
3. Name new and old laws that *directly* affect you. Why do you think they were made? Describe how they affect you and your freedom.
4. Name new and old school policies that directly affect you. Why do you think they were made? Describe how they affect you and your freedom. How do these laws and policies directly affect your freedom?

5. What can you do to change these policies? Begin with school policies. Describe the process step by step.

Walking around the classroom, David observes that most of the students are working diligently. The first of the Three Stooges pipes up, "I don't know how laws and policies affect me."

David encourages him to take out the student handbook, which the boy says he has never read. Together David and student look at the new policies. The boy is surprised. He then begins to write. Almost immediately, he calls David back to his desk asking, "Who will get this paper? Will I get in trouble?"

"No, I am the only one to read these papers. You will not get in trouble," David replies with a smile. "By the way," he continues, "what do you feel you are learning from this activity?"

"You are teaching us that we have rights and that we can make our school and our life better," he responds to David's delight.

Although most of the class becomes involved in the process over the course of the term, the Stooge who took his shirt off during the first class reverts back to his role as class clown, taking the lead to encourage his buddies to crack jokes and mouth strange-sounding noises. At this point, David feels he has no other choice than to intervene, asking the class to address the issue.

Several students urge David to "take control" of the class. Two students request that David send these boys to the office for punishment. Others suggest that they sit in front of the room for ten to twenty minutes, so that they become embarrassed and humiliated.

"Gosh, no, I can't do this," David blurts out.

Even though David questions the effectiveness of such a policy, the class unanimously adopts it as a discipline procedure. David believes that some, including the Three Stooges, passively go along with the decision. After all, through years of schooling, they have been conditioned to bite the bullet; maybe they cannot believe that as students they have the right to make decisions regarding their class. Possibly, they feel the policy won't work anyway; the teacher will take charge just like in every class.

This policy they adopt will be used for disruptive behavior, which includes chatting, talking out of turn, silliness, rudeness, and disrespect.

- 1st offense—10 minutes sitting in front of the classroom facing the blackboard
- 2nd offense—20 minutes sitting in front of the classroom facing

blackboard plus one half-hour of detention during which the student and teacher try to resolve the conflict
- 3rd offense—referral to the guidance counselor
- 4th offense—sent to the principal's office with a behavior referral completed by the teacher

The class agrees that any student as well as the teacher has the right to assign punishment according to the class-established rules. Within minutes following the acceptance of the this policy, the girl who has been moderating the discussion gives one of the Three Stooges ten minutes detention in front of the classroom for booing her. He reluctantly does what he is told. When he returns to his seat, he is more cooperative for the remainder of the period.

Throughout the year, the Three Stooges continue to be an enigma to David in relation to classroom discipline. The few students who take responsibility and try to punish them receive little or no support from their classmates. Even though each has signed the agreement to which David attached his signature, they continue to violate it. Several students say they will not stop any of these kids, because it is fun to see them distract the teacher when the class becomes boring.

When the class discusses control issues, students come up with the idea that respect comes from the heart. Control, as they understand it, is doing what they are supposed to do out of fear of punishment. David relates this concept to the large number of youth in the class who have on various occasions been stopped by the police. When he asks how they felt the moment they saw the cops approaching, they say they felt scared, intimidated, angry, misunderstood, and not trusted. Some tried to run away. When he asks how they responded when questioned by the police, several admitted to the offense, some say they lied, others say they were framed by friends who wouldn't take the blame.

The group discusses these issues in relationship to the class contract they have created and agreed upon unanimously. All agree that the contract is not working because some individuals fail to cooperate, while others leave the discipline in the hands of the teacher. Finally, the class agrees to give up on detention, with the exception of maintaining it for the Three Stooges. These three will be given a half-hour of detention every day until they begin participating in class. Should lack of cooperation begin again, so would detention.

David decides that he will try to make a special contact with the ringleader of the Three Stooges. Discovering that they both have the same free period, the following morning David stops to buy a doughnut at the local bakery for the leader. The boy agrees to meet with David in the cafeteria, the only free space during that period.

David jestingly tells the leader that the doughnut is both a bribe and an indication that he admires his creativity, intelligence, and leadership ability. Therefore, he would like to explore with him ways in which this student can conduct the class. The boy comes up with a great idea for the class that day. At the time, the Clinton-Lewinsky scandal is dominating the national news. The lad will hand out pieces of paper on which the students will write their definition of sex. Then the class will discuss these to see how similar or different they are as a means to understand the controversy over President Clinton's definition of sex. In this way, David argues how language can be manipulated and how difficult it is to come up with a solid definition. During the class, David ignores silly comments made by the leader's buddies. Both teacher and the leader of the Stooges are happy with the outcome of the class.

Within days the leader is "suspelled" from school for having been caught together with two other students in possession of drug paraphernalia and a small amount of marijuana. During the time the leader is absent, the two remaining Stooges are considerably more cooperative. The class seems more harmonious. Students who have been reluctant to speak up contribute significantly to the class. Upon the leader's return, the silliness resumes. Yet, sometimes it is intertwined with a powerful and meaningful discussion led by the returned Stooge, and now and then assisted by his buddies, who provide additional insight.

The following year, with a master's degree in hand, David ends thirty years of teaching at Madison High School. On completing his book, *Schooling for Humanity: When Big Brother Isn't Watching*, he accepts a part-time job as an adjunct professor at Thomas College, a small former business college in Waterville. Here he has considerably more freedom to explore his ideas about the democratic classroom. During his fifth year of teaching at Thomas College, David embarks upon evolving a process to negotiate a semester grade with each student.

The spring semester during which David has been teaching English composition is ending. David gives no exams, but he does require a conference with each student to negotiate a grade. The first morning of grade conferences, he pulls all his records from his bag: notes on each student's papers and attendance sheets that also indicate the level of student participation and involvement for each day. He looks at his appointment sheets to see who will be first. His office hours begin at 9:00

a.m., but he has scheduled the first appointment at 8:30 to accommodate Frieda (not her real name), who was not able to come at a later time. However, 8:30 a.m. comes and goes. Frieda does not show up for her appointment. *By gosh,* he muses, *you obviously care about a grade, so why aren't you here?. Do I have any other choice than assigning you a grade? Nope. Then, I bet you'll bitch and moan because you feel the grade I give you is unfair. Well, Frieda, that's your loss for not negotiating your grade with me. After all, how can I justify a decent grade when we can't even talk about the progress or lack of which you have made in this course?*

At 8:45 David catches sight of the rather unkempt hair and dark brown eyes of Bob peeking in the door. David warmly greets him, urging him to enter the office. "Sit down," he encourages, pointing to the more comfortable, cushioned, swivel chair at his desk.

Not quite sure what to say, Bob quickly asks, "So you said, we gotta negotiate a grade?"

"Yeah, that's right," David replies gently.

"I can't do that," he says firmly, looking at his instructor straight in the eye.

"Why not?" David asks with sinking heart. "You know what progress you have made throughout—"

"But you're the teacher. You should make a grade presentation, which we then can debate," Bob explains, resolutely adding, "Don't leave it up to me."

David feels a combination of defensiveness, disappointment, frustration, and anxiety. He has imagined that Bob, an elementary school teacher-to-be, would appreciate his approach. David suggests, "I'd rather ask you some questions. Then, if our thoughts differ, we can explore the specific issue further. I might ask you additional questions for clarification. In this way, we should be able to come up with a fair grade. Do you think this'll work for you?"

"We can try," he responds noncommittally.

"Let's begin by talking about the essay you wrote that you liked best," David encourages. "Which was it and why did you choose the topic you did?"

"Well, the one where the Maine Principals' Association violated Title 9 because they wouldn't let a boy play on the girls' field-hockey team. The boy had the guts to take his case to court. It really ticked me off when the judge ruled that the boy was taking a female's spot thereby preventing a female to play."

As Bob talks, David feels his student's resentment toward the judge and the Principals' Association. "You certainly feel strongly about this issue," he says reassuringly. "Did you enjoy writing this piece? I am eager to know."

"Because I'm pissed by the situation, I'm motivated to write," Bob says with emotion.

"What made this a good essay?" David persists.

"Well, it was easy to write. My thoughts just came flowing out," Bob responds with satisfaction.

"That's great. That's what leads to good writing," he acknowledges. "Your paper, which is filled with passion, flows naturally. Your use of dialogue is captivating. Your thoughts are clearly organized and well developed."

As their discussion moves along, David asks Bob to identify the needs he had when he entered this course and whether these were met. David is eager to learn from him whether he benefited from the class critiquing each other's work in small groups.

"I like the specific directions you gave us for critiquing our classmates' work, because they ranged from general questions to particular grammatical issues. In the small group critiques, I gained insight from those who read my work carefully," he explains, causing David to feel a little more confident that this approach works well if students are prepared.

Yet, David's mind begins to drift momentarily to those students who make little effort, as well as to those who do not complete their rough drafts on time. Even if he were to punish students for not getting their work in on time, he thinks to himself, the impact will only be negative. He must find positive ways to encourage these kids. *Lay off, David, we are discussing Bob's grade. You can have your solitary monologue at another time.*

Looking up, he sees Frieda standing at his door with anxious expression. "I'm awfully sorry that I am late. I—"

"I'll meet with you right after I finish with Bob," David says with irritation. She leaves the office to wait in the hall.

"Oh, yes," coming to again, David says to Bob, "could you comment on the two books we have read, Frankl's *Man's Search for Meaning* and Rushkoff's *Coercion*?" He is delighted that Bob likes Frankl's book, which explores the emotional struggle of those who endured the torture of being incarcerated in a Nazi concentration camp.

As David brings their conversation to a conclusion, he asks Bob whether he got all of his work in on time, including rough drafts, teacher-corrected versions, and revised copies. David checks his record of Bob's work.

Bob admits that at first he had difficulty getting his rough drafts in on time, as he really didn't know how the class was going to develop. "Your approach is new to me. Not being criticized and graded makes it harder to get my work in on time. Yet, when I realized that your intent is to be encouraging, I really got into this course. I never used to like writing. This is the first time I came to class looking forward to those ten-minute free writing sessions. It was a good experience for me."

With their fifteen-minute time slot running out, David asks, "Do you now feel comfortable enough to come up with a grade for yourself?" Anxiously awaiting his reply, he looks him straight in the eye.

"Maybe a little better," Bob replies with hesitation.

"Just try. Don't you think from our conversation that you now have some feeling from where I might be coming? Don't you think you have a better framework by which to make a judgment?" David persists.

"High B. Does that seem fair?" Bob asks with more confidence than when they began their dialogue.

"Well, yes it does. I would go for an A–. Is that OK with you?" David is eager to know as he looks at him intently.

"If you say so. You're the teacher," he responds happily, though still appearing unsure as to whether this approach really works. As Bob gets up to leave, he shakes David's hand, saying, "I really enjoyed your classes. I feel I made real progress in my writing."

With these words, he departs. David's mind is reeling with doubts about the grading process. He appreciates Bob's humility, but, by gum, he wants these kids to take ownership for their studies. *No, Bob, you nor any other student is going to bully me into the position that as teacher it is my duty to assign you a grade. You have never been empowered to grade yourself nor given the responsibility for doing so. Since grading yourself is part of both the learning and empowerment processes, I will have to give specific instructions at the onset of the course. On the course syllabus given out on the first day of class will be the questions each student will have to answer in writing prior to our grade conference. Will you take this more seriously? Who knows*? Just give us a grade, *I imagine some of you saying. Then, if you are not satisfied with the grade, you will complain that the teacher isn't fair. You'll downgrade him on your evaluation form of his course, or you'll find some other way to protest. Oh, here you go again, David; paranoia is taking over; you are trying to convince yourself that students are out to get you—*

As Bob leaves, Frieda enters, not daring to take a seat.

"Sit down, Frieda," David pleasantly says. She apologizes profusely for being late. Unprompted, she recalls that some of her work was late, that she didn't work to her ability, and asks whether a C– or even possibly a C would be fair.

He asks her what she really feels would be fair.

"I'm not good at judging, but 'cause my work was late, and I didn't try that hard, I guess I gotta take a C–."

Appreciating her honesty, David cannot justify assigning her a C–.

"Frieda," he says, "I appreciate your self-reflection and your honesty. For that alone you deserve a C."

Relieved, she looks up, trying to crack a little smile. "Thanks, Dave." She turns scurrying out of the office.

As David reflects on the grades just negotiated, or, more accurately, bargained with two students, he feels comfortable with the outcome. The students were both honest and humble, two qualities he has found to be rare and, therefore, he is inclined to reward.

Oblivious to what is going is going on around him, he catches Saundra out of the corner of his eye. Her tall but rather chubby figure is hovering over him. Her blonde hair is pulled back into a ponytail. Her blue eyes appear dull; her expression seems bored. Maybe she is just sleepy. She is clad in a tight gray T-shirt, white pajama pants with a floral pattern, and flip-flops. David wonders why her appearance doesn't seem to matter when she meets with her instructor. He wants to ask her, *"Do you really dress so tastelessly when you meet with your teachers?"*

Without so much as a greeting, she slouches into the office. David feels less comfortable with her than with Bob. He brusquely says, "So, you're here to negotiate a grade, eh?"

"Yup. I think I should get at least an A–," she says quietly but firmly, as if she is demanding the grade. *Oh no, young lady,* he says to himself, *you are not going to get away with murder. You don't make demands like this of your teacher. Who the hell do you think you are?*

Trying to conceal his irritation at her challenge and hide his feeling of insecurity, he grabs all of his students' records to demonstrate a show of *I am in charge.* He responds as quietly and tactfully as he can, "Really, why do you think you deserve such a high grade?"

"You mean to say I don't deserve even an A–?" she demands, causing his irritation at her to rise rapidly. "You didn't make a fuss last semester about my grade."

Wondering whether Saundra might have received an A– from him last semester and needing some time to be able to respond, he asks, "Well, tell me why you deserve this grade?"

"I did all my work. I can't help it that my grandmother was sick. It's not my fault that I'm on the softball team and we had a lot of games. 'Sorry.' You said these are excused absences. You have no right to lower my grade like you are doing. So there!"

No way will you get your way, David says to himself, feeling rising defensiveness and rage towards her. He feels some relief in checking last semester's records and seeing that she and he had agreed to a B+. Trying to control his annoyance and attempting to appear not too harsh, David's voice reveals tension as he speaks at a rapid clip. "Yes, I did say your absences are excused. But having missed—let me check—" as he pulls up his attendance sheets, "nine classes must have some impact upon your grade."

"That's not fair," she responds with big tears beginning to stream down her face. "I was expecting an A– at least. It's not my fault I was absent, and you didn't give me make-up work when I asked you."

As David's level of frustration rises, his entire body becomes tense. No longer is he friendly. His impatience now becomes evident, as his tone turns to anger. "No, I did not give you make-up work. But let us review my notes regarding your work." He opens his record book. "Paper #2 has a check minus: 'Interesting thoughts that need substantiation; needs organization; chaotic paper.' Paper #3 is late, plus my comment that the 'paper would be more meaningful if personal examples were offered.'" He concludes his tirade by reminding her that she handed in the rough draft of her research paper late, and that it was not typed—not even written in pen—had no citations and bibliographical references, and contained no connection to personal experiences, all requirements of the assignment.

In a hostile tone Saundra demands, "Well, what then do you think my grade should be?"

With effort, David quietly replies, "Based on the evidence, I would say that a C+ would be very generous. It could go up to a B– if you really get your act together and do a fine job on the research paper that is due [in place of the exam] before, but no later than, 8:00 a.m. on Friday morning."

"I can't accept that for a grade."

As tears now drop out of her eyes like a leaking water faucet, David asks himself, *How much more generous can I be? This is supposed to be college not high school. This young lady has no humility. But keep in mind your romantic notions: since this school apparently takes in all students who apply, many of whom come from the lower academic groups, most of whom are from low-income families, they are at college trying to make a better life for themselves. Live up to your ideals, old man, don't be so harsh on Saundra. After all, some of her work was really well done.*

"Why can't you accept a C+?" he asks, trying to be a little gentler.

"Because C is an unacceptable grade. B is average, not even a B," she insists between sobs. Before he can respond, Saundra, with pursed lips, gets up, snatches her book bag, and storms out of his cubicle mumbling so that he can hear her clearly, "You are the most unfair teacher I have ever had."

He calls out behind her, "Well, let's see how your research paper develops. I'm sorry you feel this way."

She suddenly stops, turns around, and amidst sobs sputters, "You have your mind made up. You don't believe in negotiating," and then continues on her way.

Once again, anger like electricity rises throughout his body. His entire being is as tight as a high-tension cable holding a very tall pole.

As David looks back on this incident several years later, he wonders how, as the teacher, the adult, he could have defused her anger and helped her to come up with a grade they could both agree upon. He realizes that he took Saundra's anger personally. He felt blamed, guilty, and defensive—a serious mistake. His first clue that things were going badly for her was her sloppy appearance. He needed to understand her frustration. Why hadn't he asked her, "Are you afraid your parents will be disappointed with you if you bring home a low grade?" She might have answered yes.

"Why do you think things haven't gone as well as you had hoped?"

"Cause my grandmother was sick, and I had lots of sporting events that also took me out of class?"

"So this must have affected your ability to concentrate on your school work."

"Yes, it sure did. I was really stressed."

"If things had gone better for you this semester, do you think you could have done better?"

"Of course."

"So under all of these tough conditions, what do you think a fair grade should be?"

"I don't know."

"Try! I'm sure you'll come up with a reasonable grade."

"A B," she might have hesitantly said, "if I get my research paper in to you as we talked about."

"If the paper is well done. That means it is thoroughly researched and effectively organized. You will analyze your research, your experiences, and your ideas to reach a persuasive conclusion. I'm sure you can do this and achieve at least a B–."

The days of early May are breaking forth with the warmth of spring: lush green grass; tender light-green buds sprouting from warm, brown tree limbs; puffy, pink clouds floating across a robust sky. David happily departs from the college for a long summer vacation.

Upon returning in the fall, armed with several stapled pages of "Preparation for Grade Conference" sheets in hand, David enters his Introduction to Sociology class. To his surprise, Saundra is sitting among his thirty new students. *Why is Saundra in my class?* he wonders. *After all, there are several divisions of Sociology, taught by two other instructors.*

Throughout the entire semester, Saundra is actively involved in class, doing all of the required readings, thoroughly and thoughtfully preparing written assignments (although two are slightly late), participating in class discussions, and respecting opposing viewpoints. Choosing to do her research project on homophobia, she attends a session of David's evening adult education class, Experiencing Diversity, at which a gay pastor is guest speaker. She asks numerous thoughtful and thought-provoking questions.

When it comes time to negotiate a grade, unlike many students, she hands in three, single-spaced, typewritten pages responding to the questions on the grade preparation sheets handed out on the first day of class. The last question, "Write the grade you feel you have earned. Explain why you deserve this grade," she has answered as follows, in writing: "I think I earned a B in the class due to my active participation and regular attendance. I even attended one of your night classes for my final project. There was not a class that I did not participate in, and I feel that my final project went well. I worked on it over the course of the class and didn't have to rush at all. The only thing that doesn't work in my favor would be a few absences and two late papers. Other than that I believe that everything went well."

"Do you really feel a B is a fair grade?" David asks.

"Yes," she humbly replies.

"I disagree," David says solemnly. "I can't justify any grade lower than an A," he continues.

"You what?" she says, her face brightening up with excitement. "An A?"

"Yes!"

"I can't believe it!" she says with pride and joy. "I really appreciated this class. I learned a lot how to think and question and appreciate all sorts of different people, even though I disagree strongly with some."

Because of Saundra's change in attitude and his experiences with a wonderful English composition class that semester, where the chemistry was comfortable, a trusting atmosphere for sharing, David looks forward to the coming semester.

Two years later, as the semester draws toward an end with warm spring days upon the campus, David has a gut feeling that some students may not take grade negotiation seriously. Therefore, as students sign up for their conference times with him, he gives each a copy of the class sign-up sheet with the following statement from the syllabus.

> GRADE CONFERENCE
> In order to have a grade conference you <u>must</u>:
> - Attend the meeting at the time for which you signed up.
> - Bring with you your *completed* GRADE CONFERENCE questions.
>
> You will NOT be issued a grade, not even an incomplete, without attending and participating at this conference. As a result you will fail the course.

Because one student didn't show up when his alarm clock failed to wake him for his 9:30 a.m. appointment, and another forgot to bring her completed grade conference questions, these students failed the course. Yes, spring is in the air, David reminds himself. Although only these two students neglected to follow directions, he feels something seems terribly wrong. Why must he threaten and even have to remind his students that they will fail the course should they neglect attending the scheduled meeting?

David thinks of his father in Germany. He recalls that his father as a child lived through World War I, the Great Depression, and the rise of Nazism. It never occurred to him to escape to America, his mother's native country. Conditions had been terrible in Germany; they would continue to be bad, but surely they wouldn't get worse. However, his arrest and internment at Dachau were his belated wake-up call.

Recognizing the importance of taking personal responsibility to remedy social ills, on coming to America he became politically active. He, therefore, wrote letters to the press, corresponded with syndicated columnists and journalists, and participated in the presidential campaigns of Adlai Stevenson in 1952 and 1956 against Dwight Eisenhower.

David realizes that, although circumstances are very different in

America then and today, he observes that more and more individuals fail to take responsibility, as they feel no need to. As kids grow up in an environment in which only governments and administrations hold everyone accountable for their actions or inactions, they do not develop a sense of personal responsibility—a deeply rooted feeling that their life choices, good or bad, are entirely in their own hands. Rather, they only act when they are reminded that others are holding them accountable at all times.

In our consumer and materialistically-oriented society, they can get much of what they desire instantaneously. Credit cards are a prime example of instantaneous satisfaction, allowing people to behave irresponsibly. Consumers accept high interest on debt while businesses offer zero-percent financing up to a year on a major purchase. One can purchase a new or used car, according to an advertisement, for "bad credit, no credit, new credit, or low credit score." Families who have already maxed out some of their numerous credit cards can still pretty much purchase what they want. The message is that one can have everything now, pay later. Therefore, through osmosis children learn that it is not necessary to work in order to instantly fulfill their material desires for video games, the newest iPod, or the fanciest cell phone.

Under these circumstances, why should a student, or anyone for that matter, be concerned about a political election or the passage of laws that limit each of our personal freedoms as established by the Patriot Act of 2003?

Finally, why should he, or for that matter anybody else, bother to put a doctor or dental appointment on the calendar? After all, he or she will receive a postcard ten days in advance of the appointment and a phone reminder the day prior to his visit. If he or she doesn't show up, they may complain—poor me, pity me—because they must now pay the full amount for the office visit. Sounds like his or her grade conference requirement, eh?

David also knows, if a public school teacher fails to abide by the recent Maine law that requires all public school teachers to be fingerprinted, he will lose his license to teach. When the law came into effect, rather than complying, he retired after thirty years of teaching at the same public high school.

The argument for fingerprinting is to keep pedophiles from teaching. He recently read on the front page of his local paper that the longtime popular assistant principal, athletic director of a nearby public high school, who also was pastor of an evangelical church in the same small community, was arrested for sexual misconduct. This individual since has confessed, been fired from his educational position, resigned from the ministry, and is awaiting trial. Without this new law, the educator would still have been caught, while at the same time not all educators would be under suspicion of being child molesters.

When this man is eventually released from prison, he will be labeled on a sex-offenders registry available to all to see on the Internet. Even if he is psychologically cured of his deviant behavior, bearing the sex-offender label for life will make it difficult for him to start a new life, find a new job, and especially a new place to live.

On a recent visit to a public high school, David was surprised to see that not only do students bear photo IDs around their necks, but teachers sport them as well. The rationale is that by being able to quickly identify who belongs in the school, the risk of an abductor or a terrorist entering the school is reduced. Like the fingerprinting law, the effect is growing paranoia, suggesting that any person may be suspected of criminal intentions.

David senses the potential of a similar effect arising in America as he reflects on the Jews in Nazi Germany, who were forced to wear the yellow Star of David on their sleeve. He also recalls that on all community and state lists, including tax rolls and residential addresses, Jews were identified by the capitalized word ISRAEL following their surname. This system did work to more easily identify Jews and facilitate their persecution.

David thinks of the present. Why should public school students take responsibility for their grades, when school administrators have established a system by which parents can monitor their children's status at any time online, and then blame the parents if their children do poorly? Parents can log onto such programs as classroll.com or infinitecampus.com. By typing in their child's name, his or her school district and password, they can find their child's assignments—whether due, completed, or missing—and his or her grade to date in each subject. Parents can keep nagging each of their children with statistical evidence day by day that often fosters hostility within a family. Feeling angry and unworthy, with teachers and administrators who blame parents for their children's difficulties, quite a few parents take their anger out on their children. With parents taking on the responsibility for their children's school progress, teachers have an additional weapon with which to blame parents if their children falter. Furthermore, administrators have another tool by which to hold accountable teachers whose students are doing poorly.

Teachers, too, no longer are responsible for coming up with creative classes that excite and motivate their students. Rather, they have to teach to the standards of the national No Child Left Behind law and similar state-mandated norms. If their students do poorly on the state and national tests—the results of which are published in the press—teachers, administrators, students, and even parents are held accountable. If test scores remain low, schools are in jeopardy of losing at least federal funds, while teachers and administrators are at risk of losing their jobs.

With all of these thoughts in mind, over the next few years David continues to revise the grade negotiation process. Instead of having students answer questions, an essay approach might be more effective. He realizes the need to emphasize that writing a well-developed reflective essay along with attending the scheduled grade conference are valuable for both student and teacher. The insights of students help him improve his approach to teaching. In the fall of 2006, he presents the following method:

ASSESSMENT

In this course, you *evaluate yourself.* You are REQUIRED to meet with me a minimum of 3 (three) times:

- At the BEGINNING of the semester to become acquainted and to discuss your needs
- Mid-term evaluation
- Final grade conference
- *(and)* At any time you feel you need help with your writing and/or just want to talk

Just as you keep all of your of your papers including your notes throughout the semester, I, too, keep notes on your work including class participation, your writing, punctuality of work, effort, and attendance. At our final meeting, you and I will negotiate and agree upon a grade.

At our mid-term evaluation meeting, show me log notes you have taken to date. Make sure you have responded to all questions thoroughly.

Prior to our final (grade conference) meeting, you will hand in:

End of semester/self-evaluation, approximately 5 pages, 1250 words

Learning is a process that should reflect your development as a maturing individual and, in this course, as budding writer. For instance, although you have nine papers, flexibility is important.

Example: if you wish to *continue* to develop the finished piece of an essay, e.g. essay No. 3, you are encouraged to do so. In addition to my comments on your paper, we can meet to explore the growth that is evolving. It is important that you keep all of your papers to determine the progress you are making.

Assessment includes:

- Short (1 to 1.5 pages, approx. 375 words) papers
- Longer (3 to 5 pages, approx. 750 words) papers
- Final self-evaluation essay
- Writing exercises in class
- Reading assignments
- Conferencing with me
- Critiquing/active class participation/listening and responding
- Attendance
- Punctuality of work

Final *self-analysis essay:* In this well-organized and developed essay, include the following factors:

Since education is more than getting a degree to secure a suitable job, what else should your education, especially in this course, include? Did you make progress in this direction? Explain.

How did this course help you understand yourself, your classmates, and others?

How did this course help you develop as a unique individual?

What needs did you have on entering this class? What did you do to try to meet these needs. Did you succeed? Explain. If not, what could you have done to make sure they were met?

What challenges did you face in this class? Explain and how you tried to resolve these.

Did you meet with me at least 3 times as urged in the syllabus?

Did you ask for help when you needed it, for instance, with grammar, sentence structure, and organization?

Did the feedback you received from other students help you improve your writing?

Explain ways in which the feedback was helpful to you as well as instances in which it was not.

What do you consider your best paper? What factors helped to make this succeed?

What did you like about this course?

Summarize specific improvements you made in your writing this semester.

What readings were most valuable to you? Why? Which were least worthwhile?

Explain. As the major reading this semester is Mark Salzman's *Notebooks,* a good part of your essay should include a discussion of the book, providing detailed evidence from the reading of what you liked and/or disliked about the book. In what respects was it valuable to you in terms of understanding others, as in breaking away from stereotypical responses we often have toward incarcerated youth. In reading the boys' essays, what did you learn about them, their feelings, and writing in general? What did you learn in regards to your writing, especially in terms of writing from the heart?

Were the films of value to you? Explain why, referring to specific films.

Did you get all of your work in on time, including rough drafts? If not, explain.

Describe your class participation in the class: attentiveness, listening, speaking?

Did you attend class regularly? Why or why not?

What did you dislike about this course? What attempts did you make to bring about the change(s) you felt were necessary?

What grade do you feel you have earned. Explain why you deserve this grade.

Even though David does keep his policy that students will fail the course should they not attend the grade conference, several positive changes have occurred. He realizes the causes for student passivity. He discovers that a structured series of three meetings with each student during the semester provides necessary consistency for students to better understand his approach and develop the accompanying responsibility. In rare instances when students disregard the final meeting, he can negotiate with them to either take the course over with him meeting once weekly, continue the research paper further if interested, or start a new one that inspires them, or repeat the course with another teacher.

David continues to revise his grading procedure. Two years following his retirement at Thomas College, he now teaches at a community college in the Waterville area. He still allows students two unexcused absences. However, the student will lose five points from the final semester grade for every additional absence following the two that are permitted. For failing to attend the final grade conference, David will assign the grade he would have proposed—if necessary—at the grade negotiation session. He will also deduct five points from the final semester grade.

David concentrates on finding joy in one-to-one contact with his students. The compassion he experiences in working with students of diverse emotional states and varied cultural backgrounds becomes more and more rewarding as he tries to let go of his ego, his need to be recognized as a great teacher. He remembers his father's humanitarian passion, his fervent desire to foster peace in a war-torn world, and his compassion for people, especially the oppressed. These are the ideals that David is trying to emulate.

17

Give Me Poison

A month and a half after Jing, David, and his mother met on his 50th birthday in China, he starts a new life in Madison, the town in which he continues to teach. His son Oliver, who is a loner, has become engaged. Elly likes his fiancée. She is pleased that both Jessica and her parents warmly accept her. She seems relatively content at the retirement community where she is living in Topsham, directly across the river from Brunswick.

Although each of their lives appears to be taking a turn for the better, David's old baggage still lingers. Elly reminds him that she misses living among younger people. She repeatedly laments how terrible it is to get old. She has also developed a habit of making a ticking sound with her lips that irritates David. Once again, as he becomes enveloped in old feelings of annoyance and resentment toward her, he begins to distance himself from her. Her bitterness, which he helped to cause, feels like a wound infected with poison. He doesn't want to become contaminated with bitterness, self-pity, and hostility.

When Jing arrives in early October, Elly welcomes her warmly. On their visit with her at the Highlands, her retirement home, she brings them to L.L.Bean in Freeport. There she joyfully buys Jing an expensive, nonstick wok and a winter parka.

Elly's friends at the Highlands receive Jing well. They especially appreciate her graceful demonstration of Tai Chi. David and Jing's visits with Elly become relatively frequent. Either they visit her in Topsham or she visits them in Madison, an hour and a quarter from her home. She spends at least one night every few months with them at their one-bedroom apartment.

Having to pay child support, make car payments, and pay rent, along with all other expenses, Jing and David have little money. It is Elly who comes to their rescue. She even offers to and buys their wedding rings: for each a band of blue sapphires embedded in gold.

David and Jing spend their first Christmas together with Elly in Madison. They had purchased Christmas ornaments in China. Except for the lack of candles on the tiny fir tree David has cut, their Christmas Eve celebration is similar to the ones of his childhood. As David tries to revive old family traditions, he is insensitive to the fact that Christmas is a foreign and meaningless event for Jing.

Over the years, David becomes more flexible and open to new experiences. As he experiences Jing's sadness at being unable genuinely to celebrate the Chinese New Year in Maine, along with her Chinese birthday that occurs on the third day of the new year, he better understands his mother's desire to observe Christmas. In spite of being Jewish, her parents had always set up a small Christmas tree illuminated with candlelight. At least this was one tradition she could salvage from her motherland and pass on to her son and later share with his family. The continuity of tradition helped Elly adjust and even assimilate more easily into American culture.

In early March 1994, Elly is hospitalized. Believing that she has a severe bout of the flu, she didn't take the illness seriously. As she becomes weaker, medical tests determine that she has bladder cancer. She refuses surgery, and her doctor predicts she has only six months to live. Therefore, when she is released from the hospital in late June, David and Jing bring her to stay with them in their new home in Waterville. Both Jing and David want her to die in their presence at their home. They also are eager for her to experience the birth of May, their daughter, who arrives that September ninth.

Although Elly is at first quite weak, she quickly recovers her strength. Her cancer is in remission. In spite of having a newborn baby, Jing takes exceptionally good care of her mother-in-law. She prepares three delicious meals a day for her. These include freshly baked bread that she makes from scratch, Elly's favorite English orange marmalade, ripened tomatoes picked from the garden just before lunch, and the German cakes for which Elly longs. Never thinking about herself, Jing prepares western-style dinners for Elly, including pot roast and baked chicken, instead of the Chinese food with which she grew up and that she and David cherish. Jing always sits and talks with Elly throughout lunch. Unfortunately, depressed by her growing loss of independence, Elly seems uninterested in learning about Jing. However, May bonds sweetly with her grandmother, a relationship that remains close through the end of Elly's life in 2004. Elly also contributes greatly by paying David and his family a monthly rent that helps to pay off the mortgage on their newly purchased house. When she decides to give up her apartment at the retirement community in Topsham, she offers and then pays off their entire mortgage.

During her first two years with David's family, Elly is able to travel by bus to visit friends in Topsham, as well as in Cambridge and David's only relatives in Wellesley, Massachusetts. She even travels to visit friends in Princeton, New Jersey. However, her ability to appreciate life is deteriorating, as is her memory. An avid letter writer, she gradually gives up corresponding with her friends.

Following a trip to her native city of Hamburg, accompanied by David, Jing, and May, her love for life declines more rapidly. While in Hamburg, she tries to telephone Gertrude, her closest friend from her youth and art school, who tried in vain to save her parents from the concentration camps. When a new tenant in her apartment tells her that Gertrude died over a year ago, she is devastated. From this shock, Elly never recovers.

On returning home, Elly completely gives up paying her bills. This is most unusual, as she has always been meticulous about managing her finances. She spends more and more time in bed. She seems to be drifting away into another world. David finds himself becoming increasingly annoyed with her. The warmth and tenderness that he had felt for her especially during her illness becomes mixed with emotions of frustration.

Eventually, Elly no longer cares for her personal needs. She falls several times as she goes to the bathroom. She is no longer able to bathe in the tub by herself. Her doctor, who has seen her regularly at his office, now prescribes medicine over the phone. He appears unable or unwilling to treat her condition, which includes constant coughing, decreasing appetite, and intensifying weakness. Finally, on New Year's Eve of 2000, as her coughing intensifies and she no longer will get out of bed, David brings her to the hospital just down the road from their home.

During the five days Elly is there, David hires an attorney to draw up papers, so that he will have power of attorney to care for her finances. Her living will needs to be updated according to new regulations in Maine law. She is able to sign the documents from her hospital bed before her attorney and two witnesses. As she appears very weak, her physician recommends that David bring her to a nursing home for rehabilitation. Although weak, she travels in David's car to the Glenridge Nursing Home and Rehabilitation Center in Augusta, a part of the Maine General tax-free corporation. She happily observes how beautifully the sun shines from a sparkling clear blue sky onto glistening snow. Within a few days at Glenridge, her condition worsens. She repeats time and again, "I don't want to live; let me die." Confusion mounts. At first she thinks her son is her brother who died nearly ten years before. She refuses or maybe is unable to acknowledge that the fellow by her bed is her son, David.

David speaks with her elder-care physician, Laurel Coleman, who immediately takes a liking to Elly. Under no circumstances would Dr. Coleman let Elly die. "Although her condition remains grave," she quietly explains, "she is a strong-willed person. She might very well come through." *If she wants to die, shouldn't she?* David asks himself. *She has always led an independent life; she has always been strong—a survivor in the truest sense of the word. After all, to be hospitalized, weak, and maybe having to live her life out in a nursing home, is the condition she most fears. Don't let her suffer; let her die,* he prays.

Although she does recuperate, Jing and David no longer are able to provide the care she needs at their home. Both are working full time and May is at daycare. Nor is it possible to have an attendant live with them.

David arranges for his mother to move to the Evergreen, a new retirement community in Waterville that opened in February 2000. As she has regained much of her memory, she does not fit the candidacy for the Alzheimer's unit in which she is placed. The unit, consisting of about thirty beds, is quiet, comfortable, and as homelike as is possible for an institutional setting. All floors are carpeted. Artificial flowers, sofas, comfortable chairs, and large windows with fancy curtains create a reasonably pleasant atmosphere. Yet David feels that having his mother, whose mind is becoming clearer, live among people who, if they are not screaming, are talking nonsense, is demeaning to her.

Fortunately, she has her own room with a private bath. Although her room is on the dark, north side of the building, she loves the view from her bed onto a sloping field and woods. In the spring and fall, she sees deer grazing. Yet, she is unhappy there, often speaking of wanting to die. She asks David to give her poison. Impossible. Even though David feels her pain, he doesn't have the authority to put her out of her misery. He remembers her telling him numerous times before she moved in with his family: Don't ever put me in a nursing home. I will never walk with a cane. I don't ever want to be in a situation where my mind fails.

On a bright, crisp autumn day, David brings Elly to one of her favorite spots by the ocean, Bailey Island. They have lunch together, her favorite lobster stew at Cook's Lobster Pound and Restaurant. After lunch they drive to the tip of the island. She remarks, looking out at the open sea, "This will be the last time I will ever see the ocean I so much love." Pointing to the horizon where sea and sky meet she adds, "That's where I come from; that's where I'll return with my Walter."

As David often visits the nursing home, he becomes upset with the residential facility's management. In spite of his complaints, the staff fails to cut his mother's fingernails or toenails. They wash her wool skirts with all other laundry in hot water, lose some clothing, and don't provide activities for her. He finally decides to move her in July at considerable cost to a Catholic nursing home which has an excellent reputation. The large, multistoried brick building, at one time a convent, is dismal. Not only is Elly distressed to have a roommate, but being a Jewess in a Catholic facility causes her to be all the more unhappy. She is very angry with David for having moved her to the Mount. She insists that if he fails to give her poison, she will take her own life; she says that she knows how.

Within two weeks, David brings Elly back to her room at the Evergreen, where she becomes happier. Apparently eager to have her back, the staff attempt to do more things with her. On a hot day, they take her on an outing to China Lake for ice cream. Nursing assistants look at pictures with her, as suggested by a psychiatric evaluation David ordered. The staff even begin to take proper care of her nails. She no longer talks of dying. Seeming to accept her fate, she does remain lethargic—never taking any initiative in talking with others, reading, answering letters. When David brings her a drawing pad and pencils as well as her watercolors, she shows no interest. She does ask about David's family, especially May, seeming to enjoy their visits. She is especially delighted when her grandson Oliver visits.

After her return to her old room in the Alzheimer's unit, she falls at least three times. On one occasion, she breaks several ribs, on another she puts her head through the wall in her bathroom making a big hole near the baseboard, and then in November she falls again, breaking her hip. Following surgery, her hip recovers remarkably quickly. Within weeks, she is walking with a walker. However, she never remembers that she has broken her hip. Not wanting to send her back to the same facility, David places her in the nursing home attached to the osteopathic hospital at which she is a patient. Although she again wants to die and is not happy that she has a roommate, she bites the bullet as she has throughout her life. Nursing home existence has now become her bitter fate.

During her recovery period, David and his family visit her frequently. Finally, he develops an interest in learning about her past.

18

Quiet Thunder Returns in August

SINCE BEING AT LAKEWOOD MANOR NURSING HOME following her broken hip, David's mother has become considerably weaker. She barely eats. Her weight has dropped from her normally slender 140 pounds to 80 pounds. Her once full cheeks are hollow. Her skin has become wrinkled, appearing like paper poorly pasted onto her frail skeleton. She continues to refuse any medications, except occasionally to control pain.

Following three months of beautiful, sometimes scorching hot, summer days without a drop of rain, in September the weather turns crisp and clear; the nights are finally cool. On this morning, shortly after the September 11, 2001, terrorist attack, leaves on the oak tree outside her window happily absorb the heavy rain that has been falling intermittently since the afternoon before. By mid morning the storm's gray pallor still casts darkness over Elly's room at the nursing home. Lying in bed on her side facing the wall, clad in a white hospital nightgown, her slender, withering body appears barely visible under the white sheet. Not sure whether he is waking her from a deep sleep, David quietly but firmly says his usual hello. She gradually turns, supporting herself on her elbow to greet him with a surprisingly broad smile.

"Oh, David, so good to see you!"

According to routine, he heads toward the green high-backed, plastic upholstered chair positioned by the window. Removing the absorbent paper placed on the seat for Elly, he sits down. Crossing his legs, he makes himself comfortable as he gazes out of the window before looking toward her. His patterned entry into conversation, "How are you doing?" escapes from his lips.

Returning to lethargy, she haltingly says, "I'm not sure where I am and where I should go!"

"Where would you like to go?" David asks.

"Into the woods," she tells him, and thoughts of elderly Eskimos come to his mind. Realizing they are no longer useful to the community, they disappear on an ice floe, never to return.

"And then?" he asks.

"To the ocean," she replies, bringing tears to his eyes as he imagines her walking into the waves on a cold rainy day, to be engulfed by the monstrous gray, swirling sea.

"And then?" he asks.

"Try to catch a boat," she replies as David suddenly is brought back to reality, no longer fearing her imminent demise.

"Where would you go?" he wants to know.

"To America!"

"Oh, but you are in America now, aren't you?" he asks, hoping that she realizes where she is.

"No, London," she responds with assurance.

"You do love London," he sympathetically adds.

"I like London. The British were so good to us. They saved us."

"If it weren't for the British, I wouldn't be here today," David jests.

"I know very little of the English countryside because we didn't have a car. But Walter and I loved to walk in the country. I loved the rolling meadows, the hedged-in fields, the horses. My brother loved horses."

As Elly speaks, David imagines heavily laden storm clouds engulfing London with dampness and smog, foreboding the tempest of war. He asks his mother, "Do you like America?"

"I like America, too," she replies with clarity. "America has been good to us. But I haven't made many friends."

"Are people nice to you here?" he queries, referring to the staff at the nursing home.

"They are not un-nice," she replies curtly. After a moment's pause she continues. "It's noisy. No manners, nothing. Nobody cares. Nobody is decent. Not anything."

As she speaks, the deeply imprinted television images of a plane crashing in a ball of fire and smoke into New York City's World Trade Center just a few days ago emerge in David's mind. He asks his mother whether she heard about the attack.

Without any sign of emotion, she remains quiet for moment. Looking away from her son, she calmly says, "At first I thought it was just one of those terrible TV shows. Then I realized it was real."

"How do you feel about it?"

"The government must take strong action against these people," she replies.

Astonished at her response, trying to understand how she must feel, David ponders, *At a time of great need, you were welcomed, cared for, and appreciated in America. You felt safe in this nation far away from the war that was devastating Europe. You were able to raise your family without fear of reprisal. Now the America that has given you citizenship, sanctuary, and hope seems to be under attack by angry, unappreciative people. You feel hurt; you feel America's pain. You want the United States government to take the necessary action to stop this madness. I see from where you are coming.*

A nurse tells David that his mother intuitively reacted to the terrorist attack by wanting to telephone her Walter. She knew he would be agonizing over this event. She longed to be with him, to console and reassure him. She also wanted his comfort at such a difficult time. She definitely experienced vivid flashbacks of their past together in Germany, their honeymoon in Bavaria cut short, as the landlord of the cottage they rented had joined the Nazi party. She remembered his anxiety: "What will happen to you and me? To all Jews? Will those who hate us exterminate us like mice?"

In what should be her golden years, Elly is alone once again. When she was forced to leave her native Germany, losing her parents at the hands of the Nazis, she was still strong. Although physically distanced from her brother in England by the Atlantic Ocean, she visited him several times and talked with him over the phone. They were close. However, now he is dead.

David asks his mother, "What would you really like?"

In a deeply calm and gentle voice she answers, "What I would like best is a nice quiet day, to go to sleep, and never to wake up."

Christmas 2001

David has become close to his mother over the past two years. As she no longer lives with them at home, it is easier to feel love and compassion for her. If she were still living with them day in and day out during which they must take care of her, change her diapers and bed linens, listen to her groaning, tensions would mount. David's relationship with Jing and even May would become strained. He can imagine how he would become easily irritated, engulfed in frustration and anger, and even resentment. Alas, he dares admit, it is best that she is now at Lakewood

Manor nursing home just five minutes by car from home. He can visit her easily and regularly.

For Christmas Eve of 2001, finally David writes this poem and gives it to her.

Acknowledging Mummy
To my mother, Elly

Short, straight hair,
Bodily erect, spiritually tender and honest,
Blouse, skirt, walking shoes,
My Mummy: comfortable, reassuring.

In a forest opening
Amidst wild blueberries
Crouching, jar in hand,
At your side: Daddy, Beagy, and me.

On a rocky ledge by the sea,
Nestled on grassy knoll,
Beneath a stately oak tree,
Watercolors, brush, and pad in hand,
Mummy, my teacher
Of nature's beauty.

A protected bay, gentle ripples,
Calming;
Open sea, pounding waves,
Heart throbbing;
Sorrows past and ever present,
My Mummy,
Standing strong for Daddy and me.

England 1954
Walking—old canals, over stiles, through nettles,
Cathedrals and palace gardens;
Mysterious Turner paintings fond memories evoke,
Rain with sunny intervals,
Yellow mildewed buildings;

Boston,
Rembrandt, Van Gogh, Monet, Picasso,
Variety, vitality, and hauntingly bold;
Public Gardens' Swan Boats.

Cambridge,
Miss Kennan's Toyshop, British Dinky Toys,
Strolling through Harvard Yard,
Yummy pastries at the Window Shop.

Maine,
Seascapes, quaint villages,
Mighty rivers, many lakes,
Rolling hills, and rugged mountains.

Bored and lonely at school,
You gave me Beagy,
My friend and companion;

Passion for Francine,
No, you said;
Disputes with Esther,
Suggestions you offered;
Submitting to Susan,
Pained your heart;
"Mummy knows," you wisely said,
Now I know, thank you, Mummy.

You are my Mother, my Mummy,
An artist, a seer, a feeler,
Wise, delicate, beautiful, strong;
Mummy, we are no longer estranged,
We are together,
You and I,
Your son.
I love you.

David wonders what is going through her mind. *Is she beginning to find peace with herself, with her life, so that she will be able to let go? I want so much to know what she is feeling and thinking. I wonder whether her feelings are deeply locked inside, so that she doesn't have to continue to endure the pain of her lifetime. I want so much to help her. I want her to die peacefully in her sleep with a smile on her face, believing that she finally has found peace from her tormentors. I wonder what is holding her back. What does she fear? "Mummy, don't be afraid," I say to myself. "I am with you. I love you even though I have abandoned you before. I will never abandon you again. Will you ever be able to forgive the pain and anguish I have caused you? You did everything for me, your son. When I graduated from college, you arranged to send me to Switzerland because you believed that was best for me. You didn't want me to take care of you. You would start your new life all by yourself. You never thought about re-marrying, as you could only love one man, your Walter, my Daddy. You were absolutely loyal to him, as you still are to me, and to Oliver. In you are loyalty; you are forever alone. How you must be suffering. Would you like to return to the love of mother and child, especially the time I was a baby and small child, before tensions in early adulthood erupted and I disappointed and abandoned you? How can I help you find emotional balance, so that your soul will be able to leave your frail and withering body?"*

Still David cannot look at her in the face, hold her hand, and tell her how he feels.

A Plane is Dropping Bales of Hay to Feed the Elephants

On another visit, this time during the winter of 2002, May and David find Elly's thin, frail body erectly propped on a piece of absorbent paper in the chair by the window. Dressed in her favorite summer dress, her usual beige decorated with brown ducks, she cracks a faint smile as she notices May and David standing before her. Son and granddaughter unzip their heavy winter gear on this damp, biting cold February afternoon.

"How good to see you," her voice barely audible with meager strength, she is delighted to see them.

Feeling uncomfortable in the nursing home setting, David responds with a gruff "Uh, huh," unable to respond with the warmth with which he would like. In contrast, May, age six, with outstretched arm, hands her grandmother a lively card picturing the two of them standing together holding hands. It reads:

> Dear Elly,
>
> I hope you are feeling well. I like reading and writing at school. I wish you are still living with me, Mummy, and Daddy.
>
> Love,
>
> May Aihua Ye

"How nice," Elly smiles. "I'm delighted to see my little granddaughter. She's OK?" Her voice expresses a twinge of anxiety.

"OK, why shouldn't she be OK?" David asks with concerned curiosity.

"Last night I heard your daughter screaming. I got up, walked down the hall, but couldn't find her room. I so much wanted to comfort her."

Stunned, David stares at his mother for a moment before he can utter in astonishment, "May woke up crying profusely last night. Jing and I rushed to her room. No matter how we tried to console her, between sobs she said over and over again, 'I miss Elly.'"

How could Elly possibly have known what May was feeling? he wonders. After all, they live several miles apart from each other. May must have picked up on something about her grandmother. Maybe Elly was in pain, maybe especially lonely. Elly surely must have felt her presence.

Elly's sunken, gray-green eyes, encircled with red, wander away from May and David onto the snow outside her window. Out from nowhere comes: "A plane is dropping some hay bales to feed the elephants."

"Oh, really?" David asks.

"And the cows, too," smiling at May as she drifts into sleep.

Acceptance

January 2004. After four years of living passively in nursing homes with an occasional hospital stay, Elly seems to have accepted the reality that she no longer can care for herself. She seldom talks anymore about the birds or squirrels that eat from the bird feeder near her window. She rarely comments on the weather, "such a bright sunny," day as she used to. However, she once remarks with a faint glow of energy that when she gets better, she will visit her friend in Denmark. Her comment arises following a visit from Irene, a hospice volunteer in her eighties. She, the wife of a deceased Colby College professor, was born and raised in Norway.

Still, the nursing staff reports to David that his mother remains stubborn. Head nurse Marie, explains, "She refuses to eat, though she does like to drink her chocolate health shake, some juice and water. But she barely touches any food. She *does* love chocolate; it's how she seems to survive. She never gets out of bed on her own, except to struggle to go to the bathroom. But the alarm we put on her goes off, so we can help her to get to the toilet with her walker. And she still refuses to take her medications. We are amazed that she is doing so well without any medications at all."

I'm Just Work for Them

February 3, 2004, after days of frigid weather, the thermometer has risen to the low thirties. A few puffy pink clouds are scattered across a sky bearing a tint of warm yellow in its pale-blue winter.

David enters his mother's room. The smell of urine combined with that of ammonia fills the air, as if scolding him for allowing Elly to end her difficult and painful life in the one place in which she hoped never to be confined. She is sitting in her green chair, covered with a blanket, her head tilted back against the rear of the chair. Her eyes are partially closed; she is moaning. David says hi, as he approaches her. An unusually broad smile comes over her face.

"Oh David!" she says. Sitting down on the newly-made bed, he takes her hand in his. Tears uncontrollably burst forth from his eyes.

"I like your shirt," she says, referring to his burgundy turtleneck. "And your pants, too," she continues, noticing his beige wide-wale corduroys. "You are also thinner?"

"Yes, that's because I now exercise a lot. Thanks to Jing. But I want to know how you are?"

"Not well," she replies firmly. "I want to die. Can you tell my doctor?"

"No, I can't do that. He can't give you an injection. If he does, he will go to prison."

Saying nothing, Elly looks towards the floor.

"Are you in pain?" David asks.

"Yes," she says touching her stomach with the palm of her hand.

"Your bladder?"

"Yes."

Holding her hand tightly with tears now gushing down his face, he says: "I love you dearly. I am so sorry for the tensions between us."

Her head again props against the back of her chair. She looks directly at him. Through tear-swollen eyes, David distinguishes her hazel eyes deeply sunken into her skull. The thin, wrinkled skin around her eyes is deep red. Matter of fact, Elly replies, "I am, too."

David is now sobbing uncontrollably. Wiping his tears with a tissue fails to stop them from continuing to flow down his cheeks. "I love you so much. I only wish our estrangement had never happened. Do you remember the good times we had together?" He is so eager for her to tell him about her fond memories of them together.

"I do. But I am still sad about the tension. You are still my son," she says in a calm monotone.

"Are people good to you here?" he asks, feeling she will be blatantly honest with him.

"They are OK. I am just work for them," she replies insightfully. "Your former wife cares for me." David is shocked to hear this, knowing the relentless conflict that existed between Elly and Sally. She doesn't even work at Lakewood Manor.

"Really? Is she good to you?" David is eager to know.

"Yes!" she replies.

"But tensions were so great with her?" David adds.

She chuckles, cracking a smile, "She is always pleasant."

Elly suddenly shifts subjects to ask about his family, about May, and "your wife."

As usual, when David tells her about May's incredible progress as a student of the piano, she replies, "Does she really like it?"

"Yes," David tells her. "Tomorrow, May goes to Portland, where she will have a master class with an internationally celebrated Russian pianist. Her teacher feels that May is that good!"

Elly doesn't respond. She, however, after a long moment does add, "And your wife?"

"She's fine, working hard, and a good mother," David tells her.

"What does your wife do?" she asks, as she does every time.

"She's a psychological counselor at Colby College," he explains with pride.

"Why doesn't your wife like me?" she asks.

"Jing cares a great deal for you. It was Sally with whom you had conflict, not Jing. Do you remember that you used to live with us, that Jing baked delicious bread and cake for you, cooked your favorite meals, and the two of you looked after baby May?"

"No," she replies curtly.

"You really don't remember living with us and how good Jing was to you?" David asks again.

His mother continues, "I am very lonely here. Nobody comes to even say a friendly word," as his tears stream forth again. She then adds, referring to the tensions that had existed between herself and her son, "But we weren't compatible. I am now in a nursing home."

Never before has she admitted that she has become a resident at a nursing home. She has previously asked when she will be dismissed from this "hospital."

"You surely remember visiting Jing and me in China?" David reminds her.

"No," she says, looking at him with confusion.

Gosh, she doesn't remember coming on a cruise ship to Shantou, the first such ship ever to come to this seaside city in Guangdong province, on my 50th birthday? She doesn't remember meeting Jing? They both liked each other instantly. Mother was happy for me.

"May I have a paper hankie?" she asks. He gives her a tissue, and she wipes her nose as a solitary tear descends from her right eye.

When it is time for David to depart, he firmly holds her hand, kisses her warmly on her lips. Tears again pour forth. "I love you dearly," he tells her amidst sobs.

As he stands up to leave, she longingly asks: "Do you really love me?"

"I do," David says wiping tears from his eyes as more stream forth. *Gosh, I hope so much that Mummy feels how deeply I love her, how sad I am for having caused her so much suffering—pain, anguish, utter loneliness. Of course, Mother feels abandoned by her only son and angry with me for placing her in a nursing home. I am not asking for forgiveness. I simply want her to feel my love. I want us to feel securely bonded.*

I Want to See a Rabbi

A few days later the nursing home calls: "Your mother would like to see a rabbi."

"Of course," David says, believing that his mother must be ready to die. Never before has she expressed any interest in Judaism. *You needn't ask me for permission*, he thinks.

Following the rabbi's visit, he asks her, "Did you meet with the rabbi?"

"Yes," she says. "He's an awful man. I do not like him."

"Why did you want to see the rabbi?" David asks, hoping that he and she can talk about death.

"I am Jewish, you know. I am very old; sometime I will die," she explains.

"How do you feel about death?" David wants to know.

"I don't want to die, because I need to take care of my grandchildren."

Really, David wonders. Lying here in a nursing home? He recalls Raskolnikov in Dostoyevsky's *Crime and Punishment*, who murdered the old pawnbroker in order to use her money to save the poor and destitute. He thinks of his son Oliver, who wants to study full-time, so he can get his degree in architecture and give up being a paramedic. After seventeen years driving an ambulance, dragging 350-pound people on welfare down several flights of tenement steps, patients suffering from emphysema from cigarette smoking, liver failure from alcohol abuse, or other apparently self-inflicted ailments, Oliver is burning out. Elly would love to care for him and support him in any way she could. David imagines his mother might feel that she has been abandoned by her parents and her husband who has died before her. Therefore, she should not abandon her grandchildren.

As David continues to sit on the bed, he sees her as if she were standing in a long line waiting for life to end. She watches her friends before her drop one by one. When it is time, the door opens into darkness and shuts waiting for the next person to enter. Sometimes the line moves a little more quickly, for instance, upon the sudden death of Walter's nephew Fred, to whom Elly was close, while her friend Eileen is still waiting as she drifts further into Alzheimer's. During her long wait, Elly has become more peaceful, yet still anxious, as she doesn't know what happens when each person in line goes through the door into darkness. Holding her hand, David knows his mother now is just as tenacious as on those cold, dark November and December days of 1938, when she successfully fought for the release of his father from Dachau.

David loosens his grip on her hand. Sensing he might be leaving, she asks, her smile pushing back creases on her face, "How is your wife?"

"Fine," he says.

"Visit me again when you can." The clarity in her voice assures David that she will never give up. Eventually her body will dissipate, but David and those who knew her will forever feel her tenacious yet gentle presence.

Fading

June 21, the first day of summer, her head lies back on the pillow, her mouth wide open, her eyes closed, her collarbones, shoulder blades, and sternum almost bare except for a thin layer of skin, wrinkled and onionskin-like, covering both the bones and cavities between. The remainder of her body is invisible beneath a sheet and blanket. Not even a slight bulge appears where David imagines her body lies.

"Hello," David shouts on entering the room. She shows no sign of waking up. His eyes focus on her upper chest beneath the covers, trying to observe if she is breathing.

"Hello," he yells again. No response.

On the third "hello" her mouth starts to close in synchrony as her eyes open.

"Oh, David," she moans, as a smile pushes dry, flabby wrinkles upward on her gaunt face.

David sits down beside her on the bed, taking her hand into his. Her grasping it with such strength, he finds it hard to imagine that physically she still is holding onto life as she has throughout 93 turbulent years.

"I love you," she murmurs. Wow, never before has she ever uttered these as the first words on seeing her son. They come from her parched lips amidst moans of pain with each breath that she takes. Tears stream from his eyes as he offers, "I love you!"

With waning smile, her eyes begin to close. Yet, the grasp she has on his hand remains firm.

"How are you?" David asks.

"Not well," she sighs.

"Your bladder?" he asks.

"Everything," she moans, as her head droops away from him toward the wall.

Passage

Torrential, wind-driven rains pound against the north side of David's family Waterville home. As David, his wife, and daughter are discussing whether to brave the storm to attend a youth concert in Camden more than an hour away on the coast, a yellow warbler smashes against their north-facing picture window. They decide to go. After all, the son of a friend will be performing, and May will most likely be a participant the following year with Bay Chamber Concerts' Next Generation Program.

The drive to Camden amidst hills enveloped in fog and driving rain is slow. Wipers are unable to clear the windshield from such heavy rain, while the wind frequently tosses the car as if it were a ship on a wild ocean. On leaving the concert in the late afternoon, the storm has subsided. Driving home, the sky is reminiscent of a painting by William Turner, an artist Elly deeply appreciates. The western horizon has become a warm yellow while storm clouds of various shades of gray still hang above the car.

PAINTING BY MAY FOR HER ELLY'S BURIAL, SEPTEMBER 5, 2004

On arriving home, the red light on the answering machine is flashing. Lifting the receiver to hear the message, a woman's voice announces, "This call is for David. This is Lakeview Manor. Your mother passed away this afternoon."

What a way to go! Elly had throughout her life survived one horrific storm after another, often all by herself. Her final departure, alone—without her family—during a powerful, natural storm brought her taxing life in this world to an end. As her worldly life ceased in sorrow, the energy of this storm, David imagines, brought her more quickly and easily to a new, more peaceful existence together with her parents, her husband, and others to whom she was close. Actually, her life ended within a day of that when her husband took his life forty-two years before.

As she wished to be cremated and to have her ashes scattered in the sea, her remaining family, a few old friends, and the remaining relatives of her husband from the Boston area arrive at a little peninsula on Bailey Island, Maine. September 5, 2004, is a warm, bright, cloudless day. Each person present will toss her ashes into the Atlantic Ocean that she so much loved.

Often, when together with Walter and David, she used to drive the half hour to Bailey Island, upon seeing the open sea for the first time, she would exclaim, *Oh, how blue!*

It was that same ocean across which she sailed from England to freedom in America in 1940. It was that ocean that separated her tortured life in Germany from a new, yet challenging life in her new homeland. Yet, she crossed that same ocean several more times—including a visit to her friend Gertrude from her art-school year in Germany, David in Switzerland, and her brother in England. That vast ocean, sometimes calm and sometimes tumultuous, was her connecting link between her old world and new one.

At the little gathering, her granddaughter May, age ten, presents each of assembled with a painting she created entitled *Elly's World and Mine: A Life of Two Worlds.* In the painting, with eyes closed, her grandmother is lifted from a grassy island in a fish-filled ocean, through storm clouds, into the heavens above. There she is greeted beneath a rainbow by smiling faces of varied races.

In Memory of My Mother, Elly
August 10, 1910 to August 21, 2004

Frothing clouds wrench in an angry sky.

Like a fierce bull, World War I rages;
Elly's father, Herman,
Drafted into the Kaiser's army,
Returns silent, dejected,
Haunted by dark, foggy images.

Murkiness lingers.

The wrathful bull sounds like distant thunder.
Mother and daughter leave Hamburg for Lübeck.
Elly cuddles with grandmother Schlomer,
Plays at the Baltic with Adelheid—a Protestant.

Through melancholic, ashen-gray clouds, slivers of sun peek,
Instilled with Weimar hopes,
Short hair, beige skirt, robust gait
Dancing through purple heather,

Down narrow lanes,
Amidst yellow hayfields,
Frolicking in farmers' haylofts
With her *Wandervoegel.*

In bright sun,
Her poster "Light and Air"
On butterfly wings
Uplifts underprivileged children.

From pinstriped dignitaries,
Hamburg's highest honor
Becomes her golden crown.

Flashes of lightning crash through oppressing blackness.

Swastika-bearing brown shirts
Rifle her art career.

Huddled by the open oven,
Herman is intentionally
Overwhelmed by gas fumes.
Later, clad in suit and tie,
Stepping off the embankment
Sinks to Elbe's depths;
Saved by angels.

Nazi bayonets propel Walter to Dachau.
Forging her way through fire
Elly liberates him from untimely death.
Unable to save her parents from Theresienstadt.

Eerie images
Loose flesh over skeletal remains,
Slow, languishing death.
Burdened by guilt.

Warm, sunny smiles appear:

Safety at last in London.

On to America for dreams to unfold,
Walter secluded in ivy-covered Harvard,
Rejoicing at David's birth.

Three years hence,
Disembarking in drenching rain
In Brunswick
On the Boston & Maine
Into Walter's arms.

White clapboard house, porch with Navy hammock,
10 Bowdoin Street becomes our home,
A black 1941 Ford coupe in the driveway,
"Life, liberty, happiness," at last
"Oh, the ocean so blue!" she exclaims
Stretching over the horizon
To her motherland—lost.

Morning red beckons the tempest.

Depression, hospitalization,
A razor blade ends Walter's life.

Her hair falling out,
Skin blotched, red and flaky.
Mother and son estranged,

Cancerous cells forming
All alone
Except grandson, Oliver,
In whose cocoon warmth she rests,
Unconditional love she returns.

Slivers of sun appear.

At 84 off to China
Celebrating David's 50th
With Jing, the unifier,
Reaching to ancient Chinese sages
Bringing forth balance and harmony

Helping heal David's and Elly's wounds.
Darkness blankets once again.

Cancer, hospitalization, remission, cancer, remission,
Scar tissue becomes irritated,

Depression sets in,
Disassociates from friends and correspondence.

Anger and defiance rage,
Having escaped death many times,
Now desperately trying to ward off final humiliation
Like a buzzing fly she can't swat.

Clouds burst their pent-up anguish.

August 21, 2004
Sheets of torrential rain pour
Morning—a female gold finch slams into our window
Lies motionless atop shrubs.
Afternoon—Elly's soul leaves her body.

Cleansing,
Poisons of anger,
Cancer of disappointment,
Inflammation of fear.

Cobalt blue heavens welcome

Her healthy, spirited soul
Rising like a white dove's feather
Touching each of us gently
As she joins her parents, Walter, her brother John,
Adelheid, her grandmother . . .

I feel my mother's love,
Bonded forever,
We'll meet again.

September 5, 2004, Bailey Island, Maine

Epilogue

At Home in America and in Foreign Lands

The late afternoon sun of mid August 2004 is on their backs—May's, Jing's and David's—as they, a family, head north along country roads, past large cornfields, through deep coniferous forests. Bright spots shine, light gray amidst dark, lengthening shadows of trees that stretch over the pavement. Wispy cirrus clouds move gently across the cobalt blue sky. A huge trailer truck laden with spruce logs groans up the steep hill as they head down to stop at the intersection of Dover-Foxcroft's main street. They turn left, and then bear left past a monument with a Civil War soldier. The large, white, wooden Congregational Church with its tall steeple sits just ahead, bordered by ancient maples. As they pull into the parking lot, Antonio De Innocentis, an internationally known guitarist, arrives. May will perform her second of four summer recitals before his performance.

An old baby grand piano is moved in front of the pulpit for May to practice the piece that she will soon perform. By 7:00 p.m. the old church begins to fill—a mixture of elderly churchgoers, natives of the area, some summer visitors who have cottages on the lake, and even a smattering of teenagers.

At 7:30, May, to a warm applause, walks gracefully onto the stage, bows, and with a smile distinctly says, "I am May Ye. I am almost eleven years old. I will play Beethoven's Contra Dance in three movements. I hope you will enjoy."

Dressed in a simple, beautifully tailored green dress, designed and made by a Vietnamese woman who has had her little storefront in Boston's Chinatown for twenty-five years, May sits at the piano and adjusts her bench. With both hands resting meditatively on her knees, she prepares herself for her feat. Fully concentrating, she plays the

May performing with Italian guitarist Antonio De Innocentis, Bucksport, Maine, August 2004

lively dance with fine technical skill and feeling. As she concludes her presentation, a generous applause erupts from the audience, lasting well beyond her second bow. Proudly, but with shyness, May joins her parents among the spectators, as Antonio comes onto the stage. Playing Scarlatti, Paganini, Fauré, Joplin, and others, his performance is like a dream—delicate, precise, and filled with sensitivity, causing the family of three to feel completely uplifted.

David thinks of his parents listening to classical music. Occasionally on Sunday mornings, his father carefully put Handel's *Water Music* or Mozart's *Marriage of Figaro* on the phonograph. Every November throughout his childhood, his parents took him to hear the Juilliard String Quartet play at Bowdoin College. When he was quite young, his mother drove him home at intermission, while Walter returned home on foot following the concert. In December, Bowdoin students and townspeople performed Handel's *Messiah.* Although he enjoyed these concerts, he was mesmerized at age eleven by a performance of *Messiah* at London's Royal Festival Hall.

At the same time, David is fully aware the he is living in the shadow of his young wife, who lived through the turmoil of Mao Tse Tung's Cultural Revolution. Like his parents, she loved music, dance, and literature. Yet in order to dance and sing, she had to perform the only music and dance that was permitted—patriotic creations glorifying the greatness of Mao and the motherland. When in her late teens the possibility arose for her to study classical music in Shanghai, her parents forbade her. They feared she would not be able to make a living.

Now, as David writes, May is playing Bach's *Six Suites*. The music fits her personality, especially her gentle, loving, humble, insightful, and creative aspect. Her teacher, originally from Japan and in this country only three years, told Jing and David at today's lesson that May has become more mature, listens better, and thinks less, since her recent concerts. Earlier in the summer, May participated in an International Music Festival with students from Russia, Eastern Europe, and the United States. This year, because of the War on Terrorism, our government denies visas to most foreign students. Fortunately, the master pianist from Russia, under whom May has studied, has been coming to this country for many years and is allowed to come again. However, most of those who had applied, especially from Eastern Europe and Asia, were refused visas.

Recollecting his childhood, David remembers his parents telling him of great musicians, some of whom were Jewish refugees from Nazi Germany, who played summers in the coastal community of Camden. As Maine continues to draw distinguished musicians to music festivals and summer camps, he is delighted that music is alive and well in his home state.

Had his father listened to classical music as he was contemplating suicide, his life might have been saved. However, David's family only had a phonograph and an ancient radio to which they rarely listened. In the early sixties there was no daily radio program like the daily three-hour morning program of classical music on public radio. The family phonograph only played 45s and 33s, meaning that every ten minutes to half an hour the record had to be changed.

Had the recent discoveries by the Japanese scientist Masaru Emoto been known, that vibrations from lovely music form beautiful water crystals, while ugly music creates deformed crystals, David's father might have taken this knowledge to heart. After all, since 80 percent of our bodies consists of water, it is clear that music has a significant impact on us.

The August day in 1962 when Walter took his own life was as beautiful as the days during which May performed her concerts. The petunias that David had planted earlier that summer on islands on Brunswick's Maine Street were in full bloom. Fifty-two years later the town's public works department continues the tradition. In spite of the gorgeous weather, August 23, 1962, was a bad day for Walter. He had given up hope.

Both May's enthusiasm and the weather remain superb throughout her final concert. The setting for her grand finale is quite different from the rural communities in which she has played. She is now performing in Bar Harbor, an old resort community on the Maine coast where the Rockefellers and other magnates built summer homes in the early 20th century. Following the concert, May and her parents join a few other guests at the home of one of the benefactors of this annual music festival. They gather around a gigantic granite island in the kitchen of a patron's new, multimillion-dollar mansion, that he inhabits from June through October.

As David nibbles on crackers with fresh basil, tomato, and Brie, he is reminded of the film, *Cradle Will Rock* in which Nelson Rockefeller commissioned Mexican artist Diego Rivera to paint a mural in the lobby of Rockefeller Center, which he then had destroyed because Rivera refused to remove Lenin's portrait. Often in American movies, David sees famous business magnates formally attired, partying and dining in their elegant city mansions. At this gathering, the host is informally clad with an open-collared shirt covering a widening belly. Dockers and loafers complement his shirt. An older woman with graying hair in a bun, wearing a black skirt and gray blouse, is taking Brie cheese out of a wall oven. David wonders, is she the host's wife or a maid? The ebullient musical and executive director, wearing black slacks and a maroon shirt, an internationally acclaimed violinist, has all the skills to keep the conversation flowing. David, however, feels uncomfortable in this milieu.

Although he may not be in the presence of any high-society players like those during the Red Scares of 1919, 1936, and the mid-1950s, David feels in his bones that the new war on terrorism that is raging in the United States is eroding our freedoms. He wonders whether this benefactor would support artists whose messages might question the status quo. After all, the arts are vital to the advancement of humanity. They bring creative spirit that touches our soul and fosters appreciation and understanding for one another. To survive, artists rely on the wealthy for patronage. Of course, this is nothing new—either in America or in Europe. However, as government support for the arts dwindles, as fear takes over, the ability of courageous artists and musicians to foster harmony among humankind is more and more limited.

May, at least, is happily eating away at Maine shrimp, while Jing heats water to prepare sesame paste wrapped in sticky rice. The director's wife, a recognized violinist from Shanghai, unable to attend this gathering, sent these along from her home, knowing Jing would enjoy them.

Recalling that his mother had died during a storm exactly a year ago, David thinks that this is not the America to which she and his father fled in 1940. It is now a country torn apart, once again, by panic and fear, loss of civil liberties, and a belligerently imperialistic government trying to make the Middle East safe for American exploitation. At the same time, David recently heard on public radio that the cost of sustaining refugees in Germany, especially from Afghanistan, has become such a serious economic problem that Hamburg and other German cities are sending these people back to the country from which they fled. According to the broadcast, their chances of facing arrest and the death penalty are very high.

David's combined experiences of amazement at Germany's sensitivity toward the environment but coldness toward immigrants, especially those in most need, create contrasting emotions. David, who was born in the safety of this country, as the Holocaust was still escalating abroad, wonders, How could vast numbers of people in the land of Brahms, Schiller, Goethe, Heine, Mann, and others allow Hitler to come to power? At this gathering with patrons of the arts, he wonders about the discrepancy that arises when the well-intentioned feel threatened and submit to the political power that opposes their values.

David is reminded of the present, when warriors against terrorism prevail in cultivating fear and hysteria. By making sure that fear of a terrorist attack is constantly etched in everyone's minds, these warriors remind us that they are protecting us from evil terrorists. For instance, David experienced in New York and Boston that public announcements are plastered on buses and in subway stations with the slogan, "If you see something, say something." Regardless of the erosion of Americans' civil liberties by the Patriot Act, many people feel safer that the FBI is looking after them.

Fear continues to infect every corner of American society. Daily articles in the press heighten people's angst. The police blotter relates the type and location of 911 calls such as burglaries, domestic violence, and arrests. Front-page headlines in the local Waterville daily pronounce such crimes as CHURCH BURGLARIES: POLICE SAY STRING OF CRIMES MOTIVATED BY RELIGIOUS DISLIKE, HISTORIC GRAVESTONES VANDALIZED, PRISON GUARD ARRESTED FOR SMUGGLING HEROIN TO INMATES that naturally bolster public tension. These conditions demonstrate the need for compassionate methods to resolve the problems that foster crime and fear.

David visualizes his father today writing letters to the newspaper, to national columnists like David S. Broder, and to political leaders. Walter would lament the rationale that to resolve all of these problems a tough and forceful stand must be taken. Instead, he probably would suggest that the United States develop, together with the United Nations, peaceful means to defuse the increasing rage against our country and its Western allies.

In regard to increasing government control over public education, such as the No Child Left Behind Act, David believes that attempts to micromanage children with standards that in most cases meet the needs only of corporate America are shortsighted. Seeking the death penalty for gangsters and terrorists among others, he considers as an act of revenge that does not deter crime. In both instances, he is confident his father would hold the same views.

David envisions his father offering his college students questions and ideas to inspire their passion for living and learning. He sees him awakening their conscience, nurturing their humanity, and evoking their inner sense of responsibility. In spite of worsening conditions, he may see rays of hope, as does David. For instance, as depressed and troubled as Walter would be that his country is going through a period of fear that fosters mistrust, lack of civility, and belligerence, as a student of history and philosophy, he would agree that such periods are cyclical. Like the seasons, following fall when the trees become bare and winter rushes in, without fail life is renewed each spring.

Both David's parents would be impressed by the growing number of scholars who are seeking alternative approaches to work successfully with our growing number of troubled youth. In the late 1950s Elly was actively involved with a project to reform Maine's Reform School for Boys. Today his parents might enthusiastically read James Garbarino's book, *Lost Boys: Why Our Sons Turn Violent and How We can Save Them.* This book is fine example of contemporary thinking on seeking healing approaches to "lost boys." Gabarino argues that America's socially unequal, consumer-oriented society focuses upon titillating sensationalism and instant gratification, resulting in the drug trade, gangs, violence, and broken families. These boys, he insists, need fair, caring adults who will protect them. Traumatized boys also need a calming and soothing environment to function effectively. Garbarino sees evidence that meditation successfully helps many of these troubled youth discover inner peace. David envisions his father's "thinking walks" as having been an initial form of meditation—a forerunner of the Eastern meditation that is becoming increasingly accepted in this country.

Walter was interested in Eastern philosophy. Among the books David found on his father's shelf as a high-school student were the wisdom of Lao Tzu, the sayings by Mencius, Confucius, and the teachings of the Compassionate Buddha. Walter had read and underlined some of the Buddha's teachings:

> If instead, one can identify in feeling with the experience of others who similarly suffer, he will be freed from his own grief by and in a compassionate oneness with all living beings. This oneness intrinsically brings an enduring peace and joy that are superior to grief—superior because they spring not from hopelessly trying to evade its causes or stoically steeling the mind to its impact, but through overcoming the evil to oneself by the good of a deep and fully satisfying love for others. (Burtt 1958, 44)

David recalls that his father introduced him to the more general concepts of Eastern philosophy, as did Hermann Hesse's *Siddhartha,* which he read as a high-school junior. No wonder that as a college student David chose to spend two summers working as an orderly at state institutions for the mentally challenged and initiated his hometown's first-ever project dealing with poverty. Since his parents never told him about their experience under Nazi rule, nor did he ever ask, he could only subconsciously surmise their suffering. Nor did he then know that thirty-five years later he would marry a Chinese woman who survived the Chinese Cultural Revolution as his parents had the Nazi Holocaust, and who actively practices Buddhist meditation.

David's father became interested at an early age in the philosophies of religion and Eastern thought. When Walter was a teenager at the Odenwaldschule, the school's founder and director, Paulus Geheeb, introduced him to Gotthold Ephraim Lessing. Lessing, an 18th-century German poet, philosopher, and critic, died in Walter's hometown of Braunschweig. The philosophical questions that attracted Walter are beautifully expressed in the parable of the "Three Rings," as narrated in Lessing's play, *Nathan the Wise*. The parable deals with the question: Is there a true religion? As if in justification of Walter's never-ending intellectual search for truth, Lessing concludes that the moment one has found the truth, it no longer exists. Someone cannot own truth; it is always a process of seeking and approaching.

> A man from the East received a special opalescent ring. This ring had the secret power to make the person who wore it pleasing to God and everybody he encountered. The man realized the ring's value. Therefore, upon his death, he gave it to his favorite son under one condition. This son, for generations forth, would give the ring to his most beloved son. Finally, the ring came into the hands of a father who loved each of his three sons equally. Not to disappoint his sons, he secretly had a famous goldsmith make two identical copies of the original. Just before he died, he gave each son a ring. Immediately upon their father's death, each son claimed to be the sole owner of the original ring. Unable to determine the true ring, the three brothers, accusing each other of deceit, brought their case to court. The judge carefully listened to the case. Asking the three brothers whether they love each other, he quickly realized each loved himself the best. Thereupon, he declared that all three brothers were deceived, that none of them possessed the true ring. The judge concluded:
>
> If each of you received his ring as stated,
> Let each believe his ring is genuine.
> Maybe your father would not tolerate
> The tyranny of one ring any longer
> To rule his house! And it seems certain
> That he has loved you all equally well.
> To favor one he could no longer use
> A means that would oppress the others.
> Let it thus be! Let each of you aspire
> To be his unprejudiced impartial love.
> Let each *attempt* to make the power shine forth
> That proves his ring to be quite genuine.
> Let him support this power with gentleness,
> With peace of heart, good deeds, and with faith in God.
> If then the powers latent in the stones
> Will prove their worth in children's children's children,
> I bid them in a thousand, thousand years
> To come again before this judge's chair;
> A wiser man than I will speak the verdict.

> Thus spoke the modest judge and then dismissed the three brothers. (Koelln 1953)

Lessing's moral is that one would like to have the truth, but the pure truth is for God alone. However, it is the task of each person to strive after the truth. The means and pains one takes in trying to approach the truth enhances the person's value.

These words of Lessing remind David of his father's philosophical, political, educational, spiritual ideals and practices that were inspired and influenced from ancient Eastern and Western civilizations. A former Bowdoin College philosophy major, John Welwood, who told Jing he regretfully never had Walter as a professor, is now a nationally recognized psychotherapist. In his practice and teachings he integrates Western psychology with Eastern spiritual wisdom. In an 2003 article "Double Vision: Duality and Non-duality in Human Experience," Welwood wrote,

> While the East emphasizes liberation from the human condition, the Western Spiritual traditions place special value on human incarnation in its own right, and are more interested in fulfilling the meaning of this incarnation than in going beyond it or find release from it . . . Instead of liberation, the West focuses on humaneness as an evolving vehicle through which the divine, or unconditioned being, can progressively manifest in conditioned, earthly existence. (Welwood 2003)

Being so caught up in his own anxieties, Walter became ever more hooked to his intellectual struggles that "reinforced inner division between the flow of experiencing and the ego-mind trying to control or manipulate that experience" (Welwood 2003). At the same time, in thinking about Lessing's fable, David realizes that his father had become fixated on the thinking process in order to achieve broad goals, for instance, world peace. In fact, his professors' critique years ago in Germany was that he took on too broad a topic. Instead of narrowing it down, he evolved more and more new ideas, so that the project became unmanageable. Therefore, as Walter solely pursued the thought process, the search for the truth that Lessing declared is for God alone became insurmountable. Walter seemed to understand the differences between religion and spirituality about which Eckhart Tolle wrote in *A New Earth: Awakening to Your Life's Purpose*:

> Many people are already aware of the difference between spirituality and religion. They realize that having a belief system—a set of thoughts that you regard as the absolute truth—does not make you spiritual no matter what the nature of those beliefs is. In fact, the more you make your thoughts (beliefs) into your identity, the more cut off you are from the spiritual dimension within yourself. (Tolle 2005, 17)

Yet, Walter was by no means dogmatic, one who claimed to be in sole possession of the truth. Nor was he in any way distorted by ego-based consciousness. For that reason he may well have been considered by many—his students, the underprivileged and the poor, his colleagues, his wife, and his son—a noble person. His suffering occurred because he thought too much, because he did not trust himself in a competitive, egocentric society. Nor did he allow himself to experience the transformative power arising from his consciousness. Aside from this, nowadays there is progress on the biochemical aspects of depression as a disease.

Were Walter alive today, by now Jing would have introduced him to books by John Welwood, Eckhart Tolle, and others, such as Stephen Levine, author of *Turning Toward the Mystery: A Seeker's Journey*. Perhaps he would come to understand that the rational form of thinking to which he as a philosopher had devoted his entire life actually caused him to become mired, depressed, and unfulfilled—to acknowledge Levine's insight founded in Buddhist teachings that the heart rather than the mind provides rationality. According to Levine, the heart offers "an inclination toward healing that even acknowledges the value of our pain. It learns to let go and trust the process. It knows there is an alternative to our well-guarded suffering. It recognizes love" (Levine 2002, 48).

Reading about a meeting between Levine and the Dalai Lama, David is reminded that his father was often disappointed and hurt, but he rarely appeared angry. He was always seeking peaceful solutions among individuals and throughout the world. The Dalai Lama, according to Levine, said: "Rid yourself of anger for the benefit of all sentient beings. It is better to express the pain before it turns to suffering and erupts as hostility. To bring forth world peace there must be mental peace" (Levine 2002, 158).

Jing has helped David understand the Dalai Lama's message. As we express our pain, the anguish no longer eats away at us, triggering bitterness and anger and causing suffering amongst those we encounter.

By staying with our pain, Jing explains, the energy of the suffering will transform into tranquility. Therefore, the pain will have its own appropriate place instead of consuming, dominating, and immobilizing our emotional and physical life.

If only Walter could have expressed his pain and come to experience mental peace, life for both of David's parents would have been happier. Elly would not have had to suppress her feelings, bringing about physical reactions such as severe psoriasis and almost total hair loss. David wonders how else his mother could have emotionally survived her unwavering support of her husband through the Nazi era. How could she endure his persistent torment as well as her own suffering without disassociating from feelings?

David imagines that both of his parents might be a little bothered by many of those who teach spirituality—by their seeming to "instruct" others how to achieve enlightenment through meditation even when their *advice* comes from their own experience in the form of an autobiography. He can understand why one might object to such instruction, as he David, like his parents, at home, at school, and in the workplace, has always been told what to do: to *follow, look up to,* and *obey* your teachers, bosses, and leaders. The reality, David agrees, is that teachers, role models, those who inspire are badly needed. The great teacher is the one who has gained much knowledge, understanding, and wisdom through a balance of study and experience. And the best teacher is the listener who then asks questions. From David's own experience as a teacher and from his correspondence with his father's former students, David realizes that Walter was such a teacher. Had he been able to travel the path described by the Dalai Lama, finding peace with his pain, he would have had even greater impact upon those around him.

Walter did personify Victor Frankl's experience as a Jewish concentration camp inmate:

> It becomes clear that the sort of person the prisoner became was the result of an inner decision and not the result of camp influences alone. Fundamentally, therefore, any man can, even under such circumstances, decide what shall become of him—mentally and spiritually . . . The way they bore their suffering was a genuine inner achievement. It is this spiritual freedom—which cannot be taken away—that makes life meaningful and purposeful . . . Without suffering and death human life cannot be complete. (Frankl 1971, 105–106)

Unfortunately, Walter seemed to linger in suffering in spite of his great love for humanity. The German-Jewish Buddhist nun, Ayya Khema writes:

> The point of living and loving is to develop more fully our heart's capacity to love. Just as the intellect is trained by our efforts to understand information, the heart needs opportunities to evolve, too, and any effort at love allows the heart to mature. The heart's only purpose is love. (Khema 2002, 116)

Had Walter adhered to the Buddhist teachings expressed by Khema and taken her advice to practice meditation, a practice with which he was probably wholly unfamiliar, he might have been able to overcome some of his torment. Ayya Khema also writes:

> The meditator has the opportunity to experience thoughts as movements of the mind, just as the breath is movement of the body, to see that both phenomena just come and go. It should then become clear that thoughts certainly don't equal truth. (Khema 2002, 123)

The grave of David's great-great-grandfather, Alexander Wolf Sanders, in Dessau, Germany, 2009

Even though David was born and raised in the United States, he never felt he fully belonged in this country. He identified with his parents, who, like so many Jews throughout history, were victims of diaspora. Growing up as an only child of Jewish immigrants in Brunswick, Maine, during the mid 1940s through the mid 1960s, he adopted his father's sense of feeling alienated in America. Walter's awareness of isolation was certainly understandable. Coming as a Jewish refugee from Germany to a small, provincial Maine community immediately following the end of the Second World War, Jews were still victims of discrimination. On one occasion for example, when David was four years old, the family friend Ella (from Braunschweig and then New York), visited for several days, as she often did throughout his childhood. His parents accepted her offer to look after him while they went away for the weekend. A few hours later, to his surprise, they came home. They had been turned away from an inn in Wiscasset for being Jewish.

In spite of living in Maine since the age of three and teaching for thirty years at a rural Maine high school, David has never considered himself to be a Mainer. After all, to be a true Mainer, he would not only have to be born in this state, but also have ancestors whose roots are deep in Maine soil.

Besides his parents being immigrants, his feeling of not being a true Mainer is reinforced by his experiences during his childhood—including Boston, New York, Chicago, England, and Switzerland. Therefore, he can easily relate to the Nigerian novelist, Ben Okri, who now lives as an immigrant in London and who stated in a recent interview in *Ode* magazine:

> Traveling challenges you to change your provincial perspective. Travel begins by altering your sense of the assumptions that you make about the world. Traveling enables you to see how different you are from your next-town neighbor, and how similar you are . . . That is why it is important to teach children to think clearly, but it is also important to travel with them. I think that moving children gradually away from where they originate is an important influence on freeing the mind and reducing the amount of prejudice. (Okri 2006, 61)

David's parents also encouraged him to experience and understand the arts. His mother often took him to Boston's Museum of Fine Arts, and, during their year's stay in London, the family visited the British Museum and the Tate Gallery. His parents helped him appreciate the simple beauty of a Greek sculpture in comparison to the more ornate Roman copy. David developed a fondness for Van Gogh, Monet, Manet, and Cézanne at a young age. That year in London, they took him to a performance of Spanish dancers. Back at home in Maine, they took him to the Fine Arts Theater in Portland to watch foreign movies such as Ingmar Bergman's *Wild Strawberries*.

Jing, David, May in Sicily, Feb. 2008

In 2009 David and May, nearly 15 years of age, are visiting Dessau, located in the former East Germany. After driving on smooth, often newly resurfaced roads from Braunschweig in the western sector, David notices by the rougher, less well-maintained roads of the eastern region. Having passed through old, beautifully restored villages in the West, David is struck by the contrast in the East. Once beautiful buildings that date back to the mid 1500s, if not dilapidated, lie in ruin.

However, while stopping in an old village in the East, David and May come across a delightful little bakery and café. Here they relish hot chocolate and the most delicious homemade pastries. The woman at the counter, like other folk they encounter in the East, is genuinely friendly.

On entering Dessau, David and May are taken aback by this wide, open city, still bearing many of the monstrous, concrete, prefabricated apartment buildings of the Communist era. A few large commercial buildings still stand, now decorated in gaudy colors, between the few prewar survivors, saved from the devastation of the Allied bombs. But within this desolation, a community of tree-lined streets, consisting of small, functional, white houses, appears. Designed and built in the 1920s by Walter Gropius of Bauhaus fame, this and several other eco-villages remind David that amidst Dessau's gloom, a permanent expression of hope, creativity, and planning for a better future remain solidly intact.

In one house, like the rest on the street of "Bauhaus" design, is the home of the Moses Mendelssohn Society. Mendelssohn (1729–1786) was born and raised in Dessau. A prominent Jewish philosopher, he was also the grandfather of composers Fanny and Felix Mendelssohn. Through the low window that extends about three feet below the flat roof and stretches across the full width of the house, geraniums and other plants are visible. Successfully designed to preserve the privacy of the residents from those outside, each house has a huge window in the rear facing the large garden. Not only can one enjoy the beauty of the garden with its vegetable beds and fruit trees, Gropius meant to encourage people to become more self-sufficient. Although the house, like all others, was equipped with city water, an attached outhouse was designed as a composting toilet to fertilize the garden.

In the garden of the Mendelssohn Society's home, to a small but enthusiastic gathering, David gives a lecture on his great-grandfather Sanders and his family who were born and raised in Dessau. The talk was arranged by two gentlemen, Werner Grossert and Bernd Ulbrich, neither

MAY AT 16 (2010) IS A PIANO MAJOR AT INTERLOCHEN ARTS ACADEMY IN INTERLOCHEN, MICHIGAN.

of whom is Jewish, who during the past three years have researched the Sanders family history in Dessau. They actually have found, to David's surprise, in a badly bombed and overgrown Jewish burial ground, the gravestone of his great-great-grandfather Alexander Wolf Sanders.

While David lectures, May and Renate Grossert, an elderly artist and a lover of classical music, and mother of actor Thomas Kretschmann, go shopping in Dessau. The two bond beautifully and begin a correspondence. On returning home to Maine, May sends her friend and her husband a CD of her piano playing. They tell David, "We are most surprised by your daughter. Not every pianist dares to play [Beethoven's] Waldstein Sonata. May plays it with such precision and feeling."

Upon returning home from his trip to Europe with May, David thinks over his experiences in other nations: living in Switzerland for two years following college, marrying a Swiss woman, living in China for a year, marrying a Chinese woman, traveling in 2002 with his family in Eastern Europe, and most recently experiencing both East and West Germany with his daughter. He realizes with a sense of pride that he is a citizen of the world.

Finally, he is able to identify with a remark attributed to the Roman Emperor Hadrian, "I have never had a feeling of belonging wholly to any one place, not even to my beloved Athens, not even to Rome. Though a foreigner in every land, in no place did I feel myself a stranger" (Yourcenar 1963, 123).

This volume has related numerous connections David has discovered on this journey—connections have taught him that all of us on this small planet Earth are interrelated. Now more than ever David cherishes his connection to his motherland, to his European and American roots, his Asian bond and beyond. As these worlds infuse his experience of American culture here in Maine; he is grateful and feels at home. He continues to look forward to many new journeys both internal and external: letting go of his ego, allowing his heart's capacity to feel compassion and to love, and cherishing the new connections he experiences.

Music of Debussy is wafting into the upstairs study, as David completes the final pages of this book. Jing is gently supporting May, as she is refining her playing. David imagines that his parents are looking from above at him and his family. His parents have already, in the words of Ayya Khema, met "a crucial requirement for peace and insight [which is] the accurate recognition of what is going on in ourselves, otherwise we wouldn't learn anything from it" (Khema 2002, 171).

Afterword

Few historians in the 21st century have been fortunate enough to publish their memoirs. The Internet system sacrifices the careful narrative for speed in acquiring more and more facts.

I met David Solmitz fifty years ago when he was a freshman at the University of Maine in Orono in 1961. Then I had just begun teaching European History. I retired forty years later from Ohio University, having published on the German intervention in the Spanish Civil War and teaching a popular course on Hitler and the Nazis. Throughout the years, David and I kept up an intermittent correspondence after I left Maine in September 1964.

Both David and I were personally touched by Adolf Hitler and his creation of the Third Reich. In my case, Hitler's shadow began about age nine, when Hitler seized Prague on 15 March, 1939. For me the subject of the Holocaust was a story of detached curiosity. I was raised as a fundamentalist Methodist who believed in high school that the Jews were "the chosen people."

Born as a Jew, David Solmitz presents a more intense account of the Holocaust. He has written a book which is a double memoir—his own and a recovered memoir and diary of his father, Walter.

I now agree with the apologetic conclusion of the German Lutheran (Evangelical) Church made in 1961. That church's official statement is that Judaism is a sister religion. The German Evangelical statement on Jews was comparable with Pope John XXIII's Encyclical Letter on the status of Jewry, made about the same time. Throughout my life, I could never understand how some Christians could become anti-Semitic. Two Jews, Jesus and Paul, were the most important founders of the new religion, which became an evolving, growing Christianity over the centuries.

David Solmitz has given the people of Maine (and of Germany, Mexico, China and beyond) a personal account of the discovery of Hitler's War against the Jews of Europe, 1939 to 1945—usually called the Holocaust.

David's father, Walter Solmitz, was a professional philosopher educated in Germany in the decisive years 1933 to 1940. After World

War II he taught classical Western philosophy at Bowdoin College, integrating ancient Jewish thought with the philosophy of the ancient Greeks. I only met David's father once, briefly, in my Orono office. I was still learning about things German, despite serving for a year in postwar Germany as an American soldier.

Reading this manuscript showed me how unique both David and Walter Solmitz were in 1961–62. Few Jews who survived Dachau remained pacifists after Hitler. What is really surprising is that Walter to the end of his days, despite bouts of depression about the fate of the world, remained a pacifist Jew. And despite wars in Israel, Vietnam, and Afghanistan, David still maintains the pacifist faith of his father.

Still other dimensions of Walter's story are touched upon in the years 1940 to 1962 that relate to the wider Jewish community, particularly insights on how the Warburg Library and Institute was moved from Hamburg to London in 1940. Also readers can learn something about the history of psychology and psychiatry as they developed in the US and Germany up to Walter's death in August 1962.

David began his teaching in Europe and Maine prep and high schools—art, philosophy and literature. I was never an observer in his social studies classes, but those classes must have been unique because his mind was molded by European ideas. David Solmitz's neighbors in his home town of Brunswick and the Bowdoin College community made a much deeper impression on him than did Orono and the University of Maine.

As the title and table of contents imply, David's travels to China and Mexico expanded his thoughts about his parents, Germany, and Jews. I am glad that David and I have maintained a faith in pacifism to this day.

Prof. Emeritus Robert H. Whealey
Ohio University, Athens, Ohio.

Appendix A

Report About Dachau

By Walter Moritz Solmitz
London, March 10, 1939

Translated by David O. Solmitz

I want to report about the concentration camp at Dachau, as I have been told that this information could be of help to those who want to assist prisoners who are imprisoned in Dachau, as well as others who are being threatened to be sent to a Nazi concentration camp.

Although I cannot report on the overall conditions at Dachau, I can only tell about some of the things I experienced and witnessed there. I was arrested as part of the well-known "action against the Jews" (Kristallnacht) in November 1938. I was arrested together with many others, while others under similar circumstances as mine suffered under much worse conditions. I estimate that about twelve thousand Jews were arrested in Bavaria. To be brought to Dachau together with so many others was a great psychological relief, as I did not encounter this adversity alone. At least, we were able to provide support to one another. Furthermore, there was a certain guarantee that we would not be overlooked. Twelve thousand people cannot just disappear, but one individual along with other persons can be ignored. In addition, by being completely handed over to and at the mercy of the SS (Storm Troopers) who were to guard us, to be part of a significantly large group was to our benefit and a great emotional relief as well. Thousands cannot be as badly treated as one individual. There simply were not enough personnel for that. Besides, a certain degree of public awareness exists in such collective action. Therefore, after several weeks, the SS was apparently instructed to their chagrin to repress their emotions and restrain to some extent their brutal behavior toward us. Alas, in spite of this directive, they had sufficient latitude to act arbitrarily and brutally toward us.

I was arrested on the 10th of November, 1938. I was released on December 21, 1938. I am grateful to a number of auspicious circumstances that allowed me to survive detention in completely good health, with the exception of an inflammation of the tendons in my feet and slight rheumatism. In comparison to many others, I was lucky, as I did not get severe frostbite or become seriously ill, or suffer severe emotional anguish. Of the two hundred people with whom I was together in a group, six died during the six weeks I was at Dachau.

Eight days after my return to Munich, where I lived and had been arrested, I developed a severe case of the flu. This illness appeared to be a typical reaction following imprisonment. Other prisoners had similar experiences following their release. Except for the rheumatism, I was able to overcome these handicaps. For others this certainly was not the case—especially for those who were ailing and whose illnesses became dangerously worse. At the age of 33, naturally, bearing considerable hardship was easier for me than it was for the many elderly and old people. There were prisoners who were over 70 and even 80 years of age. Luckily, only the day after my release it snowed. Therefore, I was most fortunate that such bad weather had not set in earlier. I have good reason to believe that had we had such bad weather—considering our clothes were thin and our way of life stressful and unhealthy—I would not have remained in good health. The sick were never released from Dachau.

Another aspect of great help was the fact that after two or three weeks, my wife was allowed to write to me. In her first letter, she wrote that my friends in England were working through the British Home Office for us to come to England. This was a necessary precondition for my release. This news greatly calmed my nerves as well as revived my physical and emotional strength. None of us had any notion as to what was to happen to us. We had no idea whether we had been arrested for 24 hours, for three days, for three weeks, for three months, or forever. We did not know whether we would ever come home again. We didn't even know whether home still existed. We did not get any news during our first three weeks. After the 1st of December, we could subscribe only to the *Völkischer Beobachter (the People's Observer)*, a revolting Nazi publication, and a similar paper, the *Münchner Neueste Nachrichten* (Munich's Latest News). Our letters were, of course, censored. While letters were not allowed to be longer than ten lines, occasionally, pieces of a letter were actually cut out. We weren't permitted to receive more than two letters per month. Therefore, during these first weeks, we had absolutely no idea as to what was happening in the world—not even how our relatives and friends were faring and where they were.

On the day we were arrested, *Kristallnacht*, the planned plundering of Jewish shops and the destruction of synagogues took place. Access to all Jewish businesses including food stores was forbidden. On this same day, large numbers of Jews, in part relatives of those arrested, were given the order to leave Munich, Bavaria, and all of Germany within 24 hours. Without our knowledge, these directives were withdrawn.

Actually, two days after my arrest, our apartment was raided. At 8:30 p.m., four, raging, shouting, bullying neighbors ransacked the somewhat remote little house in which we rented two furnished rooms. My wife was alone with the maid of the landlord who had also been arrested. These men ordered my wife and the maid to clear out the house. The guys set aside a number of valuables, including our typewriter, Leica camera, and record player, that they intended to take with them, since they couldn't find any "gold and silver," which they had hoped locate. After two and a half hours, the police arrived with much caution and hesitation. They had been called by a friend of ours, who by chance had telephoned my wife and had become aware of the commotion. During the period of November 9th through 12th, the police were forbidden to leave the station, despite being called out for an emergency. Even after this measure was lifted, the police, as just described, were particularly reluctant although well-intentioned. However, they would not enter the house in which the four fellows were raging. Yet, when the police appeared at the garden gate of the house, the raiders, who were intimidated, left. They abandoned the treasures they had set aside to take with them. The names of these men remain unknown.

I was not at home at the time I was to be arrested. The SA [Social Action recruits] waited for four hours at our apartment. During this time, they searched my papers and scholarly work. They rifled through personal letters and photos. They threw everything together and took along a number of books including works by Heine, Tolstoy, and Thomas Mann. I am aware that in other places the SA executed a lot more damage. In Munich, as far as I know, only one private house was set on fire and demolished. Also, while an acquaintance of mine was imprisoned, twenty-two crates of scholarly books were removed from his home. The SA left the order that I was to report immediately to the *Gestapo*, Secret State Police, at the Wittelsbach Palace. I had no choice but to turn myself in, as there was no prospect to escape. All railroad stations and roads were blocked. Trying to stay with non-Jewish friends would have placed them in danger. Therefore, I turned myself in between midnight and one a.m. My wife, who accompanied me, had to stay behind in the admitting room. When I was hauled away, she was informed only that I was taken into "protective custody."

I, then, along with others had to undergo a very thorough, bureaucratic admissions procedure carried out by a civilian official. We had to give specific information about all sorts of things, including our finances. As the officials claimed to have lost our files, the procedure was repeated again after several hours. Meanwhile, a lot of people had gathered here. We spent the night in the so-called gymnasium of the palace. It was a big, clean, dungeon-like room, sparingly and theatrically illuminated by one lamp. About thirty of the arrested Jews lay on the floor or were leaning against the wall. A black-uniformed SS man walked with even steps through the hall. I along with others had to stand at attention for a long period of time. Later we were allowed to lie on the floor. Nazis dressed in civilian clothes came and left throughout the night. They appeared criminal-like: mean, insidiously vulgar, the most evil and depraved creatures. They looked like murderous actors in the theater; their facial expression depicted sadism, and their conduct lacked that of the typical actor. They whispered, ridiculed, and reprimanded us, making threats, all with the intention to frighten us. During this night, we had no idea what they were going to do with us. We were not even given a clue that we would be sent to Dachau. This we first learned about 11 o'clock the following morning, after we had been sent outside.

From 5:00 a.m. to about 10:30 a.m., we had had to stand at attention again. A particularly fat SS officer of somewhat higher rank than others swaggered into the hall and promptly left. Shortly thereafter, he came back again. Amidst reprimands, he interrogated us: "Are there any attorneys among you?" A very small, old man announced that he was. "Do you know Judge B?" the officer asked. "Yes," answered the elderly man. "He has already been shot," replied the SS officer. This official resembled a wild boar, yet he did not appear to be as deeply corrupt and depraved as the Nazi civilians. The SS officer discovered among us a man, evidently a real estate broker, to whom he had not yet paid off his debt. He promptly reproached the poor fellow of usury and promised him severe punishment. In an outburst, the SS official said that he had become utterly down and out as a result of this debt. It was the Jew's fault, he claimed. If this officer had not received his present position with the SS, he would have been completely destroyed. I don't know whether this actually happened. I do know, however, that this inmate later died in Dachau.

The most unpleasant moments of this night were when we heard screams from a distant room. Obviously someone was being tortured. Luckily, we only had to stand still for hours. Even so, for the first time an older man collapsed. He was laid against the wall. Upon coming to, he once again was forced to take his place in line.

We were transported to Dachau in open trucks, in which benches had been placed. Throughout the trip, we were yelled at, insulted, and humiliated, although we were not physically mistreated. As long as the transport was supervised by regular police, all went properly and smoothly. Serious abuse began only when the SS took control. However, we never encountered such maltreatment on the short trip from Munich to Dachau. It was very different among other groups. They were transported in unlighted freight cars. There was standing room only, for they were tightly squeezed together. They were both verbally and physically abused. Some, for instance, received broken legs. The SS in charge threatened to pour gasoline over the entire wooden boxcar and then set it on fire.

Upon arriving, we had to line up facing the wall while SS troopers with bayonets and revolvers stood behind us. We were then once again submitted to a very bureaucratic admissions procedure. We were shaved, then separately photographed from both the front and the side. We were then marched outside, where we were required to remain standing. When we were brought back inside, we had to empty all the contents of our pockets. Suitcases and small bags had already been taken from us in Munich. We were only allowed to keep our eye-glasses and wedding rings. Medicine was also taken from us, an act that was of catastrophic proportions to those who relied on it for survival. Money was counted and properly recorded. We were allowed to keep about ten Reichsmarks. At this point, we were ordered to undress completely. All of our clothes, including our shoes, were put into a sack, to which a label was attached. Upon our release, this sack containing all of our clothing was returned to us in good condition. We were allowed to take along a handkerchief, our wallet, suspenders, trusses, and arch supports. Naked, except for these remaining items, we all had to go to an adjoining room. Here our heads were shaved. At the door to the next room an SS enlistee, a young hoodlum, stood. As we passed through the door, he gave each of us two severe whacks with a ruler. Even the most elderly were hit. Then we entered a large, very clean, modern shower room. Each of us was given a hot shower. Following our cleansing, we were led into a room where we were examined by a doctor. Initially, elderly, "Aryan" prisoners determined and recorded our weight, height, serious or contagious diseases, operations, and accidents we had had. Then we were sent on to the doctor who sat behind a table. We had to announce our presence by yelling: "Jew in protective custody, Maier, Eduard (fictitious name) obediently announces his presence here." An SS official, who was standing in front of the table cursed, insulted, and kicked each of us regardless of our age. Again we had to yell this information, this time even louder. As we departed we were given a few additional kicks. For clothes we were issued a pair of tattered socks, a jacket and a pair of pants made out of light denim, a cap, so long as the stock lasted. I was one of the last ones to get a cap—a great advantage as our heads were shaven. We were also given a thin shirt, otherwise no underwear.

After we got dressed, we had to line up outside, where we were assigned to barracks. That meant we stood around in the camp streets for the remainder of the day. Towards 5:30 p.m., we were ordered to line up at the roll-call square. Only at about 7:00 p.m. were we given our first meal since our arrest.

(I have to insert here that prisoners who arrived alone had been treated with considerable brutality. In this regard, we were better off. Jews who had arrived earlier were beaten upon entry with twenty-five blows with a cane.)

To fully describe life at the camp would take up an entire booklet. Although only a detailed description of daily events would give the reader an informative, overall picture of the atmosphere at the camp, I have to limit myself to describe only some of the external details and some individual characteristics.

The concentration camp at Dachau was very large, modern, and neat. I was able to get a view of the place as a whole only upon my arrival and departure. Around the camp a small, tidy and clean town has been erected. The streets on which the SS resided included bright, friendly appearing cottages and houses as well as a marketplace. The area that was closed off, as far as I could tell, included, administration and housekeeping buildings, warehouses, garages, a large bakery, a sawmill, a carpentry shop. The actual prison camp was separated and closed off from the outside world by a moat. Friendly appearing poplar trees were planted along its banks. Next to the moat was a whitewashed wall approximately the height of an average man capped by barbed, electric wire. A few meters inside this wall was another electric, barbed-wire fence. In front of this was one more moat before which well-maintained grass had been planted. Stepping on the lawn was forbidden. Whoever did so would be shot, to my recollection, from one of seven watchtowers situated along this wall. These high towers were manned by SS personnel armed with machine guns. Because of this tight security, placing bars across the barracks windows was unnecessary. As a result one would not get the impression that this is a prison. In comparison to traditional prisons, Dachau was similar to a modern zoological garden. Here animals seem to roam freely except that they are separated from the observer by a moat, in contrast to the conventional zoo in which the animals linger in cages behind iron bars. We entered this prison portion of the camp through an iron gate that was physically attached to the guard house. The gate would be opened for each individual or group passing through, and then it would be immediately closed. The gate was not decorated with conventional iron grating, but rather with a tasteful iron ornament in which the words WORK WILL MAKE YOU FREE [ARBEIT MACHT FREI] were inscribed.

This gate led from the west to the great roll-call square. It was bordered to the north by huge, one-story housekeeping and maintenance buildings. Towards the south the first barracks appeared. The camp was planned precisely according to the four points of the compass. It was designed as a large quadrangle, the walls of which extended exactly from north to south and from east to west. The wide camp street stretched from the north to the south, heading straight toward the buildings established for domestic purposes. A little tower accompanied by a large entrance to the kitchen accentuated these structures. On both sides of the camp street were barracks; their windowless ends faced the street. Alleys that are about as wide as the barracks themselves, approximately 7.5 meters, separated the barracks from each other.

Grass and flowerbeds bordered the camp street, which was about 20 meters wide. At the beginning of November, a few pansies were still blossoming. In front of each barrack were two large poplar trees. The camp street led onto the huge roll-call square that was approximately 150 to 200 meters in size. The architects designed the square to be closed off by the rectangular, horseshoe-shaped construction of the housekeeping buildings. These buildings were constructed of whitewashed masonry. In typical Bavarian design, the storage rooms on the second floor had brown, wooden beams set tastefully into the whitewashed masonry. One wing of the building contained the foyer, where we had to undress and where upon our departure we would be given back our civilian clothes.

Here the sacks with our possessions were hung on long rods. In the west wing of the central building are the heating plant and the large shower room. In this building, one also finds a modern, model kitchen equipped with huge, impressive kettles—all extremely clean.

The barracks were approximately 7 to 8 meters wide and probably about 80 meters long. There was a total of thirty-four barracks. The first two buildings on the east side of the roll-call square consisted of the infirmary. On the west side, one barrack was used as a canteen and a fourth as a school. Although this building had a room for instruction and a library, we were not allowed to use this barrack. The remaining thirty barracks housed prisoners. Each single barrack, called a "block," had a large number painted with black on a white background attached to the side facing the camp street. Every barrack was divided into four rooms. Each set of two rooms had a common entrance to the camp street. From the lobby, which had a brick floor, two doors—one on the left and the other on the right—led to the two rooms. To the left at the back was the door to the toilet, while to the right was the entrance to the washroom. Toilet and washroom were for both rooms. They, like the entrance, were tiled with brick. Both very practically and hygienically arranged. The toilet had six hoppers made from brown, artificial stone. They had metal handles and were flushed with water. The waste went into an underground tank. This tank was emptied every few weeks from the camp street by a truck that had a big tank along with its own vacuum system. The washroom had two big "fountains" shaped like a tree with six large faucets and a large, round basin made of white enamel. At each of these two sinks, six people could wash at the same time. On the wall, were four or six movable basins made of artificial stone with faucets above. These were used to wash our feet, clean our boots, and wash our dishes. Under these basins was a cleverly designed open gutter to prevent plug-ups. For fresh air, each of the two rooms had two large windows.

Meticulous cleanliness was demanded. Both rooms were thoroughly cleaned by inmates three to four times a day. Each living area consisted of two rooms: a self-styled day or living room and a so-called bedroom. In the living room was a big, beautiful tile stove. With wooden floors, the room appeared bright and friendly. The north and south walls towards the camp alleys each had two large windows. The window frames like the ceiling were painted white. Electric lights emanated from a functional yet tasteful glass ball attached to the ceiling. There were big, strong, yellow, lacquered tables. Pine, darkly stained cabinets and stools were just as sleek, clean and functional. As each room was designed to fit fifty people, there were fifty of these for each section. Therefore, every barrack was to house two hundred men. The walls were made of prefabricated, artificial materials that were screwed together onto a masonry or cement base. They were painted in a friendly gray or linden green. We often said that this entire, huge, functional, and in its way almost beautiful layout, would have been ideal for a large youth camp or for some other similar purpose. This arrangement had existed in its present form only since 1938. Previously the prisoners were held elsewhere. The new design was built by inmates under the most strenuous exertion and most severe torture.

Externally the camp appeared nice and neat. I doubt that the artificial materials of which the barracks were constructed were of solid quality. I question whether they will be able to withstand weather conditions over a long period of time. As the walls, for instance, are very thin, we were forbidden to lean against them. Although the barracks have been standing for only a few months, there were already numerous cracks in the walls. Next to these cracks, the word *defect* was written in pencil. Above all, the beautiful appearance of the camp gave no indication as to its intended use or what was to take place there. The rooms that were designed to house fifty men were quadrupled during my stay at Dachau. As there were now two hundred men in each room, there were eight hundred of us in every barrack. Four men shared the same locker as well as the same towel. Because of these conditions, hygienic precautions were illusory. Washrooms and toilet facilities for such a large group were, of course, much too small and narrow. Of what use were the most beautiful toilets, if we were not allowed to use them? For many of us, especially those who were sick, it was terrible torture not to be able to use the toilets. Even if they could use them for only short, predetermined periods, they still would suffer greatly. This overcrowding and being forbidden to use the toilets meant that the bureaucratic recording of all contagious diseases upon or arrival was purely a formality and an entirely superficial act. In reality, all sick people including those with active tuberculosis shared the same room with all others, used the same blankets, and the same eating utensils that were supposed to be functional, pleasant, and appetizing. Although the pleasant and clean arrangements were misused, I would like to emphasize here that this aspect of the camp atmosphere was on the whole beneficial to our survival. To be in a bright, friendly room was helpful to me, especially when I imagined the many dismal barracks that had been erected for the wounded and prisoners in time of war [World War I]. Under normal conditions, there were fifty bunk beds to a room, with straw sacks covered with white sheets. To house four times as many people, these beds were put aside. Instead, crates with straw sacks were placed on the floor, the others one meter above the other in both the sleeping and living quarters. Although we lay very close to each other, we slept well after the rigors of the day. Those who usually suffered from sleeplessness usually slept well at Dachau, in spite of all the disadvantages that occurred in such a camp for the masses, such as snoring and the groaning of the sick and dying. Certainly some people lost sleep due to the fact that the sick and healthy shared the same room. In spite of all these factors, the nightly rest regularly increased and strengthened our resistance. We were able to sleep just about nine hours from 8 p.m. to 4:45 in the morning. At first we had only one blanket, later two. Since we lay together at such close proximity, we generally felt warm enough. An exception occurred at times when we were punished. As the windows were removed from their frames, those who slept close by the windows were the ones who suffered most. We slept in the same jean suit that we wore during the daytime. During the entire six weeks that I was at Dachau, we never once changed this single outfit. We did, however, get clean shirts every two weeks.

We were awakened at 4:45 in the morning. Then we washed and were given coffee. At about 5:30 a.m. we lined up in the camp alley. From the moment we got up until roll-call time, we had to clean all the rooms, including the washroom, toilets, and lobby. These jobs were rotated about every two weeks among us. At 6:00 we marched to the roll-call place. From about 6:15 to 8:00 roll call was taken. We had to stand still and at times at attention. From 8:00 to 11:30 we had "work time." This meant lining, standing in the camp street, and marching throughout the camp. From 11:30 to 12:50 was our time for dinner and rest. Upon returning to the barracks, we could at best rest until 12:20, because at that time cleaning duty began. At 12:50 we lined up in the camp alley again. From 1:15 to about 2:00 p.m., we endured another roll call, called "distribution of work." Actually, this meant standing still at the roll-call square. From 2:00 to 4:30 was officially considered "work time." At 4:45 we lined up once more in the camp alley. We stood there from 5:00 to 6:00, 6:30, or 7:00, though sometimes even longer, depending on the mood of the evening guard. Finally, we experienced our last roll call of the day. We had to stand in rows, very still and sometimes at attention. This roll call was supposed to last several minutes, but it often lasted from a quarter to half an hour. Saturday afternoon was officially work free. Still, we had to line up much of Saturday afternoon. On one Saturday we had to stand at roll call from 2:00 in the afternoon until 8:00 at night. We did not have to be on duty on Sundays, except for the usual roll call, which was somewhat shortened. We were only awakened at 6:00 a.m.

During the week we were outside from 5:30 in the morning until 6:30 in the evening and sometimes later, as I have already indicated. The only break was the brief lunch hour. We had, however, to stand in line for food, then again in order to wash our plates and utensils amidst a large crowd. As a result, we spent the entire time on our feet—most of the while standing still.

For us the central focus of Dachau's daily routine was roll call—particularly the morning and evening count. Everybody had to come to roll call with the exception of those in the infirmary. These, with the rarest of exceptions, were the candidates for death. This did not mean that all candidates who were on death's bed were actually admitted to the infirmary. A few at doctor's orders were given bed rest in the barracks. Only the very sick were given some leniency, such as being freed of "work duty": marching about the camp. However, they were usually forbidden to be in the barracks during this time. Therefore, as an utterly miserable group, they had to stand around freezing in the camp alley. They were also required to attend roll call. Such severely ill people often had to be carried to the roll-call square, propped up by their comrades, and remain the entire time at roll call. I can immediately recall one man who had severe arthritis, another who had clubfeet, and others who were so exhausted from their illnesses, while still others suffered from the consequences of maltreatment. Even for those of us who were healthy, these roll calls were both exhausting and torturous. We never knew, particularly in the evening, how long we would have to stand around in the cold, in the wind, and during inclement weather.

In the morning and evening it was dark. We were dressed, as I said before, in an outfit of light summer material. Seen from the outside, such a roll call had the imposing appearance of a massive parade. Each block marched as a separate unit in rows of ten to the huge roll-call square. Here a mass of twenty thousand people stood in silence. When it was dark or foggy, spotlights illuminated the square. Although there were many stationary spotlights on the surrounding buildings, the spotlights on the watchtowers were on swivels. The guards played with them, shining blinding light into the crowd below.

The intent of the role-call count was, just as its name implied, to determine that no prisoner has disappeared. Each barrack supervisor gave his account to an SS official who then double-checked every count by walking along each row of ten. "Stand at attention! Caps off!" he ordered. He then handed the final check over to another yet higher SS officer. Although this was actually the "holy rite" of roll call, we often had to endure another period of standing at attention—sometimes for a short period of time, sometimes longer. On occasion, the motive was punishment because we coughed too much or too loud at roll call. Sometimes there appeared to be no reason at all. Once an additional roll call was announced, our section leader cursed and cuffed us, adding insults and threats as SS personnel appeared. We again had to straighten up in our rows of ten.

Although roll call at midday sometimes occurred during a warm sun, the mornings and evenings were terribly cold. Our limbs became completely stiff as we stood freezing. The terrible cold was made a little more tolerable when some of us received underwear. We were informed after two to three weeks that we could purchase underwear. In spite of paying five marks, several weeks passed during which we heard no word. Finally, the undershorts arrived, but far from enough. Those who did not receive any were denied a refund of their money. They could, however, pay a few extra marks to buy a knitted vest. By means of a self-help organization we started, we made arrangements so that those upon their release would leave their underwear and knitted vests for those inmates who stayed behind. At the time I was released, most but not all prisoners had some extra piece of clothing. During my last ten days, I had a pair of warm underpants and for the last few days, also a knitted vest. This was most beneficial, since a significant cold spell and sharp east wind had set in.

There was hardly an evening roll call at which somebody didn't collapse. On the 10th of December, a large Christmas tree was placed at the roll-call square. It was illuminated with electric lights both in the morning and in the evening.

There were considerable advantages to being outside during the day as much as we were. We breathed fresh air, looked up at the sky to see stars in the early morning and evening. During the mornings of my last weeks when the weather was clear, we could watch Venus rise. We also witnessed beautiful sunrises. On particularly clear days, we could distinctly see the Alps, as they appeared to be close by. As prisoners we experienced everything of beauty twofold, for which we were doubly grateful. One evening at roll call we witnessed a huge meteor with a long tail. Many inevitably interpreted this as a heavenly omen. There were even times ranging from a few minutes to a quarter of an hour during the monotony of standing still and marching, our so-called work duty, during which we could calmly gather our thoughts. This, of course, was a rare occurrence. We were usually too exhausted as a result of constantly standing, severe hunger, and above all the biting cold. I have to add that during the early days some inmates tried to protect themselves against the cold by putting newspapers or dust-cloths inside their shirts. This was immediately forbidden. Those who were caught received a severe caning consisting of twenty-five blows. Although a major portion of our work duty consisted of standing about freezing in the camp alley, other than monotonous marching about the camp, these were relatively the best moments of the day. Light gymnastics quickly lost its appeal as the SS soldiers gained special pleasure in interfering with and bullying us.

It is hard to distinguish between chicanery and incompetence. Were those in charge of us adhering to poor or excessive organization? For instance, it was probably a bureaucratic mistake when money, which was usually distributed during "work hours," was handed out after evening roll call on one of the coldest nights. Even after the temperature dropped below minus 20 degrees Celsius, we were still forced to stand in the bitter cold for hours after evening roll call. Normally, on such a cold day, we would finally have been allowed to go inside the barracks. I recall another instance. On a cold, foggy day, we had to stand in line to wait to be shaved. Shaving took place in a very clean, practical room that had running water. "Aryan" inmates, some of whom were barbers, shaved us on a weekly basis. We had to stand around for hours in the penetrating cold, wind, and fog, only to learn that we would not be shaven after all. Often we had to grab our morning coffee and drink it out-of-doors. Sometimes as punishment we were not allowed to go into the barracks to eat our midday meal. Therefore, on such days we lost our opportunity to rest a little and warm up.

Such ordeals were hard on our nerves and drained our energy. In addition we were all depressed as to the uncertainty of our fate. As far as I know, Aryan prisoners were also never informed when and if they would be released. One cannot consider such additional strain on our nerves and energy as maltreatment. The assault on my wife that I described earlier could be viewed similarly. Finally, after the intruders left, they did return once more to say, "We haven't taken anything with us. We didn't do you any harm. The action has been ended." In spite of their repulsive deeds, they still wanted to have a clean conscience. Since they didn't want to admit that they had done wrong, they allowed themselves to be drawn into such wrongdoing. For instance, the Nazis didn't immediately kill us. Rather they let us perish. Causing us to stand about and freeze is nothing short of carrying out the slogan: *Jude verrecke!* (Die, Jew!)

We were extremely lucky in regard to weather conditions during my six weeks at Dachau. November was unusually beautiful. We were grateful for this fine weather. Otherwise, many more of us would have become sick. Except for two terrible days, during one of which snow and rain fell heavily, and the other was bitterly cold with a strong east wind, the days were dry. We even had some beautiful sunny days. Luckily, both of these terrible days fell on Sundays, during which we had to be outside for relatively short periods of time. To make it easier on us, on that frightfully frigid Sunday, roll call was held at noon. When the biting cold set in, those of us who had been here for some time were already somewhat toughened by the harsh weather conditions in contrast to those who had just arrived.

On the whole, we were probably fortunate that we had not come to Dachau during the hot season. Heat could have caused epidemics to flourish among the masses of people who were tightly packed together. Without any shade, we really wouldn't have been able to tolerate the heat at the camp. Even now on windy days, dust was blowing about. Because the camp was located on marshland over which gravel and sand were spread, dust readily formed. Water, however, water being in short supply was sparingly used.

In order to gain a picture of the ordeals our nerves endured, I have to describe little incidents that added stress to our living conditions. Imagine what it was like when four hundred of us, within a very limited time slot, had to wash the top portions of our bodies in a room the dimensions of which are 5.5 x 3.5 meters. Another example to illustrate my point pertains to the directive that we were not allowed to enter the rooms wearing our boots. However, we must wear our boots when entering the washroom or to use the toilets. Each time we had to step into the washroom, for instance, just to rinse our eating utensils we had to put on our boots. We had to go through the process of removing and donning our boots about ten times a day. This was unpleasant because these boots were heavy. It was particularly painful, as most of us had swollen, frostbitten feet. As we had to perform this task under great stress and pressure, constantly being rushed, the pain was terrible. Many could not handle this procedure alone, as their hands were also swollen and frostbitten—not to mention those who were already sick upon arrival at Dachau. For instance, a man whose hands were paralyzed due to a spinal-cord illness needed assistance.

Delivering the meals was a vexing chore for those of us assigned to this task. The food was transported in tubs with two handles. The contents weighed about two hundred pounds. As it was a considerable distance from the kitchen to the barracks, we were ordered to hurry. At times the SS directly in front of the beautiful-looking kitchen assaulted us. The containers were thermoses but without lids. Once at the barracks, the contents would be poured into smaller pails. Those on duty for the evening meal had to get the food and empty the containers prior to the evening roll call. When we finally came "home" to the barracks after standing for hours in the cold, the food, of course, was now cold. The food wasn't bad, consisting largely of one-dish meals and soup. At first we were given a quarter-loaf of army bread on a daily basis, while later we were provided with one-third loaf. At first, when the camp became overcrowded, there was too little food. Later, when more people were released, the amount of food was sufficient. Under normal circumstances, the food probably would have been adequate in spite of the fact that one undoubtedly received too few vitamins, too little sugar, and not enough fat. However, due to the extra stress placed on our bodies and because of the cold, our diet was insufficient. Therefore, we became dependent on buying supplemental food at the canteen. In this way the canteen did good business benefiting the camp's entire administration.

The canteen was pleasantly set up; it was appetizing and airy. It was about half to three-fourths the length of a barrack. On one of the long sides, there were seven or eight counters at which one could buy bread, yoghurt, milk, sweets, and articles needed for smoking. One could also purchase sewing materials, toilet articles, even socks, and skin cream. Also available were butter, sausage, cheese, marmalade, honey, dextrose, pastries, dates and figs. Particularly popular was the very good coffee that cost fifteen *Pfennig*. As the times when we could go to the canteen were very limited, directly after midday and evening meals only, there was considerable congestion here as well. To get our turn, we had to stand for a long time. Later, small subsidiary canteens were set up in certain barracks.

We were allowed to have fifteen marks sent to us on a weekly basis. We were also permitted to use the money that initially was taken from us on our arrival that turned out to be considerably more than the prescribed limit. Still, there were numerous inmates who did not have any money for their own use. Much secret begging occurred at the canteen especially between the Aryan prisoners and Viennese Jews. As no money was distributed during the first three weeks of my incarceration, we were starved and therefore less capable of resisting illness. Once we received money, our physical condition improved. The coexistence of agony and imminent danger on the one hand and the "good life" with coffee and cake on the other is one of the significant irrational contrasts of life at Dachau. I ate as much as I possibly could to maintain my immune system. Upon my dismissal from Dachau my weight was checked indicating that I had not lost any during my internment. A man from Vienna, who was weighed after me, had lost ten kilograms.

Of the camp regulations that were repeatedly read to us, a few come to mind:

- Every prisoner must behave in a principled and respectful manner.
- Dachau is governed by martial law. If anybody's behavior appears to be insubordinate in any way, he can be shot without any court proceedings.
- If an SS soldier hits a prisoner in the face and the inmate instinctively raises his arms and hands to protect his face, this is considered as resistance and insubordination against the authority of the state.

Other punishments for inmates included:

- Placed in isolation in darkness.
- Given twenty-five whacks with a cane.
- Being hung upside down from a tree for several hours.
- Attempts at suicide are forbidden and will be severely punished.
- Visiting other camp alleys or barracks is prohibited. One may, however, meet with prisoners from other barracks during one's free time.
- It is strictly forbidden to be in the vicinity of the isolation barracks. To try to sneak in cigarettes or food, for instance, to these prisoners mandates severe punishment.

There were three isolation barracks that could house from six hundred to twenty-four hundred people. These barracks, to which only the SS have keys, were barred off to the rest of us. The prisoners who were kept there had none of the "privileges" we had. They could never leave the isolation barracks, never use the canteen, and if I have been correctly informed, may not receive mail, at least less than the rest of us may get. That the isolation barracks were occupied, I do know for certain. How many people were incarcerated there, I do not know. We never saw anybody on the alleys by these barracks. Only once did I see somebody make a delivery of bread or something to that effect to one of these barracks.

Furthermore, giving presents to prisoners of higher rank such as section heads or barrack leaders was forbidden. To help other prisoners polish their shoes whether paid or unpaid, was prohibited. To eat or smoke during "work hours" was also outlawed. We were allowed to smoke during our free time outside the barracks. Here there was much smoking.

During the entire night the light remained on in the toilets. Entering the washroom during the night was prohibited in order to prevent homosexual activity. Such doings had to be reported and were punished.

Each inmate was required to take care of his own clothes, keep them clean and in good repair. We had to mend our own garments. Since damage to the clothing was considered as sabotage to state property, it was punishable.

We had to address camp personnel and officers of the SS as *Herr Blockführer* (Mr. Block Leader). We had to answer all questions with a short and loud, Yes, *Herr Blockführer.* Whenever a barrack leader or SS recruit appeared or passed us by, we were required to stand at attention and remove our caps. Our salutations were never answered. We were required to carry out all orders at a running pace. Actually, this was my first glaring impression as we arrived by truck at Dachau. I observed individual groups of prisoners at this clean and bright place frantically running as they pulled carts or were involved in other activities. The visual impression I got was of monkeys being degraded.

During the time I was at Dachau, nobody to my knowledge appeared to have been shot. As we did not hear about such incidents, they probably did not happen. Even so, killing was permitted as part of the daily routine. One barrack leader, an Aryan prisoner, reported that he had to be present when his father was shot. To the best of my knowledge, no Jew received any of the official punishments while I was there. An Aryan inmate received twenty-five blows, having smoked on the return march from the work place to the camp. Work time at the camp ended only when one was dismissed. The punishment was carried out before all the prisoners in front of the barrack to which he belonged. In addition, the entire barrack was punished by having to forgo their evening meal and being forced to stand for several hours.

The Jews were clearly differentiated in dress from the Aryan prisoners.

Our light denim outfit had broad blue-and-white stripes. That of the other prisoners consisted of two different shades of dark gray-green. For those Jews who just arrived, the blue-and-white outfits had come to an end. They either wore their civilian clothes or were given some more or less unmatched pieces of colorful clothing. Those last to arrive were mostly Austrians, suffering miserably both emotionally and physically. They were clad in rumpled, collarless, civilian clothing or in patched pieces of rags. The outfits of the other inmates were warmer than those of the Jews. Besides, they had underwear, knitted vests, gloves, and earmuffs.

Each prisoner had to have his prison number attached to his jacket and pants. Beneath the number was a symbol of colored material identifying the category to which he belonged. A red triangle with the point facing down designated the political prisoners. "Professional" criminals wore black patches, while those branded as "averse to work" wore brown. Others, such as immigrants or those who studied the Bible seriously, had their own colors, while homosexuals bore the color pink. Those of the prisoners who were suspected of trying to escape bore a particular circular mark. Jews had to wear the red political triangle with its point facing down and a yellow triangle with the point facing up, creating the appearance of a red-and-yellow Magen David.

Jews, whenever possible, were kept in separate barracks from the Aryan prisoners. Only occasionally did we come into contact with them, for instance, during the weekly shaving routine in which the Aryans also had to participate, in the canteen, and sometimes on the camp streets. To talk with them was frowned upon, while communicating with those bearing black or brown symbols was, I believe, forbidden altogether. Some of the Aryan prisoners, who were brought here, were permitted to work in their own occupations, including carpenters, locksmiths, and barbers. Others did deskwork or took care of the sick in the infirmary. Most of them worked in the dreaded gravel pits or on the moor. The prisoners performed almost all tasks that were usually carried out by animals, motor vehicles, or machines. For those working on the moor, there was a huge truck called the Moor Express. However, it was wagon pulled by twelve men. Special groups of prisoners, particularly the new arrivals, were marched about the camp like us for hours at a time at the same pace. Often they had to sing "Say hi to Lore again," or a more appropriately melancholy song. I am not quite sure as to how the text goes, but it is something like this: "The clouds move, the waves roar, and the songs blow far across the sea." I still strongly hear the recurring melancholic refrain of the song. Those who sang most beautifully were groups from the Sudeten part of Germany. Jews also were required to make an attempt at singing, for instance, "Lore" or "To Wander Is the Miller's Joy." However, such attempts were short-lived. Most of the time we marched to the monotonous "Left, 2, 3, 4, Left 2, 3, 4," yelled out by the commander at the time, except to be broken only when we were ordered to speed up to a run.

The groups in brown suffered the most. Accused "as those who shied from work," their communities or even the Reich itself sent them to Dachau. Under the previous administration, they would have been put to work in almshouses or would have been cared for by the social welfare system. Some of these were elderly people, others terribly poor and wretched, tramps, the hopeless, others limping or otherwise crippled. They were forced to clean the streets, usually without appropriate tools. They had to bend over to pick up each blade of straw and each little piece of paper. After work hours, they continued to stoop, searching for each tiny bit of a cigarette butt that they could find for their own use.

Once I spoke with a young fellow in the canteen who was designated as brown. He appeared to be an especially nice, serious, and vigorous youth who had already been in the camp between three to five years. When he was seventeen, he had been hauled here from his place of work, probably for political and social education. Because of this, I didn't ask any further questions. I imagine that he had participated in a Communist youth group. He expected to be released in March of 1939, "That is if they don't designate me as Red, a political prisoner, and decide to keep me here." I asked him why two of his fingers on his right hand were bandaged. As he apparently lacked skill on the job, his boss punished him by smashing his fingers with a hammer, breaking two of them.

Among the Reds, the political prisoners, we encountered the most varied types, including hard, brutal, mistreated, raw and vulgar men, then again sturdy, handsome youth, along with skinny, small, wretched folk, as well as coarse and cunning characters, mixed among young and old, serious, sensitive, considerate individuals. There was a group of Viennese among which was the former mayor of Vienna. As a team they had to pull a heavy street roller. Also on the road crew was the son of the archduke who was assassinated at Sarajevo. If we did not consider the very hard work that these people were doing, on occasion envy emerged among the Jewish inmates towards those who could at least work. Keep in mind that such work was usually under the direct and close supervision of the SS, who often abused the workers.

We, the Jewish prisoners, had relatively little directly to do with the SS. Even though each barrack was under the command of an SS officer, he did not live there. He only appeared occasionally to make sudden revisions. Our immediate supervisors were the older Aryan prisoners. Each room also had a Red senior commander, who in turn answered to the SS barrack commander. There was a certain degree of solidarity between the supervisory prisoners and their subordinates. Even upon our arrival at the camp, these prisoners gave us orders and barked at us as viciously, especially when the SS were in sight. They then quietly added, "You must realize that you are in Dachau. I mean well with you and want everything to run smoothly. If you do something obvious, you will be hung from a tree. We are also just prisoners. If you behave decently, you will be treated decently; if you behave like pigs, you will be treated like pigs. Those who do not promptly obey our commands will immediately be reported."

The section leader to whom I was assigned had already been at Dachau for three years. For the three previous years, he had been imprisoned at hard labor. These six years had transformed him into a completely brutal, nervous savage. He had become demoralized and was no longer of sound mind. Prior to his assignment at hard labor and then internment at Dachau, he had been a miner in Bavaria and leader of the local branch of the Communist Party. Although he was not very intelligent, he was, in a primitive sense, good-natured. He also demonstrated a typical Bavarian sentimentality. He, however, also had a violent temper resulting in fits of brutality. Undoubtedly, these frightful outbursts had become severely worse during his years at hard labor and at Dachau. All he seemed able to do was hit and scream. He was simply not bright enough to deal with the daily details in these overcrowded rooms. He was unable to properly organize us, for instance, to line us up for food, to clean, remove, and put on our boots, let alone letter writing. Each tiny bit of noise caused him to become wild. Above all, when things did not go as he imagined or wanted them to, he knew of no other way to accomplish these other than lash out at us. Someone varied the dictum: "Just at the moment when ideas fail, there comes a hard blow." If somebody by chance roused his anger, that person could suffer severely for a long time. Our section leader particularly could not tolerate the elderly. He thrashed them more than others because of some real of imagined clumsiness or sloppiness on their part. For instance, an old man, over seventy years of age, had by mistake entered the wrong room and was unable to find his way around. The room leader became frightfully enraged. As he began beating the victim, he became more and more enwrapped in his fury, throwing the man to the ground and stomping on him. His rage was not premeditated. The results were usually not too serious as he appeared to be worse than he really was. No serious bodily injuries did occur. He had these outbursts on many varied occasions. For instance, when a philosophy professor did not have his locker in the prescribed order or when a doctor gave a cup of coffee to a sick person, he would lash out. A few days later he was especially nice to this sick man. There were times that he unexpectedly and simultaneously lashed out at all of us. Suddenly we were no longer allowed to be in the room or lobby. We immediately were required to put on our boots and go outside. His behavior was not really anti-Semitism. He did, however, have resentment and held contempt for the bourgeoisie. I clearly recall an instance when he discovered a sad, little old man, previously a judge, who was severely paralyzed, that he treated with great inconsideration. Although this small, certainly good-natured judge had dealt only with trifling incidents, he was to the room leader an evil magistrate. To him all judges had to be condemned to prison.

Fortunately, among us there were people who could do hands-on work. These people were able to relate socially to our section leader. Among these was a furniture packer, father of seven children. Another was the leader of a gym squad at a Jewish gymnastic organization. As the section leader did listen to them, at least to some extent, they were gradually able to take control of the internal organization of our section. This very small group gained a somewhat privileged position acting just a little like bigwigs. They did, however, have a calming effect upon all of us.

Our section leader was under constant pressure from the barrack commander, a similarly malicious and yet good-natured, raw and debilitated fellow like himself. He lived in dread of his superior. This barrack commander was in turn under pressure from the SS, who demanded ruthless treatment to all Jews.

Evenings, when we were lying down and the light was out, our section leader would give us an occasional speech consisting of all kinds of instructions. Some were good-natured, warm, and even touching, while others consisted of threats and curses. He would often threaten to report somebody to his superiors, but never did. When such a threat was made, we clearly understood the danger it implied to all of us at Dachau. “A sharp wind blows through Dachau,” he was fond of saying. “If you want to come out of Dachau alive, you have to do as I command, or I shall personally kill you. Good night to you all!”

The section leader's and barrack commander's brutal and mad actions controlled the day. However, in general, these two men did not possess the SS's cynical and intentional meanness, accompanied by their contemplated and cruel pleasure in torturing people. Under normal circumstances, it is hard to imagine that such human beings exist. Among the SS, there were other types as well. Some appeared smart, fit, and adept with disciplined brutality. Yet they looked as if they were bright, healthy, and normal. Another type consisted of civilians who were in the service of the Gestapo. These were dismal, miserable, and repulsive men. I can imagine their insidious, hideous nightlife. They were degenerate, perfidious, foul through and through as well as perverted. A third variety was a combination of these two. We saw these barrack commanders daily walking about the camp. The others operated in the background and in the dark. They were robust, strong cretins with a healthy complexion though somewhat retarded, untalented idiots possessing nothing more than cynical bestiality in their expression. Isn't there just a little spark in such faces representing the soul of humanity? I sometimes tried to find this spark. If it was there, it was completely helpless and powerless. The greatest pleasure these fellows seemed to have been to frighten the inmates and demonstrate how powerless they were. These men would ride their bicycles into a marching or stationary column without giving any signal so that the people would have to jump apart. They addressed us only as "you Jewish swine," or "you asshole." Later, apparently due to new directives, they used the form of address with the formal *Sie* (you). At times, they would force us to do exercises or gymnastics. Sometimes we had to do seventy to a hundred knee bends in ten stages. We had to stand for long periods of time at half height. Those who could not do this, especially the elderly, were boxed or kicked into the dirt. I remember an old man who was doubly harassed for begging to be excused since he had recently had an operation. I don't know whether keeping their eyes on the elderly was a special form of sadism, a sadistic form of behavior that was especially hard to understand. Or did they consider the elderly to be old criminals, and, therefore, that such abuse was an indirect and easier way to kill them? Perhaps this was the easiest way for them to carry out orders to reach the largest number of deaths possible.

Already on *Kristallnacht*, the elderly were treated particularly badly. On that day, November 10th, homes for the elderly in Munich and throughout Germany were vacated with intense vigor as their occupants were thrown into the street. In the evening, the SS were dancing inside these homes. Perhaps it was the intent of the Nazis to kill off the elderly as quickly as possible, as they no longer were able to emigrate.

Our supervisors and commanders took great pleasure in letting the inmates who were to be chastised struggle as long as possible before the flogging began. Those who wore glasses found that their spectacles were always damaged resulting from such maltreatment. Nobody escaped flogging. I, personally, was fortunate to be beaten only once and quite harmlessly. Insults and curses were directed to us almost always around monetary issues. The topic of money was a popular means to instigate more hatred toward us among the "Aryan" prisoners and the SS. I recall a pale and bloated senior SS officer who was leading a group of SS officials through the camp. He interrogated individual prisoners before a gathering of SS soldiers and prisoners, asking our profession and how much money we had.

I can only tell about what happened at Dachau during the daylight and what took place in public. If however one could have seen what went on behind the scenes and the expression on the faces of the SS soldiers, one would realize that anything is possible, much more than our normal imagination could possibly dream of—everything.

It was certainly likely that the SS themselves were taught and drilled in a very brutal, cynical, and chastising manner. In part this may be intended to be a Spartan-like toughening process. The result of the pressure of this cynical and unconstrained system, which perhaps may also be intentional, corrupts all humane characteristics, causing and progressively intensifying their need to take revenge for their suffering, disgrace, and pain. This training creates a lust for power way beyond natural limits. This indiscriminate lust for power allows a person to justify that everything he does in order to satisfy his needs is acceptable. Furthermore, such training encourages the person to develop and express a conviction that he is serving a great cause, for which he is not responsible.

The result is continuous extortion and far-reaching destruction of natural solidarity. Everybody is affected. For instance, when conditions are already terribly bad, and my spoon is not in my locker, the spoon perhaps was mistakenly taken by somebody next to me. However, when the spoon is still missing upon locker checks, I am in danger of punishment that can have the most severe consequences. Therefore, I am tempted to and do consciously take the spoon of a comrade. Who would resist such a small temptation realizing that otherwise he would face the danger of being killed? Few.

I often ask myself: What does the National Socialist regime want to achieve by establishing the concentration camps? I think more of the political prisoners than I do of the Jews. It is inconceivable that after years of being treated as described above, the original opponents of Nazism will leave the camp as enthusiastic believers and followers of the National Socialist ideology. It is not to National Socialism that they feel converted, although its exclusive infiltration may have had its persuasive power. *Since they have gotten the power, they must have understood it better than we did. Thus, they must be right.* It is not the ideology to which they turn or of which they have become convinced, rather it is the mentality of their daily life that affects them and forces them to submit to Nazism. Since life and death are no longer a matter of consequence, Nazism under these circumstances has something in its favor. At the very least it holds power. But more important than the ideology is the mentality. Such a state of mind is more contagious because it is less consciously adopted and therefore unknowingly and easily passed on. When we marched with our group and the person in front of you had his hands in his pockets or was talking with his neighbor as an SS officer was approaching who observed these flaws, none of us had the opportunity any longer to warn that comrade of forthcoming danger. Instead, we gave him a powerful punch. Our blow was particularly vigorous, because we were annoyed that this stupid fellow, due to his chatting or negligence, could not just get himself but all of us, including myself, into serious trouble. As a result there was a great deal of frustration and irritability among the Jews. I noticed in myself, contrary to better habit, that I, like others, rarely used words on such occasion any more. Rather we made ourselves understood by scolding and punching. Since there were no appropriate means of communication and expression at Dachau, we either whispered or yelled. Besides, it was obvious that the voices among those who had been imprisoned at Dachau for some time were ruined. Our voices deteriorated not only because of yelling and smoking in the cold, harsh, air, but also from lingering colds and coughs. We made ourselves understood at Dachau not with words but with pushing and shoving.

For a while, I had the job of cleaning the foot grate in front of the barrack door, as well as the container for drainage, a task I had to do three times daily. One day as I was bending over to do this chore, I was poked in the back and pushed to the ground. The room leader of the next section promptly snatched the pail with which I was working. He simply needed the pail and did not make the effort to ask for it.

Since relief from responsibility was extremely contagious, irresponsibility destroyed solidarity. I did not naturally lean towards dodging my obligations. However, at Dachau, whenever possible, I consistently and consciously shirked additional work, especially if I would be exposed to the elements, for instance transporting food. Maybe I would have acted differently were I not married. If possible, under different circumstances, I would have gladly relieved another comrade who might have been in worse physical shape than I was. It was, however, more important for me to return home healthy. The situation may have been similar during wartime, though the perspective may be different. A terrible, constant deadening of feeling coexisted with a beautiful readiness to be of help. With only a few exceptions, there generally was a wonderful sense of comradeship among the Jews in our group. There were always some who were readily available and unhesitatingly helpful. Possibly later, I will have an opportunity to tell about the truly wonderful and most helpful individual Aryan inmates.

The tendency of the system was to destroy any sense of solidarity. As we were always on the outermost edge, forever on the border of imminent danger, the basic, elementary drive for self-preservation that set in created this system of extortion. Accompanying this system was the need of the supervisors, even though they were prisoners themselves, to harass the inmates beneath them. They did this to make themselves popular with those above them, but also to save themselves from the pressure and danger imposed on them by their superiors. And above all, as previously stated, the need for power increases and becomes more brutal throughout.

A yellow band worn around their upper arm recognizes the commanding prisoners, called "capos." There were certain capos that provoked as much fear as the SS themselves. Since we did not have to work, we were not under their command. However, we could occasionally observe a variety of brutal incidents. On one occasion, we were marching about the roll-call square as a capo was busy harassing a subordinate fellow prisoner. The man was small, pale, and weak. The capo forced him to hop around on his haunches, a particularly popular punishment exercise at Dachau. It is both especially strenuous and humiliating. As he was hopping around, the capo would push, shove, and throw him to the ground. Then he would make him run, hop again, and finally let him go. Now that the man believed he was free, the capo, however, commanded him to return and start the whole affair over again. We continued to march. On returning a quarter to half an hour later, these practices were still continuing.

Although this coercive, contagious state of mind achieved an imposing orderliness on the outside, its totalitarian system did work its way by degrees onto the Jews as well. The speech and tone of the Jews approached the Dachau dialect. I have already spoken of the growing exasperation among us as there was a tendency among the Jews to lack discipline. I do not mean anything terrible like intentional lack of discipline, rather a certain degree of indifferent indolence evolved. I do not mean that those people, who by nature are amiable, were completely militaristic. These people, who had a more meditative and dreamy temperament, had a terribly hard time to adjust to the military marching and drill routine. They would arouse fierce anger, due to their lack of understanding, among those whose zealous pride demanded that they become militant Dachauers. After all, these former soldiers demonstrated great pride for having served in the First World War. Such a natural inclination against militarism is not a typical Jewish tendency. I observed this in varying degrees, especially among the Sudeten German prisoners. Rather I found this attitude toward lack of discipline to be typically Jewish. This apathetic manner provoked Dachau officials causing them to react by beating and taking other abusive actions.

A combination of being ill bred, together with a lack of seriousness, made it very difficult for many to understand what it meant to be at Dachau. How often we had to listen to the section leader or barrack commander telling us: "Remember, you are now in Dachau!" a fact that most us were constantly aware of. There was, however, a type of people, not individuals, but a type who simply could not understand that self-discipline was required even in small matters among such a massive amount of people. These folk just couldn't be quiet when they were supposed to be quiet. They crowded appallingly in front of the barrack or canteen doors, or at shaving time as if their entire happiness depended upon getting in a second earlier. They failed to realize the importance of navigating the dangers at Dachau as smoothly as possible. Nor did they seem to comprehend that in the extremely serious situation we all were in at Dachau their behavior antagonized both Aryan and other Jewish prisoners. It was, for instance, terribly noisy in the canteen in spite of warnings and threats made by the SS and inmates who were in charge there. Once I asked a friendly, elderly man to tone down his conversation. He had been shouting from quite a distance to an acquaintance or a relative. He lacked the consideration toward all of us, as an SS officer had just threatened to punish us by demanding that we stand in line for the evening if we did not quiet down immediately. This fellow inmate didn't understand me, nor had he any idea as to what I wanted. He immediately gained support against me from another group of comrades. He thought that I also wanted take command, as if the commands of the SS were not enough. Everyone now wanted to give orders. I was not the only person to have had this experience. However, many of us tried repeatedly to correct similar situations for both the benefit of those who were out of line as well as for the entire group. These people seemed unable to understand the predicament, yet they were the same who were terribly afraid as soon as the SS came into sight. Yet as soon as they disappeared around the corner, they again immediately felt completely comfortable and safe. When the sun shone on a beautiful Sunday morning, they stood about comfortably and self-confident. They were pleased to meet acquaintances and relatives from the whole of southern Germany as if nothing had happened and nothing was going to happen. This ability to forget was astonishing and perhaps a very healthy reaction. Really all of us experienced this sensation when we first came out of the cold into the warm room or even were "in bed." At this moment, the cold and the horrors of the day would seem to be forgotten and nearly impossible to imagine. But among the type I just described, this kind of forgetting went much too far. I felt that their behavior, consisting of numerous bad habits, was like that of the Children of Israel in the desert as they were complaining and sullen. But if by chance things went well, they were overly joyous, felt confident, and *ignored the commandments.* Of course, they were punished again. They were humbled and frightened. Insofar as this behavior or type of person could be considered typically Jewish, it becomes clear, however, that if this considered to be a typically Jewish trait, it was newly accentuated at Dachau. It came about simultaneously because of the great suffering and loss of responsibility we experienced. Many other traits were branded as "typically Jewish" by the anti-Semitic regime. These included cowardice, worrying, being international, adhering to a close family lifestyle, being adaptable, and even charitable. Primarily people from small towns or from the countryside represented this type. City folk were usually better educated. But among these city people, there, too, were those about whom one had the feeling that they had not learned anything from their internment at Dachau. After their release from Dachau, they were found to be completely self-confident and proud of themselves. Ironically, release from Dachau with its bureaucratic procedures gave them a sense of security being in their fatherland. They felt proud even though they had nothing whatsoever to do with their release.

My wife also observed again and again during this time a delusional lack of instinct, especially among Jewish women, when she went to the Gestapo in regard to my release. Many women in the same situation appeared before the Gestapo dolled up with fancy makeup, wearing the latest fashion and expensive fur coats, while the SS could not afford to buy such luxuries for their wives. Of course, there were more women who struggled their way through quietly, simply, and seriously. The same can be said of those at Dachau. The type of which I have spoken were not in the majority. Unfortunately, it is in the nature of such situations that the few who do stick out give the appearance that we are all like them. I have written in considerable detail about this, because we were not only concerned, but also preoccupied with the need to promote, educate, and encourage self-discipline among the Jews. If one regards being conspicuous and lack of discipline as typical Jewish traits, one must also recognize the other extreme: being inconspicuous, withdrawing into oneself, being quiet, modest, and serious. However, here one speaks less of these kinds of people.

I have already spoken about the majority of comrades who were always ready to be of the utmost help to anyone. However, in order to give an accurate picture, one has to talk about each of these different kinds of people. There were people here of all ages, mostly the very young and elderly over fifty and sixty years of age. The group in the middle and all those who were physically fit had already emigrated. There were people of every kind, healthy and strong, weak and sick, optimists and pessimists, clowns and the luckless, psychopaths and very normal people, cattle dealers, university professors, small and large businessmen, lawyers, doctors, former high officials, butchers, bank directors, locksmiths, pharmacists, and *chalutzim* [pioneers]. Really, then, our groups as a whole were not typical. If we were considered typical, then we would be less typically Jewish and more typically Bavarian. During the first weeks, I was together mostly with people from Munich and Regensburg.

This compelling, contagious mentality at Dachau even affected those of us who were most aware of it. The effect of this debilitating environment was undoubtedly the most serious and dangerous. As Jews we did not have the opportunity to pass the effects of this constant pressure onto anyone beneath us. I do not regret this at all. However, the foundation is laid for a primitive and secretive wish to take revenge later. I, myself, perhaps unnaturally, had no wish to seek revenge. But I, too, had to learn to admit that at Dachau there really were *evil* people; just as there are poisonous plants, as well as there are conditions in which people do become evil and depraved. However, those who were disinclined to become bad, eventually were forced to give in to fantasies of revenge. For these people the question remained: How is it possible that these malicious people and criminals succeed in rising to power and control? It has become very clear to me that in this way the great movement of the poor and disadvantaged rose to the top. Therefore, during this period of crisis and unemployment, National Socialism became so influential. The need for power and the hostility of those who were disadvantaged to this point were in essence directed against *capitalism, capitalists,* and their money. The regime accused the Jews of being representative of this greedy, moneyed class. They became the lightning rods for the threatening storm.

Fascistic German anti-Semitism was further symbolized as a panacea against capitalism. If the capitalists had introduced at the appropriate time possibilities for reform, the present conditions in Germany would not have been possible. This phenomenon became very visible at Dachau, but on the whole it was not understood. Those who dwelt under intense pressure at Dachau in an atmosphere of the blind hatred of German Fascists toward the Jews, responded with blind revulsion toward all Germans. This evolving hatred of all Germans is no less blind than the German hatred of all the Jews. Therefore, this loathing can be considered to be the same delusion of a national racial phenomenon, which actually was a social occurrence. Yet it is the thorough bureaucratic procedure in which the persecution of the Jews took place at Dachau that can be regarded to be characteristically German.

Among those of us who did not react to Dachau simply with wishes of revenge or passivity were those whose moral view of the world, our *Weltanschauung,* was shaken by this experience. How is such injustice possible, we wondered? These people had worked their entire life as successful, decent, and well-intentioned businessmen. They had dealt kindly with their employees. They could not be blamed for anything bad. Why should they be punished? These truly upright and honest people found it impossible to imagine that there was a personal connection to blame. They believed that they couldn't be punished for their own faults, but probably for the sins of their fathers and fellow human beings. They seemed unable to understand that this blame would include them. After all, they always fulfilled their obligations, did what was expected of them, and never were controversial. They failed to see the connection between the lack of social equality and anti-Semitic fascism. In this situation in which we found ourselves as Jews, on this earth, we no longer could formulate the problem of social inequality as a political phenomenon. All the more important to understand was that our own comrades provided the social balance through extensive mutual and charitable help that we needed. Even so, there was not sufficient organization among us to help each other satisfactorily. Yet at Dachau and due to the conditions under which we were released, we did not acknowledge all the support we got, because we could only think of ourselves first.

When we were released from Dachau, we left our fellow Jewish prisoners behind. The most we could possibly do was to pass on a few messages to some relatives. We also left behind the Aryan prisoners, for whom we could not even perform this little service. On the day I was released, two hundred Jews were freed, while only four Aryans were set free. On certain days before Christmas, only Aryans were supposed to be released. However, the same day that we were liberated, a group of twenty Aryans, apparently Sudeten Germans, were brought to the camp.

Were Jews or "Aryans" treated worse? The Aryans were more warmly dressed than we were. They did, nevertheless, say that they too had to go through a period of terrible cold. However, they did not have to endure the extra long time in the bitter cold that we had to. During my stay in Dachau, the newly arrived Sudeten German prisoners were immediately given appropriate clothing. They were even provided with coats. The Jews, except for cleaning our rooms and carrying food, were not allowed to work. The Aryans did not experience quite as much individual brutality imposed by the SS and capos, nor did they have to submit to the same kind of punishment directed toward us. We were constantly informed that we had come to Dachau during a "golden age."

An even crueler commander had been called away a short time before my arrival. The period before and during which the new camp had been constructed must have been terrible. Frightfully harsh treatment with the toughest work was the rule. At the same time there was little nourishment, only a sip of coffee and a piece of bread.

The Austrians, who just before our arrival were shipped to Buchenwald, were also maltreated. On the whole, the Aryans were more harshly treated, tortured, and even killed. However, they were not let *perish* as were the Jews.

Morally the Jews were treated worse. We were not treated as human beings. At least the Aryans were regarded as a kind of prisoner of war and as enemies. They were dealt with on the same level as members of the same system of extortionists and torturers of human beings to which the SS belonged. May it be true or false, the SS assumed that had these prisoners been the conquerors, the SS would not have been treated any better. Not even this assumption could be made of the Jews. Therefore, the Jews were even more degraded, as Fascists did not even consider them to be enemies or criminals.

The Aryans, or at least the "Reds," were prisoners in Dachau because of their political convictions. For some, it might have been just by chance that they had become Communists instead of Nazis. For the most part, they were Communists out of conviction and held firmly to these beliefs. The seriously religious followers of the Bible were martyrs to their beliefs. They were the only ones who as a group in Germany steadfastly refused to "Heil Hitler" and who unwaveringly held to their pacifist principles. These religious people were treated especially harshly, while the Jews who were brought to Dachau on November 10th submitted to the Fascist regime.

I could not and cannot resist my impression that in spite of the cruel treatment and intentional degradation we Jews suffered, we did occupy a privileged position. The Jews who were arrested on November 10th were in Dachau for weeks or months, while the Aryans were there for years—maybe forever. The Aryans had to work for us: to cook, write, clean, and repair the streets, even serve as barbers. The "Browns" had to clean the septic system and transport the foul smelling refuse in open carts. We were spared all of these things. Even the SS seemed worse off than the majority of Jews. They seemed to look at the Jews with some envy, as they were able to leave.

I do not see any reason to complain about Dachau, as I would not know to whom to complain. Thousands, if they aren't being tortured, being separated from their families, thinking about life under extreme threats, can envy those in Dachau, because they are regularly fed, have accommodations, clothing, and "no worries."

When we were brought by truck to Dachau, the truck ran out of gas. [Dachau is only about twenty minutes from Munich] The young, smart-aleck SS officer who drove the truck got a can of gas from a nearby gas station. He poured it into the tank. Next to him stood one of the repulsive men in civilian dress, smoking a cigarette. He was one of those who had been busily occupied with us during the night at the Wittelsbach Palace. The SS officer told the driver so that all could hear, "Stand back with your cigarette or else the whole caboodle will go up in flames. That wouldn't be a shame at all, but I can't take responsibility for it." I asked myself, *Would it really be a pity? Would it really be a shame if this little heap of Jews should no longer exist?* No. *If that's really the case, maybe it wouldn't be so bad if the SS officer himself were no longer either.* If one begins to think in this way, that is, "what would be a shame or what would not," then there is little left that would truly be a shame. The National Socialists think that way: In regard to the Jews, it would not be a shame. On the contrary, it would be their good fortune if there weren't any Jews left. They are bad luck! They alone are the blight, the vermin that spoils everything. They must be destroyed; why don't they exterminate us in the same way that rats and mice are wiped out? They could line us Jews up and shoot us! Why don't they do that? Why can't they take the responsibility? Is it the rest of humanity that prevents them from doing it? Not at all. For if there should be traces of humanity present, they cease in regard to the Jews. Everything becomes permissible toward the Jews, even if one may be an upright citizen and good father to his family. For instance, the morning after her apartment had been ransacked, my wife saw one of the culprits taking a peaceful Sunday walk with his wife and two children. He, the owner of a villa, was wearing a fur coat.

The gruesome torture and obliteration of the Jews can be neatly separated from the daily lives, visible personality, and humanity of these people. At the same time, they are compensated for their service to mankind. Yes, as I stated earlier, why do they behave so furtively, and why is our torture drawn out in such length? Why don't they shoot all the Jews at once? Why not do it openly? They are not disturbed by it. Are they secretly afraid of the Jews? How many people in Germany are not taking part in the persecution of the Jews? Are they reacting without emotion, feeling, and understanding because they are afraid? Will they take revenge on all of us one day? Well, if they want to rob the Jews of everything they have and take all of life's possibilities away from us, why not do it with a single stroke of the pen? Why did they create a thousand bureaucracies? Why did they first bring the Jews to Dachau and then send a notary public and a lawyer to the camp? We were required to give the lawyer complete authority to "Aryanize" our possessions. The notary public had first to explain the entire procedure to us and then witness our signature. He was a simple Bavarian who obviously found the proceedings to be embarrassing. He told us, "You have free choice as to whether you do or do not sign this authorization. However, it is urgently recommended that you do sign!" Why do they put us through this encounter, use this tactic, manipulate and deceive us with "free will?" Why do they force us to sign, when they have the power to do whatever they want to do with us? Why did they return every penny of our money that we brought with us to Dachau, when otherwise they take everything from us? Why did they create this entire, complicated bureaucratic apparatus at the time of our arrest? To know that we won't disappear anonymously, that our wives will be duly notified if their husbands die at Dachau surely is comforting to us. But why do they fabricate this false humanity and complex bureaucratic system if they are simply gaining enjoyment to notify a wife that her husband had died when in reality he is still alive? Why are we told that we are in "protective custody" to shelter us from angry masses when the people aren't at all angry at us? After all, only the SS is being used as a vehicle to demonstrate the people's rage.

At the same time, we are told, "You are coming to Dachau as punishment. Now we can proceed against you." Why do they imprison the Jews, when in reality they could just as easily hand us over to the angry SS?

Did von Rath have to be murdered before the Jews could be arrested? Instead, everything had already been prepared for our arrival following the 1st of October, just in case the crisis in Czechoslovakia should lead to war: uniforms sewn while barrack and section leaders had been fully trained. As war didn't come about, everything was made ready for November 1st. Von Rath, however, died only on November 8th. Therefore, we could only be brought to Dachau on November 10th, instead of the previously planned date of November 1st.

I have no answers to these questions. I can only clarify these facts for myself. The same kind of dual behavior can be seen when Hitler made an intimate friendship pact with Chamberlain one day, while on the next day he set out to weaken and ruin Chamberlain. This is evidence of the best intent coupled with evil, criminal motives, always carried out under the banner of a justified, holy, and noble cause. Of the greatest importance to these criminals was to receive praise for their crimes. They wanted to feel morally proud of the crimes they were committing. Capsulated in Hitler, one finds the bad conscience of humanity—at least that of the European capitalistic world. I am referring to the guilty conscience, not conscience itself. True conscience recognizing a guilty conscience tries to come to terms with it. The aim is to make the guilty conscience no longer appear burdensome but good. Therefore, the bad conscience must be made to disappear, not by denying, suppressing or combating it, but on the contrary, placing a high value on the evil act by making the act appear as if it were a good deed.

I will try by giving an example to clarify my point. A poor pickpocket steals a wealthy lady's pocketbook, which contains twenty marks. He is arrested and confronted by the lady. His excuse is that he desperately needs money. If he were to return the money, it really would make no difference to the lady if she had twenty more or less marks. Besides, she belongs to the rich who keep the poor oppressed. To this, the lady has no answer. The man is right; he appealed successfully to her guilty conscience. He not only used it, he embodied it. He has become her guilty conscience. To carry this example further, the man having had success with this excuse continues to steal even when stealing is no longer urgent. He always gives the same reason: to help the holy cause of the oppressed classes until in the end he believes his excuse himself. Even after he has become a real criminal, the rich who have been robbed will accept his arguments. Their own social guilty conscience has become no better. The ideologically sanctioned criminal embodies the guilty conscience. He knows instinctively how to touch the sore spot. The guilty conscience allows no peace of mind. It must constantly renew and document its morality by committing new crimes. To carry the example even further, a factually justifiable, historically necessary movement of the disadvantaged classes steps into action. The movement will serve the ideological criminal and it in turn carries him to new heights. So the politically justified movement becomes an "historic necessity." The argument pertaining to the "historical necessity" and the mission of a just cause fits the guilty social conscience of those who are attacked. In this way, one can understand why the attacked nations and social classes feel insecure and conflicted when ideologically sanctioned criminals judge them. There is also a connection between anti-Semitic fascism and a guilty conscience, about which I have already spoken. There is also a discrepancy, a twofold combination of crime and law, of bureaucracy and despotism. For instance, the Nazis tortured us under the Christmas tree placed at the roll-call square at Dachau. These connections or differentiations may help to understand several more points about which I still want to report.

Although clearly observed from a distance, the following scene took place at the roll-call square. As we marched through that area in the morning, standing in front of the scrubbing room, we saw columns of newly admitted Austrian Jewish prisoners. A little to the side stood another column of prisoners who were being beaten and shoved about. Looking on was an important SS official, probably the doctor. A stretcher arrived from the infirmary to bring a sick member of this group to the doctor. The poor man was forced to get up. He must have been a member of the newly arrived as his upper body was still clad in civilian clothing. He wore nothing to cover the lower part of his body. The patient was then forced down onto his knees and severely beaten.

I still have to report about the treatment of the sick. The infirmary was efficiently set up and kept immaculately clean. Not only could we observe this from the outside, but we also learned this to be true from reports by patients who had been there. For a patient to be admitted to the infirmary was an exception. When a sick person finally was allowed in, as a rule he did not leave alive.

I will now report three separate exceptions that were told to me. The first concerns the elderly judge, whom I have already mentioned, who was severely paralyzed. Finally, after four weeks or longer, he was brought to the infirmary. After a few days, showing no signs of improvement, he was returned to the barracks to participate as before. After three more weeks, he was released from Dachau. Secondly, one of us was admitted to the infirmary with pleurisy. After some time, we heard that he was getting better. He was still at the infirmary when I was released. The third situation occurred on the same day that I was released. A small, elderly and charming man from Nürnberg-Fürth was released directly from the infirmary. He, who had had a severe case of pneumonia, had just overcome the crisis a few days before. On the day of his release, he, as we all were, was terribly grateful. We were amazed at this miracle, as he was the first person among us who had overcome such an illness at the infirmary. He told us that he had been cared for very lovingly and well by those attending to him, namely prisoners.

Daily and usually several times a day, we saw the hearse pass from the barracks to the infirmary or from the infirmary crossing the square. The stretcher was a simple device with two rubber-rimmed wheels on which a flat bier was fastened covered by a hood of gray canvas. The cart had a handle, so that one could easily maneuver it with one hand. The corpses were burned at Dachau and the ashes sent home to relatives.

In order to be admitted to the infirmary or to see a doctor, we had to follow a set procedure. We had to notify our section leader the evening before we wanted to go the infirmary. There were only two hours daily at which we could go to the infirmary, once at noon and once late in the afternoon. The section leader would at his own discretion allow or forbid a person to go. On arriving at the infirmary, one would either be turned away or examined by hospital attendants. Wounds were bandaged, frost-bitten hands were painted with a tincture of iodine, inflammation of the throat would also be painted, and pills were issued as well as castor oil. One could be given an appointment with the doctor. Those who finally were given an appointment were only permitted to be brought to him following evening roll call. The doctor prescribed lenient treatment or bed rest in the barracks. Following bed rest, the doctor might admit him to the infirmary, give him pills, or prescribe nothing at all.

Surgical cases including hand injuries and breaks were without hesitation taken care of. Only those visible surgical cases were considered as illnesses. Everything else was passed over as being bogus.

The first to die was a diabetic who did not get his regular insulin shots. Only later were diabetics treated.

On the whole, we were astonished by the ability of our bodies to adjust, considering all we had to endure. Each one of us at some point suffered from a severe cold with fever. Recovering quickly in most cases from a cold under these living conditions is indeed surprising, although a chronic cold or cough tended to linger on. Of course, such recovery was true only for those of us who were in good health.

I recall an elderly man, a victim of tuberculosis, who after several weeks asked to be allowed to go to the infirmary. Having been an actor, whatever he said sounded a little theatrical. Therefore, the section leader became suspicious that he might be faking. Since the section leader accused him of being a fraud, he was forbidden to go to the infirmary. Only some time later was he permitted to go, however, without success. He not only had to return, but also participate in everything we were required to do. As his condition continued to worsen, he was given a little reprieve by only having to be dragged to roll call. Finally, after it was already too late, he was assigned to bed rest. One morning it became apparent as he was still calmly lying in bed while we were already standing about the room drinking our coffee. Four people always shared the same bowl. The section leader came in. Observing him with experienced eyes, he said, "Don't you see, you idiots, he is dead?" The body was examined and death was confirmed. We continued to drink our coffee.

On the whole, Jews were not directly killed at Dachau. In one barrack, it was said that the section leader actually beat a Jewish prisoner to death. Although this incident was convincingly reported, I can not prove its veracity.

During my sixth week, the majority of us in our block had to do afternoon punishment exercises. Allegedly, the barrack commander ordered these because our lockers were not satisfactorily straightened out. My knife wasn't shiny enough. There is no doubt that the pretext for these exercises and the orders to carry them out were given by the SS. The day before, the same punishment exercises took place in a neighboring barrack. They were charged for the same reasons as ours and carried out in the presence of SS bullies. While we had to do these, two SS men appeared, directed and watched us exercise. Punishment exercises consisted of doing a variety of activities without pause that included running, throwing oneself on the ground and jumping back up, knee bends, and hopping around on our haunches. For those of us who were young, these exercises were strenuous but not bad especially since the barrack commander occasionally shut an eye. On the contrary, we would finally become warm. Yet a terribly oppressive atmosphere prevailed. The older people were after some time given a little consideration and were separated from us. They had to stand still in the freezing east wind facing the barrack wall. This so-called form of protection resulted in one man fainting and in the death of another. Occurring during the sixth week of our "protective custody," newspapers reported that the "protective custody" of Jews had been lifted, and the SS were given orders to lay off of us.

In hindsight, having survived these exercises, they no longer seem as terrible as when we were right in the midst of them. Not knowing what might lie ahead was indeed unpleasant. Nor did we know how long such punishment exercises would last, how much further they would be escalated, whether the SS would return, and what they might have in mind to do with us. However, when these were over after one and a half to two hours, these events became the past and were forgotten. Yet we knew the situation for our relatives at home was quite different. They did not experience these moments when the exercises were all over, nor did they sense our sighs of relief. They constantly remained under the pressure of not knowing what lay ahead, just as we knew that at Dachau anything was possible.

In the barrack next to us, a lawyer from Munich had a nervous breakdown. We heard his continued and extreme screams. He was brought to the infirmary, where he was told, "We are going to drive your craziness out." He then was placed in a bathtub filled with cold water. Without being dried off, he was wrapped in a few woolen blankets and returned to the barracks, where he died a few days later of pneumonia.

The barrack's four rooms came together during marching and chiefly at roll call. Directly in front of us from the neighboring rooms stood the smallest men, including the very young and the very old. Among these were twin brothers. Each looked more miserable and wretched than the other. Both were totally sick. I was under the impression that they had been brought here either from a hospital or from a home for the elderly.

They were quiet, modest men, faithful to each other and lovable. Finally, one morning after four weeks, the more severely ill of the two brothers was released. At noon, he had returned. As an SS soldier, upon his arrival, had hurled him against a wall causing him to acquire a black eye; he was sent back. In order for him to be released, his eye had to heal completely. Supported on his brother's arm, he dragged himself to roll call. From day to day he grew weaker and weaker until one morning he was found dead. Attendants hauled him to the infirmary on a stretcher. He was covered with a blanket, his feet sticking out. His brother walked three paces behind him, then stood at attention and returned to the ranks.

A few days later another of these small people from the neighboring section could go no farther on the way to the roll-call square. We supported and massaged him as best as we could during roll call. Afterwards, two young men from our group, who always and energetically seized the opportunity to help, brought him to the infirmary. As he was not admitted, he was sent back to the barrack. As he had not been able to eat for days, episodes of weakness occurred again and again. He was brought back to the infirmary, but not admitted. He was returned to the barrack where the room leader kicked him out. The capo was a baker from Mainz, a powerful, huge man. He had a sly countenance, a humorous expression, an indifferent good nature, and a furious, brutal chin. He was at the camp because his wife had denounced him. Although this capo could be quite pleasant and cheerful, this totally inconspicuous little man became the target of his scorn. On the third time that he went to the infirmary, he was physically removed with blows and kicks. Brought back to the barrack, the section leader promptly kicked him out. As on that evening money was distributed, we had to stand in the cold long after the evening roll call had concluded. I have already talked about this. We at least wanted to put this man in the lobby until his turn came. This would be late, as his name started with S. Comrades did bring him into the lobby. After a while the room leader noticed him and kicked him out again. He had to stand with us. During the following night he died. In view of these cases, we assumed that high officials gave section leaders a quota demanding that a specific number of people die. Although our assumption was not improbable, it cannot be confirmed.

In another situation, matters developed differently. There were two very big, fat brothers in our group. They were generally and for good reasons not well liked. Had they been in the Orient, they might have been popular pashas. However, as comrades at Dachau, they were hard to tolerate. They were egotistic, fault-finding, demanding, and nosy. In short they were un-comradely. After a while, one became sick, while the other was released. I can still see how touching and with such longing the one brother waved to the other as he was being released. From this day on, his illness, apparently a kidney ailment, worsened. Someone said that with his brother's departure he lost all of his depraved support. Almost instantly, attention toward him changed in his favor. He was married and father of a child. Now he had become a childlike, helpless creature. Several times he was refused admittance to the infirmary. Finally, he was given bed rest. At this time, he was running a high fever, experiencing excruciating pain, and was no longer able to make himself understood. As he could only babble, nobody was able to understand his wishes. Four strong men brought this big, heavy, motionless man to the toilet. Even the section leader now touchingly tried to care for him. We presumed that there was some kind of sepsis, which probably was the case. When he was finally admitted to the infirmary, open wounds were discovered on his back. He died a few days later at the infirmary.

Because of the nature of this report, I speak mostly about the sad, horrible, and unpleasant aspects about our predicament at Dachau. Because our experiences here were terrible, everything that is pleasant is experienced all the more intensely. The following are such examples. The longed-for moment, about 11:30, when the announcement was made: "Food carriers out," when a quarter of an hour later we really were allowed to enter our room; when we received a warm meal; when at night we could lie peacefully on our backs; when on Sunday morning we could quietly talk with a comrade for half an hour; when finally we began to receive money with which we could buy a cup of hot coffee, following an icy-cold and wet evening at roll call; when after a cold, unpleasant morning, the warming sun came out, so that we were able to enjoy the mild yet rich light in which a few beautiful fir trees stood outside the wall; or even the lawn; or if one could see a few sparrows flying by.

There were no animals at all at Dachau, except for a mysterious monkey that a prisoner led around on a leash, and the unpleasant dog in the canteen. There were no birds, only innumerable planes that preferred to fly over the camp. To receive a letter from home was awesome, but most wonderful of all was the moment at which we were informed that we would be released.

Whether this moment would ever come, we did not know until the last minute. During the first three weeks, we had no idea as to whether we might be released in the foreseeable future. Nor did we know during our first three weeks whether we would be released in large numbers. Finally, after three weeks, individuals began to be freed, followed later and more often by one large group at a time. However, for days following a release, nobody would be freed.

Sometimes during the first part of the morning, during mid morning, or in the afternoon, an announcement was made that all Jews were ordered to report to the roll-call square. We could not help but hope that something good would happen, that an announcement would be made in regard to our future, even though we were often disappointed at the reason for the roll call. These dealt with such matters as jersey material, owners of automobiles from upper Bavaria, or anyone who knew Jew M. in L., or all people from L. Finally, when the actual release began, a lot of guessing took place, for instance, from which category will the first be chosen? Maybe the first will come from amongst the elderly over sixty or seventy years of age, or those younger than eighteen. It is true that there were men in their high seventies who remained at Dachau for weeks. Were they soldiers from the front line of the First World War? There were, however, many released from R. to whom this category did not apply. Would people be first who had all their papers together in order to emigrate? Yes, but among these folk, there were people who had sailing tickets for the beginning of December and were not able to use them, as they were not released from Dachau.

We learned of our release early in the morning. At first, however, when the releases started, names were called out, and then those prisoners were summoned to the roll-call square. We never knew for sure whether we were notified that we would be released or whether the summons had to do with other issues. When the barrack scribe appeared in front of the door to our room in the early morning prior to roll call, he seemed to be like a messenger from the gods. As he read off the names, I will not describe the nervous tension and joy we experienced. At that point we quickly tore off all of our warm clothing, including our underwear and knitted vests, to be left for those who were staying behind. We still had to participate in the morning roll call, but only until 7:00 a.m. Although the day continued with uninterrupted standing, we were in warm rooms. Part of that time we were already dressed in civilian clothing, until all formalities were completed. We were informed that we had to report to the Gestapo immediately upon our return to our home town. Those like me, who were released because we would emigrate, had to present to the Gestapo our emigration papers within three weeks. We again had to appear before a doctor, a pure formality, to be sure that nobody who had evident traces and effects of abuse or illness acquired at Dachau would be released. Thus, when I was freed, there was still a man who was to have been liberated weeks earlier, but still could not leave, as his hands were completely bandaged due to severe frostbite. I cannot imagine how such frostbites could disappear during the winter at Dachau. Furthermore, we were to be released only if we testified that we had not had an accident, or if we had we did not have any physical evidence that would reveal maltreatment.

At that point our clothes, money, and other belongings were returned to us. At this juncture, once again, those who owned an automobile were commandeered off and forced to run. As a result, an acquaintance of mine, who had been standing for nine hours without food, suffered a severe heart attack. Towards 4:00 p.m. those of us who were to be released had the opportunity to participate in a new privilege that had just been established, namely, to buy cookies or chocolate at the canteen. Once again we were required to then stand at the roll-call square, marched across it, to stand for an hour in front of the administration building. About 6:00 p.m. an SS officer appeared amidst a swarm of SS soldiers. He gave us a short speech in which he explained that those of us who planned to emigrate must do so as soon as possible. "Don't ever let yourselves be seen here again. Should you ever return to Germany, you will be returned to Dachau, this time for life. Furthermore, don't give gruesome accounts of Dachau, certainly not while you are in Germany. Once outside, you may say whatever you want." Again, following another short period of standing, the gate opened, and we marched through the broader campgrounds. Once again, we went through another heavy, iron gate, from which the SS led us in a close column for about an hour's march to the railroad station at Dachau. There were two special cars waiting for us that were attached to the local train headed for Munich. At the Munich railroad station, special representatives from the Munich Jewish community met us. They gave us medical advice for our transition into normal living conditions. They also looked after the needs of those who were going to continue on their long journey from Munich. These represented the great majority. The representatives from the Jewish community secured tickets for those who did not have the money for the journey. These people came mostly from the Rhineland and from Austria. All others, of course, had to pay their own way. By the way, we did not have to pay for room and board while we were at Dachau.

What I have reported so far represents only one side of Dachau. To describe the other side thoroughly, by which I mean the efforts made by our wives to secure our release, would be as manysided and lengthy as that which I have already covered. As only men were arrested, women remained at home. For the first ten days, our wives had no idea where we were! Then they received a post card with the following prescribed message.

> Dear Wife,
>
> I am in Dachau and am healthy. You may send me 15 RM [Reichsmarks] weekly."

A note followed this as to how to address the money and how to properly sign. Not knowing what was to happen was equal on both sides. However, probably the feeling of uncertainty for our wives was greater, as they had no idea as to how Dachau appeared and what it was like there. We who were incarcerated at Dachau simply had to passively wait. Our wives had to make all decisions, take all action, and to do everything necessary to try to secure our release.

Indeed, it was true that those over seventy and those under eighteen were released first. Next to be freed were those over sixty and those who had fought on the front lines during the First World War, followed by those who were over fifty. Finally, those of us whose emigration was underway were released. The Gestapo once told my wife that they receive different instructions on a daily basis. Even after the instructions seemed definite, only tremendous luck determined whether all of these categories would really be carried forth. All of this depended entirely upon the good or bad mood of the officials on duty at the time. Due to the quick action of my friends in England and with the help of the British consul in Munich, who confirmed in writing that we had permission to go to England, I was supposed to have been released on November 24th. However, I was only released four weeks later. Among the officials with whom my wife had to deal, was one of those civilians about whom I spoke earlier. He was a fat, gray-faced, malicious, perverse, and thoroughly repulsive character. He simply refused to recognize the certificate from the British consul. He insisted that "your husband will not be released a day sooner than he has a passport, visa, and tickets." In order to secure a passport, my wife had to provide a number of documents from such bureaus as the Office of Foreign Exchange, as well as from a great variety of departments. Here again, the Gestapo that had ruthlessly arrested us were the same officials who brought about our release through strict, *legal*, bureaucratic methods. This bureaucracy was suitable to legitimize every kind of malice. When, finally after weeks of intense effort on my wife's part, she had received her passport while mine was at the passport police office awaiting my signature, the same officer who refused my release insisted that my passport be sent to Dachau, where I could sign it. My wife informed the passport police officer of this information, who in turn urgently advised her not to have the passport sent to Dachau. He explained, "We have had very bad experience with this. Passports disappear in Dachau. No one knows where they are kept. We are certainly prepared to send the passport to Dachau if you insist, but we strongly urge you not to." Thus it became clear that the Gestapo official wanted my passport sent to Dachau so that it would disappear there and therefore block my release. My wife, of course, refused to have the passport sent to Dachau. At a later visit to the Gestapo, by good luck, she encountered a well-meaning official who on the same day gave orders for my immediate release from Dachau.

The fascist bureaucracy is the organization of legal crimes. The crime, where evil acts are not supposed to appear to have been done, acts as the instrument of the bureaucracy, an administration that had once been a vital part of a civilized, humane nation. Now, in an irrational way, crime and humanity function as one and the same.

On the day following my return home, I had to report to the Gestapo. My wife waited for a few minutes on a bench outside the room to which I had to report. The SS official, who was on duty at this central nerve system of this center of hell, invited her to wait in another room that was a little warmer. He had already greeted us in a friendly and sympathetic manner, "Well, there he finally is!"

Without the intervention of this well-meaning official and my wife's efforts, I would, if at all, have only been released in January. I doubt whether I would have been able to stay healthy, as during this period the weather turned for the worse. Therefore, I might very well not have been in a condition in which to be released.

It was of the utmost importance that we be released as early as possible. Each day counted. Without the permit to enter England, I probably still would be in Dachau. When I was released, all the Jewish prisoners between the ages of eighteen and fifty who did not have any emigration papers remained at Dachau.

Sometimes, now, we have heard rumors that all have been released. Although I am sure that many may have been freed, I have reason to doubt that this rather vague report regarding "everyone" is actually true. First of all, there must still be sick people at Dachau. Secondly, I heard only last week of a man who is still in a German concentration camp, although he has a ticket for passage to Bolivia. He is supposed to be kept at the camp until September. It is these solitary individuals who tend to be forgotten or overlooked who are in the greatest danger.

If we were released on the grounds of our forthcoming emigration, we had to be prepared to leave the country within three weeks. In most cases that was impossible, for to complete all the formalities took considerably more time. Although in my case everything had long since been taken care of, still all of these three weeks were used to take care of more details, including a visit to the customs search department. The same German authorities that on the one had demanded immediate emigration on the other hand delayed it. Those whose emigration to another country had not been cleared were in serious jeopardy of being returned to the concentration camps. On rare occasions, the deadline was extended but never unlimited.

Reports via word of mouth from Germany suggest that certain well-known Jews, who had not only completed all formalities but also had sent their belongings abroad, are being held hostage in Germany. Furthermore, the following case has been reported to me. A Jewish pharmacist's little drugstore, on which he and his family survived, was taken from him. As he no longer had any means by which to survive, he had to turn to public welfare. This he could only get if he worked in the countryside, trying to improve conditions there or work on the roads. He landed up doing road work and living in a barrack together with about forty people. The workday consisted of nine hours of terribly strenuous labor. Only on Sundays could he visit his family. He was paid 15 RM a week, of which seven were taken to pay for room and board at the work camp. Only eight marks a week remained to support his wife and child.

With those Jews who remained in Germany, the Nazis dealt indirectly. For instance, Aryan landlords were forbidden to house Jewish tenants. Jews lost ownership of their real estate. From this one can conclude that eventually all Jews will be placed in concentration camps. Those Jews for whom it was impossible to emigrate, who must remain in Germany, will end up at forced labor camps and at concentration camps.

A book has recently been published in Paris entitled *Nazi-Bastille Dachau.* I have not yet seen this book.

I would have liked to sign this report with my full name. I must, for the time being, waive my signature in consideration of my relatives, who are still in Germany.

Appendix B

The Frog King

A Chapel Talk
By Walter Moritz Solmitz

Bowdoin College
December 5, 1961

The professor's privilege is that he may ask more questions than he can answer himself. Perhaps, he ought not to do so on the occasion of exams, but here—on this island of free speech, free thought and free imagination—he may be allowed to do so, even in public, for a few brief moments.

This is the season to be jolly—or, at least to prepare for the season to be jolly—the preparation including such questions as, "What should I give my younger sister?" To this question the professor will give an answer today. For, as you will see in a moment, I shall suggest Grimm's Fairy Tales as a colorful and charming gift.

More seriously, this is the season to prepare for THE season—for that season which presents and represents to us "peace on earth and good will among men"—and not only among men, but where and when swords are turned into plowshares, also the lion will lie next to the lamb, and even the ox and the donkey join in the cosmic celebration of hopes and wishes to be born, and reborn, and realized.

This being predominantly the children's season, the child's season, I had thought of making it jolly and taking it easy myself; I'll read you from one of my favorite fairy tales—and afterwards tell you some of the reasons why I read it—and ask my unanswered questions.

I once had a friend whom, in talking to myself, I found myself calling the Frog King one day—and it was he who by his very nature, his appearance and character, made me understand better.

The Story of the Frog King or Iron Henry

In olden times when wishing still accomplished something—when wishing still helped—there lived a king whose daughters were all beautiful, but the youngest was so beautiful that the sun itself, which has seen so much, was astonished whenever it shone in her face. Close by the king's castle lay a great, dark forest, and under an old linden tree in the forest was a well, and when the day was very warm, the king's child went out into the forest and sat down by the side of the cool well, and when time got long for her, she took a golden ball, and threw it up on high and caught it, and this ball was her favorite plaything.

Now it so happened that on one occasion the princess's golden ball did not fall into the little hand which she was holding up for it, but on the ground beyond, and rolled straight into the water. The princess followed it with her eyes, but it vanished, and then the well was deep, so deep that the bottom could not be seen. At this she began to cry, and she cried louder and louder, and could not be comforted. And as she thus lamented, someone said to her, "What ails you, king's daughter? You weep so that even a stone would show pity."

She looked around to the side from whence the voice came, and saw a frog stretching forth its big, ugly head from the water. "Ah! Old water-splasher, is it you?" said she; "I am crying for my golden ball, which has fallen into the well."

"Be quiet, and do not cry," answered the frog, "I can help you, but what will you give me if I bring your plaything up again?"

"Whatever you will have, dear frog," said she. "My clothes, my pearls and jewels, and even the golden crown which I am wearing."

The frog answered, "I do not care for your clothes, your pearls and jewels, nor for your golden crown, but if you will love me and let me be your companion and playfellow and sit by you at your little table and eat off your little golden plate and drink out of your little cup and sleep in your little bed; if you will promise me this, I will go down below, and bring your golden ball up again."

"Oh, yes," said she, "I promise you all you wish, if you will but bring me my ball back again." But she thought, "How the silly frog does talk! All he does is sit in the water with the other frogs, and croak! He can be no companion to any human being!"

This must suffice to remind you of the story. You'll remember that the frog brings the ball back, the princess wants to forget about her promise, but is reminded when the frog appears at meal time. Her father insists, "That which you have promised, you must perform."

The king's daughter began to cry, for she was afraid of the cold frog, which she did not like to touch and which was now to sleep in her pretty, clean, little bed. But the king grew angry and said, "He who helped you when you were in trouble ought not afterwards be despised by you."

So she took hold of the frog with two fingers, carried him upstairs, and put him in a corner. But when she was in bed, he crept to her and said, "I am tired; I want to sleep as well as you; lift me up or I will tell your father."

At this, she was terribly angry, and took him up and threw him with all her might against the wall. "Now, will you be quiet, odious frog!" said she.

But when the frog fell down, he was no frog but a king's son with kind and beautiful eyes. He by her father's will was now her dear companion and husband. Then he told her how he had been bewitched by a wicked witch, and how no one could have delivered him from the well but herself, and that tomorrow they would go together into his kingdom. Then they went to sleep, and the next morning, when the sun awoke them, a carriage came driving up with eight white horses, which had white ostrich feathers on their heads, and were harnessed with golden chains, and behind stood the prince's servant, faithful Henry! Faithful Henry had been so unhappy when his master was changed into a frog that he had caused three iron bands to be laid round his heart, lest it should burst with grief and sadness. The carriage was to conduct the prince into his kingdom. Faithful Henry helped them both in, and placed himself behind again, and was full of joy because of this deliverance. And when they had driven a part of the way, the prince heard a cracking behind him as if something had broken. So he turned around and cried, "Henry, the carriage is breaking!"

No, sir, not the carriage is breaking
It's a band from my heart which was aching
In pain when you were a prisoner in the well
And there as a frog had to dwell.

Again and once again while they were on their way something cracked, and each time the prince thought the carriage was breaking, but it was only the bands which were springing from the heart of Faithful Henry, because his master was set free and was happy.

The bands were springing from the heart of Faithful Henry.
His master was set free and happy.

I think this is one of the reasons why I read this story. Because I feel this is such a good picture of being freed—of relief—and because it shows how one person can feel with another, and can suffer when the other one is not free, when the other one is bewitched to be something different from what he could be and ought to be and from what he really is, and how the friend can feel freed when the other one is freed.

As I said, it was the nature and appearance of my friend which made me see the story in a new light. For his was a princely soul in a froglike body. I have never seen anybody who looked as much as a frog as he did—his face, his sudden movements, his clumsy and clownish behavior—and who still, and perhaps because of this, was so full of good cheer and full of fun, the melancholy clown from a Shakespearian play, at the same time a man of fortitude, great civil courage and kindness.

The "Let the little children come unto me" was part of his nature and extended also to the teenagers. He played with them, and clowned with them—and must have helped them a hundred times when they were crying because their ball had fallen into the water. But among them it seems there was no princess, or, perhaps, when there had been one, there had been no father around who insisted on fulfillment of a given promise. Or more likely: When he helped them, he would not make his assistance dependent on the fulfillment of any condition. He was too noble for that. Thus, he died a bachelor—a few years ago—and I would like to regard these remarks as a small memorial to him, leaving him anonymous because that befits his modesty. I would call him self-effacing, if there had been any selfishness in him to be effaced.

And now there comes my professional question: Is it true that sometimes some humans remind us of some animals—and some animals of some humans—in their looks and in the way they seem to act?

Is there any significance to that? And as my friend's appearance made me see better the fairy tale of the frog and the bewitched prince, can conversely the fairy tale help us to see appearances better and to look through appearances?

Of course, we are scientific in our thought, we must be scientific, and make the scientific distinctions, but cannot the fairy tale complement and supplement our everyday, scientific outlook?—

Let me with the omission of some steps, which might have made my thought more easy to follow, still jump to a few reflections on this.

The philosopher finds it sometimes desirable to supplement his critical thought by the free play of the imagination. Plato tells also some fairy tales, and he tells one about the life hereafter, and the choice one has to make himself of the form in which to spend one's next life. One who was a singer in this life, chose to be a nightingale in his next life. A fighting hero who had gone through some tragic experiences in this life chose to become a lion in his next life: so that we may say that Plato saw in a lion a tragic hero who had been despaired too much to become a human again. And is it by chance that Nietzsche in describing the transformation and metamorphoses through the individual's phase of the lion must create for himself the freedom to be free for new creations?

And in one of the masterpieces of contemporary prose, Hermann Hesse, the Nobel Prize winner of 1946, describes what happened to him one July day in 1955 while he was working in his garden. While he was standing and breaking wood and was lost in memories of his childhood and the parrot they used to have at home,

> Suddenly like a golden flash from the blue sky of the summer morning, something came shooting down, bright in yellowish green, whizzed past my head . . . came flying back, set down on the branches by my feet—and was a parrot. "Yes, where are you coming from?" and it was only good that I still knew the parrot language from my childhood.

And after a detailed description:

> Never had anything happened to me as fair, as unlikely and like a fairy tale as this visit that lasted perhaps for ten minutes—this visit from the virgin forests of distant lands, the virgin forest of my distant childhood in which I still knew the language of the birds.

Is all this only by chance? As is it by chance only that since ancient times the Aesopian fables have used lions and mice and ants when they wanted to characterize outstanding human characteristics? And what about the comparative behaviorist and psychologist? The current issue of *Scientific American* has an essay with drawings of animals whose style would fit any fairy tale or fable book—and which ends with a moral teaching as a conclusion as would fit any Aesopian fable. And since ancient times have not the astrologers described humans as lions or black widows or scorpions and the like?

And is it then by chance that we ourselves in our everyday talk speak of Adenauer as a fox, or ourselves as pigs, of others as chicken, or somebody as catty, or a wise owl, of others as funny birds—and furthermore of the Russian bear—and of some people even as polar bears?

Is it not true, is it not strange that sometimes we may say something essential about a human being if we see him as that "kind of animal" that he is. Might it not be true that just when we do that, at the same time, we become all the more aware of the transcendental—of the kingly soul in the animal form?

What is it that is behind these strange correspondences and tensions between the animal and the truly human animal? What is it that makes us truly human animals? What is it that makes us truly human? What is it that sets us free? What is it in us that wants to be set free?

The professor—freed here from the scientific rigor and the scholarly discipline of the study and the classroom—allows his hopes free rein. And his hope is—which is always a teacher's hope—that the questions he could raise but not answer, the quests his generation has not yet been able to fulfill, will be taken up by you to put you into the mood, open your minds and hearts, to the possible realization that at least the human lion and the human lamb will get along in peace—and in this sense let me extend to you the season's first greetings and far-reaching warm wishes.

Appendix C

Obituary for Moritz Solmitz

Braunschweiger Gazette, 27 July 1879

On the evening of the 21st of this month, one of the most honorable citizens of our town, one of the most revered members of the Jewish community, passed away in his 69th year. He was Mr. Moritz Solmitz, merchant and partner of Aronheim and company, a commission firm. The deceased was deeply trusted and held in high esteem by his religious brethren, the commercial world, and above all by his fellow citizens.

Twenty-six years ago the Jewish community elected him as a member of the board of directors and accountant of the synagogue, an office to which he was always reelected. In this capacity, he carefully administered and successfully doubled a significant bequest from the deceased banker Nathalion. Due to his meticulous management of that account, the city of Braunschweig takes pride in the magnificent new synagogue at the corner of Stein and Knochenhauer Streets. The Jewish community fully acknowledged his merits when their representatives and the rabbi formally announced the formation of a charitable foundation bearing his name on the occasion of his silver jubilee as a board member.

In the world of commerce, the deceased enjoyed the highest admiration. That is why he was elected as a member of the managing board of Braunschweig's Chamber of Commerce. He contributed to this office with his typical unselfishness, passion and success. Therefore, following the departure of its past president, Selwig, the merchants of Braunschweig elected him consecutively for many years as president of the Chamber of Commerce.

His fellow citizens acknowledged his value as well when they elected him several times as a member of the city council. In this position, too, the deceased performed his tasks with diligence and perseverance.

He was not a person who delivered long speeches, nor was he an outstanding orator. Yet, he always made his point of view clear and stuck to it when he was convinced of the correctness of his opinion. He never became irritated, even when opposing views or conjectures were made. His demise will be felt by his fellow citizens for a long time to come. By the way, Solmitz was not a Braunschweiger by birth. He was born in Peine in 1810. As he came to Braunschweig at the age of thirteen, we feel entitled to count him as one of our community.

References

Aby Warburg Library, Hamburg, Germany. Walter M. Solmitz papers.

Adelysevein, www.cbnsa.net/celiahayes/Adelysevein.htm-bok

Anastas, Peter. 1983. Untitled column. *Gloucester Daily Times*, 22 September.

Asekoff, Louis. 2001. Interview by author. Waterville, 12 August.

Bein, Reinhard. 2004. *Ewiges Haus: Jüdische Friedhöfe in Stadt und Land Braunschweig.* Braunschweig: Döringdruck.

———. 2007. Letter to author, 20 July.

———. 2008. Letter to author, 18 October.

Bein, Reinhard. 2009. *Sie lebten in Braunschweig.* Braunschweig: Döringdruck.

Bircher, Ralph. 1966. Letter to author, 3 December.

Blakney, Raymond Bernard. 1955. *The way of life Lao Tzu/Wisdom of ancient China, a new translation.* New York: The New American Library.

Bowdoin Orient, 8 December 1957.

Braunschweiger Gazette, 27 July 1879.

Brister, Louis. 2010. Adelsverein. *The handbook of Texas online*, www.tshaonline.org/handbook/online/articles/AA/ufa1.html.

Brunswick Record. 7 March 1954.

Brunswick Record. 5 May 1965.

Brunswick Record, 20 July 1965.

Brutt, Edwin A., ed. 1958. *The teachings of the compassionate Buddha: Early discourses, the Dhammapada, and later basic writings.* New York: The New American Library.

Cahnman, Werner J. 1964. In the Dachau Camp. *Chicago Jewish Forum* 23, no. 1.

Carr, Edward Hallet. 1963. *What is History?* New York: Alfred A. Knopf.

Conway, Jill Ker. 1994. *True north: A memoir.* New York: Alfred A. Knopf.

Dachau Concentration Camp, Dachau, Germany. Archives.

Dachau Concentration Camp, Dachau, Germany. Documents on the "Judenaktion vom November 10, 1938." Index P-II d. No. 750.

Emoto, Masaru. 2004. *The hidden messages in water.* Hillsboro, Oregon: Beyond Words Publishing, Inc.

Epstein, Helen. 1979. *Children of the Holocaust: Conversations with sons and daughters of survivors.* New York: Bantam Books.

Frankl, Viktor E. 1971. *Man's search for meaning.* New York: Washington Square Press.

Frankenstein, Curt. 2006. Telephone conversation with author, December.

Friederichs, Nellie H. 1974. Sixty-six happy years: My story told to our children. The Friedrichs Family Web Site, www.friedrichs.us/History-Nellie-66-

Happy-Years-Full.html.

Garbarino, James. 2000. *Lost boys: Why our sons turn violent and how we can save them.* New York: Anchor Books.

Geheeb, Paulus. 1923. Letter to Sophie Solmitz, 11 April.

Gordon, Jennifer. 1996. Life. Term paper, Madison High School.

Grolle, Daniel. 2004. *Tai chi verstehen: Ein Spielweg zu den Quellen der ursprünglichen Freiheit,* Schiedlberg, Austria: Bacopa Verlag.

Grolle, Joist. 1994. *Bericht von einem schwierigen Leben: Walter Solmitz (1905 bis 1962): Schüler von Aby Warburg und Ernst Cassirer.* Berlin: Dietrich Reimer Verlag.

Hanley, Daniel, F., Dr. 1963. Letter to Attorney Frederic G. Corneel, 3. January.

Hart, Basil Henry Liddell. 1971. *Why don't we learn from history?* New York, NY: Hawthorn Books, Inc.

James, William. 1910. The Moral Equivalent of War. *McClure's Magazine*, August, 463-468.

Jowitt, William Allen. 1953. *The strange case of Alger Hiss.* London: Hodder and Stoughton.

Jung, Carl Gustav. 1954. Letter to Walter Solmitz, 24 August.

Kabat-Zinn, Jon. 2005. *Coming to our senses: Healing ourselves and the world through mindfulness.* New York: Hyperion.

Kamp, Jurriaan. 2006. Treat life as a workshop to find out who you are. *Ode,* May.

Khema, Ayya. 2002. *Come and see for yourself: The Buddhist path to happiness.* London: Windhorse Publications.

Koelln, Fritz Carl Augustus. 1957. Translation of "The Three Rings" from Lessing's *Nathan der Weise.*

Koelln, Fritz Carl Augustus. 1962. Memorial service for Walter Solmitz, 3 October.

Kranzler, David. 1976. *Japanese, Nazis, and Jews: The Jewish refugee community of Shanghai, 1938–1945.* New York: Yeshiva University Press.

Lessing, Gotthold Ephraim. 1779. *Nathan der Weise.* Munich: Wilhelm Goldmann Verlag.

Leue, Mary. Chapter 19, www.thoughtsmemories.net/myrems19.html-38k.

Levine, Stephen. 2002. *Turning toward the mystery: A seeker's journey.* San Francisco: HarperSanFrancisco.

Martin, Henry. 2001. Letter to author, 27 September.

Mora-Torres, Juan. 2001. *The making of the Mexican Border: The state, capitalism, and society in Nuevo León, 1848–1910.* Austin: Texas University Press.

Morning Sentinel. 2008. In Israel, debate over hitting Iran nuclear sites. 2 November.

Okri, Ben. 1996. *Dangerous love.* London: Phoenix.

Olmsted, Frederick Law. 2004. *A journey through Texas: Or a saddle-trip on the southwestern frontier.* Lincoln, NE: University of Nebraska Press.

Oomen, Sheena. 2010. *Hin nach Texas! (Off to Texas).* Houston Institute for Culture, www.houstonculture.org/cr/germans.html.

Pols, Edward. 1962. Memorial minute (pdf p. 42) read at the meeting of the faculty of Bowdoin College, 8 October.

Pols, Edward. 1963. Affidavit. 8 January.

Quirk, Patrick, Dr. 1963. Affidavit. 10 January.

Ray, Benjamin. 2004. Letter to author, 4 April.

Roberts, Jeff. 2005. The passing of a moral titan: Raymond Klibansky. *The McGill Reporter,* 25 August.

Rousseau, Jean-Jacques. 1963. *Emile.* Translated by Barbara Foxley. New York: Dutton.

Sanders, Arthur, ed. 2000. *Henry Sanders: An autobiography of amusing and entertaining anecdotes from 1868 to 1912.* Little Rock, AR: Thumbprints Publishing.

Sanders, Alexander Wolf. 1840, Letter to the Duchess Frederieke of Anhalt-Dessau, 23 April.

Sanders, Fred. approximately 1869. Untitled story.

Schlomer, George, Dr. 1956. Letter to Dr. Daniel F. Hanley, 14 January.

Scmit, Frank. 2002. Letter to author, 34 September.

Shakespeare, William. 1937. *The comedies of Shakespeare.* London: Oxford University Press.

Shirley, Dennis. 1992. *The politics of progressive education: The Odenwaldschule in Nazi Germany.* Cambridge, MA: Harvard University Press.

Shufang, Yui. 1939. *Chinese children at play.* London: Methuen and Co. Ltd.

Skillings, R. D. 1974. What's True? *Antaeus* 13-14, 318-319.

Solmitz, David. 2001. *Schooling for humanity: When big brother isn't watching.* New York: Peter Lang Publishing.

———. 2006. Letter to the editor. *Morning Sentinel,* 12 February.

———. 2006. Letter to the editor. *Morning Sentinel,* 5 May.

Solmitz, Elly. 1992. Unpublished manuscript.

Solmitz, Walter M. 1939. Report on Dachau. Translated by David O. Solmitz.

———. 1942. Some supplementary notes on anti-Nazi propaganda in Germany. Unpublished notes.

———. 1943a. Declaration of intention for a lasting peace. Unpublished notes, 18 April.

———. 1943b. Outline on some obstacles to the establishment of a lasting peace. Unpublished notes, 11 April.

———. 1945. Eulogy for Ernst Cassirer.

———. 1948. The redemption of the outcast. Chapel talk delivered at Bowdoin College, 6 March.

———. 1952. Letter to Dorothy Thompson, 31 November.

———. 1953. A wheelbarrow: In defense of the 18th century. Chapel talk delivered at Bowdoin College, 14 March.

———. 1954. Letter to Carl Gustav Jung, 21 August.

———. 1957, Letter to the editor. *Bowdoin Orient,* December.

———. 1961. The frog prince. Chapel talk (pdf p.363), unpublished manuscript, December.

Spriggs, Kent. 2001. Letter to author, 3 September.

Thompson, Dorothy. 1952. A vote against Trumanism. *Boston Globe,* 24 October.

———. 1952. Letter to Walter Solmitz, 3 November.

Tolle, Eckhart. 2005. *A new earth: Awakening to your life's purpose.* New York: Plume Books.

Villoldo, Alberto. 2008. *The four insights: Wisdom, power, and grace of the Earthkeepers.* New York: Hay House, Inc.

Warburg, Aby. (1886–1929) The survival of an idea. Astrp.uni.bonn.de/probesche/persons/pers_warburg.html-4k.

———. Biography, members, chello.it/Warburg/scritti/inglese/test/biografiang.html-29k.

———. 1995. *Images from the region of the Pueblo Indians of North America.* Translated by Michael P. Steinberg. Ithaca, NY: Cornell University Press.

Waskow, Arthur. 1966. *From race riot to sit-in, 1919 and the 1960s: A study in the connections between conflict and violence.* Garden City, NY: Doubleday and Company.

Welwood, John. 2003. Double vision: Duality and nonduality in human experience. In *The sacred mirror: Nondual wisdom and psychotherapy,* edited by J. Prendergast, P. Fenner, and S. Krystal. St. Paul, MN: Paragon House.

———. 2006. *Perfect love, imperfect relationships: Healing the wound of the heart.* Boston: Trumpeter.

Whitehead, Alfred North. 1929. *The aims of education and other essays.* New York: The Macmillan Company.

Yourcenar, Marguerite. 1963. *Memoirs of Hadrian.* New York: Farrar, Strauss and Giroux.

David Solmitz grew up in Brunswick, Maine, home of Bowdoin College, from which he graduated in 1965 and where his father taught philosophy. Following in his father's footsteps as an idealist, while a high school student he planted flowers on traffic islands on his town's main street, developed Brunswick's first antipoverty project in 1964, taught at Germany's first coed and progressive boarding school, which his father had attended as a boy, and continued for forty-plus years in his dad's footsteps as a creative teacher and social activist. In 2001 Peter Lang published his book, *Schooling for Humanity: When Big Brother Isn't Watching.* From his mother, an artist, he learned the joy of watercolor painting, a hobby he continues today. He lives with his wife Jing Ye in Waterville, Maine.